Indices and Identity

Linguistic Inquiry Monographs
Samuel Jay Keyser, general editor

Indices and Identity

Robert Fiengo and
Robert May

The MIT Press
Cambridge, Massachusetts
London, England

This book was set in Times Roman by Asco Trade Typesetting Ltd., Hong Kong and was printed and bound in the United States of America.

Library of Congress Cataloging-in-Publication Data

Fiengo, Robert, 1949–
  Indices and identity / Robert Fiengo and Robert May.
    p.   cm.—(Linguistic inquiry monographs; 24)
  ISBN 0-262-06166-X.—ISBN 0-262-56076-3 (pbk.)
  1. Grammar, Comparative and general—Syntax. 2. Anaphora (Linguistics)
  3. Dependency grammar. 4. Government-binding theory (Linguistics)
  5. Grammar, Comparative and general—Ellipsis. I. May, Robert, 1951–   .
  II. Title. III. Series.
  P295.F54   1994
  415—dc20   93-37789
                                                                    CIP

Contents

Contents

Series Foreword

We are pleased to present this monograph as the twenty-fourth in the series *Linguistic Inquiry Monographs*. These monographs will present new and original research beyond the scope of the article, and we hope they will benefit our field by bringing to it perspectives that will stimulate further research and insight.

Originally published in limited edition, the *Linguistic Inquiry Monograph* series is now available on a much wider scale. This change is due to the great interest engendered by the series and the needs of a growing readership. The editors wish to thank the readers for their support and welcome suggestions about future directions the series might take.

Samuel Jay Keyser
for the Editorial Board

Preface

The topic of this book is *syntactic identity*: Under what circumstances can bits of a syntactic structure be said to be the same as or different from other bits of a syntactic structure? The answer we give in this book is that occurrences of expressions are syntactically the same just in case they are *reconstructions* of each other. The grounds on which expressions are identical in the sense of reconstructions are twofold. One, there must be lexical identity—they are composed of the same lexical expressions; and two, there must be structural identity—the constituent elements that dominate the lexical expressions must be syntactically organized in the same way. That is, occurrences of expressions are reconstructions just because they have the same formal structure. Thus, in the sentence *Max saw Harry, and Oscar saw Harry, too* the verb phrases are reconstructions—there are two occurrences of the verb phrase *saw Harry*—but the subject noun phrases, for instance, are not reconstructions, since they are not lexically identical. But although such a characterization intuitively sets forth necessary conditions on syntactic identity, the precise application of these conditions has been an issue of broad discussion in the literature, primarily because of unclarity about what it means to be a "lexical expression" and for these expressions to be "organized in the same way." Our goal in what follows is to give a degree of precision to these two notions.

This goal arises from our interest in the theory of anaphora. There is an intuition, dating back in the contemporary literature at least to Geach, that the pronoun in a sentence such as *Max saw his mother* stands in for the name and that it should be taken as just an alternative linguistic way of expressing what the name otherwise expresses. So taken, this means that in the sentence above there are two occurrences of an expression that denote Max. Viewed in this way, issues of anaphoric connection are issues of syntactic identity. It is well known, however, that we cannot be too literal minded about this identity. For instance, it would not do to take the pronoun as a mere *façon de parler*, so that the logical form of the above sentence would be the same as that of *Max saw Max's mother*, since these two sentences are not synonymous; there must be some way in which names and pronouns differ. Accordingly, we need to find a more articulated way of establishing identity of lexical expression that allows pronouns to be appropriately nondistinct from names, yet does not distort their pronominal character. What allows us to do this is the notion of an *index*.

Formally, in what follows we will understand indices to be a structural part of the "feature content" of a category in a phrase marker. We will represent indices, or more precisely, a constituent part of indices that we will call their *indexical values*, by numerals. Although indices could be represented in various ways, numerals have the important advantage of readily satisfying the desideratum that indices formally express a notion of occurrence. Thus, we can distinguish various occurrences of an index, or *coindexing*, by distinguishing occurrences of a numeral. By this light, coindexed expressions such as the name and the pronoun in *Max saw his mother* are, in a sense appropriate to the theory of anaphora, identical; because they will bear occurrences of a given index, they will stand as occurrences of a given expression. Coindexing, therefore, will provide sufficient grounds to establish identity of expressions, and hence identity of reference, but it will do so in a way that is sufficiently abstract so as to allow certain sorts of differences in lexical realization, for instance, as a pronoun or as a name. A theory of the distribution of indexical occurrences in syntactic structures is called a *binding theory*. The theory of anaphora will at least encompass a binding theory, along with a way of appropriately interpreting coindexing and noncoindexing, itself a task not without its pitfalls, as we will show.

A theory of anaphora so construed, however, will still not be sufficiently discriminating for our purposes, since there are contexts that offer grounds for taking a given expression as being repeated—for there being reconstructions—but not with the same index. These cases center around the phenomenon known as "sloppy identity." Perhaps the most well-known illustration of this is with verb phrase ellipsis; thus, in *Max saw his mother, and Oscar did, too* the second clause can be understood in the same way as *Oscar saw his mother* with coreference. The issue, then, is this: although the elided verb phrase is a structural repetition of the unelided verb phrase, this repeated material cannot, for the reading in question, include the index of the overt pronoun, since then what would be obtained would be a strict reading, namely, that Oscar saw Max's, not Oscar's, mother. Thus, when we look at identity of pronouns within the more general notion of syntactic identity—that is, the context of reconstruction—more subtle notions are required. These will turn on reorienting ourselves from considering the distribution of indexical occurrences to considering their *relations*, given a distribution. These relations are of two sorts; occurrences may be independent or dependent, the indication of which will form a second constituent part of indices, their *indexical type*. The theory of indexical types we call *Dependency Theory*, and along with a binding theory, it will constitute the formal part of the theory of anaphora.

Theoretically, in the six chapters to follow we will be exploring the theory of anaphora as just described, and its role in characterizing identity of expressions and identity of structures. In chapter 1 we explore the "meaning" of coindexing and noncoindexing in sentences and discourse. Our thesis is that coindexed expressions are determined in virtue of grammar to be covalued, but for noncoindexed expressions the grammar makes no such determination. In chapter 2 we introduce Dependency Theory, providing a formal presentation of its tenets and placing it in the context of a formal semantics encompassing indices. Dependency Theory remains the topic of discussion in chapter 3, where we examine conditions on identity of dependencies. In this chapter we present our initial results on strict and sloppy identity, picking up the thread of investigation of verb phrase ellipsis, which we showcase in the subsequent chapters. In chapter 4 we focus on a group of central empirical issues that arise in ellipsis with respect to strict and sloppy identity; we call these the *eliminative puzzles*. Their importance is twofold: they show the empirical limitations of previous approaches to ellipsis, and in providing an adequate account for them, we can illustrate the workings of Dependency Theory. Reconstruction, or the general issue of syntactic identity and how indexical identity embeds within it, is the topic of chapter 5. There we treat a range of matters, including strict reflexive phenomena, quantifiers within ellipsis, and what we call *vehicle change*—the nondistinctness of certain sorts of expressions under ellipsis. Finally, in chapter 6 we explore the interaction of logical representation in grammar and grammatical constraints. We do this by presenting our research into a particular type of ellipsis, namely, antecedent-contained deletion, and this chapter itself stands independently as a study of this construction.

Acknowledgments

Although the issues discussed in this work have been on our minds in one form or another for many years, its genesis dates back to the summer of 1986, when we participated in the Workshop on Semantics and Logical Form held at the Linguistic Society of America's Summer Linguistic Institute at The Graduate Center of the City University of New York. Although we found the workshop tremendously stimulating, it failed in our eyes to make much progress on one of its goals, to explore empirical issues arising in the relation of anaphora and ellipsis. Thus, in the fall of 1988, when RF spent a sabbatical leave visiting at the University of California, Irvine, and in the fall of 1989, on another visit by RF to UCI, we decided to undertake research in this area, initially focusing on anaphora in antecedent-contained deletion constructions. By the end of RF's second visit, we had made sufficient progress to warrant preliminary presentations to seminars at UCI. We would like to thank Hagit Borer, Alec Marantz, Barry Schein, and Ken Wexler for their comments at that time. By the spring and summer of 1990 this material had matured, and we had the opportunity to present it at conferences in Paris, sponsored by the Centre national de la recherche scientifique; in Cambridge, at GLOW; and at an invited lecture at the University of Osaka (on a memorably hot and muggy July day). The content of these presentations will be included under the title "Anaphora and Ellipsis" in the Proceedings of the GLOW conference, to be published by Mouton de Gruyter; it is found here, in revised form, in chapter 6.

By the summer of 1990 the overall research in this book had been put together in rough form, and at that time we were fortunate to be able to present it in a week of lectures at the International Summer School of Linguistics in Girona, Catalonia. We especially would like to thank Irene Heim for her patience in sitting through the presentations of what was quite unpolished material and offering a wide range of enlightening and thoughtful comments. During the following year we continued to refine our ideas, and in the late spring and summer of 1991 we were able to present rather more worked out material on the theory of anaphora and on ellipsis. We are grateful for invitations to speak at Semantics and Linguistic Theory I at Cornell University, at the Conference on Logic and Language, jointly sponsored by the Linguistic Society of America and the Association of Symbolic Logic, and held at the University of California, Santa Cruz during the 1991 Linguistic Institute, and at a workshop at the University of Tromsø, Norway. Thanks are due to Tarald Taraldsen, who organized the workshop, and to the other participants for their helpful feedback.

We were also very pleased to have been able to present selections from this material at a number of departmental colloquia. We would like to thank the following institutions for their generous invitations: UCLA, University of Connecticut, MIT, University of Arizona, UCI, Princeton University, State University of New York at Stony Brook, Stanford University, and University of Maryland. From our interactions with the audiences at these presentations we learned a great deal for which we are grateful. We have been similarly edified by the students in our seminars over the last five years at The Graduate Center and at UCI, and to them we also owe a vote of thanks.

In June 1991 a preliminary draft of this work was circulated for comments. The response we received was invaluable in leading to significant improvements in the content and organization of the manuscript. It was read with great care by Richard Larson's seminar at SUNY Stony Brook and, with discussion led by Steve Berman and Arild Hestvik, in Rainer Bauerle's seminar at the University of Stuttgart. The participants' comments and reactions, relayed to us by Larson and Hestvik, were of great help. Of equal value were detailed comments on this draft sent to us by James Higginbotham, Stephen Neale, Mats Rooth, and jointly by Mary Dalrymple, Stuart Shieber, and Fernando Pereira. We trust that all these individuals will recognize the care we took with their comments, and the ensuing developments they stimulated in our line of thinking.

In March 1992 Steve Berman, Arild Hestvik, and Hans Kamp organized a workshop on ellipsis at the University of Stuttgart to which they were kind enough to invite us. The workshop, which brought together researchers currently working on ellipsis, was extremely lively and stimulating, and our interactions with the attendees led us to work more deeply on a number of crucial aspects of our approach. Our presentation, drawn from chapter 4, appears in the workshop proceedings, circulated by IBM Germany.

There are many people to thank personally, besides those already mentioned. Special thanks are due to Richard Larson, who spent many hours talking to us about all parts of this book. We are extremely grateful for his ongoing interest and his enlightening criticisms, as well as specific assistance in getting straight on various matters. Our gratitude is also due to Arild Hestvik, who kept up a lively e-mail correspondence, and to Shalom Lappin, whose input led to numerous improvements. Particular thanks are due to the following, who gave freely of their time and insight: Sylvain Bromberger, Gennaro Chierchia, Noam Chomsky, Hans Kamp, Bill Ladusaw, Howard Lasnik, and Ivan Sag. We also benefited from comments by Mark Baltin, Andy Barss, Barbara Bevington, Russell Dale, Naoki Fukui, Jim Huang, Jerry Katz, Richie Kayne, Terry Langendoen, Peter Ludlow, Taisuke Nishigauchi, Dick Oehrle, David Pitt, Ruth Reeves, Stephen Schiffer, and Ed Stabler. Barbara Bevington has given much-needed assistance with the manuscript. To all these people, along with those others who are mentioned at various points in the text, our thanks. Finally, we would like to acknowledge our profound intellectual debts to the writings of Gareth Evans, James Higginbotham, Howard Lasnik, and Tanya Reinhart on anaphora, and those of Östen Dahl and Ivan Sag on ellipsis. Their scholarship, which sets the critical background for what follows, is a testament to the depth that research at the confluence of syntax and semantics of natural language has achieved.

Support for this research was provided in part by a University of California, Irvine, Faculty Research Grant.

In the end, projects like this come to fruition with the support of family and friends. Thus, from RF to Ruth, and from RM to Virginia, with deepest thanks and love.

Chapter 1

Reference, Coreference, Not-Coreference

1.1 Indices and Coreference

In characterizing syntactic relations, there is no notion more central than that of an index. This is because it is this notion that allows us to speak of various elements in a structure as "going together" in some sense, as somehow being the same or different. What is an index? A familiar way of answering this question is that in syntax indices are numerals appended to elements in a structure, although one could imagine other representational forms that would do equally well in fulfilling the *function* of indices. What then is the function of indices? Clearly, it is not anything connected to their mathematical roles, as ordinal or cardinal numbers. In syntax we never encounter relations that are legitimized, say, by whether the sum of indices is greater than 10 or less than the even prime. Rather, the function of indices in syntax is to afford a definition of syntactic *identity*: elements are the "same" only if they bear occurrences of the same index, "different" if they bear occurrences of different indices. The key notion here is *occurrence of an index*: any given index may be realized in a structure through indefinitely many occurrences. Numerals are particularly suited for this task; by representing indices in this way, we can directly ascertain that in (1), for instance, there are two occurrences of one index, notated as "1," but only one occurrence of another, notated as "2":

(1) John$_1$ believes he$_2$ saw him$_1$

Although in syntax, occurrences of indices can be used to characterize any number of identity notions, such as being members of the same or different categorial projections, or being in the same or different argument structures, we will be looking at indices as they are employed to mark off anaphoric relations, as in (1).

One of the central themes in the study of anaphora has been to reduce the question of what are possible and impossible anaphoric relations to a question of the structural distribution of indexical occurrences. A theory of this distribution is called a *binding theory*. A well-known approach to binding theory, which we will assume, derives from ideas of Chomsky. Indices are partitioned into those appended to anaphors, to pronouns, and to other expressions that are neither anaphor nor pronoun, including names, demonstratives, and other referential expressions. Binding Theory is then given by the following clauses (Principles A, B, and C):

Binding Theory
A. Anaphors must be bound in their governing category.
B. Pronouns must be free in their governing category.
C. Other NPs must be free in all categories.

An element ψ is *bound*, for purposes of Binding Theory, if and only if there is a coindexed element (i.e., one bearing an occurrence of ψ's index) that c-commands ψ. ψ is *free* if either of these conditions is not satisfied. We gloss *governing category* as an "appropriately local syntactic domain."[1] By this theory, the indexing in (1) is permissible, but the indexing in (2) is not:

(2) *John$_1$ believes he$_2$ saw him$_2$

The problem with (2) is that the embedded pronoun *him* is not free in its local domain (its clause), and this contravenes Principle B. An anaphoric relation between the pronouns in *John believes he saw him* is thus to be precluded, in virtue of the ungrammaticality of the indexing of (2).

---

1. See Chomsky 1981, 1982, 1986b. There are many important theoretical issues surrounding the theory of binding. These include, but are not exhausted by, matters pertaining to the definition of c-command and to the definition of governing category. Discussion of these matters falls outside the scope of our inquiries here, but for concreteness we will assume the definition of c-command (or m-command) established by May (1985), developing original ideas of Aoun and Sportiche (1983). By this definition, α c-commands β iff every maximal projection dominating α dominates β, and α does not dominate β, where domination is determined relative to category segments. (For our purposes in this chapter, however, older definitions based on branching node (Reinhart 1976) would work just as well.) We will gloss the governing category of a constituent in a rough-and-ready manner as the smallest NP or S containing that constituent, although there are well-known cases such as embedded predications (see below) and long-distance anaphora that show this to be too narrow a characterization. See Chomsky 1986b for one precise characterization of this notion.

In order for a theory of indexing to suffice as a theory of the structural determination of anaphora, it is necessary to map the syntactic notion of identity that indexing affords onto a semantic notion of identity: When do elements in a structure have the same or a different "meaning"? The answer that immediately suggests itself is that elements that are coindexed are covalued, and those that are not coindexed are not covalued. For (1), this would mean that in virtue of the fact that *John* and *him* bear occurrences of the same index, they have the same reference, but because *John* and *he* bear different indices, they have different reference. Succinctly, coindexing is coreference, noncoindexing, noncoreference. There would appear to be a simple rule at work here, linking syntactic and semantic identity: Sameness of index, sameness of reference; difference of index, difference of reference.

It is well known that this simple picture is not the right picture. This is because we can very well make utterances whose primary communicative import is to leave open whether there is coreference or not. A particularly revealing form of the argument is due to Higginbotham (1985). Suppose that Max sees a man leaving the room but cannot see his face. Max asks his friend who that person is and his friend says, "I don't know, but he put John's coat on," with the intention to imply that the person who left the room *is* John. We now have the air of paradox. In virtue of Principle C, we must have the indexing in (3):

(3) He$_1$ put John$_2$'s coat on

And in virtue of the rule above, this implies that *he* and *John* differ in reference. But on the contrary, it is perfectly consistent with Max's intention in uttering this sentence that *he* and *John* have the *same* reference. Difference of index, it would appear, does not entail difference of reference.

In contrast to our judgments about (3), it remains a fact that when considering them in other contexts, we most commonly have the intuition that sentences such as *He put John's coat on* or *He thinks John is crazy* express noncoreference between the relevant NPs. But why should this be so, given what we have just seen? To answer this, let us state the rule linking occurrences of indices to their interpretations as follows:

Linking Rule
The coindexing of NPs in *S* contributes to the meaning of *S* that the NPs are covalued.

The intent of the Linking Rule is to say that coindexing grammatically causes, or determines, covaluation. That is, it is part of the *linguistic meaning* of S that $x = y$, and that for any utterance of S, it will be determined by the grammar that the value of x will be the same as the value of y. Now, what if the NPs in S are not coindexed; what follows then? What we have argued to be incorrect is that noncoindexing causes or determines noncovaluation. The mistake here is to hold that noncoindexing is just as much a relation between expressions as coindexing and hence is grammatically causal or deterministic. Rather, noncoindexing is the absence of the relation that triggers the Linking Rule. Hence, all that noncoindexing tells us is that the Linking Rule is not in force for the NPs in question; noncoindexing does not cause or determine covaluation. The converse of the Linking Rule is thus as follows:

The noncoindexing of NPs in S does not contribute to the meaning of S that the NPs are covalued.

By this condition, if it is not part of the linguistic meaning of S that NPs are covalued, then it is left open by their indexical structure whether, relative to an utterance, x and y have the same value or not. We now understand a speaker who uses a sentence that contains noncoindexed referential NPs, which otherwise meet the requirements of Binding Theory, as using a sentence for which we cannot specify—*in virtue of indices*—any meaning in which the NPs are coreferential.[2] Thus, given the Linking Rule, one effect of Binding Theory is to eliminate certain meanings from the set of linguistic meanings that a sentence might otherwise have, those meanings in which the two NPs have the same reference.

Given the Linking Rule, it follows that if the speaker uses a sentence with coindexing of NPs, then coreference must comport with his communicative intentions, since coreference is grammatically required for such structures. On the other hand, structures in which there is noncoindexing say nothing grammatically about coreference or noncoreference. Speakers, however, want to say *something* by the use of their language, and the sentences they utter must allow for the expression of their communicative intentions. Now, the primary circumstance in which a speaker might choose to use a sentence containing noncoindexed NPs is one in which fulfillment of the speaker's communicative intentions demands that the

---

2. We gloss *covaluation* here as "coreference," deferring discussion of quantification until chapter 2. There we turn to the semantics in a more formal vein, showing how the Linking Rule and its converse follow from the interpretation of NPs relative to their indices. Thus, bear in mind that the Linking Rule and its converse are not strictly speaking "rules" at all, but statements of generalizations.

NPs not be taken as coreferential. This circumstance is by far the most common, since typically speakers' communicative intentions are not consistent with leaving the reference of an NP open. Speakers will normally know what they wish to refer to by the NPs they utter, and accordingly will utter sentences consistent with this knowledge. Thus, speakers will normally exclude coreference in the face of noncoindexing in favor of structures that grammatically determine coreference, that is, those with coindexing. This leaves noncoreference as the normal assumption when a structure in which there is noncoindexing (as this is determined by Binding Theory) is encountered.

But circumstances may deviate from the normal in various ways. For instance, suppose the speaker wishes to remain uncommitted about whether two NPs corefer or not, as in the situation described above. When the speaker utters "He put John's coat on," he might do so in a state of doubt about whether *he* and *John* corefer. What the speaker wishes to accomplish by his utterance is to cancel the normal implicature and *argue the conclusion* that the person who left the room *is* John, by relying on the tacit assumption that typically people put their own coats on and not other people's. If the speaker intends that his statement imply that the person who left the room is John, then clearly he would not make a statement that could be taken to mean this in the first place, since the implication would then follow trivially. To make the argument in a nontrivial way, the speaker must avoid using a sentence that could have this as its meaning, since if he asserted this, he would not accomplish his intended speech act. If a speaker does not wish to commit to whether expressions corefer, then he will not assert a sentence for which coreference is determined by its grammatical form. Rather, he will use a sentence for which it is not part of its grammatical meaning that the expressions do indeed corefer. That is, he will use a sentence in which the NPs are not coindexed.[3]

A different set of circumstances is presented by what has come to be called the "masked ball" situation. Suppose A, who is attending a masked

---

3. Notice that in the context described it is less felicitous to say *I don't know, but John put his coat on*, even though *John* and *his* might not be coindexed. Speakers normally strive to avoid unclarity in their statements, however, and this sentence might equally well have these NPs coindexed. Since the latter option is precluded for *He put John's coat on*, it will therefore be the sentence of choice. Also, observe that the latter sentence may be used when there is no doubt on the part of the speaker that the person who left the room is John, so long as the speaker only wishes to implicate and not assert this. Thus, "He put on John's coat; you figure it out" could be a response to the initial question.

ball, hears another person B, who is masked, claiming that John is crazy. A, hearing this, asserts the following (without ostension):

(4) He₁ thinks John₂ is crazy

There are two circumstances that may in part underlie A's use of this sentence. Either A has no beliefs concerning who B is and wishes to leave this open, or A believes that B is not John, so that A's utterance of (4) carries the normal implicature that B is not John. If A had believed that B was John, then A would have uttered a different sentence, one that grammatically indicates coreference, such as (5):

(5) John₁ thinks he₁ is crazy

Now suppose B takes off his mask and A discovers that the person he heard is indeed John. What has gone wrong? If A had no beliefs concerning the identity of B, then nothing has gone wrong—(4) is true, since A has left open the possibility of coreference between the pronoun and the name. But what if A sincerely and firmly believed that B was not John and hence spoke in a way comporting with that mistaken belief? A's statement of (4) remains grammatically impeccable and true, but nevertheless it does not have the same status as in the previous circumstance. This is because in the second case A's utterance gave rise to a conversational implicature —namely, that B is not John—which has turned out to be false. In this case there is a sense in which we can label the coreference as "accidental," but we do not regard accidental coreference as anything more than this sort of failure of such conversational implicature.[4]

The grammar, then, makes available two indexical options: coindexing and noncoindexing. These two formal options correspond to three semantic possibilities: coreference as part of linguistic meaning, on the one hand; coreference not as a part of linguistic meaning, and noncoreference, on the other. Under these interpretations, sentences of the two indexical types may be used by speakers to express their communicative needs. That the semantics makes available just these interpretations is a consequence of how we go about assigning values to the relevant expressions of the language. Suppose a domain of individuals D, and suppose that we define σ as a (finite) sequence of those individuals, assigned to the positions of σ. Let $\sigma(i)$ stand for the ith position of σ. We then interpret NP_i, that is, an NP bearing an occurrence of the index i, as picking out $\sigma(i)$, the ith

4. We postpone to footnote 12 discussion of the differences between this notion of accidental coreference and others found, for example, in Lasnik 1976, Evans 1980, Reinhart 1983, Roberts 1987, and Soames 1990.

position of σ. This NP will refer to the individual assigned to that position. This will be so for *all* NPs that bear occurrences of the index i; thus, in that they each pick out $\sigma(i)$, they will be coreferential. This is coreference in virtue of linguistic meaning—what we mean when we say that coindexed elements are covalued. NPs that bear occurrences of different indices, on the other hand, will pick out different positions of σ: $\sigma(i)$ and $\sigma(j)$. Logically, there are just two ways of assigning values to these positions: either different individuals are assigned to $\sigma(i)$ and $\sigma(j)$, or the same one is. If different individuals are assigned, then noncoindexing is interpreted as noncoreference: NP_i and NP_j in S are understood as noncoreferential. But if the same individual is assigned, then occurrences of NP_i and NP_j in S are interpreted as coreferential. This coreference is not part of the linguistically determined meaning of S, however, since it is not determined strictly in virtue of indexing. Rather, it depends on what assignments of individuals are made relative to indices, and nothing in the grammar determines in this case which constitutes an appropriate assignment for a particular use of a given sentence.[5]

Given these considerations, we take it as inaccurate to describe the anaphoric relation that holds in *He saw John* or *John saw him* as disjoint reference or noncoreference. Rather, what the indices determine about such sentences is that it is not part of their linguistically determined meaning that the NPs corefer. As a technical term, therefore, we will refer to these cases as displaying *not-coreference*, understanding this description as not precluding coreference, under appropriate conditions of use. We

5. Note that the semantics of coreference/noncoreference is local in the sense that it depends only on the evaluation of indices actually used in a given sentence. The assignments to positions other than these are immaterial to their valuation. We leave aside here issues that arise with how indices are activated or otherwise raised to salience in a discourse, and how this relates to anaphora with definite and indefinite expressions; see Heim 1982. In giving the semantics, we take all NPs as sensitive to sequences, following Larson and Segal (forthcoming), although the interpretation scheme as stated in the text is incomplete, at least for names. This is because the lexical content of a name determines a constraint on the individual assigned to $\sigma(i)$. Thus, $[_{NP} John]_i$ fixes the assignment of the ith position to John. In this regard, names contrast with pronouns, which place no such inherent constraint. They pick out a position otherwise constrained, either by a name, or via context or demonstration. (We leave quantification aside here.) A truth clause for a sentence will read something like: The sentence *John_i left* is true relative to σ if and only if John is the individual assigned to the ith position of σ, and that individual left; that is, if and only if John left. We present this more formally in chapter 2.

thus reinforce a lesson due to Evans (1980), that although expressions may be anaphorically related by the grammar, and hence coreferential, if they are not so related, they may be either coreferential or noncoreferential, and that speakers may intend to use sentences indexed in this way to either referential end.[6]

In saying that noncoindexing is not-coreference, we do not mean to say that languages preclude any ways of grammatically expressing the stronger noncoreference condition. Indeed, languages do provide ways of saying just this; for example, the expression *other* found in sentences such as *John saw someone other than himself* has this effect. That grammatical disjoint reference is involved here can be seen by comparing *John resembles him* with *John resembles someone other than himself*. Whereas the former sentence could involve coreference (e.g., if the speaker had been unable to discern that the referent of the pronoun was in fact John, or, as with the example above, he wished to argue the conclusion that John is him), these are simply not options for the latter sentence. Its truth requires that the referents of the subject and object NPs be disjoint. Such required disjoint reference constructions are to be classified with required conjoint reference constructions; thus, paired with *John saw someone other than himself* is *John saw himself*. Whereas the use of the reflexive generates truth conditions that say of the predicate x *saw* y that $x = y$, the use of the counterreflexive *other* adds the condition that $x \neq y$.

Notice that both disjoint and conjoint reference constructions contain an occurrence of a reflexive element. Syntactically, this imposes a strict locality condition on both grammatical disjoint and conjoint reference— in either case the locus of the referential identification/nonidentification is the subject NP. This follows from Binding Theory (Principle A), which requires that reflexives be bound in their governing categories, resulting in the indexings in (6):[7]

(6) a. John$_1$ saw himself$_1$

    b. John$_1$ saw someone other$_2$ than himself$_1$

---

6. Our proposal for characterizing this insight, however, diverges from Evans's in fundamental ways, including how the grammar characterizes anaphora—for us, this is a symmetrical relation (coindexing), for Evans, an asymmetrical one—and in the relation of anaphora and dependencies. See chapter 2 for discussion of the latter issue.

7. There is also a nonlocal indicator of disjointness, as in *John came in. Someone other than him left*. Here, Binding Theory leads to use of a personal, rather than a reflexive, pronoun.

In (6b) there is also the additional index borne by *other*; as indicated by the semantics, its index is some index other than that of *John*. Notice that it follows in virtue of this indexing, and the meaning of *other*, that whereas disjoint reference is local, only the weaker relation of not-coreference holds for nonlocal environments. Since *other* is subject to Principle C (it is neither a reflexive nor a pronoun), a sentence such as *Max said John saw someone other than himself* has the indexing in (7):[8]

(7) Max_3 said $John_1$ saw someone $other_2$ than $himself_1$

The truth of (7) is compatible with the other person's being Max, although this is not determined by the grammar (*Max* and *other* are not coindexed), and hence the identity of the other person is left open to contextual determination.[9]

On the approach we are advocating, the role of the grammar in determining anaphoric relations is purely formal: all the syntax has responsibility for is determining the distribution of occurrences of indices. Reference only comes into the picture with respect to the semantic interpretation of the patterns of indices syntactically observed. This approach includes no *grammatical rule* of disjoint reference or noncoreference, and none of the attendant problems made quite clear by Evans (1980), in criticizing views of Lasnik (1976).[10] Assuming such a rule would mean that rather than just not committing the speaker to coreference, as we have it, noncoindexing

---

8. Rather than coindexing *himself* with *John*, as in (7), we can take the reflexive (perhaps more marginally) as a long-distance anaphor, coindexed with the matrix subject *Max*. It would then be compatible with the reading so represented that the other person is John, although this is again not required to be so.

9. Whereas in English disjoint reference is expressed through a complex NP, in other languages this is lexicalized; see Saxon's (1984) discussion of disjoint anaphors in Dogrib, which share the distributional properties just described. Our views on disjoint reference develop from the work of Heim, Lasnik, and May (1991b), who discuss the plural variant—the reciprocal pronoun *each other*—analyzing *The men saw each other* essentially as each of the men saw some man other than himself. Our views also place us in contrast with those who hold that such elements indicate that coindexing is to be disassociated from coreference; see Enç 1989 and Roberts 1987.

10. Evans (1980) offers two central arguments against such a rule as proposed by Lasnik (1976). First, it makes true identity statements ungrammatical. Second, if *he* and *Oscar* corefer in *Look, fathead. If everyone loves Oscar's mother, then certainly he must love Oscar's mother*, then the latter sentence is ungrammatical. But clearly there is an understanding of this sentence in which coreference obtains and it is grammatical. We address these cases in section 1.3.

would grammatically *commit* the speaker to noncoreference. But as we have argued, noncoindexing is not incompatible with coreference, it is only incompatible with coreference being determined in virtue of the indexical structure of the sentence. It is thus a consequence of our view that the name/pronoun pair in *He put on John's coat* can corefer just as well as the pair in *John put on his coat*, although the uses of these sentences will be appropriate to quite different communicative circumstances. Where the sentences differ is that only for the latter is coreference determined grammatically as a matter of coindexing; for the former, we must rely on context to establish coreference in the face of noncoindexing.

The difference between grammatically determined and context-determined coreference can itself have an effect on truth conditions of sentences. Thus, consider a sentence in which *He put on John's coat* occurs in an embedded position:

(8) John said he put on John's coat

Here the pronoun is open to anaphoric binding, with Binding Theory allowing the indexing in (9):

(9) John$_1$ said he$_1$ put on John$_2$'s coat

By Principle C, the embedded occurrence of *John* cannot be coindexed either with the pronoun (as in its unembedded counterpart) or with the subject occurrence of *John*. The latter NP and the pronoun, on the other hand, can be coindexed, since Principle B is satisfied. In regard to indexing, (9) is to be contrasted with (10):

(10) John$_1$ said he$_1$ put on his$_1$ coat

In virtue of this difference in their syntactic form, (9) and (10) differ in their truth conditions. This is because they report on utterances of different sentences. Suppose that Max walks up to John and asks him, "Are you John?" John, somewhat sarcastically, replies, "Well, I put on John's coat," letting Max draw the obvious conclusion. John's having made this utterance will be sufficient for the truth of (9), uttered by Max; the embedded clause of (9) reports the sentence uttered by John, save the difference in point of view signaled by the change in person. On the other hand, it is John's saying (the uninformative in the context) "I put on my coat" that is sufficient for the truth of (10). Conversely, the former utterance will not be sufficient for the truth of (10), nor will the latter be for the truth of (9). But this is all so even though John's utterances agree on their truth conditions, in virtue of *John* and *my* having the same referent. Where they differ is in their indexing; although there is coreference all around in each sentence, it is only for the coreference between the coindexed elements that this follows in virtue of grammar.[11] Hence, there is a difference in what sentences John *said*, and thus what is reported through indirect speech.

That noncoindexing does not mean noncoreference can also be seen by examining inferential patterns such as that in (11):

(11) People think that only they (themselves) are crazy
      He thinks that John is crazy
      Therefore, he is John

By Binding Theory, the pronoun and the name in the second premise must bear distinct indices. But if this were to be interpreted as noncoreference, we could not reach the identity statement as a valid conclusion. This result holds regardless of whether or not the noncoindexing is grammatically forced by Binding Theory. Thus, the conclusion of (12) is nontrivial, but only presuming that *his* and *John* in the second premise are not coindexed:

(12) Only people's mothers love them
      His mother loves John
      Therefore, John's mother loves John

Here, since in the second premise neither *his* nor *John* c-commands the other, coindexing is possible as well. But if there were coindexing, then the conclusion of the argument would follow trivially, just as it does in (13):

(13) People respect only themselves
      John respects himself
      Therefore, John respects himself

Also trivial in this way is the inference in (14), where we take the pronoun as bound, comparable to (13):

(14) People think only they themselves are crazy
      $John_1$ thinks he_1 is crazy
      Therefore, John thinks he, John, is crazy

Note that the coindexing that gives rise to the triviality afflicting (14) does not depend upon binding:

11. Soames (1990) points to the sentence *Mary told John that he isn't John*, observing that it does not mean that Mary told John that he isn't himself. Essentially the same considerations hold for this example as for that in the text, although one must take into account the role of the embedded identity in determining the possibilities of reference vis-à-vis the indexing of its arguments. See discussion in section 1.3.

(15) Pictures of people's fathers belong only to those people
       Pictures of John$_1$'s father belong to him$_1$
       Therefore, pictures of John's father belong to John

The conclusion of (15) is also trivial, although *him* is not bound by *John*; *John* is not in a position in which it c-commands *him*.

   One consequence that we can draw from the properties of these inferential patterns is that the relation of coindexing is grammatically meaningful, independently of whether there is also binding—that is, coindexing *and* c-command. Coindexing, therefore, is a syntactic relation that is interpreted by the grammar (in the cases given, to indicate coreference), whereas noncoindexing is not interpreted by the grammar, as specified by the Linking Rules. But what if it were to be held, to the contrary, that only binding, the stronger notion, is grammatically meaningful? On this view, held by Reinhart (1983), all that is grammatically meaningful is the binding of one occurrence of an index by another—that is, where one c-commands the other. (Reinhart characterizes this relationship as bound variable anaphora, but whether this is the correct description of coreference is immaterial to the issue at hand.) Thus, in sentences such as *John's mother loves him* the coreference of the NPs cannot depend on indices, since there is no binding. Rather, coreference (or noncoreference) can only be established pragmatically, through whatever mechanisms establish (actual) reference. Thus, the possibility of coreference in *John's mother loves him* is not grammatically determined coreference, just as the coreference in *He put on John's coat* is not.[12] On this view, it would follow that the inferences in (13) and (14) are of quite different status from that in (15). The conclusions in (13) and (14) will follow as a matter of language per se, since only in these cases is coindexing grammatically meaningful. On the other hand, in (15) the conclusion would not follow as a matter of language (in the narrow sense of grammar); rather, it would follow as a

---

12. Reinhart calls coreference in these cases accidental coreference, since coreference with some other noun phrase in the sentence is just one among any number of referential options for the pronoun; see also Roberts 1987 and Soames 1990. This is the normal manner of obtaining coreference if there is no c-command. Lasnik (1976) holds a more sweeping view; since he eschews any grammatical marking of pronominal anaphora, coreference will always arise in this accidental manner for pronouns. This notion is to be contrasted with the one we put forth above, by which accidental coreference is, so to speak, an abnormal case, arising from the failure of an implicature based on a mistaken belief. For us, there is no accidental coreference in Reinhart's sense.

matter of the *use* of language. On this view, the conclusion of (15), whether it is trivial or not, is nongrammatical, since coreference here is a matter of the pragmatics of language. Thus, if what is grammatically meaningful is just binding, we cannot generalize across the intuitively comparable (13), (14), and (15) as inferences that follow as matters of language. Rather, what such cases appear to show is the significance of coindexing, since it is this notion that ties together their logical properties as a matter of grammar.

If binding (or, as she terms it, bound anaphora) is the grammatically meaningful notion, as Reinhart claims, then what the grammar must specify are the contexts in which this holds. For reflexives, these are local domains; for pronouns, nonlocal domains only. These conditions correspond to Principles A and B of Binding Theory. However, Reinhart's approach does not have an analogue to Principle C—since bound anaphora is the grammatically significant notion, only conditions pertinent to binding are required. The slack in the theory is to be taken up by pragmatic considerations; loosely, if you intend coreference, use a bound anaphora structure; but if you avoid bound anaphora in that structure, then no coreference is intended, unless there is some reason to avoid bound anaphora (Reinhart 1983:167). Reinhart understands this pragmatic strategy as just an articulation of the Gricean Maxim of Manner. This may very well be so, but if it is, it is not an innocent articulation, since it introduces a transderivational aspect to the theory of anaphora. This is because for a token sentence S, there is not enough information in S itself to evaluate it anaphorically. We must also have access to at least one other token sentence S' to determine whether the bound anaphora property holds of that type of syntactic structure. Thus, *He saw John* is understood with intended noncoreference only because there is a bound anaphora derivation of another sentence, *John saw himself*, which presumably the speaker and hearer will know to be appropriately of the same type as that actually uttered in the discourse. Moreover, it is not altogether clear to us just how the notion of "sentence of the same structure" is to be characterized. For example, are *John believes himself to be smart* and *John believes he is smart* of the same structure? In certain senses they obviously are, yet the existence of the first sentence does not give noncoreference for the second. Also unclear is what counts as good "reasons" to avoid bound anaphora. As an example of the sorts of problems that arise in making this notion precise, consider Reinhart's proposal (1983:168) that sufficient reason for allowing *He is Zelda's husband* with coreference is that the bound anaphora alternative, *Zelda's husband is himself*, being a tautology, doesn't express what the speaker intends to say. But if this is so, then the bound anaphora option should require noncoreference for *Zelda's husband is Zelda's husband*, which is a tautology. But this sentence is well formed, with the NPs coreferential. In using this sentence, the speaker has avoided bound anaphora, but there is no reason for avoiding it, since this sentence means just what *Zelda's husband is himself* means. Note also that in the initial case there is no way simply by observation of the sentence to know that it is nontautological. Consider it in the following context: *You know who Zelda's husband is? He is Zelda's husband.* Here the sentence is tautological, but again it is grammatical with coreference. (See section 1.3 for further discussion of identity statements.)[13]

On our theory, unlike Reinhart's, sentences themselves contain sufficient information for their anaphoric evaluation. Understanding of *He saw John* is based directly on the indexing assigned to this sentence by the grammar, where this assumes that there is some principle determining what is a possible indexing of its NPs—to wit, Principle C of Binding Theory. Utterances, in turn, are based on the following pragmatic principle: Use whatever sentence the grammar makes available that suits your communicative intentions. With anaphoric language, implementing this principle will depend upon whether the speaker wishes to be committed to coreference or not. If so, he will use a sentence that grammatically expresses this, one in which there is coindexing; if not, he will use a sentence that does not grammatically express this, one in which there is not coindexing.

1.2 Indices and Discourse

Our statement of the Linking Rule in section 1.1 is, in fact, too narrow. This is because it holds only for occurrences of indices within sentences; however, we want it to hold more generally *among* sentences in a dis-

---

13. Reinhart (1983) presents arguments for her position based on the distribution of strict and sloppy readings in elliptical contexts. We discuss these in chapters 3 and 4. Grodzinsky and Reinhart (1993) present an emendation of Reinhart's (1983) proposal that abandons the pragmatically based comparison of sentences of the language in favor of a grammatical rule that directly compares possible interpretations. Leaving aside the particulars of this rule, the idea is that if a sentence could have a bound variable interpretation that is indistinguishable from a coreference interpretation, then only a noncoreference construal is available for that sentence. As far as we can see, the criticisms above, as well as those presented below, hold equally well for the modified theory.

course. Thus, we construe *Superman* and the pronoun in (16) as covalued in virtue of grammar just as much as we would if they occurred in a single sentence:

(16) Superman$_1$ is faster than a speeding bullet. He$_1$ also leaps tall buildings in a single bound

Similarly, we find expressions that occur in sententially embedded environments related across discourse:

(17) Lois Lane thinks Superman$_1$ is a super hero. Lex Luthor thinks he$_1$ is a super heel

Here again, we take the covaluation of the coindexed elements as a matter of the linguistic structure of the sentences within the discourse.

Let us extend our semantics to cover this case by saying that if a sentence S is evaluated relative to a sequence σ, then σ is a *context* for S.[14] Let us furthermore say that a *discourse* is any set of sentences for which σ is a context. The domain of the Linking Rule will now be a discourse in this technical sense, with the evaluation of indices extending across the set of sentences that make up the discourse. Thus, relations among indices perseverate through a discourse, although not necessarily between discourses, defined relative to distinct contexts of assignments. An NP bearing index i in one discourse may be linked to a different value than it is linked to in another.[15] Now, following the reasoning we applied to the intrasentential cases, if NPs in distinct sentences are not coindexed, then covaluation is an open matter grammatically; it would be a discourse environment of not-coreference. As with single sentences, there are circumstances in which we want just this matter left open. Adapting an example

14. We should make clear here that this is not intended as a comprehensive notion of context, but rather a minimal notion that any more general notion will have to embed as part of its structure. This more general notion would seek to include other factors such as time and location of speech act, associated demonstrations, and pluralities of individuals. Additionally, our brief remarks do not address the dynamics of contextual change in connected discourses. In a more fleshed-out theory, we would want to allow for incremental updating of a context at linking points of discourses, that is, for alteration in the structure of σ. We briefly address this point in chapter 2.

15. What we are *not* holding is that indices are part of the *lexical* semantics of words, since then indexing would be independent of assignment. Also, coindexing in discourse differs from coindexing within sentences in that the distribution of occurrences between sentences is not subject to Binding Theory.

of Richard (1983), suppose that a man A is talking to a woman B on the telephone. Suppose further that A sees a woman in a telephone booth across the street threatened by some danger. The woman in danger is B, but A does not know this. Relative to this circumstance, both of the following can be true, uttered by A into the telephone:

(18) I believe that she is in danger

(19) I don't believe that you are in danger

By the use of the third person, A refers to the woman across the street, and by the use of the second person, to the woman on the telephone (both in fact B). In order for both (18) and (19) to be true, it is necessary (but not sufficient) that the pronouns *not* be coindexed. If they were coindexed, then they would be occurrences of the *same* pronoun, and consequently, the embedded sentences would be, in an appropriate sense, the same sentence. But then (19) would be the negation of (18), as a matter of their linguistic form, and these sentences would be inconsistent. This is not so, however, if the pronouns bear different indices. Since they are different pronouns, nothing in their linguistic structure makes (18) and (19) inconsistent. That the pronouns in these sentences are not coindexed jibes with A's communicative intentions. That *she* and *you* pick out the same person is precisely what A does not want to commit himself to, since he does not know or believe this, and his use of indexically *different* pronouns conveys this. Therefore, he will not use sentences in which the pronouns are coindexed, and hence coreferential as a matter of grammar.

Sameness versus difference of indexing, then, provides a criterion for when linguistic expressions are the same or different. Application of this criterion might be thought to be unnecessary for distinguishing (18) and (19). Rather, that they contain different pronouns could be taken to be manifested directly in their superficial linguistic form, in virtue of the appearance of the second versus the third person forms. The idea would be that the morphological forms of the words used would be a sufficient difference between the sentences. But in fact this would not be sufficient, since the problem also arises when morphologically (and semantically) nondistinct pronouns are employed:

(20) I believe that she is in danger

(21) I don't believe that she is in danger

The problem is that these sentences appear to be of the form p and $\neg p$. However, both sentences can be rationally believed by the speaker (that is, A when not on the phone) who is in the state of ignorance described for the puzzle, since for him, in (20) *she* points to the woman across the street, whereas in (21) it points to the woman on the phone. This is so even though the embedded sentences in each case employ the same words. In a similar vein, (22) and (23) can both be true, again when uttered by A not into the telephone:

(22) I believe that I can inform her of her danger via the telephone

(23) I don't believe that I can inform her of her danger via the telephone

For (22) to be true, the two instances of *her* must be distinct, the first pointing to the woman on the telephone, the second to the woman across the street. In contrast, for (23) to be true, the pronouns must *not* be distinct, since what A does not believe is that he can inform someone of her own danger via the telephone. In a parallel way, both (24) and (25) can be true, but in this case when said into the telephone:

(24) I believe that I can inform you of your danger via the telephone

(25) I don't believe that I can inform you of your danger via the telephone

A may truly say (24) if the first *you* points to the person on the telephone and the second *you* points to the person across the street. Again, A does not believe that he can inform anyone of her own danger via the telephone; hence (25).

We can identify the problem we are encountering with this alternative view. It is the assumption that since the clauses embedded below *believe* in pairs like (20)/(21) and (22)/(23) are homophonic (as well as categorially isomorphic), they therefore constitute the same sentence. Taking this to be so prevents us from saying what we need to say here, that the pronouns in (20) and (21) are different pronouns, and that (22) contains one occurrence each of two pronouns, but that (23) contains two occurrences of a single pronoun. Therefore, we must have some mechanism that will distinguish homophonic occurrences. Indexing is just such a device. That there are different pronouns in (20) and (21) follows from differential indexing, as does the fact that there are two pronouns in (22):

(20′) I believe that she$_1$ is in danger

(21′) I don't believe that she$_2$ is in danger

(22′) I believe that I can inform her$_2$ of her$_1$ danger via the telephone

(23′) I don't believe that I can inform her$_1$ of her$_1$ danger via the telephone

In (23′), in contrast, there is coindexing. By the Linking Rule, it is a matter of grammar that the pronouns bearing these occurrences are coreferential. Moreover, it follows that they are coreferential with the occurrence of *her*₁ in (22′). Nothing follows from the grammar, however, about their referential relation to the occurrence of *her*₂ in this sentence. Thus, given their indexing, there is nothing in the linguistic forms of the pairs (20′)/(21′) and (22′)/(23′) that would make one the negation of the other. This is because, superficial appearance aside, they do not employ the same expressions.

The dangers inherent in not sufficiently distinguishing homophonic occurrences can be seen by considering an argument tendered about these cases by Richard (1983). It is agreed that (18)—*I believe that she is in danger*—is true when said by A. Now B can say (26) over the telephone to report this belief A has about her:

(26) The man watching me believes that I am in danger

A can then truly assert (27), given what B has said to him over the telephone:

(27) The man watching you believes that you are in danger

(28) is also true as said by A:

(28) I am the man watching you

Then, from (27) and (28) we can conclude (29) by substitution:

(29) I believe that you are in danger

But this contradicts (19)—*I don't believe that you are in danger*. But then (19) ought to be false, by reductio. In the context of the puzzle, however, (19) is true; hence, this argument must be invalid.[16]

---

16. Two assumptions underlie this argument, as given by Richard (1983). One is a definition of validity according to which if ψ follows from ϕ in context c and ϕ is true in context c, then ψ is true in c. The second is that A is the unique man watching B. Richard assumes this to "simplify" the argument, since "nothing hangs on this." But the uniqueness assumption is in fact essential to this argument. Suppose that there are many men watching B, so that use of the definite is not appropriate; rather, all that is warranted is use of an indefinite. But then from *A man watching you believes that you are in danger* and *I am a man watching you*, we clearly cannot infer (29), *I believe that you are in danger*. Thus, the argument holds at best only for a special case. In discussing this argument, Richard himself maintains that it is valid, and that as such it shows our intuitions to be misguided. In Richard 1983, he uses it as an argument for a property-based theory of belief; in Richard 1990, as an argument for Russellian propositions. Although extended

The problem with the argument stems from a confusion over homophonic occurrences of pronouns that arises from inattention to their indices. To see this, look again at (26). This sentence is intended to report on A's belief, which he reports himself by (18). We can ensure that this is so by employing the same pronoun in (26) as in (18). We can indicate this by (30) and (31):

(30) I believe that she$_1$ is in danger

(31) The man watching me$_1$ believes that I$_1$ am in danger

(30) and (31) must report on the same belief; all that changes is the person of the pronouns, to reflect the shift in point of view. A's subsequent utterance will just show another shift in point of view:

(32) The man watching you$_1$ believes that you$_1$ are in danger

From this we can now conclude (33), on the basis of (28):

(33) I believe that you$_1$ are in danger

But this is clearly circular; what we have deduced is no different from (30), since *you* here still points to the woman on the telephone (albeit with change in point of view). In order for the inference to go through, we must have (34), not (31), as a premise:

(34) The man watching me$_2$ believes that I$_2$ am in danger

Then we can deduce (35), which contradicts (36):

(35) I believe that you$_2$ are in danger

(36) I don't believe that you$_2$ are in danger

But (34), although homophonic to (31), does *not* report on the belief expressed by (30). This is because the pronouns in (30) and (34) are different linguistic expressions, in virtue of bearing different indices. Thus, this step in the argument involves an illicit substitution of one pronoun in a belief context for another. And for this reason, the argument fails.

---

discussion of these views would take us far afield, we simply observe here that one can just as well conclude, taking our intuitions as evidence, that the puzzle argues *against* these views. (We return in chapters 2 and 4 to various problems that arise with appealing to properties in linguistic analysis.) Richard (1990), although maintaining that the argument is formally valid, proposes that it does fail when taken in the context of a conversation between A and B. The cause of the failure is attributed to a restriction proscribing any substitution in first person belief ascriptions. But comparable cases can be shown in which the same issues arise with third person ascriptions; see examples (37) and (38) in the text.

Just given considerations of the syntax of belief contexts, it follows that substitution is guaranteed in such contexts under coindexing, since what we have is simply the same expression twice over. It is not guaranteed on this basis, however, in the face of noncoindexing, since different expressions are involved.[17] We have no more right to expect that distinct but coreferential pronouns can be freely substituted one for another in such contexts, than we have to expect substitutivity of distinct coreferential names. Thus, suppose that A and B, both of whom are apprised of Superman's secret identity, see him stepping out of a phone booth. Seeing this, A says to B:

(37) Lois Lane thinks he is a superhero

Later, as part of the same discourse they see Clark Kent back at the *Daily Planet*, and now A says to B:

(38) Lois Lane doesn't think he is a superhero

Use of different pronouns is called for here precisely because A does not want to attribute to Lois what she takes to be false, that Superman is Clark Kent. Use of the same pronoun would give this, and make (37) and (38) contradictory. In the situation described, matters would be no different had A said in the first place

(39) Lois Lane thinks Superman is a superhero

and in the second:

(40) Lois Lane doesn't think Clark Kent is a superhero

Insofar as it is a matter of the contribution of linguistic form to the theory of belief that (39) and (40) contain different proper names, so too it is a

17. The possibility of such substitutions will depend on stronger conditions than coreference. For instance, it will be allowed if the agent of the beliefs knows that the noncoindexed expressions are coreferential. But this is just what is not the case in the phone booth context. Short of such licensing conditions, we would want a theory of belief to entail that noncoindexed elements cannot be substituted one for another (unlike in extensional contexts). We leave open at this point how best to integrate indexical structure in a theory of belief, but see Larson and Ludlow (1993) for an approach that allows the substitution principle to be directly sensitive to the structure of the linguistic vehicles of belief. (Richard (1990) presents a similar view, although his particular approach is problematic, we believe, because of inattention to the fine structure of linguistic form.) Also, bear in mind that guaranteed substitutivity under coindexing holds only for a given discourse context; different discourses may involve distinct assignments relative to an index.

matter of linguistic form that (37) and (38) contain different pronouns. Thus, how we employ different pronouns in discourse is directly comparable to the way we employ different names. What consideration of the pronominal cases brings into focus is the need for a more abstract way of distinguishing expressions, given the homophony problem, than the sorts of superficial differences that might be thought to sufficiently distinguish between names. By the use of indices, syntactic structure makes available for pronouns just as much information as for proper names with respect to identity of expressions. Independently of its particulars, any semantic theory of belief must therefore incorporate at least as much linguistic information as is given by indexical relations.

To summarize, on the view we have developed, substitution in belief and other related contexts is a matter that sits on the interface of the theory of anaphora and the theory of belief (more generally, of propositional attitudes). Our concern here has been to isolate the formal contribution of the theory of anaphora. The cases of discourse anaphora we have considered serve to show the role of indices in individuating linguistic expressions, to say when they are the same or different, even when they have the same (superficial) form and the same reference. These considerations fall in with more general concerns pertaining to the role of indices as a formal aspect of linguistic structure, within the purview of the theory of anaphora. What has tied together the various matters we have discussed in this section has been two concerns: (i) how indices afford a notion of syntactic identity in sentences and discourse, determining what counts as the same or different expressions; (ii) how this notion of syntactic identity maps onto semantic identity of reference. Our view is that although identity of indices maps onto identity of reference, nonidentity of indices does not necessarily map onto nonidentity of reference. Coreference in virtue of coindexing, then, is a matter of grammar, but coreference or noncoreference in the face of noncoindexing is left open by the grammar. It is rather a matter of context and principles of rational discourse. This relation of syntactic and semantic identity is at the heart of our understanding of anaphora. We now turn to another issue: How do notions of anaphoric identity apply in environments in which identity is independently asserted?

1.3   Identity Statements

In discussing the theory of anaphora put forth by Lasnik (1976), Evans (1980) observes that a problem arises because the grammatical noncoreference rule assumed in the theory is stated in terms of an extensional notion of disjointness of reference. Evans observes that it follows from this assumption that all true identity statements are ungrammatical. This is because in *Cicero is Tully* the two names must be referentially disjoint; but if this sentence is to be true at all, they must in fact be coreferential. The point here is indeed even more general, because it also follows from Lasnik's theory that *Cicero isn't Tully* is analytic, since by grammatical principle *Cicero* and *Tully* are noncoreferential. That is, what this sentence asserts is determined to be part of its meaning as a matter of language. Clearly, we wish to avoid these results. Note that appeal to intentionality of reference would be of no use here. As Evans points out, matters of intentionality are of no moment, since by sincerely uttering an identity statement, the speaker manifestly intends that the NPs corefer. Thus, in uttering (41),

(41) Griswold is the best cook in town

the speaker may very well mean to say that there is someone who is the best cook in town and that Griswold is that person; *Griswold isn't the best cook in town* is true provided that the person who is the best cook in town isn't Griswold. Clearly, if (41) is to be used to make an assertion at all, it is asserting that the arguments of *be* have the same value.[18]

Let us consider such identity statements from the indexical point of view. Given that the argument NPs of a true identity statement corefer, it might be thought that they bear occurrences of the same index, so that in (42) it would be the case that $i = j$:

(42) Griswold$_i$ is [the best cook in town]$_j$

Now, since the referents of NP_i and NP_j are the same, (42) is true. But we clearly do not want to impose it as a grammatical requirement that $i = j$, since then (42) would be analytic, because it would be part of the meaning determined by its linguistic form that the NPs in this sentence corefer. When coupled to the meaning of the verb *be*, this will make (42) in effect of the form $a = a$, and hence uninformative. Moreover, such an indexing would not allow us to account correctly for the inference in (43):

---

18. We must be careful to distinguish the reading of (41) that interests us here from a prominent predicational reading also available for this sentence. On this reading, *Griswold isn't the best cook in town* might merely mean that he is a very bad cook, without implying that there are any other cooks in town. We discuss such readings in section 1.4.

(43) People respect Cicero
      Cicero is Tully
      Therefore, people respect Tully

The conclusion of this argument is nontrivial, since it is an instance of the inference schema (44):

(44) People respect X
      $X = Y$
      Therefore, people respect Y

If, however, the NPs *Cicero* and *Tully* of the identity premise were co-indexed, we would have an instance of the trivial schema in (45), trivial in the sense that the conclusion follows directly from the first premise:

(45) People respect X
      $X = X$
      Therefore, people respect X

Note that (43) may be stated, and typically would be stated, by someone who perfectly well knows the reference of the individuals under discussion. There is no question of mistaken belief or ignorance on the part of the speaker. Therefore, it would be mistaken to hold that noncoindexing always indicates noncoreference.

What these arguments show is that the NPs in identity statements are not to be coindexed. This result is exactly what follows from the grammatical principles governing indexing: Principle C of Binding Theory requires that i and j be distinct, since it cannot distinguish (41) from any other arbitrary transitive clause. This means that such an identity statement will be indexed as in (46):

(46) Griswold$_1$ is [the best cook in town]$_2$

Given that the NPs of identity statements are not coindexed, it follows that they are different expressions. It will now follow, for instance, that (43) will properly be an instance of (44). Care is needed, however, in how we interpret identity statements so indexed. Thus, suppose that we interpret the indexing in (46) to mean that the referent of NP$_1$ is not the referent of NP$_2$. This leads to an unfortunate result: that (41) is a contradiction, and, more generally, that identity statements can never be true. We would appear to be in something of a quandary regarding the indexing of identity statements: if their indexing is exceptional vis-à-vis Binding Theory so as to allow coindexing, they are uninformative, but if they are indexed as prescribed by Binding Theory, they are necessarily false. We assuredly wish to adopt a method of treating indices that avoids these untoward results for identity statements.

The theory of interpretation we sketched above has this consequence. As we have stated matters, it only follows that a sentence of the form NP_i be NP_j (for $i \neq j$) does not carry as part of its *meaning* that NP_i and NP_j are coreferential *in virtue of the interpretation of indices*, just as it is not part of the indexically determined meaning of NP_i *saw* NP_j or NP_i *hit* NP_j. Saying that it is not part of the meaning that the NPs corefer does not preclude that they do, in fact, corefer. Identity statements assert that a relation holds between the reference of the NPs, the identity relation expressed by *be*. Because *be* has this meaning, coreference between the NPs is required for truth. Other relations like *say* or *hit* cannot be employed to make such assertions of coreference between their arguments. But this is just as much a matter of what they mean as coreference is a matter of what *be* means. Thus, we conclude, an indexing of identity statements can be consistent with Principle C; hence, they can be informative since coreference is not indexically required as part of their meaning. And since noncoreference is not the interpretation of noncoindexing, they can be true.

A further argument that the NPs in identity statements are not coindexed can be garnered from examples like the following, which allow coreference between the pronouns:

(47) She is the daughter who her mother likes best

Now suppose that the NPs flanking the copula are coindexed, in apparent violation of Principle C. Then, given the indexing of relative clauses, the following structure would result:

(48) She$_1$ is [the daughter who$_1$ her$_1$ mother likes e_1 best]$_1$

Relative to this structure, however, anaphora should not be possible, since it violates various restrictions on the occurrence of pronouns. Among other problems, the pronoun and the trace of the *wh*-phrase in the relative clause are coindexed; there is a weak crossover violation.[19] As such, this is not a well-formed structure. In contrast, the following is well formed:

(49) She$_1$ is [the daughter who$_2$ her$_1$ mother likes e_2 best]$_2$

---

19. "Weak crossover" is used to designate the absence of a bound variable interpretation for the pronoun in questions like *Who does his father love* or relative clauses like *everybody who his father loves*, where the *wh*-phrase, in moving to its superficial clause-initial position, crosses over the pronoun. Thus, there are contrasts with *Who is loved by his father* and *everybody who is loved by his father*, in

Here the NPs flanking the copula are not coindexed, and hence there is no crossover. Consequently, an anaphoric connection between the pronouns is possible.

In identity statements, there are also structures of the form NP_i be NP_j for which Binding Theory requires that $i = j$; these typically have reflexive pronouns:

(50) $John_1$ is $himself_1$

But there are other identity statements that do not contain the reflexive, but appear to be of the form NP_i be NP_i. Consider (51):

(51) John is John

This sentence can be understood in two ways. On the one hand, it might be used when it is being wrongly assumed that two Johns are under discussion, and the speaker wishes to correct the assumption. This reading is straightforwardly representable by the indexing in (52):

(52) $John_1$ is $John_2$

In contrast to this interpretation, there is also an analytic construal, where (51) is understood as utilizing occurrences of the same name of the same person. This reading would presumably be represented as in (53):

(53) $John_1$ is $John_1$

The problem, of course, is that the latter indexing appears to contravene Principle C, yet clearly this is a possible reading of *John is John*.

One moral we could draw from this is that Principle C is somehow counterexemplified by (53). We do not believe, however, that this is the correct lesson to be learned. Rather, this sentence is to be seen as drawn from an attenuated part of the language in which the operant referential principle is that the "shape" of an expression determines its reference anywhere it occurs. To see what we have in mind here, consider what may seem a somewhat exotic case, the arithmetical statement in (54):

(54) $2 \times 3 = 2 \times (2 + 1)$

(55) gives an English "translation" of (54), where the parenthesis—close parenthesis "construction" is used to mark overtly the structural relations of the arguments:

---

both of which the pronoun can be read as a bound variable. For various approaches to the analysis of weak crossover, see Chomsky 1976, Higginbotham 1980b, Koopman and Sportiche 1982, and May 1985, 1989, among others. Note that *who* or its trace in (48) may also violate Principle C with respect to *she*.

(55) Two times three equals two times parenthesis two plus one close parenthesis

(55) is of interest in that it contains three instances of the argument *two*. We think it is clear that at least the second instance of *two* c-commands the third, yet there is no doubt that these two instances of the numeral have the same referent, the number two. We thus have a language of arithmetic to which binding principles do not apply. Not only is Principle C inapplicable, but our language of arithmetic also lacks reflexives and pronouns, although we might construct an arithmetic that contained those elements. For instance, we could translate (56) as either (57a) or (57b):

(56) $3 + 1 = 2 \times 2$

(57) a. Three plus one equals two times two

b. Three plus one equals two times itself

This freedom from A-binding in arithmetic that English may preserve is suggestive. It appears that we may adopt a way of speaking in which the referent of a name is fixed irrespective of the structure in which it appears. Principle C is inapplicable to (55), since it makes no sense to ask whether the second and third instances of the numeral *two* refer to the same number; the referent of the numeral is invariant.

The view we are taking of the analytic *John is John*, that is, under the indexing in (53), is that it has the character of being taken from this metafragment or register of language that lets occurrences of a name refer uniformly, regardless of where they occur syntactically.[20] Names with different shapes, but with the same reference, will naturally fall outside this fragment: *Cicero is Tully* is not analytic, so that it is represented as in (58), not as in (59), consistent with Binding Theory:

(58) Cicero_1 is Tully_2

(59) *Cicero_1 is Tully_1

---

20. The distribution of this effect is to some extent determined by linguistic context. Thus, the nomic (i), which admits coreference, contrasts with the eventive (ii), which does not:

(i) Men_1 think that men_1 are rational

(ii) *Men_1 said that men_1 were getting fired yesterday

If we include nomic statements within those of arithmetic, we may advance the generalization that in nomics a name may have invariant reference.

On our view, *John is John* is a sort of quasi-mathematical statement, of a piece with *Two is two*, and to be distinguished from the nonanalytic *He is John*.

Notice that a sentence like *He is John* can be placed in a syntactic environment in which the pronoun can be bound by an occurrence of *John*. Doing so, however, does not give results equivalent to those obtained with repeated names, as is shown by examples due to Perry (1977). Observe the contrast in (60):

(60) a. Hume believes he is Hume

     b. Hume believes Hume is Hume

Even though the pronoun here refers to Hume through its anaphoric connection, the two beliefs ascribed to Hume are different. In (60a) Hume merely believes something that is true, whereas in (60b) he believes something that is analytic. This is captured by the indexings in (61):

(61) a. $Hume_1$ believes he_1 is $Hume_2$

     b. $Hume_1$ believes $Hume_1$ is $Hume_1$

(61b) is part of the mathematical fragment, as is (62), which attributes to Heimson the same belief as (61b) attributes to Hume:

(62) $Heimson_3$ believes $Hume_1$ is $Hume_1$

(63), however, does not ascribe to Heimson the same belief as (61a) ascribes to Hume:

(63) $Heimson_3$ believes he_3 is $Hume_2$

This is because the complements of *believe* differ in syntactic form relative to their indices.[21] Anaphoric reference, therefore, is not the same as repeated reference within the mathematical fragment.

The idea behind our discussion here is that in the "mathematical" register of the language multiple occurrences of a name can be utilized to repeat reference. To do so, Principle C must be overridden, so as to allow the names to be coindexed, and hence coreferential as a matter of gram-

21. (61a) and (63) do, however, exemplify the same indexical pattern, and hence are the same sorts of beliefs relative to their agents. Lewis (1979) employs these examples as part of his argument for *de se*, or self-beliefs. See Higginbotham 1991a for telling criticisms of Lewis's views; our treatment captures the spirit of Higginbotham's positive remarks on these cases, we believe. The status of *de se* belief is discussed at greater length in chapter 3.

mar, as in the analyticity of *John is John*. Because this metafragment allows for "anaphoric names," it is well suited for use in technical discourse. For instance, linguists commonly use it to report judgments of pronominal anaphora. Thus, we can report the anaphoric reading of *Jane thinks she is happy* by (64), where clearly we want to preserve the indexing assigned to the sentence on which we are reporting:

(64) Jane$_1$ thinks Jane$_1$ is happy

(In order to indicate the appropriate register, we normally accompany the repeated expression with emphasis.) A device corresponding to repetition of proper names is used for reporting on occurrences of bound variables by the use of demonstratives (again with emphasis to mark the register). Thus, a logic teacher may describe one reading of *Every man loves some woman* by saying *For every man, there is some woman, such that that man loves that woman*. This contrivance can also be used in order to explicate pronouns employed as bound variables. This allows (65) to stand in for *Every man thinks he is happy* in technical (or other appropriate) discourses:

(65) Every man$_1$ thinks that man$_1$ is happy

Another technical application is in elucidating the description of logical reasoning, so that we can report instances of the inference from "$\forall x(Pxa)$" to "$P(aa)$" as in (66) (adapting an example from Evans 1980), where the former repeats a numeral, the latter, a proper name:

(66) a. If every number is greater than two, then two is greater than two

   b. If everyone admires Oscar, then Oscar admires Oscar

In the metafragment the occurrences of *two* in the second clause of (66a) and of *Oscar* in the second clause of (66b) can be coindexed, in each case expressing grammatically determined coreference.[22]

   In order for the metafragment to be efficacious, it must be sufficiently expressive to report on pronominal anaphora in the language. To do this,

---

22. Bear in mind that the communicative import of cases like (66) is to illustrate an instance of the law of universal instantiation. Some authors have cited examples such as Evans's *Everyone has finally realized that Oscar is incompetent. Even Oscar has realized that Oscar is incompetent* and have argued that coreference is possible because of the interpretation of *even*. (See for instance Grodzinsky and Reinhart 1993, where *even* plays a truth-conditional role.) But this is to miss the point about such examples, since coreference is possible when *even* is missing, as shown in (66). Since these examples are illustrations of inferences via universal instantiation, no matter of presuppositions or implicatures is involved here.

there must be some way of marking coreference other than by means of the pronoun whose anaphoric status is being reported. This can be achieved by taking the metafragment as being defined by the inapplicability of Principle C of Binding Theory. Notice that although this characterization permits repetition of coindexed proper names as in the cases above, it does not exclude pronouns from the fragment. Thus, we can have not only the inferential illustration in (66b), for instance, but the one in (67) as well, as Evans (1980) also observes:

(67) If everyone admires Oscar, then he admires Oscar

As a sentence of the metafragment, (67) can have a representation in which the pronoun and the occurrences of *Oscar* are coindexed. In contrast, the indexing in (68) would not serve to illustrate the relevant inference:[23]

(68) If everyone admires $Oscar_1$, then he_1 admires $Oscar_2$

This representation would not express what the speaker wishes to say, since it would leave open as a matter of context whether the two occurrences of *Oscar* name the same person. But this is something the speaker does not wish to leave open at all. Given that (67) reports an inference in virtue of the sentence's logical form, the speaker will use a form in which coreference is determined as a matter of grammar. In general, in the metafragment nothing is to be left referentially open via-à-vis indexing, so that it will never be the case that noncoindexing is anything but noncoreference.

To summarize, identity statements fall into two categories. The first class consists of those whose indexing conforms to the strictures of Binding Theory. Such identity statements will be informative (save those with reflexive objects), since noncoindexing does not entail noncoreference. The second class consists of those that are drawn from the "mathematical" register of the language. They conform to Binding Theory as it applies to this register—that is, without Principle C. These identity statements will typically be uninformative, although they will be appropriate in discourse contexts in which analytic statements play a role, such as descriptions of logical proofs, or where the speaker wishes to assert a triviality, as in the aforementioned *You know who Zelda's husband is? He is Zelda's husband.* Where these two types of identity statements differ is that for the former coreference is not grammatically determined in virtue of indices, but for the latter it is.

---

23. (68) reconstructs the treatment of these cases by Evans (1980), who proposes that although the pronoun cannot anaphorically depend upon the second occurrence of *Oscar* for its reference, it can depend upon the first.

1.4 Predication

Identificational sentences are to be distinguished from another sort of copulative sentence illustrated by (69):

(69) Griswold is a cook

We refer to (69) as a *predicational* sentence. In it, *a cook* does not refer to a particular cook that Griswold is; the truth of *Griswold isn't a cook* cannot be secured by finding a particular cook that Griswold isn't. Rather, *is a cook* is a predicate whose reference is not an object. Let us call its reference a *concept* (remaining neutral here on the metaphysical status of such things). Sentence (69) then states that the referent of the object word *Griswold* falls under this concept. Many sentences of the form *NP be NP* are ambiguous between the identificational and predicational interpretations, the ambiguity often only being resolved contextually. For instance, *Griswold isn't the best cook in town* can be read either identificationally or predicationally; in the latter case it is taken as saying, perhaps in a somewhat sarcastic way, that Griswold is certainly a bad cook, perhaps even the worst cook around. There is a similar ambiguity in sentences such as (70):

(70) Griswold isn't my friend

This might mean that a particular friend of mine isn't Griswold, the question being left open whether Griswold is a friend of mine or not. Here the referent of *my friend* may already have been contextually determined. But the speaker might also mean that Griswold isn't a friend of mine; that is, (70) might merely be stating that Griswold lacks that property, without distinguishing him from any particular person.

Combinations of *be* plus an indefinite noun phrase are perhaps the most common form of predicational copulative sentence. That the occurrence of indefinites in this position is typically predicational can be shown from the fact that although the identificational sense may appear inverted, as in (71) or (72), such sentences lack the predicational sense of their uninverted counterparts:

(71) The best cook in town isn't Griswold

(72) My friend isn't Griswold

(73), in contrast, is strikingly odd:

(73) A man is Griswold

Inversion is possible only when both NPs refer to objects—that is, where they flank a relation. Indefinites in this context, however, do not refer to objects. Inversion is thus impossible for them, since English does not admit expressions of the form NP_i be NP_j where NP_i be is a predicate that NP_j falls under, although one could imagine a language constructed this way.

There are two ways in which NP_i may fall under NP_j in a predicational sentence: either it refers to an object that falls under the concept referred to by NP_j, or it refers to a concept that falls within (in Frege's sense) a higher-level concept referred to by NP_j. If we take indefinites as concept words and definites as object words, we will have predicational sentences of the form *The X is a Y*, in which an object falls under a concept, and *An X is a Y*, in which a concept falls within a higher-level concept. By this assumption, (74) and (75) differ in that in the former an object falls under a concept, whereas in the latter a concept falls within a higher-level one:

(74) The chimpanzee is an animal

(75) A chimpanzee is an animal

As shown by the inversion test, (75) cannot be an identity statement. *An animal is a chimpanzee* is not synonymous with (75); in fact, it is false. Thus, just as in a structure of the form NP_i be NP_j we take NP_i as falling under NP_j, so too with the more general relation of "falling within." We can gloss the meaning of (75) as a predication as follows:

(76) If X is a chimpanzee, X is an animal

In contrast, in (74) the term *the chimpanzee* has object reference to the class of chimpanzees, saying of this object that it falls under the concept *animal*. Now it might be thought that (74) and (75) are synonymous as generic statements. But if they were, we would not expect to find a contrast between (77) and (78):

(77) The chimpanzee is a species

(78) A chimpanzee is a species

Extending our line of reasoning, (78) is unpacked as (79), which is false:

(79) If X is a chimpanzee, X is a species

In contrast, (77) is true, since it says of the object that is the reference of *the chimpanzee* that it constitutes a species.

Given that the distinction between predicational and identificational sentences is a difference between predicative and relational forms of *be*, how do these two constructions differ in indexing? One possibility is that they do not. Thus, *Griswold is a cook* would be represented as in (80):

(80) Griswold$_1$ is [a cook]$_2$

This representation has the advantage that it satisfies Principle C; but upon closer reflection, this does not appear to be the right way to look at the problem. We assume that the predicate *a cook* refers to a concept and that *Griswold* refers to the object Griswold. And we assume that noncoindexing indicates not-coreference in the sense described above. But objects fall under concepts and are different in kind; a concept is the reference of a predicate, something that an object cannot be. We certainly do not wish it to be sufficient for the truth of *Griswold is a cook* that Griswold is not the concept of being a cook, since this would make (80) true trivially, regardless of whether Griswold is a cook or not. We want Principle C to limit the circumstances under which two *object* words may have the same object as their reference, not to require or prohibit the inalterable fact that the reference of an object word cannot be the same as the reference of a concept word. We fare no better if we represent *Griswold is a cook* as in (81), with coindexing:

(81) Griswold$_1$ is [a cook]$_1$

Here we would be asserting that Griswold, that person, is the same as the concept of being a cook, which is nonsense.

The underlying problem with the approach to indexing just described is that it reduces predicational sentences to identificational ones. By indexing *a cook*, we are saying in effect that it is an argument of the copula. We have just been at pains, however, to show this is precisely *not* the role of this NP in predications. Let us therefore take seriously the notion that Binding Theory, and in particular Principle C, applies to relations between argument positions. It then follows that Binding Theory is inapplicable to predicational NPs. This would be tantamount to saying that predicational NPs have no index, as far as Binding Theory is concerned. *Griswold is a cook* will thus be represented as follows:[24]

---

24. In terms developed in chapter 2, strictly speaking, we would not say that predicational NPs have no index; rather, we would say that they have no indexical type. Thus, we do allow for representations such as (i):

(i) I know what$_1$ Griswold is e_1. Griswold is a cook

(Note that *what*, not *who*, occurs in the predicational instance since reference is to a concept, not to an object such as a person.) That this index must be present is

(82) Griswold$_1$ is a cook

The ambiguity of a sentence such as *Griswold isn't Wagner's cook* will now reduce to the difference between (83) and (84):

(83) Griswold$_1$ isn't Wagner's cook

(84) Griswold$_1$ isn't [Wagner's cook]$_2$

(83) may be taken as synonymous with (85) and does not entail that Wagner has a cook, that is, that Wagner's cook exists:

(85) Griswold doesn't cook for Wagner

(84) on the other hand does entail that Wagner's cook exists; the identificational predicate NP is an object word, an argument of a two-place predicate.

Now, suppose *Wagner* is replaced with a pronoun, giving the following sentence:

(86) Griswold is his cook

Does (86) have both predicational and identificational interpretations? That is, are both (87) and (88) allowed, where, by the indicated indexing, it would be part of the meaning in either case that *Griswold* and *his* corefer?

(87) Griswold$_1$ is his$_1$ cook

(88) Griswold$_1$ is [his$_1$ cook]$_2$

We can show that an identificational construal is possible by considering (89):

(89) Griswold$_1$ isn't [his$_1$ cook]$_2$

Suppose that we do not know whether Griswold and his cook are the same person or not. Were we to learn that Griswold is Swedish and that his cook is French, we could conclude (89). Since the identificational instance of *his*

---

apparent because principles governing $\overline{A}$-binding are operant in this construction, so that standard sorts of syntactic island effects arise ; compare *What did Wagner claim that Griswold is* with the ungrammatical **What did Wagner make the claim that Griswold is*. The point here is that $\overline{A}$-binders may bind not only arguments but also predicates (as well as adverbial expressions, if these are to be distinguished from predicates), whereas A-binding considers only relations among arguments. But whatever index predicational NPs might receive, from movement or other grammatical processes, it is irrelevant, and hence invisible, as far as Binding Theory, and the determination of reference, is concerned. With this in mind, we will simplify the exposition by representing predicational NPs without indices.

cook is an argument, (88) should be possible for the same reason that (90) is:

(90) Griswold$_1$ read [his$_1$ book]$_2$

On the other hand, it does not appear that the predicational construal is possible, so that although (88) is a possible structure, (87) is not. This is made apparent by expressions that require predicational construals:

(91) Wagner considers [Griswold his cook]

Here the pronoun is understood anaphorically to *Wagner*, not *Griswold*. The reason for the absence of the predicational reading can be garnered by observing the paraphrases of (87) and (88) in (92) and (93), respectively, where these paraphrases preserve the relevant indexing pattern:

(92) *Griswold$_1$ cooks for him$_1$

(93) Griswold$_1$ is the same person as [his$_1$ cook]$_2$

(92) violates Principle B, but (93) does not. Similarly, we take (87) as a Principle B violation, but not (88). The idea we are getting at here is that (87) is a structure in which a predicate contains a pronoun, so that coindexing of the pronoun should be no better in (87) than it is in (94):

(94) *Griswold$_1$ saw him$_1$

In Binding Theory terms, we can state the insight by saying that an NP functions as a governing category for Binding Theory only if it is an argument, and hence bears a Binding Theory–relevant index. Thus, just as the phrase *for him* is not a governing category for *him* in (92), neither is *his cook* a governing category for *his* in (87). In contrast, the containing NP is a governing category for the pronoun in (95), read predicationally:

(95) Griswold$_1$ is [his$_1$ mother's]$_2$ cook

This is because *his mother* is an argument of the noun *cook*, the composed phrase forming the predicational NP. On this reading, (95) will have the sense expressed by (96):

(96) Griswold cooks for his mother

Here the pronoun is free in its governing category, as we take it to be in (95) as well.

Recall that in section 1.3 we observed that reflexive sentences such as *John is himself* can have an identificational reading, under which it would be indexed as in (97), pursuant to Principle A:

(97) $John_1$ is $himself_1$

This analytic reading is to be contrasted with another reading where it means something like John is his usual self, a reading we take to be predicational. Interestingly, the expression *his usual self* cannot appear in extensional argument positions:[25]

(98) *John hit his usual self

Furthermore, as would be expected, *John is himself* in this sense is not analytic; neither (99) nor (100) is contradictory:

(99) John isn't himself

(100) John isn't his usual self

By our reasoning above, the relevant reading in question of (97) is represented via the indexing in (101):

(101) $John_1$ is himself

Thus, we take (97) on this construal as predicational, an idiomatic way of expressing the predication otherwise expressed by *John is his usual self*. Note that even though the reflexive pronoun bears no index in (101), it will still be required to occur locally, in virtue of the independent locality of predications of this sort that require that the predicate and its argument form an immediate constituent. Thus, *John thinks Mary is his usual self* is ungrammatical, as a failure of proper predication.

To summarize, we have distinguished two sentence types of the form *NP be NP*, the symmetrical identificational and the asymmetrical predicational, and we have shown that they are associated with distinct patterns of indexing. These do not, however, exhaust the ways in which *be* can be employed in the language, since there are sentences of the form in question that apparently do not have the collection of properties associated with either identificational or predicational *be*. Consider (102):

(102) That sound is Jane

(102) is neither identificational or predicational. It is asserted neither that Jane and an acoustic waveform are the same object, nor that some acoustic

25. There are nonextensional arguments that allow the use of *his usual self*, as in *John saw his usual self in the mirror*. Also, this expression can be used in noncopulative predicative positions, as in *John* considers Bill *his usual self*, comparable to *John* considers Bill crazy.

waveform has human properties. Rather, on the reading we are isolating, it asserts that the sound indicates the presence of Jane. Perhaps you hear a squeak from upstairs, and you know that only Jane is upstairs. Then, you can authoritatively say (102). Notice that the sound you hear that gives rise to uttering (102) need not be characteristically Jane-sounding; anyone upstairs stepping where she did could have made that sound. The use of the proper name in (102) is to be contrasted with that in (103), in which the name refers to Coltrane's music, as in *I like listening to Coltrane*, and not to the person Coltrane:

(103) That sound is Coltrane

Suppose you are hearing a saxophonist with a derivative sound; you might remark (103), meaning that the saxophonist has a Coltrane-esque sound. Taken this way, (103) is a predication. (103) can also have an identificational reading, meaning that that sound is Coltrane's sound. In this sense, it can stand as an answer to *What is that sound*, as can (104):

(104) Coltrane is that sound

The reading of interest for (102), on the other hand, is not symmetrical; it is not equivalent to (105):

(105) Jane is that sound

On this reading, (105) could only mean that Jane, the person, has properties indicating a sound, a circumstance that is rather hard to conceive of. Let us refer to the sort of asymmetrical *be* found in (102) as *indicational*. Roughly speaking, the semantics of indicational *be* is something like the following: A sentence NP_i *be* NP_j is true just in case the referent of NP_i has properties indicating the referent of NP_j.

We might extend our understanding of indicational *be* to cover cases like (106):

(106) Olivier was his father

Clearly, (106) is false a priori if taken identificationally. But what if it were taken indicationally? Taken indicationally, (106) asserts that Olivier took on properties indicating his father. This certainly could be true. If Olivier were playing the role of Olivier's father in a play, (106) on the indicational reading *would* be true. That (106) is indicational in this context is confirmed by the interpretation of (107):

(107) His father was Olivier

This sentence can be understood as asserting that Olivier's father was playing the role of Olivier, but not that Olivier was playing the role of Olivier's father.

The status of indicational *be*, therefore, is no different from that of any other asymmetrical predicate. In particular, (108), taken indicationally, and (109) are on a par both in terms of the distribution of indices and in terms of their interpretation:

(108) Olivier$_1$ was [his$_1$ father]$_2$

(109) Olivier$_1$ hit [his$_1$ father]$_2$

Although indicational sentences are unlike predicational sentences in the indexing of the NPs surrounding *be*, they are comparable to identificational sentences in this regard. Thus, regardless of whether we take (106), for instance, as identificational or indicational, coindexing will determine coreference between the NP *Olivier* and the pronoun *his*. The difference arises with respect to how we take the noncoindexing of the NPs *Olivier* and *his father*. The indicational *be*, unlike the identificational *be*, does not contribute to the meaning that these two NPs are covalued any more than *hit* in (109) does; in either case we have a context of not-coreference. For indicationals, this will normally amount to noncoreference: (108), on this reading, is not saying that Olivier was the same person as his father (an impossibility), any more than (102) asserts the absurdity that Jane (a person) and a sound are the same thing. Rather, it asserts that Olivier portrayed some other person, by taking on properties that sufficiently indicate that person to the audience. Of course, one way in which Olivier could satisfy this requirement would be to play an autobiographical role; he certainly has sufficiently indicative properties to indicate himself. Then (110) would be appropriate:

(110) Olivier$_1$ was himself$_1$

Although this is a triviality if identificational, it is not if indicational, since it could be false (if, for instance, it turned out that it was Gielgud who played Olivier, and not Olivier himself).[26]

---

26. Higginbotham (1991a) discusses a reading of *be* that is asymmetrical like indicational *be*, although it has a much more severely limited distribution. This usage is found in the context of reports of mistaken identification. Thus, if Olivier and his father looked sufficiently alike that you mistook one for the other, you could accurately apprise someone of this mistake by uttering (i):

(i) I thought Olivier was his father

1.5   Coindexing and Plural Anaphora

It has been our thesis that coindexing determines covaluation: if elements are coindexed in a sentence, then it is part of the meaning of that sentence that they are covalued. For the purposes of singular anaphora, this rule is quite adequate, but it is known to be problematic when applied to plural anaphora. The problem concerns "split antecedents" for plurals:

(111) John$_1$ told Mary$_2$ that they$_i$ should leave

It is plain that (111) can have a meaning in which the reference of the pronoun is John and Mary. In representing this reading, what value should "i" in (111) have? It clearly cannot be either "1" or "2," since the pronoun is not coreferential with either of the expressions that bear these indices. Nor, it would seem, could it be some index distinct from these two, since then it would not be part of the meaning of (111) that the NPs *John* and *Mary* antecede the pronoun.

Intuitively speaking, the reference of a plural pronoun such as the one in (111) is the reference of the conjunction of the NPs *John* and *Mary*, the

---

As Higginbotham observes, (i) and (ii) report different misidentifications; (i) of Olivier as Olivier's father, (ii) of Olivier's father as Olivier:

(ii) I thought his father was Olivier

The significance of (i) for Higginbotham is to be found in a contrast he perceives between it and (iii), which he maintains cannot report on the mistake in question:

(iii) I thought Olivier was his own father

Presumably, the argument goes, there is an anaphoric connection between *Olivier* and *his* in (iii); but if there is the same sort of connection in (i)—for us, both are matters of coindexing—then (i) and (iii) should have the same status, in the context. Ergo, there is no anaphoric connection in (i). Higginbotham's argument seems suspect to us, in part because it does not seem at all inappropriate to report the mistake by (iii); the presence of *own* only seems to amplify the stupidity of the mistake—*Can you believe it? I thought Olivier was his own father. How dumb!* Moreover, if there is no anaphoric connection in (i), then we would not expect it to behave in other ways that turn on there being such a connection. But apparently it does; for instance, it can occur in sloppy identity contexts, as in (iv):

(iv) I thought Olivier was his father, and that Gielgud was, too

Although a satisfactory general discussion of these cases, as well as the particulars of Higginbotham's discussion of them, would take us far afield, what we wish to emphasize here is that they do not raise any substantive issues with respect to indexing and anaphora, although they may in other areas, such as the analysis of propositional attitudes. (We would like to thank J. Higginbotham for useful discussion here.)

NPs that are the "antecedent" of the pronoun. Formally, we can reconstruct the intuitive notion of conjunction of NPs by taking the index of the plural to be the "fusion" of the indices of its antecedents. We represent the fusion of i and j as $i \oplus j$. The reference of an NP bearing a fusion index will be a plural reference—a collection of individuals, who are the referents of the NPs bearing the atomic indices within the fused index.[27] Now, taking for (111) $i = 1 \oplus 2$, we have (112), where the reference of the pronoun is to John and Mary:

(112) John_1 told Mary_2 that $\text{they}_{1 \oplus 2}$ should leave

Letting $j, \ldots, n$ stand for atomic indices, and $j_\oplus, \ldots, {}_\oplus n$ for the fused index composed of those atoms, we define the following natural extension of what we mean by coindexing,

(113) i is *coindexed* with $j, \ldots, n$ iff $i = j_\oplus, \ldots, {}_\oplus n$.

where in the usual (non–split antecedent) case, this will reduce to:

(114) i is coindexed with j iff $i = j$.

For (112) it now follows that the plural pronoun, bearing a fusion of indices, is coindexed with its antecedent and thus will corefer with the collection of individuals composed of John and Mary.

The lesson of split antecedence, we believe, is that it affords a deeper understanding of just what is meant by coindexing, as a semantically significant mechanism, and how it is related to binding. Although pronouns with split antecedents are coindexed with those antecedents, they are never bound by them. This predicts that the distribution of split antecedents will not be limited by Binding Theory. Although this is not apparent in (112), in which the antecedents are outside the governing category of the pronoun, it is in (115), where they are both within this domain:

(115) John talked to Mary about them

In (115) it is possible to have an anaphoric construal, with split antecedence. On our assumptions, the indexing of (115) is as in (116):

27. To clarify this, we are saying here that when a plural NP bears a fusion index, this indicates only that it is the referents of the atomic indices that stand as the arguments of the appropriate predicates and relations. Left open is whether the predicate or relation holds of each member of the collected referents individually, or holds of them as an n-tuple—roughly, whether plural reference is distributive or collective. For some recent discussion of plural reference, see Link 1983, 1987, Roberts 1987, Landman 1989, Heim, Lasnik, and May 1991b, Schein 1994.

(116) John$_1$ talked to Mary$_2$ about them$_{1 \oplus 2}$

This structure is consistent with Binding Theory, since the pronoun is free in its governing category; it is not c-commanded by another NP bearing an occurrence of that index. Coreference follows here, however, because although not bound by either NP, the pronoun is *coindexed* with them, by the definition in (113). And it is coindexing, we have maintained, that determines coreference, not binding. Thus, split antecedence is just as possible in (118a) and (118b), where only one antecedent c-commands the pronoun, and in (118c), where neither does, as in (117), where both antecedents c-command the pronoun:

(117) Watson said Crick expected them to win the Nobel Prize

(118) a. A friend of John's mother told Mary about them

    b. John told a friend of Mary's father about them

    c. A friend of John's mother told a friend of Mary's father about them

Split antecedence is even possible if one of the antecedents is contained within the other:

(119) a. Bill's best friend told an embarrassing story about them

    b. Max's wife says they are still in love

Thus, (119b), for instance, can perfectly well mean that Max and his wife are still in love, according to Max's wife.[28]

In comparison to (115), an anaphoric construal is precluded for (120):

(120) They talked about them

What accounts for the contrast? The reason is that if (120) is to have coindexing, and hence coreference, it must also have binding. But (121)

---

28. Note that it follows from our theory that reflexive pronouns cannot have split antecedents, since they cannot be bound. To take an example, (i) shows a clear contrast with (117):

(i) *Watson said Crick expected themselves to win the Nobel Prize

Some speakers find an additional contrast between (i) and (ii), although whatever the reason for this, it is clear that these two sentences cluster in (un)grammaticality against (117):

(ii) *Watson said Crick expected themselves would win the Nobel Prize

Our thanks to A. Hestvik for discussion of these points, and for alerting us to the range of relevant cases.

will contravene Principle B, as opposed to (116), the structure of (115), which lacks binding:[29]

(121) They$_1$ talked about them$_1$

Unlike the case of split antecedents, this case has just two NPs, so that its analysis is no different from that of *He talked to him*. In either case the NPs must bear occurrences of distinct indices.[30]

A further instance of linguistically determined fusion of indices is found with conjunctions, for which we assume that the conjoining category bears an index that is the fusion of the indices of its constituent parts. Given our definition of coindexing in (113), it follows directly that a conjoined phrase is coindexed with its members. Hence, the reference of a conjoined phrase is just the reference of the phrases that it conjoins. In this regard, the interpretation of coindexing, in our extended sense, treats conjunctions and split antecedents in the same fashion, reinforcing the idea that coindexing, and not binding, is the basic grammatical notion of semantic

29. An issue arises here as to whether there are plural atomic indices, in addition to fused plural indices, or whether plurals always have fused indices, atomic indices being reserved for singulars. If we hold the former, it then follows that collections of individuals can be assigned as the plural values of a given position of a sequence. In indexing (120) as in (121), we have followed this course, although which assumption we make is immaterial to the point at hand, since if we replace the atomic index with a fused one, we will still have binding, and a resulting violation of Binding Theory. Also, note that if we assume plural atomic indices, then an indexing of (111) is possible in which the pronoun bears such an index. But then it will not be coindexed with either of the other NPs, making this a context of not-coreference.

30. Consider (i), whose interest was brought to our attention by J. Higginbotham:

(i) John told Mary that they ought to talk about them

Perhaps the most salient readings of this sentence are where one of the pronouns takes John and Mary as split antecedents, and the other pronoun has some other reference. But notice that (i) can also be used to report on John's having told Mary, "We ought to talk about us." In the sentence of which (i) reports this utterance, there will be coreference, but not as a matter of coindexing, which is barred in this context by Binding Theory. Rather, there is coreference because both pronouns must refer to the speaker and hearer, regardless of their indexing. In order for (i) to accurately report on what John said, the pronouns also must have different indices, yet be coreferential. Otherwise, (i) would report John's having said to Mary, "We ought to talk about ourselves," in which there is coindexing. But (i) cannot report such an utterance. Thus, (i) can have coreference in the face of noncoindexing because only in this way could there be a report of the sort of coreference possible with repetitions of first (and second) person personal pronouns.

import. There is a distinction between the cases, however, since although with split antecedence the antecedents do not form a single constituent that would be subject to Binding Theory, with conjoined phrases they do. In a case such as (122) Principle B will correctly determine distinct indices for the subject and object:

(122) [John$_1$ and Mary$_2$]$_{1 \oplus 2}$ talked about them$_3$

In this representation the pronoun is not coindexed with any other NP; it thus follows that it is not part of the meaning of the sentence that the reference of the pronoun includes the reference of any of the other NPs. A violation of Binding Theory ensues, however, in (123):

(123) *[John$_1$ and Mary$_2$]$_{1 \oplus 2}$ talked about [him$_1$ and her$_2$]$_{1 \oplus 2}$

It is part of the meaning of (123) that *John* is *him* and *Mary* is *her*, and accordingly that *John* and *Mary* are *him* and *her*. But this structure violates Principle B, relative to the fused indices borne by the subject and object conjoined NPs (presuming conjunctions of pronouns to be pronouns themselves). To have a well-formed indexing, the object NP must be free, which it can be only if the conjoined NPs bear distinct indices. Thus, either *John* is not *him* or *Mary* is not *her*, since changing the index of one or the other would alter the value of the fused index. (124), for instance, is perfectly well formed:

(124) [John$_1$ and Mary$_2$]$_{1 \oplus 2}$ talked about [him$_1$ and her$_3$]$_{1 \oplus 3}$

Whereas it is part of the meaning of this sentence that *John* is *him*, it is not part of its meaning, as a matter of grammar, both that *John* is *him* and *Mary* is *her*.[31] (124) can be perfectly well understood comparably to *John and Mary talked about him and Sally*, with the allowed coreference. Both pronouns can be coreferential, however, in (125):

(125) [John$_1$ and Mary$_2$]$_{1 \oplus 2}$ said that [he$_1$ and she$_2$]$_{1 \oplus 2}$ went to the store

This structure is consistent with Binding Theory. It is part of its meaning that the conjoined NPs corefer, and that the conjuncts also corefer, as indicated by the indexing.[32]

31. Some speakers find that the sentence with the order of the pronouns reversed admits the simultaneously coreferential interpretation: *John and Mary talked about her and him.* (This was brought to our attention by R. Larson.) Although it is not entirely clear to us why this is so, the important point here is the contrast that turns on Binding Theory, which holds for all speakers.

32. Suppose that we were to take plurals to bear not the fusion of indices, but a summation of atomic indices, so that, for example, a conjunction would bear the

We have argued that the noncoindexing of two NPs indicates that it is not part of the meaning of the sentence that contains them that the two NPs are covalued, at least by virtue of the indexical values of these NPs. In a simple sentence such as (126)

(126) He_1 talked about $them_2$

this means that it is not part of its meaning that the reference of *he* is the reference of *them*. It is compatible with this view that the reference of *them* might, in fact, include the reference of *he*, so that their values would overlap. We take this as an empirically correct result, which manifests itself in somewhat more complicated cases:

(127) [The men_1 and $Mary_2]_{1 \oplus 2}$ talked about $them_1$

This structure is well formed from the Binding Theory perspective; just as in (122), the pronoun is properly free. What follows from this representation is that it is not part of the meaning that the subject and object NPs have the same reference; it also follows that it *is* part of the meaning that *the men* and *them* corefer, just as it is part of the meaning of (128) that *John* and *him* corefer:

(128) [$John_1$ and $Mary_2]_{1 \oplus 2}$ talked about him_1

Therefore, overlap of reference in such constructions is perfectly possible as far as grammatical determination of anaphora is concerned.

   Lasnik (1981) considers the facts in (129), noting the difficulty in obtaining an overlap reading for them:

(129) a. They like him

       b. John and Mary like him

Taking these facts as indicative, he argues that the binding principles in the grammar should be stated not in terms of noncoreference, but in terms of nonoverlap of reference. But, he points out, then it would not be

---

index that is the sum of the indices of the conjuncts. This would allow for a representation such as (i):

(i) [$John_1$ and $Mary_4]_5$ believe that [he_2 and $she_3]_5$ went to the store

Here there are NPs that bear the same total index; from this representation it follows, paradoxically, that although the two conjoined NPs corefer, it is nevertheless not part of the meaning of the sentence that *John* is *he* and that *Mary* is *she*. This shows the nonmathematical nature of indices; recall that what is significant about the use of numerals is the characterization of occurrence they afford.

possible to account for split antecedents; he therefore proposes that they are cases of "free" reference of the plural pronoun. The conclusion he draws is that one or the other of these cases will be inexplicable, if all the grammar provides is a distinction between coindexing and noncoindexing. If it is to account for examples like (129), a notion of nonoverlap of reference is needed, but this excludes an account of split antecedents. On the other hand, a notion of noncoreference will allow for split antecedents, but at the cost of not being able to distinguish them from cases like *He saw John*, since both will involve noncoindexing.

Our views diverge from Lasnik's at two junctures. First, we hold that there need not be any grammatical notion of nonoverlap of reference, since the restrictions on this construal do not appear to depend upon those aspects of grammatical form otherwise relevant to the distribution of indices. If this were the case, then we ought to find a contrast between the following cases:[33]

(130) a. I expect us to meet John at the party

      b. I expect John to meet us at the party

But in both sentences an overlap reading is possible, even though they differ with respect to Principle B—only in the former does the pronoun occur in what would be a nonoverlap environment. A similar conclusion is invited by the following examples:

(131) a. The officers expected the soldiers to leave

      b. The officers persuaded the soldiers to leave

---

33. There also appears to be an order effect on the possibility of an overlap reading. Thus, an overlap reading for (i) seems strained in a way that it does not for (130a):

(i) We expect me to meet John at the party

A similar contrast is observed in *I sent us the bill* versus *We sent me the bill*. This effect appears to be sensitive to the syntactic distance between the pronouns. Compare (ii) with (i):

(ii) We expected John to meet me at the party

To us, (ii) sounds quite natural with an overlap construal. Also acceptable are sentences like (iii):

(iii) We made John president and me vice-president

Note that the latter examples make it doubtful that the order effect, whatever its cause, turns on Binding Theory.

(132) a. The officers thought that the soldiers should leave

     b. The officers demanded that the soldiers leave

We read the (a) examples such that the officers are included among the soldiers, but not the (b) examples, under whose readings the officers and the soldiers are two separate groups. Although these pairs differ along a number of grammatical parameters, they are not ones that differentiate them with respect to Binding Theory. Indeed, if Binding Theory were the determining factor here, we would not expect any of these sentences to admit overlap of reference, since these are all alike in being Principle C contexts. Cases such as Lasnik's (129), therefore, must be considered in the context of the possibility of overlap construals of examples such as (126) through (128), which are structurally indistinguishable. For us, the status of (129) does not turn on its grammatical form per se, but on the interaction of this form with matters of lexical meaning. Thus, for these cases, the grammar is silent on the *interpretation* (as opposed to the distribution) of indices.[34]

Second, in contrast to Lasnik, we have argued that split antecedents in fact fall under coindexing, not noncoindexing, and hence are not cases of free reference at all.[35] For us, insofar as there is any distinction between disjoint reference and free reference, it consists in the interpretation of environments whose indexing could not express coreference. The only notion of free reference we have is relative to structures for which it is not part of their meaning that there is coreference. Rather than being a matter

---

34. Note that the cases just discussed need to be distinguished from examples like We_1 *like* me_2, where the possibility of an overlap reading arises because it is part of the meaning of the pronouns that their reference includes the speaker. Thus, they are to be grouped with the identificational sentences discussed above, in that coreference is possible, although not as part of the meaning of the sentence in virtue of its indexing. Such an example differs from them, however, in that this reading follows not from the meaning of the predicate, but from the meaning of the arguments.

35. Note that elliptical sentences with split antecedents admit a "sloppy" reading:

(i) John told Mary that they should get married, and Max did, too

We can infer from this sentence that John told Mary that John and Mary should marry, whereas Max told Mary that Max and Mary should marry. Now, if the sloppy reading is grammatically determined, as is usually maintained, then it follows that split antecedence also must be grammatically represented. We will turn to more detailed discussion of strict and sloppy readings in subsequent chapters, simply observing here the difficulty it poses for a theory, such as Lasnik's, that places the characterization of split antecedence outside the grammar.

of grammar, free reference turns on the pragmatics of reference and anaphora, as in the coreferential understanding of *He put on John's coat*. In a sense, our theory is just the opposite of Lasnik's. Whereas for Lasnik, overlap or disjointness of reference is grammatical, but split antecedence is not, for us, overlap of reference is not grammatical, but split antecedence is. Therefore, the theory of anaphora can allow of only two indexical possibilities, coindexing and noncoindexing, so long as it is only the former that is linguistically meaningful.

Chapter 2
Dependency Theory

2.1 Indices and Dependencies

An index may have multiple occurrences in a syntactic structure; when it does, structures will result in which there are coindexed elements, each bearing an occurrence of that index. A formal theory of such indices and their occurrences should answer at least two questions: How can indexical occurrences be distributed in a syntactic structure, and how, given a distribution, might they be related to one another in that structure? A theory of the distribution of indexical occurrences is what we call Binding Theory. A theory of how they might be related is what we call Dependency Theory. The latter part of the theory of indexing, and the role it plays in the theory of anaphora, is the topic of this chapter.

The fundamental notion of Dependency Theory is this: an occurrence of an index may be *dependent* on another or *independent* of other occurrences. Therefore, occurrences may be related either symmetrically or asymmetrically. If occurrences are independent, then a's being coindexed with b is no different from b's being coindexed with a; if there is a dependency between occurrences, then this is not the case. For concreteness, let us refer to an occurrence that is independent of others as an *α-occurrence*, and one that is dependent on another as a *β-occurrence*. On this view, the sentence *John saw his mother* is formally ambiguous, differing in the type of indexical occurrence appended to the pronoun:

(1) a. John$_1^\alpha$ saw his$_1^\alpha$ mother

    b. John$_1^\alpha$ saw his$_1^\beta$ mother

We understand that the occurrence of the index on *his* is independent of the occurrence of the index on *John* in (1a) but dependent on it in (1b). Indices, we claim, are complex objects, made up of an *indexical type*, indicated by a superscripted α or β, and an *indexical value*, indicated by a subscripted numeral. Thus, although the indexical occurrences borne by the pronouns in the structures in (1) differ in their type, they agree in their value. Because of this value agreement, in both (1a) and (1b) one occurrence of the index *binds* the other, since one c-commands the other. But only in (1b) is there also a dependency. It will be important in what follows that these two asymmetrical notions—that of one occurrence *binding* another, and that of one occurrence being *dependent* on another—be kept distinct. Binding Theory, for instance, is sensitive to the former notion, but not to the latter. The latter falls within the province of Dependency Theory.

Given that we have a formal, syntactic ambiguity of indexical type, what role does it play in the analysis of pronominal anaphora? Consider the sentences in (1). Note that both structures express coreference. Since there is coindexing, it is part of the meaning of each structure that *John* and *his* corefer, as a matter of grammar; coindexed elements are covalued. However, even though the name/pronoun pairs in (1) are coreferential, as determined by their indexical value, we will argue that in virtue of their indexical type—α or β—they come by this coreference in different fashions. Corresponding to the distinct formal ways of relating occurrences of indices will be distinct ways in which the grammar can establish covaluation. The difference is as follows. For α-occurrences, reference is established independently for each occurrence; coreference obtains for each in virtue of individual valuations of each bearer to the same referent. Because of this, in (1a) the reference of the pronoun will turn out to be that of the NP *John*, where this reference is directly established for each NP just as it is in *John left* or *He left*, except that it will be done twice, rather than once. Because reference is established in this manner, ostension can accompany elements bearing α-occurrences. On the other hand, ostension is unnatural with elements bearing β-occurrences, which find their values through the intermediation of some other linguistic element that is prior to, or *antecedes*, it. The establishment of the value of this antecedent will be sufficient to determine the value of all of the occurrences that depend upon it; reference need be established, so to speak, only once for the index, rather than for each of its occurrences. The different indexical types thus indicate whether an expression is dependent on its linguistic context (β-occurrence) or not (α-occurrence). Indexical type, when taken in combination with specification of indexical value, will constitute the content of an index, and will encompass (along with lexical content) the linguistic determinants of the values of noun phrases.

To home in on the distinction we are making here, we can contrast it with another that has been broached in the literature, but from which it must be kept distinct. This is the distinction between "accidental coreference" and "bound anaphora," as these terms are used by, for example, Reinhart (1983), Roberts (1987), and Soames (1990). On an accidental construal for *John saw his mother*, the name *John* and the pronoun *his* would just happen to corefer, without linguistic connection between the two. But this sentence can also mean, on this view, that John saw his own mother, and this involves a linguistic connection. To represent this, the pronoun is to be taken as a variable, bound up by predicate abstraction:

(2) $\lambda x(x$ saw x's mother) John

It would be facile, however, to equate the distinction between accidental and bound variable anaphora with that between pronouns bearing α-occurrences and those bearing β-occurrences. Insofar as there is co-reference without linguistic connection in our theory, it is with respect to representations such as (3), where there is an α-occurrence, but no coindexing:

(3) John$_1^\alpha$ saw his$_2^\alpha$ mother

In those circumstances in which this sentence can be used to express coreference (see chapter 1), this coreference is not accidental. Coreference comports with the speaker's communicative intentions, although it would not comport with those intentions to express this coreference grammatically. Moreover, when α-occurrences are coindexed, their coreference is also in no way accidental, but rather is part of linguistic meaning. Since this involves a linguistic connection, if anything is to correspond to co-indexed α-occurrences, it must be the bound variable representation (2). However, this representation would also have to correspond to coindexed β-occurrences, since they also involve a linguistic connection, although of a different sort than with coindexed α-occurrences. Thus, the notion corresponding to coindexing encoded in (2)—namely, occurrence of the same variable—is not sufficiently articulated to capture our intended distinction in the ways in which coreference can be part of linguistic meaning. Therefore, the theory of anaphora we are proposing here discriminates not only whether or not anaphora results from linguistic connection, but also, when it does, whether this connection is dependent or independent.

For reasons that will emerge as we proceed, we believe that predicate-abstraction is not only insufficiently articulated, but also generally inappropriate as a device for representing anaphora, and it is unclear what role, if any, it should play in the semantics of natural language. In part, our skepticism arises because abstraction leads to a conflation of notions that must be kept distinct: a semantic notion of predication—the meaning of a particular type of constituent (for example, verb phrase or noun)—and syntactic notions of indexing and dependency. It has been argued that the use of predicate abstraction to represent bound anaphora makes it possible to capture a "reflexive" sense of *John saw his mother*, in virtue of taking "$\lambda x(x$ saw x's mother)" as expressing the property of seeing one's own mother, which in (2) holds of John.[1] It is not clear, however, that there is any phenomenon here that cannot be expressed by coindexing as structurally represented. That is to say, it is not apparent why the notation in (2) captures a notion of reflexivity, since there is nothing inherent in repeated occurrences of variables that specifies that they have the meaning of *x's-own*. (This point is due to Evans (1977).) One could, of course, define repeated occurrences in such a way that this meaning is intrinsic to them. But even then, it is unclear why (2) should "give" the meaning of *John saw his mother* rather than a logically equivalent form resulting from λ-conversion, which presumably would not express the reflexive predication. Alternatively, one could postulate a primitive distinction between the properties "$\lambda x R(x, x)$" and "$\lambda x Self\text{-}R(x)$" in order to capture the relevant distinction, where this might be thought to correspond to the distinction between α- and β-occurrences.[2] But leaving aside the question of how to ensure that *John saw his mother* expresses the latter property, it is unclear that there is ever an anaphoric reading in which *John saw his mother* does not mean that John saw his own mother, or for that matter, that there is ever a reading of *John saw Max's mother* that means that John saw anyone other than Max's own mother. Therefore, what appears to be involved here is nothing about anaphora per se, but rather something about the interpretation of noun phrases of a certain form. But if this is so, then

---

1. For example, Soames (1990) rejects a theory of what he calls demonstrative anaphora in favor of a bound variable theory on the argument that the latter, but not the former, can express reflexivity. However, he leaves open just how readings that do not depend on linguistic connection are to be accounted for.

2. A distinction of this sort is stipulated by Salmon (1986) and Soames (1987). Higginbotham (1990) observes that this view would also have to distinguish "$R(x, y)$ and $R(y, x)$" from "x and y bear R to each other" (p. 14). We agree with Higginbotham here when he says that "the needed distinctions are made for us once we attend to the anaphoric, or cross-referential, connections found within the sentences themselves" (p. 14). We do, however, disagree with Higginbotham regarding the nature of these connections; see section 2.4.

predicate-abstraction cannot give us any notion of anaphora that is any more expressive than coindexing. We will return to these matters in our discussion of inference and, in particular, of ellipsis in chapters 3 and 4.

In this chapter, then, our goal is to develop Dependency Theory as a component of the theory of anaphora, making concrete the notions of indexical dependence and independence we have been sketching. Our strategy is first to formally define a notion of *indexical dependency* (section 2.2) and to see how it can be incorporated into the semantics (section 2.3). In doing so, we will try to sew together two underlying intuitions, one syntactic, the other semantic. The syntactic intuition is that there is a distinction between anaphoric relations that depend on structural relations and those that do not. The semantic one is that there is a distinction between reference being given once for a structure and reference being given many times over. Section 2.4 is devoted to the relation between Dependency Theory and Binding Theory, as independent although interrelated components of the theory of anaphora, as well as to more general issues of the role of dependencies in the theory of anaphora. We will then turn in chapter 3 to formulating the identity condition on indexical dependencies. This will allow us to begin to draw out the major empirical consequences of Dependency Theory. This discussion carries over, in the specific context of anaphora in ellipsis, to chapters 4 and 5.

2.2   Indexical Dependencies

Our point of departure, then, is the following question: Under what conditions can we recognize an indexical dependency as legitimately present in a structure? Or, to put this another way, under what conditions can we take β-occurrences to be well formed in a structure? Our answer will be that β-occurrences are licensed if and only if they are *structurally resolvable*. That is, a dependent occurrence is possible just in case there is some other occurrence in the structure for it to depend on, and through which it receives its semantic value. The central notion of an indexical dependency, then, is to be given by characterizing the syntactic relation holding among the elements bearing the β-occurrences and their antecedent. Dependencies in this sense will be realized just in case it is possible to structurally describe the dependency.

Formally, the theory of dependencies goes as follows. Let us say that an *indexical dependency ID* is any triple consisting of a sequence of elements, an index, and a structural description:

$$\langle (c_1^\alpha, c_2^\beta, \ldots, c_n^\beta), I, SD \rangle$$

The elements of the sequence $(c_1^\alpha, c_2^\beta, \ldots, c_n^\beta)$ are bearers of the occurrences of the index I; such sequences must contain one and only one element bearing an α-occurrence of I—the antecedent—and at least one bearing a β-occurrence of I—the dependents. The structural description SD specifies the structure that connects the elements that bear occurrences of the index. Following notions originally defined by Chomsky (1955), we let a *structural description SD* be an ordered string $\langle term_1, term_2, \ldots, term_n \rangle$, and let a *phrase marker P* be a set of n-ary linear factorizations, $\langle category_1, category_2, \ldots, category_n \rangle$. Then a factorization F of P satisfies SD if and only if $category_1$ is a $term_1$, $category_2$ is a $term_2$, ..., $category_n$ is a $term_n$. Further, we let a *part* of a factorization F be any contiguous substring of factors $\langle category_i, \ldots, category_j \rangle$ of F. We can now link indexical dependencies to structures by the following definition:

A phrase marker P *realizes* an indexical dependency ID if and only if:
i.   for some f, f part of a factorization F of P, f satisfies SD of ID,
ii. the factors of f bearing I of ID are $(c_1^\alpha, c_2^\beta, \ldots, c_n^\beta)$, the elements of
     ID,
iii. there is no f' for which (ii) holds that has fewer factors than f.

We will sometimes say that an indexical dependency is *encoded* in P, intending this as equivalent to saying that it is realized in P. We now define what it is for β-occurrences to be resolved:

c_i^β is *resolved* in P if and only if c_i^β is an element of an ID realized in P.

Every β-occurrence of an index must be resolved; hence, they are licensed in a structure just in case they are associated with well-formed indexical dependencies.

   To illustrate the application of these definitions, consider the phrase marker (4) and the indexical dependency (5):

(4) $[_S[_{NP} \text{John}]_1^\alpha \, [_{VP}[_V \text{ saw}] \, [_{NP}[_{NP} \text{ his}]_1^\beta \, [_N \text{ mother}]]]]$

(5) $\langle ([_{NP} \text{John}]^\alpha, [_{NP} \text{his}]^\beta), 1, \langle NP, V, NP \rangle \rangle$

We read (5) to say that there is an indexical dependency between the NPs *John*, the antecedent, and *his*, a dependent, bearers of occurrences of the index "1," whose structural relation is described by the factorization given. (4) realizes (5), since (4) satisfies this structural description; that is, there is a part of a proper analysis of (4) containing the elements bearing the occurrences that satisfy the terms of the structural description. Hence, the β-occurrence is resolved in (4), and licensed in virtue of the realization of the well-formed indexical dependency (5) in (4). Note that the β-occurrence in the embedded clause in (6) is licensed by the same dependency:

(6) Mary said John$_1$ saw his$_1^\beta$ mother

The structural description of the indexical dependency in (7) is also satisfied by this structure:

(7) $\langle([_{NP}$ John$]^\alpha, [_{NP}$ his$]^\beta), 1, \langle NP, V, NP, V, NP \rangle \rangle$

But this dependency is not realized in (6), since it does not meet clause (iii) of the realization relation. There is a smaller part that contains *John* and *his*, namely, the part that satisfies the structural description of (5). This part includes no factors other than the NPs *John, his*, and the factors that connect them. What we are capturing here is that the differences between (4) and (6) are inessential to the dependency, since the syntactic material that appears to the left of the NP *John* in (6) is immaterial to characterizing the dependency in which it occurs with the pronoun. Realized indexical dependencies, therefore, are those that give just enough structural information to pick out a dependency in a phrase marker.[3]

Besides the structure in (4), *John saw his mother* also has the structure in (8), in which there is an α-occurrence on the pronoun:

(8) $[_S[_{NP}$ John$]_1^\alpha$ $[_{VP}[_V$ saw$]$ $[_{NP}[_{NP}$ his$]_1^\alpha$ $[_N$ mother$]]]]$

Although α-occurrences will be mentioned in dependencies associated with β-occurrences, their syntactic occurrence is not licensed through association with dependencies. Thus, no structural relation is specified to hold between the occurrences of the index in (8). It is in virtue of not being

---

3. Note that we place no restriction in principle on the order of the α- and β-occurrences in an indexical dependency. Thus, consider a sentence such as *His mother saw him*, which is formally ambiguous between representations parallel to *John's mother saw him* and *His mother saw John*, as well as having the representation in (ii):

(i)   a. His$_1^\alpha$ mother saw him$_1^\beta$

    b. His$_1^\beta$ mother saw him$_1^\alpha$

(ii) His$_1^\alpha$ mother saw him$_1^\alpha$

The sentences in (i) realize the same indexical dependency, although the realization is with respect to a different correspondence of the elements to the terms of the structural description. Note that we do not preclude correspondence restrictions being built into Dependency Theory, although we have not done so here. Our comments here hold just as much for cases in which one of the bearers c-commands the other as for cases in which c-command is absent. This is because dependencies are stated with respect to linear, not hierarchical, properties of structures.

associated with indexical dependencies in our technical sense that we say that α-occurrences are independent occurrences.

Two important properties of Dependency Theory can be noted immediately. First, β-occurrences are limited to the domain of dependencies, that is, to phrase markers. Hence, pronouns anaphoric on elements outside their phrase markers must bear independent α-occurrences; β-occurrences cannot be resolved outside their structures. It follows, then, that dependencies are a property of intrasentential anaphora; they are not found in intersentential contexts.[4] Second, a dependency may not have more than one antecedent, that is, more than one α-occurrence, although it may have any number of dependents. But what about cases like (9) in which a pronoun has more than one antecedent, namely, cases of split antecedence?

(9) John's wife said they are in love

On the basis of such examples it might be thought that the condition requiring a single antecedent is too restrictive, since it would preclude a dependency whose members are the pronoun and its two antecedents, the NPs *John* and *John's wife*, both of which bear α-occurrences. But even if we were to accommodate split antecedents by allowing dependencies with multiple antecedent expressions bearing α-occurrences, it still would not be possible to characterize a dependency realizable in (9) among these elements. Let us see why this is so.

In chapter 1 we proposed that pronouns as in (9) bear fusion indices that are compositions of some number of atomic indices. For (9), this means that *they* will bear the fusion of the indices of *John* and *John's wife*. The question that now arises is what status fusion indices have with respect to indexical types. There are two possibilities: they are either one indexical occurrence distinguished as to type, or the composition of atomic indexical occurrences, each atom distinguished as to type. If we were to adopt the former assumption, then a dependent fusion index would bear a single β-occurrence, and accordingly we would have to allow dependencies with multiple antecedents. On the other hand, if we adopt the latter, then rather than having a single dependency with multiple antecedents, we could have multiple dependencies, each with a single antecedent,

4. Although there may be discourse-based conditions on intersentential anaphora (see Heim 1982, Roberts 1987), we would take issue with theories that attempt to collapse intra- and intersentential anaphora under one semantic mechanism. For example, Kamp (1984) proposes that anaphora consists just in identification of discourse referents in either case. It is unclear, however, how such theories of discourse representation would incorporate a distinct notion of dependency, applicable just to sentential domains.

for each atomic occurrence. Dependency Theory forces the latter alternative. For suppose that fusion indices were single occurrences; it would then not be possible to realize a dependency for (9) of which both antecedents of the pronoun are elements. This is because there can be no factorization of the phrase marker of (9) in which *John, John's wife*, and *they* are terms, given the embedding of the first NP within the second. However, as shown in (10), where each atom is specified as to indexical type, we can have two separate dependencies, each of which can be properly realized in the same phrase marker:

(10) a. John$_1^\alpha$'s wife$_2^\alpha$ said they$_{1 \oplus 2}^{\beta}$ $^{\beta}$ are in love

   b. $\langle ([_{NP} \text{ John}]^\alpha, [_{NP} \text{ they}]^\beta), 1, \langle NP, N, V, NP \rangle \rangle$

   c. $\langle ([_{NP} \text{ John's wife}]^\alpha, [_{NP} \text{ they}]^\beta), 2, \langle NP, V, NP \rangle \rangle$

These dependencies each have only one antecedent element bearing an α-occurrence; thus, each atomic β-occurrence borne by the pronoun in (10) is resolved relative to its own indexical dependency. Split antecedence thus amounts to the union of those dependencies defined for the pronoun's atomic indices; what distinguishes split antecedence is that there are many dependencies associated with a given pronoun. Hence, even when a pronoun intuitively takes multiple expressions as antecedents, this breaks down formally into many distinct dependencies, each with a single antecedent.[5]

A third property of dependencies is that although *linear* dependencies are in general possible, *embedded* dependencies are excluded: no single factorization of a structure can contain both a category and a category it contains as factors. Thus, in a sentence such as *John took a picture of it*, a β-occurrence borne by the pronoun cannot be resolved because there is no way to structurally describe for (11) a dependency of the pronoun on the object NP as its antecedent:

(11) John took [a picture of it$_1^\beta$]$_1^\alpha$

If, on the other hand, the contained element is an α-occurrence, then this pattern of indexical values is allowed. Suppose that a speaker holds that Mary, a songwriter, is the leading vocal interpreter of her own tunes.

---

5. Notice that although we can characterize the split antecedence in *John told Mary that they should get married* via multiple single-antecedent dependencies, a single multiple antecedent dependency would not be ruled out in the way described in the text, since one antecedent does not contain the other. However, there are reasons for generally rejecting the possibility of the latter sort of dependency, as we discuss in chapter 4.

Then, the speaker could say (12), with the meaning that the coindexed NPs corefer:

(12) Fred loves [the best singer of Mary$_1^\alpha$'s songs]$_1^\alpha$

The speaker could also have uttered (13), with the name *Mary*, the bearer of an α-occurrence, replaced by a pronoun with an α-occurrence that refers to Mary:

(13) Fred loves [the best singer of her$_1^\alpha$ songs]$_1^\alpha$

Because α-occurrences are not themselves resolved, there is no bar to an α-occurrence of an index being embedded within another α-occurrence of that index. In this way we derive the *i*-within-*i* Condition (Higginbotham and May 1981a).[6]

At this point let us consider more carefully what we understand by *the realizability of a dependency with respect to a phrase marker*. In the presentation of Chomsky 1955/1975 (references given are to 1975) a P(hrase)-marker is a set of derivations, themselves ordered sequences of linear strings of categories; see the formal development in chapter 7, and especially ¶53.6. Chomsky distinguishes between a P-marker and its "collapsed diagram"; it is these collapsed diagrams that are so familiar as labeled bracketings or trees in syntactic analysis. Chomsky observes that a collapsed diagram may correspond to more than one derivation:

> [W]e call two derivations equivalent if they have the same collapsed diagram and thus differ only in the order of development of their terms. Then the set of steps of the derivations that constitute an equivalence class of derivations can serve as the P-marker of their common product. This equivalence ... has its graphic counterpart in identity of collapsed diagrams.... (p. 182)

In abbreviating an equivalence class of derivations, a collapsed diagram may have, so to speak, more than one history specifying its phrase structure constituency. We can now state more precisely the realization condition on an indexical dependency for a sentence S:

> An indexical dependency is realized in a phrase marker of S if and only if there is at least one *derivation* of the P-marker of S in which the dependency is realized.

6. We must be careful to distinguish the sort of examples in the text from reduced relative clauses or nominal adjuncts, which, like full relatives, do not display circular anaphora effects. Haïk (1983) points out examples such as *the man next to his dog*, which is comparable to *the man who is next to his dog*. What differs in these examples is that the pronoun is bound internally to the NP. On this matter, see also Hoeksema and Napoli 1990.

In what follows, where there is no chance of ambiguity or confusion, we will speak of a dependency being realized in a phrase marker or a structure rather than in the stricter idiom of its being realized in a derivation of a **P**-marker.

Now what if there is more than one indexical dependency for S? Then there must be at least one derivation of the **P**-marker of S in which all of the dependencies are realized. To take an example, consider (14a) and the realization of the dependencies in (14b) and (14c):

(14) a. John$_1^\alpha$ told his$_1^\beta$ wife$_2^\alpha$ that she$_2^\beta$ is beautiful

   b. $\langle([_{NP}$ John$]^\alpha, [_{NP}$ his$]^\beta), 1, \langle NP, V, NP\rangle\rangle$

   c. $\langle([_{NP}$ his wife$]^\alpha, [_{NP}$ she$]^\beta), 2, \langle NP, C, NP\rangle\rangle$

The labeled bracketing (15) is a "collapsed diagram," abbreviating the derivation (16) (among others):

(15) $[_{IP}[_{NP}$ John$]_1^\alpha$ $[_{VP}$ told $[_{NP}[_{NP}$ his$]_1^\beta$ $[_N$ wife$]]_2^\alpha$ $[_{CP}$ that $[_{IP}[_{NP}$ she$]_2^\beta$ $[_{VP}$ is beautiful$]]]]]]$

(16) 1.   IP

   2.   NP, VP

   3.   NP, V, NP, CP

   4.   NP, V, NP, C, IP

   5.   NP, V, NP, C, NP, VP

   6. NP, V, NP, N, C, NP, VP

   7. . . . etc.

In this derivation the dependencies in (14) are both realized, albeit with respect to different lines of the derivation. In particular, the structural description of (14b) is satisfied by part of line 6, whereas that of (14c) is satisfied by part of line 5 (where line 6 differs from line 5 in the expansion of NP as NP and N).[7] Note that there are other derivations abbreviated by the collapsed diagram (15), and in some of them one, but not the other, of the dependencies will be realized. But these derivations (or pairs of

---

7. The pattern of multiple dependencies realized in different lines of a derivation will be found whenever the dependencies structurally overlap in any way. For (14), the overlap arises because an element of one dependency contains an element of another, but the same pattern of realization will be found for the nested dependencies in *John told Mary that she loved him* and the crossed ones in *John told Mary that he loved her*. In contrast, the dependencies in *John told his wife that Mary loved her husband* can be realized in a single line of derivation.

them) will be sufficient for the joint realization of the dependencies relative to the indexing in (14).

Notice that in (14) a dependent β-occurrence is contained within an antecedent α-occurrence. This is possible only if these elements do not bear occurrences of the same index, since if they did, a dependent would be contained within its own antecedent, an impossibility, as we have shown. Moreover, distinct indices will be sufficient for a β-occurrence to be within an α-occurrence just in case their indexical dependencies are properly realized in a phrase marker derivation. It is the latter circumstance that fails to obtain in the analysis of (17), due to Jacobson (1977):

(17) His wife loves her husband

The problem with this sentence is that we cannot understand the pronoun *his* as having *her husband* as its antecedent while at the same time taking *her* as having *his wife* as its antecedent. The reason this reading is excluded is that there is no single derivation with respect to the indexing indicated in (18a) in which the structural descriptions of the dependencies in (18b) and (18c) are simultaneously satisfied:

(18) a. His_1^β $wife_2^\alpha$ loves her_2^β $husband_1^\alpha$

      b. $\langle([_{NP}\ his]^\beta, [_{NP}\ her\ husband]^\alpha), 1, \langle NP, N, V, NP\rangle\rangle$

      c. $\langle([_{NP}\ his\ wife]^\alpha, [_{NP}\ her]^\beta), 2, \langle NP, V, NP\rangle\rangle$

Observe that the collapsed diagram assigned to (17)—namely, (19)—

(19) $[_{IP}[_{NP}[_{NP}\ his]_1^\beta\ [_N\ wife]]_2^\alpha\ [_{VP}[_V\ loves]\ [_{NP}[_{NP}\ her]_2^\beta\ [_N\ husband]]_1^\alpha]]$

abbreviates a P-marker that contains (at least) the following two derivations, which differ in line 4:

(20) 1.   IP

      2.   NP, VP

      3.   NP, V, NP

      4.   NP, N, V, NP

      5. NP, N, V, NP, N

(21) 1.   IP

      2.   NP, VP

      3.   NP, V, NP

      4.   NP, V, NP, N

      5. NP, N, V, NP, N

Now realizability in a collapsed diagram (labeled bracketing) is insufficient to establish realizability in a **P**-marker; rather, for this, dependencies must be realized in a derivation of a **P**-marker. The dependencies indicated in (18), however, are not both realized in one or the other of the derivations in (20) and (21); (18b) is realized relative to line 4 of (20), and (18a) is realized relative to line 4 of (21). ((18b) is not realized at all in (21), nor is (18c) realized in (20).) In fact, there is no single derivation of those that collapse to (19) that can realize both dependencies. Hence, it is not possible to realize both the dependencies in (18) in a phrase marker, leaving the β-occurrences unresolved and accounting for the lack of the "referentially circular" reading of (17).

Note that our remarks about (17) obtain only if both indices are taken as dependent, as β-occurrences. If there is only one such occurrence (or none), then (17) becomes comprehensible. Thus, the indexing shown in (22), where there is only one dependent occurrence, is to be contrasted with that in (19):

(22) His$_1^\alpha$ wife$_2^\alpha$ loves her$_2^\beta$ husband$_1^\alpha$

Suppose that someone is describing the sorry state of modern marriage and utters the following discourse:

(23) Virtually all marriages end in failure these days, but there are some exceptions. For instance, his wife loves her husband

This is most natural if *his* is stressed and perhaps accompanied by ostension—indicators, we assume, of a nondependent α-occurrence. Although the other pronoun, *her*, may bear a β-occurrence of its index, this would not hinder obtaining the desired reading. Since there is only one indexical dependency, it can be realized without the sort of conflict afflicting (19). From the standpoint of dependencies, (22) would be no different from *Mary saw her husband*.[8]

---

8. Notice that a discourse of the following form is possible:

(i) *Speaker A*: His$_1^\alpha$ sister$_2$ bought a car
    Speaker B: Her$_2^\alpha$ brother$_1$ paid for it

R. Larson points out that this is a somewhat odd discourse; its oddness, however, does not appear to have anything to do with crossed anaphora. Equally odd is the following discourse:

(ii) *Speaker A*: He$_1^\alpha$ bought a car
    Speaker B: Her$_2^\alpha$ brother$_1$ paid for it

It appears that conflicting discourse conditions are at work here, having to do with

What these cases show, then, is that what underlies the problem with circular reference sentences is not a problem with establishing referents for the pronouns. Nor, for that matter, is it a problem with establishing antecedents for the pronouns: in and of themselves, each of the dependencies in (18) is well formed and realizable in some derivation of the phrase marker of (18). In contrast, embedded dependencies are realizable in no phrase marker derivation. (The problem only arises with the realizability of the dependencies in one single phrase marker.) Our view of circular reference sentences differs from that put forth in Higginbotham and May 1981a and Higginbotham 1983 (see also Brody 1982 and Hoeksema and Napoli 1990), where the problem is attributed to circular anaphora, the impossibility of establishing proper antecedence. The idea is that pronouns cannot be their own antecedents and hence depend on themselves to establish their reference. To obtain this result, however, it is necessary to define an extended notion of antecedence that mentions not only antecedence in the standard sense, but also containment: *his* depends on *her husband*, which contains *her*, which depends on *his wife*, which contains *his*, which would then be its own antecedent. It is by no means clear, however, why a primitive notion of structural containment should be part of the definition of antecedence, but it is clearly required if we are to view (17) as a case of anaphoric circularity. Dependency Theory eschews this notion for a notion of antecedence *simpliciter*; consequently, circular reference is not circular anaphora.[9]

To summarize, although Chomsky is surely correct when he says that "distinct derivations differ only ... inessentially from the viewpoint of constituent interpretation" (1955/1975:180), we see here that this distinctness becomes essential when taken from the viewpoint of anaphoric interpretation. The sensitivity of Dependency Theory to derivation stands in

---

the order of pronouns and definites. Note that the following discourse is also rather strange:

(iii) *Speaker A*: He$_1^\alpha$ bought a car
      Speaker B: John$_1$ paid for it

From the perspective of indexical possibilities per se, therefore, we would hold that all three discourses are well formed.

9. Notice that we could incorporate the extended antecedence notion into Dependency Theory by having simultaneous recursive definitions of antecedent and dependency, the former being determined as described in the text. Then circular reference would reduce to the impossibility of a given element bearing both an α- and a β-occurrence. However, to proceed in this way, the definition of antecedent would have to make reference to the structure in which its associated dependency would be realized.

contrast to Binding Theory. The indexing of (18a) is impeccable from the perspective of Binding Theory, both pronouns being free in their governing category. It is problematic only from the perspective of Dependency Theory. Thus, as was originally recognized by Higginbotham and May (1981a), circular reference sentences show that a notion of dependency is necessary independently of binding. In the current context, such sentences illustrate graphically a central characteristic of our theory: the independence of Binding Theory (the theory of the distribution of indexical values) and Dependency Theory (the theory of the distribution of indexical types) as components of the formal theory of anaphora.

Given the principles of Dependency Theory we have introduced, a question arises concerning the distribution of α- and β-occurrences of indices: What types of indexical occurrences can be borne by which types of noun phrases? We can answer this question by classifying pronominal and nonpronominal elements in terms of the types of indices they bear. This projects a basic typology of nominal expressions:[10]

$$NP^{\alpha}_{[-\text{pronoun}]} \qquad NP^{\beta}_{[-\text{pronoun}]}$$
$$NP^{\alpha}_{[+\text{pronoun}]} \qquad NP^{\beta}_{[+\text{pronoun}]}$$

This typology classifies expressions along two dimensions: a featural one and an indexical one. It is a typology of argument expressions (i.e., those that occur in A(rgument)-positions) and hence classifies those expressions to which Binding Theory and Dependency Theory are applicable. The classification along the featural dimension is one relevant to Binding Theory; [$\pm$pronoun] corresponds to applicability of Principle B versus Principle C. The distinction in the indexical dimension, on the other hand, is relevant to Dependency Theory, between elements bearing β-occurrences, whose distribution is constrained by indexical dependencies, and those bearing α-occurrences, whose distribution is not so constrained. The latter expressions, however, exhaust the class of expressions that can be antecedents of dependencies.[11]

---

10. One type of expression seemingly left out of this typology is reflexive pronouns. For reasons we turn to in chapter 5, we take reflexives to be composite forms, *pronoun* + *self*, and hence to enter the typology through having a pronominal constituent. Also, bear in mind that phonetic realization will be subject to language-specific conditions. For instance, English has an empty realization of pronominal α- and β-occurrences as noncontrol and control PRO, which does not surface in some other languages. See chapter 5.

11. Note that Dependency Theory applies to coindexed argument expressions, and not to coindexing in general. Thus, it does not apply to the binding of a variable

The typology partitions the class of argument expressions into two basic categories: nonpronominal arguments, realized variously as names, demonstratives, and variables, among other expressions, and pronominal arguments. What is novel about this typology is the way in which it cleaves these classes of expressions, projecting categories of expressions that are *obligatorily* coindexed with some other expression. The example we have provided thus far is pronouns that bear β-occurrences, although there are also nonpronominal β-occurrences in the form of epithets and incomplete descriptions.[12] Although expressions bearing β-occurrences are not morphologically distinguished from those bearing α-occurrences, they differ in that they must be realized in phrase markers relative to indexical dependencies, and hence they must be coindexed with some other expression in that phrase marker. Expressions bearing α-occurrences, on the other hand, are not so constrained, and they may occur not coindexed with any other element in their phrase markers. English is unlike some other languages in morphologically conflating these two types of expressions, at least for pronouns; other languages may use morphological contrast to mark them off. For instance, other Germanic languages have morphologically distinct pronouns (*sich* in German, *zich* in Dutch, *seg* in Norwegian, *sig* in Icelandic) that cannot be bound locally—they obey Principle B in this regard—but must be bound nonlocally, as Reinhart and Reuland (1993) observe. That is, they have properties of "β-pronouns."[13] Morphology masks such

---

by a quantifier or *wh*-word, since these expressions are operators, not arguments. Nor does it apply to the binding of NP-trace found in passive and raising constructions, since this is binding within an argument, not between two arguments. For the latter, see chapter 5.

12. Notice that nonpronominal expressions bearing β-occurrences will require that their antecedents do not c-command them, since they are subject to Principle C. The evidence for the existence of such expressions is provided by Higginbotham (1993), who observes that sloppy identity is possible in sentences such as *The people of every northern city hate the traffic in the damned place, but the people of southern cities never seem to* and *I read about Russell before I ever met the man, and you read about Chomsky before you did.* That sloppy identity is a diagnostic for β-occurrences is shown in chapters 3 and 4. Bear in mind that epithets and incomplete descriptions also have homophonic counterparts bearing α-occurrences, just as pronouns do. Not all nonpronominals can bear either type of indexical occurrence, however. Thus, both names and variables bear only α-occurrences.

13. These elements are usually referred to in the literature as "long-distance anaphors," mistakenly in our view. By saying that they bear β-occurrences, we do not mean to say that this exhausts their interesting properties; it simply places them in the typology. See the contributions in Koster and Reuland 1991 for recent

behavior in English; however, the presence of β-pronouns in English will be observed once we begin to look at how occurrences of pronouns in one sentence can be compared with occurrences in others. Showing this presence will be our concern in chapter 3.

The second aspect of the typology on which we wish to dwell is that although it is based on formal distinctions, the cells projected correspond, at least intuitively, to elements with distinct characteristic semantics. Thus, in developing Dependency Theory, we have drawn on an intuition that the typological distinction between expressions bearing independent occurrences of indices and those bearing dependent occurrences corresponds to a distinction in their mode of semantic resolution. Put in a general way, this intuition is that for expressions bearing α-occurrences reference is determined directly, independently of syntactic position. Among the expressions that bear such occurrences are expressions of direct reference such as names and demonstratives. Expressions bearing β-occurrences differ in that reference is only determined indirectly, mediated through a structural relation to some other expression, which itself can directly refer. The class of possible mediating structural relations, we have argued, is coextensive with the class of structurally realizable indexical dependencies. The basic semantic split, therefore, is between those expressions whose valuation is directly grounded within the semantics—those bearing independent α-occurrences—and those whose valuation is not so grounded, and which must be linked into the semantics through the valuation of some other expression. These are the expressions that bear dependent β-occurrences. Thus, our syntactic distinction between independent and dependent occurrences of indices is mirrored by a corresponding semantic distinction between direct and indirect interpretation. Characterizing this correlation of type of syntactic expression and mode of interpretation, and how (given our typology of expressions) indexical dependence and independence can be integrated into the semantics of anaphora, is the task to which we now turn.

2.3 The Semantics of Indices and Dependencies

In chapter 1 we introduced certain basic semantic ideas as part of developing the role that indices play in determining reference and coreference. Among our goals in doing so was to be able to distinguish two sorts of

---

discussion. Some languages also morphologically mark off α-pronouns; see footnote 22.

coreference: coreference that is grammatically determined, and coreference that is determined relative to context. Thus, for the former case, if i = John, then it does so for every occurrence of i, but for the latter, the same individual is picked out relative to different indices. If i = John and j = John, too, then we have a case of coreference, but this is not determined strictly in virtue of indices. To make this difference in coreference more formally precise, we introduced the notion of a sequence of individuals over a domain D, where a sequence models a context. For an expression bearing an index i, the denotation of that expression would be the value assigned to the ith position of the sequence σ. It now follows that if $\sigma(i)$ = John, that is, if the assignment to the ith position is John, then all expressions bearing i will be coreferential. This sort of coreference is strictly determined by grammar, independently of assignments to other indices. It also follows that if $\sigma(i)$ = John and $\sigma(j)$ = John—that is, if the assignment to both the ith and j^{th} positions is John—then expressions bearing i and expressions bearing j will be coreferential, too, but this coreference will obtain only in virtue of context. Thus, we can say that the indices mediate between expressions and their reference in that they take us to sequences of assignments of semantic values. In this regard, indices are the glue between the syntax and the semantics of anaphora.

In employing the notion of sequences as we have, we have departed from the role they play in a standard semantics for a first-order language. In such a semantics, sequences are part of the interpretation of quantification; thus, the quantificational clauses say something like, "For so many sequences that differ from an initially assumed sequence in just the assignment to the ith position, P holds." But whereas sequences play a central role in the semantics of the logical constants, they do not normally play any role at all in the semantics of the nonlogical constants, expressions such as names. These expressions just pick out their reference, independently of sequences. The facts of anaphora show, however, that we need to employ sequences in the semantics of the latter expressions as well, if we are to fully explicate the ways in which referential expressions such as names and pronouns can corefer. But in employing sequences for this task, some care is needed. When sequences are used in the interpretation of quantification, we take an arbitrary sequence over the domain and then consider variants of it; it does not matter what individual is actually assigned to any position of the sequence. But if we take referential expressions as also interpreted relative to sequences in this sense, then it could turn out that "John$_i$ left" is false even if John left, if it were to turn out that $\sigma(i) \neq$ John. That is, if the truth of "John$_i$ left" requires that the assignment to the ith position is John, then if we have, so to speak, the "wrong" sequence, one in which John is not so assigned, the sentence in question will be false. Clearly, this is a result we wish to avoid.[14]

In a sense, what has happened is that although the properties of anaphora have led us to interpret referential expressions relative to sequences, in doing so we have blurred the distinction between expressions that are semantical and those that are logical. Sequences are normally part of the logical apparatus, and not part of the semantical apparatus of reference. (In model-theoretic terms, this is the difference between expressions whose valuations are "within the model," and quantifiers, which are valued "outside the model.") This conflation has occurred, however, because we have assumed that the notion of sequence employed in the interpretation of logical terms, for which assignments are arbitrary, is just the notion that is appropriate for the interpretation of the nonlogical terms. But there are fundamental differences in the semantic use to which we are putting sequences when applied to the different types of terms. For names, sequences set *contexts*; by being indexed, the reference of a name becomes part of a context for a sentence. But it is the nature of quantifiers that they are noncontextual; the identity of values assigned in a sequence is immaterial to their interpretation. In giving the semantics, therefore, we must be careful to distinguish the sense in which sequences model contexts, and the relation of such sequences to quantification.

The sort of interpretive procedure we have in mind to meet this desideratum is one that makes two passes, so to speak: the first to establish reference, the second, truth. By this procedure, a context is "constructed" by assigning individuals to indices, where the indices are limited to those actually employed in the sentence. Thus, if we have the sentence in (24),

(24) Max_1 saw $Oscar_2$

we will want the procedure to establish that the context is $\{\sigma(1) = Max, \sigma(2) = Oscar\}$, with the domain of σ restricted to "1" and "2," and undefined for all other indices. On the view we are describing, the name *Max*, when it occurs in a sentence as an NP with index i, will determine that the ith individual of a context σ is Max, and it will make this determination for any index the NP may bear. Pronouns will function in a similar way, except that since they lack any lexical content that identifies a partic-

14. Avoiding this result is of particular importance for the semantics of identity statements. Thus, recall that we understand a sentence like *John is himself* as analytic in virtue of the coindexing of the NPs. But it could not be analytic if it could be false, which it can be if the index is assigned to some individual other than John.

ular individual in all contexts, as with names, they will determine only that the ith individual of a context σ is some individual (where this individual may be male or female, the speaker or the hearer or neither, etc., depending on the feature content of the pronoun). Coreference will obtain between expressions of these two sorts when they bear occurrences of an index—that is, when they are coindexed. By such an algorithm a unique context will be constructed for each sentence, so that the "wrong sequence" problem does not arise. This is because for "John₁ left" there is only the context $\sigma(1) = $ John; no other context is possible *for this sentence* in which $\sigma(1)$ is assigned to anyone other than John, or in which John is assigned to any other index. Hence, this sentence must be true if John left.

The semantics takes the form of simultaneous definitions of context, and of truth relative to such contexts. Our basic semantic notion is the relation of *valuation*, which we write as

Val(χ, Φ, σ)

and read as χ is a *value* of expression Φ with respect to a sequence σ. Now, suppose we have an indexed structure S. Let $NP_i^\alpha, \ldots, NP_n^\alpha$ be all the argument expressions bearing α-occurrences in S, and let $x_i, \ldots, x_n$ be such that **Val**$(x_i, NP_i^\alpha, \sigma), \ldots,$ **Val**$(x_n, NP_n^\alpha, \sigma)$. Then, g is any sequence that differs from σ only in that $g(i) = x_i, \ldots, g(n) = x_n$. We will call g a *context for S with respect* to $i, \ldots, n$ if and only if $Dom(g) = \{i, \ldots, n\}$. A context, therefore, is a partial sequence of individuals of domain D restricted by just those indices that show in S. We then proceed to define

Val(t, S, g),

that is, truth of a sentence relative to a context. We extend the semantics to discourses by letting $NP_i^\alpha, \ldots, NP_n^\alpha$ be all the expressions bearing α-occurrences in some set of sentences. Then the sequence g generated from these sentences will stand as a context for the entire set, that is, for all of the sentences that make up the discourse.

The definition of valuation for a language takes the form of a recursive definition from an axiomatic base, where the axioms directly interpret the structures of the language.[15] The axioms are of two sorts: categorial axioms, which give the value of an expression in terms of the values of the

---

15. Some care is needed here, since we do not hold that it is only the well-formed, or grammatical, structures that are interpretable. Grammaticality is not necessary for interpretability, since it is plain that there are many ungrammatical sentences that are perfectly understandable, with determinate truth conditions. This is, in fact, probably the rule rather than the exception.

categories of its immediate categorial constituents, and lexical axioms, which give the values of lexical items. (25) gives a set of axioms for a simple portion of English:

(25) *Categorial axioms*

   a. **Val**(t, [$_S$ NP$_i$ VP], σ) iff for some x, **Val**(x, NP$_i$, σ) and **Val**(x, VP, σ)

   b. **Val**(x, [$_{VP}$ V NP$_i$], σ) iff for some y, **Val**($\langle x, y \rangle$, V, σ) and **Val**(y, NP$_i$, σ)

   c. **Val**(x, [$_{VP}$ V], σ) iff **Val**(x, V, σ)

   d. **Val**(x, [$_V$ Ψ], σ) iff **Val**(x, Ψ, σ)

   e. **Val**($\langle x, y \rangle$, [$_V$ Ψ], σ) iff **Val**($\langle x, y \rangle$, Ψ, σ)

   f. **Val**(x, [$_{NP}$ −*pronoun*]$_i^2$, σ) iff **Val**(x, NP, σ)

   g. **Val**(x, [$_{NP}$ N], σ) iff **Val**(x, N, σ)

   h. **Val**(x, [$_N$ Φ], σ) iff **Val**(x, Φ, σ)

   i. **Val**(x, [$_{NP}$ NP's N], σ) iff for some z, **Val**(z, NP, σ) and **Val**($\langle z, x \rangle$, *gen*-N, σ)

   j. **Val**($\langle z, x \rangle$, *gen*-[$_N$ Φ], σ) iff **Val**($\langle z, x \rangle$, *gen*-Φ, σ)

Lexical axioms

   a. **Val**(x, *Max*, σ) iff x = Max

   b. **Val**(x, *Oscar*, σ) iff x = Oscar

   c. **Val**(x, *left*, σ) iff x left

   d. **Val**($\langle x, y \rangle$, *saw*, σ) iff x saw y

   e. **Val**(x, *student*, σ) iff x is a student

   f. **Val**($\langle z, x \rangle$, *gen-mother*, σ) iff x = z's mother

T-sentences will be derived by deduction from the axioms, as determined by the structure of the sentence being interpreted, until all instances of **Val** are eliminated from the right-hand side of the biconditional.[16]

---

16. That the semantics be given as simultaneous definitions over reference and truth is proposed in the work of Heim (1982) and Kamp (1984); antecedents are also found in the semantics for demonstratives given by Weinstein (1974). In giving an axiomatic truth definition, we draw directly from the work of Higginbotham (1985), and especially from that of Larson and Segal (forthcoming), who work out such an approach in detail. Bear in mind, however, that the basic ideas embedded in the semantics are general and could be embedded in a range of semantical systems. We are especially indebted to R. Larson for extensive discussion of the material presented in this section.

To take an example, consider the derivation of the following T-sentence:

(26) **Val**(t, [$_S$[$_{NP}$ Max]$_1^\alpha$ [$_{VP}$[$_V$ saw] [$_{NP}$ Oscar]$_2^\alpha$]], g) iff Max saw Oscar

We determine first that $g = \{g(1) = \text{Max}, g(2) = \text{Oscar}\}$. This follows from the axioms for NP, from which we determine that Max is the value of [$_{NP}$ *Max*]$_1^\alpha$ and Oscar is the value of [$_{NP}$ *Oscar*]$_2^\alpha$. The derivation of the T-sentence (26) is then as follows:

Val(t, [$_S$[$_{NP}$ Max]$_1^\alpha$ [$_{VP}$[$_V$ saw] [$_{NP}$ Oscar]$_2^\alpha$]], g) iff for some x,
   Val(x, [$_{NP}$ Max]$_1^\alpha$, g) and **Val**(x, [$_{VP}$[$_V$ saw] [$_{NP}$ Oscar]$_2^\alpha$], g)
Val(x, [$_{NP}$ Max]$_1^\alpha$, g) iff **Val**(x, [$_{NP}$ Max], g)
Val(x, [$_{NP}$ Max], g) iff **Val**(x, [$_N$ Max], g)
Val(x, [$_N$ Max], g) iff **Val**(x, Max, g)
Val(x, Max, g) iff $x = \text{Max}$
Val(x, [$_{VP}$ [$_V$ saw] [$_{NP}$ Oscar]$_2^\alpha$], g) iff for some y, **Val**($\langle x, y\rangle$, [$_V$ saw], g)
   and **Val**(y, [$_{NP}$ Oscar]$_2^\alpha$, g)
Val($\langle x, y\rangle$, [$_V$ saw], g) iff **Val**($\langle x, y\rangle$, saw, g)
Val($\langle x, y\rangle$, saw, g) iff x saw y
Val(y, [$_{NP}$ Oscar]$_2^\alpha$, g) iff **Val**(y, [$_{NP}$ Oscar], g)
Val(y, [$_{NP}$ Oscar], g) iff **Val**(y, [$_N$ Oscar], g)
Val(y, [$_N$ Oscar], g) iff **Val**(y, Oscar, g)
Val(y, Oscar, g) iff $y = \text{Oscar}$

Appropriate substitutions will lead directly to (26). It should be apparent that the same truth conditions will be derived regardless of the particular values taken for the indices in S. Thus, if truth holds with respect to some g for S, it will hold for any g.

Our fragment as given thus far only provides for the interpretation of one sort of noun phrase: names. We extend it to pronouns by the following axiom schema:[17]

---

17. Although we do not treat this explicitly, we might assume that the feature content of pronouns can place restrictions on the valuation of pronominal noun phrases relative to their context of use. For example, we can take person as fixing whether the pronoun refers to the speaker, the hearer, or neither, so that we would have the axioms in (i) and (ii):

(i)   **Val**(x, [$_{NP}$ I]$_i^\alpha$, g) iff $x = g(i)$ and $x = $ the speaker

(ii) **Val**(x, [$_{NP}$ you]$_i^\alpha$, g) iff $x = g(i)$ and $x = $ the hearer

Gender we can take as limiting what sorts of individuals can be values, whereas number determines whether there is just one value or more than one. In assigning semantic roles to such features, however, we must also be careful to disentangle the purely grammatical role they play in agreement, including case agreement. For some discussion, see Bevington 1993.

(27) **Val**$(x, [_{NP} +pronoun]_i^\alpha, \sigma)$ iff $x = \sigma(i)$

We can now derive the following T-sentence for *He left*:

(28) **Val**$(t, [_S[_{NP} he]_i^\alpha [_{VP} [_V left]]], g)$ iff $g(1)$ left

What distinguishes the interpretation of pronouns by the axiom schema in (27) is that they depend on context for their values. Notice, however, that given the definition of context, it will follow that there will be no direct specification of any individual in context for pronouns bearing α-occurrences. All that will be returned as a value of $g(i)$, given the axiom in (27), will be $g(i)$. For (28), then, $g = \{g(1) = g(1)\}$, a triviality, so that relative to this index, g will contain no contextual information. This amounts to saying that there is no nonreflexive determination of a value in context for pronouns bearing α-occurrences in virtue of their lexical content, as there is with names. Rather, their values, relative to a context, must be determined in some other way. There are two basic methods. One we can call demonstration, since this notion is applicable to the use of demonstrative expressions; by this method, $g(i)$ is stipulated to have a particular value relative to particular utterances of expressions. The second method is through coindexing. Suppose that a discourse containing $[_{NP} he]_i^\alpha$ also has an occurrence of $[_{NP} Max]_i^\alpha$. Then, in virtue of the latter expression, it will be the case that $g(i) = $ Max, and this will be so for any expression that bears an occurrence of i, including $[_{NP} he]_i^\alpha$. We will now have it that, in context, they will share a value; hence, coindexing determines coreference.[18]

---

18. As we have stated the semantics, the context serves as a given background for interpretation. However, the construction of a context can be thought of in a somewhat different way, as being built up as one proceeds through the interpretation of a sentence, and as one proceeds from sentence to sentence in a discourse. Under this view, each sentence in a discourse extends the context inherited from the previous sentence, the new indices being joined with those already established for g. Such a dynamic view has been suggested by Heim (1982) and Barwise (1987) (also see Rooth 1987). In Heim's file-card idiom, for instance, we would say that as NP_i^α is encountered, its value is written on the ith file card; the stack of cards so generated then constitutes a context for the discourse thus far encountered. As Heim shows, a virtue of this approach is that it allows conditions to be stated that reflect the relation between the unfolding of context and the felicity of use of certain types of expressions—for instance, the Novelty-Familiarity Condition, a constraint on when an index in a structure keys the addition of a new card (indefinites), and when a card already in the file is to be used (definites). Although we could incorporate such a procedure in our semantics, we will leave this matter aside in what follows, since the way we have stated the semantics will be sufficient for the aspects of anaphora that concern us here.

Let us now extend our semantics to quantification so that we can provide for the interpretation of structures such as (29), the logical form of *Every student left*:

(29) $[_S$ every student$_1$ $[_S$ e_1^α left]]

Variables can naturally be treated much the same way as pronouns, so that their interpretation will be given by (30):

(30) **Val**$(x, [_{NP} e]_i^\alpha, \sigma)$ iff $x = \sigma(i)$

Just like pronouns, variables have no value directly determined in context, and in this sense they have no inherent value of their own. Thus, in g there is no assignment of a value to i, i an index of a variable. But rather than being determined in the manner described for pronouns, the values of variables are determined as a function of the quantifiers that bind them. To interpret (29), therefore, we must bring into play the appropriate quantificational axiom. Let $g' \approx_i g$ stand for those sequences that differ from g in at most the assignment of a value to i; g' may be just like g except for the assignment of a value to i where g had none:

(31) **Val**$(t, [_S Q\text{–}N_i S^\dagger], g)$ iff for Q g', $g' \approx_i g$, such that **Val**$(g'(i), N, g)$,
    Val$(t, S^\dagger, g')$

($S^\dagger$ stands for the (open) sentence that contains e_i free.) We can now derive the T-sentence for (29) in the following way:

Val$(t, [_S[_{NP}$ every student$]_1$ $[_{S^\dagger} e_1^\alpha$ left]], g)$ iff for every g', $g' \approx_1 g$ such that **Val**$(g'(1), [_N$ student], $g)$, **Val**$(t, [_{S^\dagger} e_1^\alpha$ left], $g')$
Val$(g'(1), [_N$ student], $g)$ iff **Val**$(g'(1),$ student, $g)$ iff $g'(1)$ is a student
Val$(t, [_{S^\dagger} e_1^\alpha$ left], $g')$ iff for some x, **Val**$(x, [_{NP} e]_1^\alpha, g')$ and
    Val$(x, [_{VP}[_V$ left]], $g')$
Val$(x, [_{NP} e]_1^\alpha, g')$ iff $x = g'(1)$
Val$(x, [_{VP}[_V$ left]], $g')$ iff **Val**$(x, [_V$ left], $g')$ iff **Val**$(x,$ left, $g')$ iff x left
Val$(t, [_S[_{NP}$ every student$]_i$ $[_{S^\dagger} e_1^\alpha$ left]], $g)$ iff for every g', $g' \approx_1 g$ such that
    $g'(1)$ is a student, $g'(1)$ left

By this, (29) is true just in case for every sequence that differs from g in at most the assignment to 1, assignments restricted to students, the individual that is the value of that assignment left. Thus, the determination of the truth conditions of quantificational sentences proceeds in terms of the quantification over sequences found in the quantificational clauses such as

(31). The procedure may iterate in the usual way to derive the truth conditions for sentences with multiple quantifiers.[19]

We should point out three aspects of this treatment of quantification. (i) In giving a semantics for quantification, we want to capture the intuition that although reference is "about" individuals, quantification does not care about the identity of individuals. The semantics expresses this by variables not being assigned any nonreflexive values in context. In taking sequences as modeling context, our approach differs from standard quantificational semantics, in which values are assigned to free variables, but these assignments are immaterial to the evaluation of the quantificational context in which a variable is bound. Since it is necessary to consider each variant of the initial sequence, the initial assignment of any value to the free variables will suffice. But if any initial valuation will suffice, then so will no initial valuation. The assignment of values to free variables is essentially a formal artifice in the semantics of quantification and is not a necessary aspect of those semantics. (ii) In constructing the semantics, one of our goals is to allow for coreference in the presence of noncoindexing. No comparable effect is found in the case of quantification: noncoindexed variables can only be occurrences of *different* variables. They can never be taken as occurrences of the same variable, only coindexed elements can, so that here there is a stronger relation between noncoindexing and noncovaluation. The reason for this is that with other expressions bearing α-occurrences, assignments in a context to distinct indices can be of the same value. But variables are not defined for context in the appropriate sense and hence are distinct just in case their indices are. (iii) Since any variable that remains free in a sentence will only be vacuously defined for context, no truth conditions are derivable for the sentence in which it occurs. But as has been widely observed, structures containing unbound traces are ill formed. The constraint on "no free variables" thus follows.

The semantics we have constructed is a semantics of expressions that (in our typology) bear α-occurrences. They are the expressions that establish a context, in virtue of being expressions that directly refer. However, our typology also has expressions of another type, pronouns that bear β-

---

19. (31) can be generalized straightforwardly to other quantifiers, by establishing, for a quantifier Q, that there must be Q-many i-variants g' of g. We assume the background of semantic development of quantification in Higginbotham and May 1981b, May 1989, and Sher 1991, which places this view of quantifiers within the context of the theory of generalized quantifiers.

occurrences. Whereas the semantics provides definition for expressions bearing α-occurrences, it does not establish any index in context for those bearing β-occurrences. Rather, being outside the semantics, an expression bearing a β-occurrence will be noncontextual, and will have to be linked into the semantics in order to attain a valuation through the valuation of some other expression with which it is coindexed. Thus, the interpretation of such expressions will always be indirect, as opposed to the direct interpretation of α-occurrences. The linking in of β-occurrences will be accomplished by substitution; we characterize this by the following axiom schema:[20]

(32) *β-occurrence of a pronoun*

$\quad$ **Val**$(x, [_{NP} +pronoun]_i^\beta, \sigma)$ iff **Val**(x, NP_i, σ)

This reads that x is a value of a pronoun bearing a β-occurrence of i, relative to a sequence, iff x is a value of an NP bearing i, relative to a sequence. The difference between this rule and the rule for pronouns bearing α-occurrences is that the latter is disquotational (since there are no occurrences of **Val** on the right-hand side of the biconditional), whereas the former is not. But we must still assign some value to such pronouns, and this will only be possible by substituting an NP bearing i for which a value can be assigned, which in turn can only be an NP bearing an α-occurrence. Once that NP is located, then the steps taken in deriving its value can unfold, ultimately discharging the occurrence of **Val** and establishing the same value for the dependent as for the antecedent. As an example, consider the derivation of the T-sentence for *John saw his mother*:

Val$(t, [_S[_{NP} John]_1^\alpha [_{VP}[_V saw] [_{NP}[_{NP} his]_1^\beta [_N mother]]]], g)$ iff for some x,
$\quad$ **Val**$(x, [_{NP} John]_1^\alpha, g)$ and **Val**$(x, [_{VP}[_V saw] [_{NP}[_{NP} his]_1^\beta [_N mother]]], g)$
Val$(x, [_{NP} John]_1^\alpha, g)$ iff ... iff $x =$ John
Val$(x, [_{VP}[_V saw] [_{NP}[_{NP} his]_1^\beta [_N mother]]], g)$ iff for some y, **Val**$(\langle x, y \rangle,$
$\quad [_V saw], g)$ and **Val**$(y, [_{NP}[_{NP} his]_1^\beta [_N mother]], g)$
Val$(\langle x, y \rangle, [_V saw], g)$ iff ... iff x saw y
Val$(y, [_{NP}[_{NP} his]_1^\beta [_N mother]], g)$ iff for some z, **Val**$(z, [_{NP} his]_1^\beta, g)$ and
$\quad$ **Val**$(\langle z, y \rangle, gen\text{-}[_N mother], g)$
Val$(\langle z, y \rangle, gen\text{-}[_N mother], g)$ iff ... iff $y = z$'s mother
Val$(z, [_{NP} his]_1^\beta, g)$ iff **Val**$(z, [_{NP} John]_1^\alpha, g)$

---

20. (32) is a case of the more general axiom schema that applies to [$\pm$pronoun], thereby covering incomplete descriptions and epithets, which are [$-$pronoun] elements, as well as pronominals. See comments in footnote 12.

$\text{Val}(z, [_{NP} \text{ John}]_1^\alpha, g)$ iff ... iff $z = \text{John}$

$\text{Val}(t, [_S[_{NP} \text{ John}]_1^\alpha [_{VP}[_V \text{ saw}] [_{NP}[_{NP} \text{ his}]_1^\beta [_N \text{ mother}]]]], g)$ iff John saw John's mother

The step to observe is the third from the last, where the interpretation of the pronoun is determined to be that of the NP *John*, the steps interpreting this NP then being repeated, giving rise to coreference for the pronoun.

Notice that semantically, coreference between a pronoun bearing a β-occurrence and its antecedent reduces to coreference between α-occurrences. This is because the interpretation of an expression bearing a β-occurrence involves substituting that of a coindexed expression bearing an α-occurrence, and it is through the interpretation of the latter expression that a reference is ultimately obtained for the former. That is, we can only solve for the value of a β-expression by solving for the value of a coindexed α-expression. At the point of discharge of the semantic terms, then, there is only one sort of *coreference*, essentially that between two coindexed α-expressions, since it is only such expressions that can refer in the first place. Saying this, however, should not obscure the fundamental differences in the manner of valuation of pronouns bearing α- versus β-occurrences. The valuation of a β-occurrence depends only on its linguistic environment, since it must find its value through an antecedent in the sentence in which it occurs. A pronoun bearing an α-occurrence, on the other hand, is valued relative to context and is not sententially constrained in finding its value.

There is one sort of environment in which an NP cannot stand as an antecedent occurrence establishing the value of a coindexed β-occurrence —namely, when it contains the β-occurrence. This is because the result would be a circularity of valuation, and no disquotation of the pronoun. Thus, recall the discussion of *John took a picture of it*, represented as in (33):

(33) John took [a picture of $it_1^\beta]_1^\alpha$

The inability to associate the β-occurrence of the pronoun with a well-formed dependency in the syntax is mirrored in the semantics by the impossibility of discharging a valuation. The procedure assigning a value to a pronoun bearing a β-occurrence does so in terms of the value of another phrase bearing that index, rather than directly in terms of a value, as with α-occurrences. If that other phrase is itself complex, then in virtue of the compositional nature of valuation, to compute its value, the assignment procedure must compute the values of its constituent parts. These parts may include an NP bearing a β-occurrence, which, as in (33), may be of the same indexical value as the α-occurrence. But then, given (32), it is not possible to assign any semantic value relative to that index:

(34) a. $\mathbf{Val}(x, [\text{it}]_1^\beta, g)$ iff $\mathbf{Val}(x, [\text{a picture of it}_1^\beta]_1^\alpha, g)$

    b. $\mathbf{Val}(x, [\text{a picture of it}_1^\beta]_1^\alpha, g)$ iff ... iff $\mathbf{Val}(x, [\text{it}]_1^\beta, g)$

    c. See (a)

(32) is regressive in that there will always be an undischarged occurrence of **Val**. Consequently, it must be the case that the contained element is an α-occurrence, a possibility we noted in section 2.2.

This sort of circular valuation also afflicts sentences like *His wife loves her husband*, indexed as in (35):

(35) $\text{His}_1^\beta \text{ wife}_2^\alpha \text{ loves her}_2^\beta \text{ husband}_1^\alpha$

Say that we seek to assign a value to *his*. Given the coindexing of this pronoun with *her husband*, by (32) it follows that:

(36) $\mathbf{Val}(x, [\text{his}]_1^\beta, g)$ iff $\mathbf{Val}(x, [\text{her}_2^\beta \text{ husband}]_1^\alpha, g)$

Now, to compute the value of *her husband*, values must be assigned to its constituent parts, in particular to the contained pronoun *her*, which is coindexed with *his wife*:

(37) $\mathbf{Val}(x, [\text{her}]_2^\beta, g)$ iff $\mathbf{Val}(x, [\text{his}_1^\beta \text{ wife}]_2^\alpha, g)$

But to compute the value of *his wife*, values again must be assigned to the constituent parts. However, this includes *his*, the NP whose value we were initially trying to determine. Hence, we have again reached an impasse in which there can be no complete disquotation of the semantic terms, an impasse that can be escaped if one or the other of the contained pronouns bears an α-occurrence.

Given these observations regarding the semantics of β-occurrences, we see that syntactic realizability of dependencies establishes *necessary and sufficient* conditions for meaningful occurrences of phrases bearing β-occurrences; it will be possible to determine a value for every element of a properly realized dependency. The semantic problem surrounding structures like (33) for *John took a picture of it* and (35) for *His wife loves her husband*, then, is that both, strictly speaking, are meaningless if the pronouns bear β-occurrences, since there can be no definite derivations of T-sentences for them, and this semantic failure mirrors the syntactic impossibility of resolving the β-occurrences in these structures. The sources of this unresolvability are different for the two cases, however. For (33), there is no phrase marker derivation at all that can realize the relevant dependency, whereas for (35), there is no derivation that can jointly realize both of the relevant dependencies, although there is some derivation that can realize each one separately. (See discussion in section 2.2.) Note that if we were to analyze both of these cases solely in terms of their semantic failings, as suggested by Higginbotham (1989), for instance, we would obscure their different status vis-à-vis antecedence and dependency. Thus, it appears that neither the syntactic nor the semantic part of the character-ization of dependencies is dispensable, since there are aspects of the syntax of dependencies that cannot be reduced to the semantics.[21]

Given the way we have specified the interpretation of pronouns bearing β-occurrences—namely, that they are substituted for—it turns out that they are compatible with both referential and quantificational anteced-ents. Thus, if the value assigned to an antecedent of a pronoun bearing a β-occurrence is some referent, then the value of the pronoun will ulti-mately be computed to be that referent as well. For example, in (38)

(38) John$_1^\alpha$ saw his$_1^\beta$ mother

the valuation of *his*, as specified by axiom (32), will be in terms of that of the NP *John*. On the other hand, consider a case where the antecedent of the pronoun is a variable:

(39) Everyone$_1$ [e_1^α saw his$_1^\beta$ mother]

The value of the pronoun will again be as specified by axiom (32), but in this case the result will be that the pronoun will be realized as another occurrence of the variable. That is, the valuation of a pronoun bearing a β-occurrence that is coindexed with a variable will proceed in terms of that variable. In the case of (39), this means that $[_{NP}\ e]_1^\alpha$ will substitute for $[_{NP}\ his]_1^\beta$, so that there will actually be two occurrences of the variable. This will give (40) as the interpretation of the clause standing within the scope of the quantifier:

(40) $g'(i)$ saw $g'(i)$'s mother

What the referential and quantificational cases have in common, then, is that the substitution for the β-pronoun allows the semantic terms to be

21. For amplification of this irreducibility, see the discussion of the identity condi-tion on dependencies in chapter 3.

eliminated from the right-hand side of the T-sentences by substituting a valuation statement of an expression bearing an α-occurrence.[22]

Notice that we must keep pronouns and variables distinct. A lexical pronoun can only be a bound variable pronoun insofar as it can be realized as a variable, and this is only possible if the pronoun bears a β-occurrence. Thus, a pronoun bearing a β-occurrence is a variable if and only if it is coindexed with a variable. A pronoun bearing a β-occurrence is valued in the manner of a pronoun if and only if it is coindexed with another pronoun, that is, with a pronoun that bears an α-occurrence. Bear in mind: β-pronouns are *always* substituted for. Their status, therefore, always depends upon their antecedent; in the case of bound variable anaphora, we thus have multiple occurrences of a variable (syntactically, a trace).

In this light, consider the status of (41), which is just like (39) except that the pronoun bears an α-occurrence:

(41) Everyone$_1$ [e_1^α saw his$_1^\alpha$ mother]

The pronoun here is not, and cannot be, a variable. However, given the axiom for the interpretation of such pronouns in (27), (41) could seren-dipitously come to have the same meaning as (39), since the pronoun would have the same meaning as a variable. This would be a highly marked option in the grammar, however, since the grammar—which allows for pronouns bearing β-occurrences to be realized as variables—will normally treat pronouns bearing α-occurrences as reserved for refer-ential purposes, through coreference or demonstration. Thus, in normal circumstances pronouns bearing β-occurrences will occur in quantifica-tional structures, but not those bearing α-occurrences. There will be, how-

22. In a sense, then, English is a language that collapses two elements that bear β-occurrences: bound variable pronouns and coreferential pronouns. Evans (1977) was concerned with why a language would use the same pronominal form for both functions. His answer was to reduce quantification to reference. For us, the reduction is to dependency; what these two functions have in common is their connection to their antecedents through dependencies, not the semantic nature of those antecedents. Unlike English, some languages do have a morphologically distinct referential pronoun, that is, one that bears an α-occurrence but has no homophone bearing a β-occurrence. Thus, Japanese arguably has an α-pronoun *kare*, as opposed to the β-pronoun, *zibun*, as observed by Saito and Hoji (1983); and Sells (1987) points to the pronoun *hann* in Icelandic, which contrasts with the β-pronoun *sig*.

ever, certain cases of a marked nature in which α-pronouns can stand in for variables. We will discuss these in chapter 3.

By saying that pronouns bearing α-occurrences are not variables, we do not mean to preclude the possibility that such pronouns can be anaphoric to quantified phrases. To take one example, consider (42), where the plural pronoun is understood as all the sailors:

(42) Few sailors$_1$ like the army, but they$_1^a$ like the navy

Here, the pronoun can only bear an α-occurrence, because the expression with which it is coindexed occurs in another sentence, barring its association with an indexical dependency. It is well known that the defining property of the sort of anaphoric relation to quantified phrases found in (42) is precisely that the pronoun is not construed as a bound variable. If it were, then (42) would be interpreted in roughly the same way as *Few sailors like the army and the navy*—incorrectly, since (42) implies that all the sailors like the navy. The pronoun in (42) is familiar as one kind of E-type pronoun brought to light by Evans (1977, 1980). To accommodate this particular type of anaphora, we will need to extend the semantics in such a way that quantified expressions can make available referential values for plural pronouns bearing α-occurrences. Suppose then that we can gather up the assignments of individuals that answer to the variable the quantifier binds, so that a quantified phrase contributes to a context g a value for $g(i)$, where for $[_{NP} Q-N]_i$ this is $\{x | x \text{ is an } N\}$.[23] Once established in context, this plural value can then also serve as a value for other expressions of plural reference indexed i. In the case of (42), the pronoun's

23. In the general case, the reference of E-type pronouns can be recovered from the overall clausal context of the quantificational antecedent; Evans (1977, 1980) notes many examples to this effect. Thus, in making the semantics more precise, values for E-type pronouns will have to be added to the context, so to speak, dynamically, and not introduced in the initial construction of a context, since g is initially defined only relative to expressions bearing α-occurrences, and not with respect to their syntactic environments. This predicts that there will be no backward E-type anaphora, as opposed to backward coreference anaphora, as appears to be the case. Notice that whereas E-type pronouns may depend on syntactic environment, in (42) the reference is only to be recovered from the nominal complement to the quantifier. If it were to be recovered from the entire clause, then the second clause would mean incorrectly that the sailors who like the army also like the navy. See Neale 1990: chap. 5 for discussion of what "recoverability" amounts to.

referents will be the sailors, made available in the way described by *few sailors*.[24]

24. Although many important issues in anaphora arise with respect to E-type pronouns, we leave aside a full treatment of their syntax and semantics, since our goal is just to indicate how such pronouns fit into the scheme of occurrence types. For recent discussion of E-type pronouns, including their relation to indefinites (which we do not address here), see Heim 1982, 1990, Neale 1990, among others. However, a few observations are in order. First, there are other pronouns categorized as E-type that (unlike the one in (42), which bears an α-occurrence) bear β-occurrences. Among these are certain "donkey-pronouns." In chapters 3 and 4 we show that sloppy construals of pronouns are possible only when they bear β-occurrences; thus, note the availability of a sloppy reading in *Every man who owns a donkey beats it, and every man who owns a cow does, too*. Second, in holding that a reference for an E-type pronoun is made available by, or recovered from, an antecedent quantifier phrase, we follow the spirit of Evans's approach, although Evans himself is somewhat imprecise in his informal descriptions of what this recovery consists in. In Evans 1980, he states that E-type pronouns "[refer] to the object(s), if any, which *verify* the antecedent quantifier-containing clause" (p. 340), but later says that "their reference [is] fixed by a description recoverable from the antecedent, quantifier-containing, clause" (p. 344). These statements do not appear to be equivalent, since they can be construed to make different predictions about E-type pronouns with negative quantifiers such as *no*. Evans takes it as criterial of E-type pronouns that they cannot have such antecedents, and the initial characterization of the semantics would rule out this possibility, since there are no objects that verify sentences containing negative quantifiers; *No sailor likes the army* is false if some sailor does. However, contrary to Evans's empirical claim, it appears that E-type pronouns do occur in negative quantifier contexts. Thus, *No sailor likes the army, but they like the navy* is well formed, and it has just the E-type pronoun properties described for (42). This case would apparently be allowed by Evans's second characterization because of the recoverability of the description *the sailors*. It is also allowed on the semantics described in the text. Third, Evans's approach to E-type pronouns reflects one of two main trends of thinking on this sort of anaphora. The other, championed by Neale (1990), is that the pronoun is itself (or is replaced by) a definite description. On this view, we would replace *they* by *the sailors* in (42). Neale also holds that descriptions are a species of quantifier expression, adducing arguments, derived from Kripke (1979), that such pronouns can have scope and hence are subject to the rules determining quantifier scope. We could incorporate this alternative approach here, although it is unclear to us that the scope properties are incompatible with Evans's approach. Thus, note that in (42) the E-type pronoun has distributed universal force, meaning something like *the sailors each*. But then the quantificational properties are arising from the distributed aspect of plurals, and not from how the pronoun gets its value. Note, also, that it could be that E-type pronouns, qua pronouns, move at LF and then pick up a referential value, much like the *wh*-phrase in nonrestrictive clauses like the one in *Napoleon, who won at Borodino, lost at Waterloo*. For discussion of parallelisms between E-type pronouns and such definite operators, see Sells 1986.

What we have now established semantically is that the difference between indexical types corresponds to different paths to reference, the direct and the indirect. These two paths, however, may very well lead to the same reference. Thus, regardless of whether a pronoun bears an α- or a β-occurrence in a sentence such as *John saw his mother*, the truth conditions derived will be exactly the same. Since the reference of the pronoun will be established as John for either type of pronoun, John's mother being seen by John will be sufficient for the truth of either sentence. This equivalence notwithstanding, the distinction between occurrence types can make a difference in truth conditions. Such cases will arise where not only the reference of expressions but also their formal structure is pertinent to determining truth conditions. Since indication of indexical type, along with indexical value, is what makes up an index, and since indices are formal aspects of linguistic structure, it follows that in such cases difference in truth conditions can turn on difference of indexical value (as shown in chapter 1) or of indexical type. Let us consider such a case.

Suppose we take a *wh*-question of the form *wh* $P(x)$, for example, *Who left*, where $P(x)$ corresponds to the clause *t left* in logical form. This will be a different question from *wh* $Q(x)$, if $P \neq Q$; *Who came* is not the same question as *Who left*. Now suppose we have the following procedure for obtaining *direct answers* to *wh*-questions: Delete *wh*, and substitute an appropriate nominal expression for x. The rest remains the same, up to convenient anaphoric substitutions. Thus, $P(John)$ is a direct answer to *wh* $P(x)$, and $Q(John)$ is a direct answer to *wh* $Q(x)$, but $P(John)$ is not. By this, *John left* is a direct answer to *Who left*, but *John came* is not, and *Max saw his mother* is a direct answer to *Who saw John's mother*, with *his* and *John* coreferential. Distinct questions, therefore, determine distinct direct answers.[25]

Now take a set of answers to *wh* $P(x)$, and suppose that each answer is uttered by some speaker. Then, it will be sufficient for the truth of (43)

(43) Mary answered $P(John)$

that Mary has given $P(John)$ as an answer to *wh* $P(x)$. Mary's having given this answer, however, would not be sufficient for the truth of (44),

(44) Mary answered $Q(John)$

nor, for that matter, would her utterance of $Q(John)$, which is sufficient

---

25. For discussion of the semantics of questions, and the classification of answers we are assuming, see Higginbotham and May 1981a, May 1988, 1989, Higginbotham 1991b. Also, see Lahiri 1991 for development of this approach.

for the truth of (44), be sufficient for the truth of (43). This is so even if P and Q are coextensive, because answers to questions are in part determined by their form. In this light, consider (45):

(45) Mary answered John loves his mother

(45) is true if Mary answered by uttering *John loves his mother*. But this could be an answer to two different questions:

(46) a. Who loves John's mother

     b. Who loves his mother

Clearly, these questions are requests for quite different sorts of information. But then, (45) must be reporting ambiguously on two different forms, since different questions determine different answers. The issue, then, is to determine what this difference consists in.

We can rule out certain possibilities immediately. First of all, it does not involve any difference in reference, since in each case the pronoun refers to John. Similarly, it cannot be a matter of differential indexing, since in both cases coreference is required, not simply allowed. Thus, there is no reason to think that there is anything other than coindexing of *John* and *his* in (45). Where there can be a difference, however, is in indexical type. The key here is that since there is a difference in indexical types in the questions in (46), this will carry over to the indexical types of their answers. Consider then the representations of the questions in (46):

(47) a. Who [t loves John$_1^\alpha$'s mother]

     b. Who [t loves his$_1^\beta$ mother]

In (47a) the name bears an α-occurrence, by Dependency Theory, and must not be coindexed with the subject NP, by Binding Theory. In (47b) the pronoun is a bound variable pronoun, coindexed with the variable, and hence must bear a β-occurrence. Now we can give answers to these questions by substituting some name in the manner described above. Suppose that this is *John*:

(48) a. John loves John$_1^\alpha$'s mother

     b. John loves his$_1^\beta$ mother

in order to prevent confusion that might arise because of Binding Theory, (48a) would normally be replaced by (49), since this would permit coreference to be directly expressed:

(49) John loves his$_1^\alpha$ mother

(49) and (48b) are the answers given by Mary to the questions in (47a) and (47b), respectively. Her doing so can be reported on by the following sentences:

(50) a. Mary answered John loves his$_1^\alpha$ mother

      b. Mary answered John loves his$_1^\beta$ mother

(50a) is true if Mary gave (49) as an answer to (47a), and (50b) is true if Mary gave (48b) as an answer to (47b). But, obviously, (50b) is false if it reports on an answer to (47a), since it does not report an answer to this question at all, and similarly (50a) is false as a report of an answer to (47b). The ambiguity of the string *Mary answered John loves his mother* is thus now revealed as an ambiguity of indexical type.

To summarize, in developing the semantics for dependencies, we have sought to express certain generalizations that accrue to the indexical types. Our emphasis has been on the direct interpretation of expressions bearing α-occurrences, as opposed to the indirect interpretation of those bearing β-occurrences. Moreover, we have sought to correlate this difference in their manner of interpretation with two basic properties of pronouns: (i) pronouns bearing β-occurrences must have antecedents within their phrase markers, a constraint that does not apply to α-occurrences; and (ii) pronouns bearing α-occurrences are limited to taking referential antecedents, as opposed to those bearing β-occurrences, which can take either referential or quantificational antecedents. In the chapters to follow we will be looking at differences in the interpretation of anaphora that arise in virtue of indexical types, although unlike the case we have just considered, where truth conditions are directly affected, these will be cases where the effects are indirect.

2.4   Dependency Theory and Binding Theory

The theory of anaphora we have developed in chapters 1 and 2 is based on the thesis that its formal part has two components: a theory of binding and a theory of dependencies, or, in other words, theories of the distributions and relations of occurrences of indices. These theories differ in their foundational notions. Those of Binding Theory—free and bound —are defined relative to hierarchical properties of structures, namely, c-command; those of Dependency Theory—independent and dependent —are defined relative to linear properties. The notions of the two theories are not to be confused: either free or bound occurrences of indices may be independent or dependent occurrences. This is because Binding Theory allows an occurrence of either sort to be one of many occurrences of a given index in a structure; that is, either free or bound occurrences can be *coindexed*. It is among coindexed elements that indexical dependencies can obtain, by Dependency Theory, although coindexed elements may also be independent, as singleton occurrences of indices must be. Thus, two sub-cases are subsumed under coindexing: independence—coindexing among α-occurrences—and dependence—coindexing between an α-occurrence and β-occurrences. Both of these circumstances hold for expressions that are grammatically determined to be covalued, since this is a matter solely of coindexing, which, in the appropriate sense, identifies the expressions. In contrast, when expressions bear occurrences of different indices, the grammar does not determine that they are covalued. Rather, the grammar leaves such matters open; in the case of coreference, this means that noncoindexing is grammatically compatible with noncoreference, as well as with coreference. But although this coreference is allowed, neither it nor noncoreference will be grammatically determined.

That the lack of a grammatically determined anaphoric connection allows, but does not imply, noncoreference, although the presence of such a connection does imply the inverse, is a lesson that was initially taught by Evans (1977, 1980). Evans developed a view of anaphora in which dependencies play a central role in characterizing anaphora. In his conception, the anaphoric connections determined by the grammar are *referential dependencies*, where a dependent expression and its antecedent are coreferential.[26] Referential dependencies may anaphorically connect expressions when they occur in one sentence, as well as when they occur in different sentences, and they are the only sort of anaphoric connection that can hold grammatically among expressions, although Evans does not prohibit expressions independently referring to the same object when one is not referentially dependent on the other. Although either route will allow a speaker to use a sentence when coreference is intended, only in the former

26. For Evans, it was a desideratum that the pronouns in *John saw his mother* and *Everyone saw his mother* not be seen as unrelated. He therefore sought to assimilate the cases through a theory of quantification on which it comes out that *Everyone saw his mother* is true if and only if for every x, if "$β$" refers to x, the sentence $β$ *saw his mother* is true. A referential dependency may then hold in the substitution instances between the pronoun and $β$, just as it may between the pronoun and *John* in *John saw his mother*. Thus, that the dependencies are *referential* dependencies is significant for Evans.

way will this usage be based on a sentence in which anaphora is grammatically represented.[27]

The theory we are presenting departs from Evans's in fundamental ways, and it is our goal in this section to describe these differences. The primary one is that on our theory, dependencies do not grammatically represent anaphoric connections. This role is fulfilled not by an asymmetrical notion (A being (referentially) dependent on B is not the same as B being (referentially) dependent on A), but by a symmetrical notion, coindexing (A being coindexed with B is the same as B being coindexed with A).[28] Second, Evans's *referential* dependencies are not the same as our *indexical* dependencies, and indeed Evans's notion does not surface in our theory. Indexical dependencies do not indicate any sort of referential (or valuation) relation; this is instead the role of indices.[29] Thus, what is structurally *represented* are indices, which by hypothesis are complex objects, consisting of a value and a type, and it is indices and their relations that ultimately have semantic import. The role of dependencies within Dependency Theory is to take part in the well-formedness conditions on indices of a certain type—namely, those of type β. Thus, if an indexical dependency is *realized* (not represented) in a structure, then a β-occurrence

27. Evans's theory also permits "coreference in merely the extensional sense," coreference that is "accidental" and not intended by the speaker. We are skeptical of this notion; as discussed in chapter 1, we regard accidental coreference as a matter of failure of implicature, and not some separate type of coreference.

28. Evans (1977) speaks of expressions that are anaphorically connected as "braced" or "chained together," symmetrical notions. He explicitly develops the asymmetrical notion in Evans 1980, in the context of arguments against Lasnik's (1976) proposed grammatical rule of noncoreference. Evans's arguments show —decisively, we believe—that a symmetrical grammatical notion of anaphora is untenable if that notion is coreference. They do not show, however, that a symmetrical characterization of anaphora is untenable in general. On the contrary; see the discussion of Evans's cases in chapter 1 relative to coindexing and noncoindexing.

29. One way in which the notions of dependency materially differ is in their application to quantificational structures. On Evans's theory, pronouns in such structures are referential elements, and referential dependencies are applicable to them in virtue of this status; see footnote 26. In contrast, on our theory, such pronouns are not referential, but rather bound variables, and may be associated with indexical dependencies if they bear β-occurrences of their indices, although they may also bear α-occurrences. Although on our view bound variable and referential pronouns have different semantic status, it does not follow that they are utterly unrelated; rather, they are related syntactically with respect to properties of their indices.

is resolved, that is, properly represented, in that structure. The domain in which dependencies may be realized is the phrase marker, so that the resolution of β-occurrences takes place within the sentence; coindexing, however, may hold among expressions in different sentences. Realization of a dependency, however, is not a requirement for well-formed occurrences of an *index*, since they may be α-occurrences. Note that the coreference that arises among such occurrences is just as much grammatically determined, in virtue of coindexing, as the coreference that arises with β-occurrences. Thus, this circumstance is not comparable to the one that arises when there is no referential dependency, in Evans's sense, for then there is no grammatical representation of an anaphoric connection. Insofar as a comparison can be made, it is between noncoindexing and lack of referential dependency.

If referential dependency is to be the grammatical notion of anaphora, then there must be grammatical constraints on the distribution of such dependencies. Although Evans (1980) touches on this matter, it is Higginbotham's (1983, 1985, 1989, 1992) development of Evans's conception that approaches it in depth and detail. In Higginbotham's phrasing, referential dependencies are indicated grammatically by "linking," a directed line (arrow) from a dependent expression to an antecedent expression, where semantically the former inherits its reference from the latter. The distribution of such dependencies or links is the province of Linking Theory. Dependents are subject to two conditions: roughly, (i) anaphors must be linked in their governing categories, and (ii) pronouns may not be linked in such domains. An expression E is linked in a governing category C just in case E is a dependent whose antecedent c-commands E in C.[30] We can categorize Linking Theory as a *strong* theory of dependency in virtue of having two properties: (i) dependencies are represented, and (ii) their distribution depends on a hierarchical property of structures (c-command). Thus, links replace indices, and Linking Theory replaces Binding Theory. This contrasts with our theory, which we can think of as a *weak* theory, where not dependencies, but indices, are represented. Dependency Theory coexists with Binding Theory in determining the distribution of indices; its terms are linear. In Higginbotham's view, on the other

---

30. Higginbotham actually uses different notions in the conditions on anaphors and pronouns; the former requires linking, whereas the latter proscribes antecedence. See discussion below, as well as the lucid presentation and discussion of Linking Theory in Lasnik and Uriagereka 1988:sec. 5.2.

hand, once Linking Theory is available, Binding Theory can be dispensed with: dependency and binding do not coexist.

The initial presentation of dependency theory in the form of Linking Theory found in Higginbotham 1983 contains what in our view is an important insight to be captured by any theory of dependency, that dependencies should apply only to elements that *can* be dependent. It thus ought to be applicable to pronouns and anaphors, for instance, but in particular not to names, which (having only independent reference) are never dependent. Higginbotham captures this insight by there not being any linking principle applying to names. Whereas Linking Theory has analogues of Principles A and B of Binding Theory, it has no analogue of Principle C. Rather, the empirical effects of this condition are to be attained by assuming a condition that resides outside Linking Theory, namely, that reference must be determined uniquely. A name, which inherently determines its reference, cannot also have its reference fixed through a dependency, so that in *He saw John*, the name cannot be referentially dependent on (i.e., linked to) the pronoun. It is not altogether clear, however, just what is meant by unique determination of reference. It would appear to have to be limited to linguistic determination, for a name can certainly be used felicitously in the presence of (noncontrastive) ostension to its referent. But the limitation to linguistic determination is also problematic, as Lasnik (1989) points out. Under Higginbotham's assumptions, anaphoric epithets—*the fool, the idiot*—would be expected to have the distribution of pronouns, since although they can clearly inherit their reference from some other expression—*John went to the 7-11; then the idiot robbed it*—they do not lexically determine any reference in and of themselves. Although unlike names in this fashion, as Lasnik observes, they are like names in that (51) is understood comparably to the way *He thinks that I like John* is understood:

(51) He thinks that I like the fool

Linking Theory predicts that anaphoric epithets have the distribution of pronouns and thus would allow the pronoun and the epithet to corefer. Binding Theory, on the other hand, predicts that they have the distribution of names. From its perspective, what the grammar says about (51) is that the pronoun and the epithet are not coindexed; hence, it is not part of the meaning of the sentence that they have the same reference. That is, the grammar says the same thing about this sentence (under the appropriate indexing) that it says about *He thinks that I like John*.

Higginbotham (1985) himself observes a further problem with his initial proposal. Although it would apply to the "upward" linking of a name to some other element, it still would allow "downward" linking to a name, as in (52):

(52) He saw John

Although names are prohibited from depending on some other element, nothing prohibits other elements from depending on a name, an incorrect result for structures such as (52). Higginbotham's response to this problem (and a variation of the epithets argument) is to incorporate an analogue to Principle C into Linking Theory. Although he entertains a formulation of this principle according to which expressions such as names cannot be linked with expressions that c-command them, he settles on a formulation based on the notion of *obviation*, which "forces A and B to be 'different' in some sense" (Higginbotham 1985:570). Some care is required in specifying the "in some sense" rider. It is clearly not intended to mean that A and B have different links or different referential dependencies, since it may be that they are not linked to or dependent on anything at all. A notion that does involve difference would be that "A and B differ in reference." But this would just be the theory proposed by Lasnik (1976), and would take on the attendant problems noted by Evans, which Linking Theory is intended to circumvent. Higginbotham (1985:575) thus gives the following "rough description":

(53) If X and Y are obviative, then they cannot be determined by the structure in which they occur to share a value.

Linking Theory encompasses two syntactic circumstances: linking, which is represented, and nonlinking, which is not represented. If A is linked to B or B is linked to A, then, and only then, are A and B structurally determined to share a value. If A and B are not linked, then they are not structurally determined to share a value, and hence are obviative. Higginbotham then revises Linking Theory by including an analogue for Principle C requiring that names and other "R-expressions" be obviative from any c-commanding NP, that is, not linked with a c-commanding NP. This rules out both the downward linking seen in (52) and the comparable upward linking of the name to the pronoun. Thus, in preventing an anaphoric connection in *He saw John* and structurally comparable cases, the empirical effects of this condition parallel those of Principle C.

By formulating the analogue to Principle C in terms of obviation, the revised Linking Theory still counts as a "pure" dependency theory, since there is no direct condition on linking nondependents such as names. Rather, that names are not linked to c-commanding elements is entailed by the obviation condition. Preserving this property of Linking Theory does not come without cost—namely, the cost of abandoning Linking Theory as a formal theory of anaphora. This is because obviation is a notion that is defined in semantic terms (semantic value), and this semantic notion is mentioned in the formulation of grammatical principles governing the syntax of links, namely, the Principle C analogue. (In this regard, Higginbotham's theory is comparable to that of Lasnik (1976), in which the semantic term *coreference* is mentioned in a grammatical principle, his Noncoreference Rule.) Binding Theory, in contrast, is a purely formal theory of the distribution of indexical occurrences; its formulation makes no reference to any semantic terms. One could return to a formal theory by having the Principle C analogue proscribe linking of a name with a c-commanding NP, but this would be at the cost of giving up Linking Theory as a dependency theory, since now there would be a direct condition on linking nondependents. Higginbotham (1985) argues, however, that there is independent reason for the grammatical theory of anaphora to encompass a notion of obviation. The argument pertains to the analysis of (54), with the indicated linkings:

(54) John said he saw him

It is consistent with Linking Theory for this sentence to have each of the pronouns independently linked to the NP *John*, which would presumably allow, incorrectly, coreference all around to be determined structurally. However, since *he* and *him* are not linked, they are obviative. But in both being linked to *John*, they would share a value, as a matter of structure, which, by (53), they cannot do. It is this inconsistency that gives rise to the ungrammaticality of (54), Higginbotham claims.[31]

31. In "Logical Form, Binding, and Nominals" (1983) Higginbotham seeks to rule out (54) in a different way, by an additional principle on antecedence: If X and Y share an antecedent and Y c-commands X, then Y is an antecedent of X. In (54), for *he* to be an antecedent of *him*, the latter would have to be linked to the former. Since it is not, ungrammaticality results. In "On Semantics" (1985), however, he rejects this approach, in order to allow the pattern of linking

The account of (54) is straightforward under Binding Theory, since it is not possible to have any representation in which the pronouns are coindexed, although either one may be coindexed with the NP *John*. Thus, within our assumptions regarding indexing we need not appeal to a grammatical notion of obviation. Higginbotham, however, offers other arguments to establish the superiority of Linking Theory over Binding Theory,[32] concluding that linking allows the possibility of escaping locality effects that would be enforced by Binding Theory. One example is found in Higginbotham 1989:

(55) John found himself easy [O PRO to please t]

---

in (54) where it does not lead to a conflict in value sharing. His primary examples are reciprocal sentences like *John and Mary told each other that they should leave*, where both *they* and *each other* are directly linked to *John and Mary* and hence obviative. This structure, Higginbotham argues, represents two readings; on one, John told Mary that John should leave and Mary told John that Mary should leave; on the other, John told Mary that John and Mary should leave, and Mary told John the same thing. In neither case do *they* and *each other* share a value (presuming that plural values are distinct from singular values). However, as Heim, Lasnik, and May (1991b) point out, Higginbotham's account does not give a correct analysis of these cases. See also footnote 32.

32. Besides those discussed in the text, Higginbotham (1985) presents a further argument, based on properties of reciprocal constructions, to the effect that the indexing notation of Binding Theory is deficient because it obscures information necessary for interpretation. Thus, he points out that under standard assumptions regarding reciprocals as anaphors, in *John and Mary told each other that they should leave*, *John and Mary*, *each other*, and *they* should all be coindexed. But this sentence is three-ways ambiguous. It may mean (i) that John told Mary that Mary should leave and Mary told John that John should leave; (ii) that John told Mary that John should leave, and Mary told John that Mary should leave; and (iii) that John told Mary that John and Mary should leave, and Mary told John the same thing. Under Linking Theory, there are two possible structures for this sentence: one in which *they* is linked to *each other*, which in turn is linked to *John and Mary*, representing reading (i), and another on which *they* and *each other* are independently linked to *John and Mary*, representing readings (ii) and (iii). (See footnote 31.) This argument is discussed in detail in Heim, Lasnik, and May 1991b, to which the reader is referred. Two basic problems with the analysis are discussed there. The first is that it does not properly account for readings (i) and (ii); the second is that reading (i) is grouped against readings (ii) and (iii) in terms of linking patterns, when in fact the correct groupings of readings are (i) and (ii), as cases of bound variable anaphora, against (iii), as a case of coreference anaphora. Heim, Lasnik, and May also show that cases such as these can be directly accounted for within the confines of indexing and Binding Theory, given proper attention to the logical structure of reciprocal sentences.

Higginbotham argues that under standard assumptions PRO and t will be coindexed, in violation of Binding Theory, since the antecedent of the empty operator—*himself*—and the controller of PRO—*John*—are themselves coindexed. However, under Linking Theory, it is possible for PRO to be linked to its controller, the NP *John*, independently of the trace being linked to its operator. But this account appears to directly contradict the analysis Higginbotham gives for (54). This is because PRO and the trace are unlinked, and hence obviative, yet both ultimately have their value established as John. For PRO, this would be in virtue of control by the NP *John*, and for the trace, through links to its binding operator, and then to the reflexive and on to *John*. Thus, it does not appear possible to give a consistent account of the anaphoric properties of both (54) and (55) in the context of Linking Theory incorporating a grammatical notion of obviation.[33]

A similar inconsistency in interpretation of Higginbotham's theory arises in another form of the argument presented in Higginbotham 1990, based on the use of the superficially demonstrative element in a sentence such as (56):

(56) Mary told every man that he didn't see that man

Higginbotham's point is that under Binding Theory the pronoun and the demonstrative cannot be coindexed in (56). But under Linking Theory, Higginbotham argues, this sentence is allowed because the demonstrative, rather than being linked to the pronoun, can be linked directly to (the variable bound by) the quantifier, as can the pronoun. This syntactically well formed pattern of linking, however, runs up against the same sort of

---

33. Higginbotham's argument from (55) to the inadequacy of Binding Theory is based on the assumption that empty operators in structures like (55) are coindexed with the subject of *easy*. This assumption is found in the treatment presented by Chomsky (1986b), who proposes that the index of the operator and that of the NP are identified in virtue of "predication." But what requires this identification? Presumably, it is to ensure that it follows that *John is easy to please* is true if and only if it is easy to please John. But this follows quite independently of whether *John* and the empty operator are coindexed, given that *John is easy to please* is a predication on the order of *John is a cook*. That is, given that *easy to please* is a predication that has *John* as its argument, *John* must be the value of the empty operator regardless of its index. No additional argument has been given, either by Chomsky or by Higginbotham, with the consequence that proper satisfaction of the empty operator requires indexical identification. Indeed, we can take Higginbotham's example (55) in the text as arguing, given Binding Theory, that at least in certain cases the indices must not be identified.

problems of obviation engendered by (54) and (55), since the pronoun and the demonstrative are obviative, yet both are linked to the quantifier and hence should share a value. Higginbotham's treatment of (56) in fact runs up against other difficulties, because, as he observes, this sentence contrasts with (57), in which *that man* cannot be anaphoric to *he*:

(57) He didn't see that man

Linking of the demonstrative to the pronoun in (57), Higginbotham argues, is syntactically proscribed. But on what principle is this proscription founded? It cannot be the Principle C analogue based on obviation, since presumably this would be applicable to (56) just as it presumably is to (58), in which *that man* cannot be anaphoric to *John*:

(58) Mary told John that he didn't see that man

Since Principle C effects, which the obviation principle subsumes, are upwardly unbounded, it would seem that the operant principle should be the one that otherwise applies to pronouns, prohibiting them from being locally linked. This would differentiate (56) from (57), modulo (58), allowing for a long-distance link in the former. It would, however, disallow (59):

(59) Every man saw that man

In this sentence the demonstrative pronoun can function as it does in (56); but the nonlocal linking needed to characterize this is not possible.[34]

In closing, we have tried to make clear the conceptual and theoretical differences between our theory of anaphora and that which emanates from the work of Evans and Higginbotham, in which the empirical burden shared by Binding Theory and Dependency Theory is to be carried by Linking Theory. It should be clear that Linking Theory is not Dependency Theory, since it cannot be maintained that the former is asymmetrical in nature. Whereas in his initial formulation Higginbotham (1983) attempted to justify the richer formalism of linking by its ability to express asymmetrical dependencies, by including a notion of obviation he has now added a notion that is *symmetrical* in nature: if A is obviative from B, then B is obviative from A. In doing so, however, Higginbotham has imbued Linking Theory with what is an essential property of indexing, but not dependencies; the ability to characterize symmetrical anaphoric relations. By including a notion of obviation, applicable to nondependent expressions

---

34. We have already commented on the status of "variable demonstratives" and their relation to Binding Theory in chapter 1.

such as names, Higginbotham thus gives up the analysis of anaphora as being solely in terms of linking, and hence Linking Theory as solely a theory of referential dependency. Linking Theory is also not Binding Theory. Binding Theory admits two representational states, coindexing and noncoindexing, although only the former grammatically determines anything about anaphora. Noncoindexing "means" only that the grammar is anaphorically nondeterminative. In contrast, Linking Theory allows only one representational state: linking. Nonlinking is not the representation of "antilinks," only the absence of links. Nonlinking does, however, determine a grammatical condition (obviation).[35]

To conclude, then: To reject Linking Theory is not to say that there is no role for asymmetrical notions of dependency; indeed, our goal in this chapter has been to lay the foundations for just such a role. Rather, it is to say that a dependency theory cannot replace or subsume a binding theory; the two have independent, although interacting, roles to play within the overall theory of anaphora.

---

35. The distinction we allude to here corresponds to what Higginbotham (1985) refers to as weak and strong construals of the Disjoint Reference Condition. Although we adhere to the weak construal, we find it misleading to call this a disjoint reference condition, since it admits coreference.

Chapter 3

Identity of Dependencies

3.1 Identity of Dependencies

Consider the *wh*-question in (1):

(1) Who loves John's mother
$\quad$ (= (46a) of chapter 2)

In chapter 2 we noted that the string *John loves his mother* can count as a direct answer to this question. Although we considered there the circumstance in which this answer was given by a particular speaker, other speakers may have given other answers:

(2) a. Mary answered: "John loves his mother"

$\quad$ b. Sally answered: "Max loves his mother"

$\quad$ c. Jane answered: "Oscar loves his mother"

As answers to (1), the representations of Sally's and Jane's answers will be parallel to the representation of Mary's, so that in each the pronouns bear α-occurrences and are to be taken as coindexed with the NP *John* in the question:

(3) a. $John_1$ loves his_1^α mother

$\quad$ b. Max_2 loves his_1^α mother

$\quad$ c. $Oscar_3$ loves his_1^α mother

That is, for each of John, Max, and Oscar, what is being answered is that they each love John's mother.

$\quad$ What allows us to take the sentences in (3) as a list of answers? The answer seems plain enough: aside from the part of each sentence that adds new content or information, they are the same, and so long as we keep repeating the constant remainder, a connected parallel discourse, a list, will result. In this regard, they stand in no different a relation to the question they answer than do the sentences *Max left, Oscar left, Sam left,* given as answers to the question *Who left.* By what criterion, then, can we say that the remainder in each of the sentences above is the same? Perhaps the narrowest structural identity condition that will do the job is the following: they are each occurrences of some one sub–phrase marker over a given terminal vocabulary. Let us call such occurrences *reconstructions* of one another. The sentences above, therefore, constitute a connected parallel discourse because the verb phrases in these sentences are reconstructions, and the sentences differ just with respect to those parts that provide new information.

Now consider the other question that concerned us earlier:

(4) Who loves his mother
     (= (46b) of chapter 2)

(5) represents (2) as answers to (4):

(5) a. John$_1$ loves his$_1^\beta$ mother

      b. Max$_2$ loves his$_2^\beta$ mother

      c. Oscar$_3$ loves his$_3^\beta$ mother

Here the pronouns bear β-occurrences, and hence they must be coindexed in their sentences, as shown. The answers here are that John loves John's mother, Max loves Max's mother, and Oscar loves Oscar's mother. Although intuitively the sentences in (5) count as a list of answers just as much as the sentences in (3), it is not altogether clear why this is so, since the "remainders" in (5) differ structurally. Since the pronouns bear occurrences of three different indices, it would seem that we have occurrences of three different verb phrases. But if these verb phrases are not reconstructions, then the sentences in which they occur cannot form a connected parallel discourse. There is, however, a way in which these sentences are nondistinct: *they each realize the same indexical dependency.* It is satisfaction of this condition, we will propose, that is sufficient for the sentences in (5) to count as a list of parallel answers. Our concern in this chapter, therefore, is with the identification of dependencies. Under what conditions can we say that various structures manifest the same or different indexical dependencies, and how does this interact with more general conditions of structural identity falling under the rubric of reconstruction?

We can establish straight off that a notion of identity of dependency cannot be recovered directly from the semantics; there is no "thing" in the semantics that is the dependency of a pronoun. It is true that the axiom for β-occurrences, in a sense, induces dependencies in the derivation of truth conditions, in that the valuation of such pronouns depends upon the valuation of other elements. However, it only establishes the value of the pronoun in terms of *some* other element; the axiom is blind to the structural position in which this element occurs, as well as to the order in which the value of this element was introduced into the derivation. Thus, the only notion of identity that would be available would be that dependencies are the same only if the pronouns depend on the same element for their value. But this is both too weak and too strong, because *John saw his mother* and *John said Mary saw his mother* would manifest the same dependency, but not *John saw his mother* and *Max saw his mother*. What we are failing to capture here is that dependencies are the same only if the pronouns depend on elements that are structurally parallel, so that the former pair of sentences could not display the same dependency, whereas the latter pair could. But positional information of this sort is precisely what the semantics, in and of itself, cannot provide. Rather, dependencies, insofar as they can be identified, are aspects of the structures subject to interpretation— that is, aspects of the logical form of sentences, and not of the interpretation itself.[1]

With this in mind, we define a notion of identity of indexical dependencies of the form $\langle (c_1^\alpha, c_2^\beta, \ldots, c_n^\beta), I, SD \rangle$ as follows:

Indexical dependencies *ID* and *ID'* are *i-copies* if and only if *ID* and *ID'* vary from each other in at most the value of *I*.

Indexical dependencies are *i*-copies if and only if they have the same elements and the same structural descriptions—the particular indexical value they have is not relevant to whether they are the same dependency. By this condition, which in a sense is implicit in the definition of indexical dependency, we thus ensure that β-occurrences of *i*-copies are nondistinct, since they occur in dependencies that are nondistinct. (6) and (7) realize dependencies that are *i*-copies:[2]

(6) a. Oscar$_1$ saw his$_1^\beta$ mother

   b. $\langle ([_{NP} \text{Oscar}]^\alpha, [_{NP} \text{his}]^\beta), 1, \langle NP, V, NP \rangle \rangle$

---

1. The situation here is quite parallel to the situation with multiple quantifiers. Although the interaction of the interpretive clauses for quantifiers will induce a dependency between the quantifiers in *Everyone loves someone*, this is insufficient to define the scope of quantifiers, which is an aspect of logical form. For discussion of this point, see May 1985, 1989, 1991.

2. Note that *John believes he loves his mother* and *John believes himself to love his mother* also realize the same indexical dependency, even though in one case one of the elements involved in the dependency is a pronoun, and the parallel element in the other is a reflexive. We return to the significance of this in chapter 5.

(7) a. Jane$_2$ loves her$_2^\beta$ father

 b. $\langle ([_{\mathrm{NP}} \text{ Jane}]^\alpha, [_{\mathrm{NP}} \text{ her}]^\beta), 2, \langle \mathrm{NP}, \mathrm{V}, \mathrm{NP} \rangle \rangle$

Bear in mind that dependencies hold between indexed categories, that is, between NPs, and not between their lexical contents. Thus, that the antecedent in one contains the name *Oscar*, whereas the other contains *Jane*, or that the pronouns are different genders, is irrelevant to the dependencies encoded. All that is important is that in each dependency there is one NP bearing an α-occurrence, and one bearing a β-occurrence. And although these β-occurrences are nondistinct in virtue of being associated with dependencies that are *i*-copies, the sentences in which they occur will differ in their truth conditions. But this follows solely from the difference in the lexical content of the two sentences, for they do not differ in any structurally meaningful way.

Via its characterization of identity of dependencies, Dependency Theory provides the criterion by which pronouns bearing β-occurrences are nondistinct, even though they are not coindexed—namely, just in case they are resolved in dependencies that are *i*-copies. For example, for the sentences in (5), in which the pronouns bear β-occurrences, there will now be no relevant formal distinction between their verb phrases, which will thus count as reconstructions. Hence, these sentences can stand as a connected list of parallel answers. In contrast, although the sentences in (6) and (7) encode indexical dependencies that are *i*-copies, the VPs are not reconstructions, since they are not over the same terminal vocabulary and hence cannot stand as members of a connected parallel discourse. Thus, there is no *wh*-question for which (6) and (7) can stand as a list of direct answers.[3] It is in this manner, then, that the formal identity condition on indices—*i*-copy—contributes to a more general notion of syntactic identity for a language, setting a necessary, but not sufficient, condition for reconstruction, and hence for the characterization of the information structure of connected parallel discourse.

3.2 On the Distribution of Strict and Sloppy Identity

The role of reconstruction in characterizing connected parallel discourse, then, is to set fixed points against which to introduce new information.

---

3. These sentences can stand as a list for other purposes, for example, as a list of transitive sentences. Conditions for such lists, however, are weaker than for connected parallel discourse; for instance, they do not require any lexical identity.

These syntactically determined points are of course redundant to the discourse; being just occurrences of a particular sub–phrase marker, they could not add anything new. Because they are redundant, reconstructions need not be repeated in each subsequent utterance of a conversation. There is no need to say again what has already been said; it can be left unpronounced. Thus, just as *Max left. Oscar left, too* can stand as answers to *Who left*, so can *Max left. Oscar did, too*, where the repeated verb phrase has been lexically suppressed, or elided. Similarly, we can have the ellipsis in (8), where the verb phrase contains a pronoun:[4]

(8) Max saw his mother, and Oscar did, too

We can understand this sentence to mean that Max saw Max's mother, and Oscar saw Oscar's mother. If we assume that (8) is represented as in (9a), we can then say that elision of the boldface occurrence of the VP is warranted even though the pronouns bear different indices, because the dependencies realized by (9b) and (9c) are *i*-copies, and hence the VPs are reconstructions:

4. In this chapter and those to follow, our discussion will focus on verb phrase ellipsis, given its general productivity, setting aside the more distributionally limited verb phrase anaphora found with *do so/do it/do that/do the same thing*, and so on. But see the comments on this in chapter 6. We will also gloss over the function of such particles as *too, as well*, the negative, and *either*, which occur with lists of sentences, including those in which there is ellipsis. Briefly, the generalization underlying their occurrence is that their presence indicates that the same thing is being said over again, their absence, that different things are being said. Thus, *too* signals that what is being said about Max in *Max loves Sally, and Oscar does, too* (or *Max loves Sally, and Oscar loves Sally, too* for that matter) is also what is being said about Oscar. Absence of this particle is decidedly odd: **Max loves Sally, and Oscar does*. Presumably this is because the clauses say the same thing about Max and Oscar, but this is not properly specified by the presence of *too*. Negating one of the clauses brings a return to well-formedness: *Max loves Sally, but Oscar doesn't; Max doesn't love Sally, but Oscar does. Too* is absent here because the clauses say opposite things about Max and Oscar, not the same thing. If, on the other hand, both clauses are negated, then a "same-saying" indicator, in the negative form *either*, must return; compare *Max doesn't love Sally, and Oscar doesn't, either* with **Max doesn't love Sally, and Oscar doesn't*. Notice that certain contexts prohibit the appearance of *too: John saw Max before Bill did* but **John saw Max before Bill did, too*. In the former, what is being said of Bill (that he saw Max) is not what is being said of John (that he saw Max before Bill saw Max). Addition of *too* would require same-saying; but *too* is missing in the (mind-boggling) latter sentence. In what follows, we will control for the occurrence of same-saying particles. For discussion of the functions of these particles, see Dahl 1973.

(9) a. Max_1 [$_{\text{VP}}$ saw his$_1^\beta$ mother], and Oscar_2 [$_{\text{VP}}$ **saw his$_2^\beta$ mother**]

    b. $\langle(\text{Max, his}), 1, \langle\text{NP, V, NP}\rangle\rangle$

    c. $\langle(\text{Oscar, his}), 2, \langle\text{NP, V, NP}\rangle\rangle$

(As a convenient shorthand, we give just the lexical item in the dependency, rather than its fully annotated category.) The construal represented by (9) is what is referred to as the "sloppy" reading. By extension, the set of answers in (5) constitutes a set of sloppy answers. Notice that the pronoun in (8) need not be taken as bearing a dependent occurrence. It can also be taken as bearing an independent occurrence, so that alongside of (9) we have (10):

(10) Max_1 [$_{\text{VP}}$ saw his$_1^\alpha$ mother], and Oscar_2 [$_{\text{VP}}$ **saw his$_1^\alpha$ mother**]

Here the VPs are straightforwardly reconstructions; they are the same down to indexical occurrences. Thus, alongside the "sloppy" reading represented by (9), we have the "strict" reading represented by (10), where it is understood that Oscar saw Max's mother, not his own. Again, by extension, the set of answers in (3) constitutes a set of strict answers.[5]

It follows from Dependency Theory that the elided pronouns in (9) and (10) could not bear any other indexical values than those indicated, since then the VPs would fail to be reconstructions, and a necessary condition

---

5. On the sloppy reading of *Max saw his mother, and Oscar did, too*, its truth is compatible with Max and Oscar having seen different people. The reason for this is to be found in considering the comparable interpretation of *Mary saw someone, and Sally did, too*, whose truth is compatible with Mary and Sally having seen different people. Since quantifiers and their traces bear α-occurrences, the indices of both the overt and covert occurrences of *someone* will be the same, so that *Mary saw someone, and Sally did, too* will be of the form $\exists x\, P(x) \wedge \exists x\, Q(x)$; but from the truth of this it does not follow that $P(a) \wedge Q(a)$. Since the scopes of the quantifiers do not overlap, there are instances of distinct variables, even though they are indexically identical. The same reasoning holds for (i), which also does not require that Max and Oscar saw the same person:

(i) Max saw the woman he loves, and Oscar did, too

The last step is to recognize an analysis of *his mother* on which it can come out as being something on the order of *the mother of him*. Then the analysis of *Max saw his mother, and Oscar did, too* will be comparable to that of (i), by assimilating (at least certain) possessive NPs to the class of expressions that bind variables in their logical form. (In other cases such as *John saw his brother*, the possessive would be indefinite, as in *John saw a brother of his*.) In what follows, we will by and large ignore the LF movement that this treatment entails; see chapter 5 for further discussion of this "quantificational sloppy" reading in ellipsis.

on this sort of ellipsis as a type of connected parallel discourse would not be fulfilled. For (9), this is because if the β-occurrence borne by the elided pronoun were of any other indexical value, this occurrence could not be resolved, since it would not be coindexed with any other occurrence of that index. For (10), taking another value for the α-occurrence would not lead to this problem, since α-occurrences are not resolved with respect to dependencies. But because they are not so resolved, i-copy is undefined for such occurrences. It is only applicable to β-occurrences, so that there is no way in which pronouns in distinct structures that bear α-occurrences of different indices can be judged nondistinct. That is, elements bearing α-occurrences of different values are, in a strong sense, different elements, that is, nonidentical. Thus, (11), for instance, is not well formed as a possible elliptical structure, since the VPs are not reconstructions:

(11) *Max$_1$ [$_{VP}$ saw his$_1^\alpha$ mother], and Oscar$_2$ [$_{VP}$ **saw his$_3^\alpha$ mother**]

Of course, there is no bar to seeing α-occurrences of the *same* value as identical—coindexing is, after all, the essence of syntactic identity, and if such occurrences were to be distinct, then we would have no notion of identity at all. This point holds just as well with nonanaphoric as with anaphoric pronouns, so that the theory admits only (12a) as well formed:

(12) a.   Max$_1$ [$_{VP}$ saw his$_3^\alpha$ mother], and Oscar$_2$ [$_{VP}$ **saw his$_3^\alpha$ mother**]

   b. *Max$_1$ [$_{VP}$ saw his$_3^\alpha$ mother], and Oscar$_2$ [$_{VP}$ **saw his$_4^\alpha$ mother**]

Thus, for *Max saw his mother, and Oscar did, too*, if the overt pronoun is understood with deictic reference, then the elided pronoun must be understood to have just this deictic reference as well, and no other. On the other hand, if the elided material is overt, then a representation comparable to (12b) is well formed: in *Max saw his mother, and Oscar saw his mother* the pronouns can perfectly well refer deictically to different persons.

   In what follows, we will primarily limit ourselves to cases in which dependencies can be straightforwardly decided relative to simple phrase markers. In a more complete account, we would extend the treatment to transformational relations, such as the one in (13):

(13) Jane's mother is likely to love her, but it is unlikely that Mary's mother does

(13) allows a sloppy reading for the elided pronoun, so that the right-hand clause can express that it is unlikely that Mary's mother loves Mary. As examples of a sort brought to our attention by R. Oehrle show, similar effects can be found under other transformational relations: for instance, *The cop who gave the third degree to Bill beat him up, and the one who gave*

Max the third degree did, too, with the dative alternation, and *The cop who arrested Bill read him his rights, and the one who picked Max up did, too,* with particle movement. An example due to Rooth (1992) also shows a transformational effect:

(14) First John told Mary I was bad-mouthing her, and then Sue heard I
      was

This case involves verb-raising of *told*, as discussed by Larson (1988).[6] Also falling in this category is (15), pointed out by Hardt (1992):

(15) If Tom was having trouble in school, I would help him. On the
      other hand, if Harry was having trouble, I doubt that I would

Here, the *if*-clause in the second sentence is construed as inside the scope of *doubt.* This is an instance of what has been called "protasis-lifting"; see Kimball 1970. What this class of examples shows is that in the general case, indexical dependencies are realized relative to a notion of "basic" phrase markers that incorporates an appropriate concept of transformational derivation. For example, for (13), *Jane's mother* is structurally interpreted in the position of the complement subject trace, and with respect to this structural position, the indexical dependencies for the β-occurrences borne by the overt and covert pronouns will be *i*-copies. We may imagine a number of ways of obtaining this result. For instance, dependencies could be realized in D-Structure phrase markers, or in phrase markers relativized to the structure of argument chains; see Chomsky 1993. Extensions to the other cases can be constructed along similar lines. But, whatever the particulars of the theory of phrase structure that is adopted, the point here is that indexical dependencies are realized relative to the "underlying" structure of sentences.

We have outlined the characterization of strict and sloppy identity with respect to Dependency Theory by examples in which the antecedent of the overt pronoun is a name. Now consider the construal of examples that minimally differ in the substitution of a quantified expression for the name:

---

6. Rooth (1992) proposes that sloppy identity is possible in (14) because of an implicational bridging relation between *tell* and *hear.* But insofar as a sloppy reading is possible in (14), is also it possible in (i):

(i) First John told Mary that I was bad-mouthing her. Then Sue behaved as
     though I was

In (i) there is no implicational bridge, although there is structural parallelism, modulo verb-raising, as in (14).

(16) Everyone saw his mother, and Oscar did, too

Taking the pronoun here as a variable gives the representation in (17), in which the pronoun bears a β-occurrence:

(17) Everyone$_1$ [$_S$ e_1^α [$_{VP}$ saw his$_1^\beta$ mother]], and Oscar$_2$ [$_{VP}$ **saw his$_2^\beta$ mother**]

Since the dependencies here are *i*-copies, this represents the sloppy reading of (16). Unlike the referential cases, the quantificational cases show a significant preference for this sloppy reading. A strict reading is not precluded, however, although it has a particular character, and a somewhat marked status. This can be seen most directly from examples like (18):

(18) Many students think they are smart, but the professor doesn't

Although this sentence has a sloppy reading, it can also have a strict reading under which the second clause is understood to mean that the professor doesn't think that the students are smart. As observed by Lappin (1992) and T. Nishigauchi (personal communication), what is curious about these sentences is that whereas the overt pronoun functions as a bound variable, the elided pronoun is construed as an E-type pronoun. We represent this reading as follows:

(19) Many students$_1$ [$_S$ e_1^α [$_{VP}$ think they$_1^\alpha$ are smart]], but the professor$_2$ doesn't [$_{VP}$ **think they$_1^\alpha$ are smart**]

(19) provides an instance of the observation made in chapter 2 that pronouns bearing α-occurrences can fulfill the semantic function of variables, as a marked option in the grammar. When such a pronoun is reconstructed, since it bears an α-occurrence, its indexical value cannot change. However, the elided occurrence is not inside the scope of the quantifier with which it is coindexed and hence cannot play the role of a variable. It can, however, be anaphoric to this quantifier; that is, it can be an E-type pronoun. Thus, (19) represents the observed strict reading of (18), although given the marked status of α-pronouns in this environment, this reading itself will be marked.[7]

---

7. The sort of strict reading we are describing is not limited to sentences in which the overt pronoun is plural. For instance, it appears to be possible in (i), and it can also be found in simple examples like *Everyone saw his mother, and Oscar did, too*:

(i) If every student revises his paper, then I won't have to

In the representation of this reading, the elided pronoun will be plural, although it will correspond to an overt singular pronoun. This is not problematic; rather, it is an instance of what we call "vehicle change"; see discussion in chapter 5.

Bear in mind that we take (9) to represent (part of) a connected parallel discourse, made up of a list of two sentences. Each of these sentences is a distinct domain of dependencies, and no dependency can factor across them, from one to the other. Because dependencies are domain-limited to sentences in a discourse, β-occurrences cannot be linked to antecedents in other sentences in the discourse. This rules out an impossible reading for (20), a list of three, rather than two, sentences, on which Sally saw John's father and Jane saw John's grandfather:

(20) Mary saw John, Sally saw his father, and Jane did, too

This reading would be possible if the structure of (20) were as shown in (21), because (21b) and (21c), being i-copies, would license the indexing in (21a):

(21) a. *Mary saw John$_1$, Sally saw his$_1^\beta$ father$_2$, and Jane **saw his$_2^\beta$ father$_2$**

b. $\langle$(John, his), 1, $\langle$NP, CONJ, NP, V, NP$\rangle\rangle$

c. $\langle$(his father, his), 2, $\langle$NP, CONJ, NP, V, NP$\rangle\rangle$

But these dependencies are not well formed, since in having the conjunctions as terms, they factor across sentences of the discourse. What is possible is (22), representing a strict reading in which Sally and Jane saw the same person:

(22) Mary saw John$_1$, Sally saw his$_1^\alpha$ father$_2$, and Jane **saw his$_1^\alpha$ father$_2$**

Notice that the discourses in (8) and (20) would be unchanged if rather than being uttered by one speaker, the sentences were uttered by multiple speakers. Discourses are ordered sequences of sentences, in the technical sense of sets of phrase markers. They are to be distinguished from conversations, sequences of utterances. The identity conditions of reconstruction, including those on dependencies contributed by Dependency Theory, are identity conditions on sentential structure and hence are notions of discourse, not of conversation. (See chapters 4 and 5, where we return to the relations of discourse structure, dependencies, and reconstruction in more detail.)

What holds with respect to strict and sloppy identity for α- and β-occurrences borne by singular noun phrases carries over directly to occurrences borne by plural noun phrases. Thus, *Max and Oscar said they are going to Europe this summer, and Sally and Jane did, too* can be understood as either strict or sloppy. Strict and sloppy readings are also found when we mix plural and singular antecedents; thus, consider (23), adapted from observations by Webber (1978):

(23) Max and Oscar said they are going to Europe this summer, and
Sally did, too

Quite clearly, this sentence can have a strict reading; on this reading the
second clause means that Sally said that Max and Oscar are going to
Europe. What is of greater interest about this sentence, however, is the
sloppy reading, on which the second clause is understood as meaning that
Sally said that Sally is going to Europe: although on the strict reading the
pronoun is construed as plural, referring to Max and Oscar, on the sloppy
reading it is construed as *singular*, referring only to Sally. This difference
follows directly. Consider first the strict reading; its representation is as in
(24):

(24) Max and Oscar$_{1\oplus2}$ [$_{VP}$ said they$^{\alpha}_{1\oplus2}$ are going to Europe this
summer], and Sally$_3$ [$_{VP}$ **said they$^{\alpha}_{1\oplus2}$ are going to Europe this summer**]

Clearly, the VPs here are reconstructions, since there are no differences
between them, down to indexical value. No structure comparable to (24)
is possible if, rather than two α-occurrences, there are two β-occurrences
in the second clause, since there would not be enough antecedents to
resolve both atomic β-occurrences of the fusion index. What is possible
with β-occurrences is (25):[8]

(25) Max and Oscar$_{1\oplus2}$ [$_{VP}$ said they$^{\beta}_{1\oplus2}$ are going to Europe this
summer], and Sally$_3$ [$_{VP}$ **said she$^{\beta}_3$ is going to Europe this summer**]

In this structure all of the β-occurrences are properly resolved, and the VPs
are proper reconstructions. They are reconstructions because they are
identical in terms of categorial structure, and although they contain indices of different values, the dependencies of the β-occurrences are *i*-copies.
Note that it does not matter for reconstruction how many β-occurrences
there are in each clause, so long as they are *i*-copies, nor does it matter
which clause they are in. The effect is symmetrical, because reconstruction,
defined as a set of occurrences, is a symmetrical relation; so (26) has the
same sort of sloppy reading as (23), except that the elided reconstruction
is plural, rather than singular:

(26) Sally said she is going to Europe this summer, and Max and Oscar
did, too

---

8. The VPs in (25) also appear to differ in a respect other than indexical value, in
that the pronouns, and the attendant verbal agreement, are of different number.
But such differences in terminal vocabulary are immaterial to reconstruction; these
are again instances of vehicle change (see chapter 5).

In allowing for differing numbers of occurrences in reconstructions, β-occurrences differ from α-occurrences, which must have the same number. Thus, the verb phrases in (27) are not reconstructions in the narrow sense of identity required for α-occurrences:

(27) *Max and Oscar$_{1 \oplus 2}$ [$_{VP}$ said they$^{\alpha}_{1 \oplus 2}$ are going to Europe this summer], and Sally$_3$ [$_{VP}$ **said he$^{\alpha}_2$ is going to Europe this summer**]

Thus, it follows from our theory that sentences like (23) will have a singular sloppy reading, but a plural strict one.[9]

What is common to the representations of the strict and sloppy readings is that structurally each preserves the occurrence type of the pronoun's index, whether it is independent or dependent. What is not common is what counts as identity for α- and β-occurrences of indices. This difference leads to a difference in structural sensitivity for strict and sloppy readings. Because the possibility of sloppy construals depends upon having parallel dependencies, if such parallelism fails, so that the dependencies in question are not i-copies, then a sloppy reading will be excluded. This appears to be so:

(28) Max's mother saw him, and Oscar said Mary did, too

In this sentence the elided material cannot be understood to mean . . . *saw Oscar*. This is because the dependencies involved, having different structural descriptions, are not i-copies:

(29) a. *Max$_1$'s mother saw him$^{\beta}_1$, and Oscar$_2$ said Mary **saw him$^{\beta}_2$**

    b. $\langle$(Max, him), 1, $\langle$NP, N, V, NP$\rangle\rangle$

    c. $\langle$(Oscar, him), 2, $\langle$NP, V, NP, V, NP$\rangle\rangle$

Whereas the VPs in (29) consequently do not count as reconstructions, those in (30) do:

---

9. As noted, our discussion is based on observations by Webber (1978), who, in her brief comments, gives the example in (i):

(i) Irv and Martha wanted to dance together/with each other, but Martha's mother said that she couldn't

Such cases exhibit the same sort of symmetry as (23) and (26):

(ii) Irv wanted to dance with Martha, but Martha's mother said that they couldn't

Full analysis of these examples would require bringing in notions of indexing relevant to reciprocal constructions; see Heim, Lasnik, and May 1991b for discussion. However, they do not raise any issues pertaining to reconstruction beyond those addressed in the text.

(30) Max_1's mother saw him_1^α, and $Oscar_2$ said Mary **saw** $\mathbf{him_1^\alpha}$

This represents the strict reading of (28). It is possible because identity of α-occurrences is not determined through i-copy, and hence their distribution in reconstructions is not limited to structurally parallel environments. Similar observations hold for (31):

(31) Max saw his mother, and Oscar said that Harry did, too

In addition to the strict reading, this sentence has a sloppy reading. But this sloppy reading is only the one on which Oscar said that Harry saw Harry's mother, that is, a reading on which the pronoun's antecedent is the embedded subject. The sentence lacks a sloppy reading on which Oscar said that Harry saw Oscar's mother, that is, a reading on which the matrix subject is the antecedent. For it to have the latter reading, the representation in (32) would have to be well formed, but it is not, since the indexical dependencies are not i-copies:

(32) a. *Max_1 saw his_1^β mother, and $Oscar_2$ said Harry **saw** $\mathbf{his_2^\beta}$ **mother**

   b. $\langle(\text{Max, his}), 1, \langle\text{NP, V, NP}\rangle\rangle$

   c. $\langle(\text{Oscar, his}), 2, \langle\text{NP, V, NP, V, NP}\rangle\rangle$

(33) contrasts with (31) in that the elided pronoun can be anaphorically related to the matrix subject, but just in case the pronoun is also so related:

(33) Max saw his mother, and Oscar said he did, too

This reading is possible on the representation of (33) as (34):

(34) a. Max_1 saw his_1^β mother, and $Oscar_2$ said he_2^α **saw** $\mathbf{his_2^\beta}$ **mother**

   b. $\langle(\text{Max, his}), 1, \langle\text{NP, V, NP}\rangle\rangle$

   c. $\langle(\text{he, his}), 2, \langle\text{NP, V, NP}\rangle\rangle$

By taking the pronoun *he*, bearing an α-occurrence, as the antecedent of the elided pronoun, we arrive at a representation that realizes indexical dependencies that are i-copies. Notice that we could have taken *he* as bearing a β-occurrence, but then the resulting indexical dependency would not be an i-copy of (34b).[10]

---

10. Bear in mind that resolution of a β-occurrence in a structure does not require that *all* occurrences of its index in that structure be in the realized dependency. Also, in relation to (33), we observe that a sloppy reading is possible in *Max saw his mother, but everyone else said he didn't*, although we find it somewhat marginal relative to the strict reading. The reason for this is the marked possibility for the pronoun *he*, when bearing an α-occurrence, to function as a bound variable. See discussion in chapter 2.

Counterparts of the above examples without ellipsis can have coreference in the second clause; compare (35a) and (35b), assuming the elided VP in (35a) is that headed by *saw*:

(35) a. Max says Mary saw his mother, and Oscar did, too

b. Max says Mary saw his mother, and Oscar saw his mother, too

Although (35a) can only have a strict reading for the reasons just described, (35b) also allows a reading that we would label sloppy—the second clause can mean that Oscar saw Oscar's mother. (This is also pointed out in Rooth 1992.) It can have this reading because, unlike (35a), it can be taken as a nonreconstruction context. Consequently, the conditions enforcing structural parallelism are inapplicable, so that the representation in (36) is possible:

(36) Max_1 says Mary saw his_1 mother, and $Oscar_2$ saw his_2 mother, too

The sloppy reading here does not depend upon the pronouns' bearing β-occurrences; they could also bear α-occurrences. If, however, indexical dependencies are involved, they need not be *i*-copies, since (36) is not necessarily a reconstruction context.

Therefore, we have the following basic correlation, in virtue of Dependency Theory: In parallel connected discourse, α-occurrences must have the same indexical values, but there is no constraint arising in virtue of indices that they occur in parallel structures. β-occurrences may have differing indexical values, but only if they occur in the same structural context with respect to their antecedents. This structural parallelism for identity of dependencies is blind, given reconstruction, to whether the parallel structure, that which satisfies the structural descriptions of indexical dependencies, is overt or covert. Thus, either of the discourses in (37) and (38) is possible:

(37) I didn't know that Bill was a bigamist
     Mary just said he's married to her, and Sally did, too

(38) I didn't know that Bill was a bigamist
     Mary just said he's married to her, and Sally said he is, too

In both of these cases a sloppy reading is perfectly well possible for the elided pronoun *her*.[11]

---

11. Sag (1976) claims that the sloppy reading is unavailable for sentences like those in (38); the example he cites is (i), to be contrasted with its fully elided counterpart in (ii):

In placing the parallelism restrictions on sloppy identity in the context of Dependency Theory, we are relativizing the distribution of this reading to proper factorizations. This means that sloppy identity is licensed if there is a proper *linear* relation in a structure connecting a β-occurrence to its antecedent. It has been suggested, however, that sloppy identity tracks the stronger relation of binding. There are two ways this stronger condition can be understood. One is that sloppy identity tracks environments in

---

(i)   John said Mary hit him, and Bill said she did, too

(ii) John said Mary hit him, and Bill did, too

We doubt this judgment, especially given examples like those in (38), but insofar as there is an effect, we believe that it can be traced back to circumstances of use that would lead one to employ a partially elided form when a more inclusive ellipsis is possible. On Sag's account, (i) follows from the condition on alphabetic variance that prohibits VPs from being elided whose corresponding λ-expressions contain variables bound from outside by different token operators. Thus, in (iii) the λ-expressions indicated as "λy" and "λz" are not alphabetic variants:

(iii) John, $\lambda x(x$ said (Mary, $\lambda y(y$ hit $x))$), and Bill, $\lambda w(w$ said (she, $\lambda z(z$ hit $w)))$

Only deletion of the entire λ-expression "$\lambda w(\ldots)$" is possible, since it is an alphabetic variant of "$\lambda x(\ldots)$"; hence, sloppy identity should be possible only with maximal possible ellipses. Cases like (38) stand as counterexamples to this claim, however. (For further discussion of this aspect of the alphabetic variance condition, see chapters 4 and 5.) Partee and Bach (1984) point to (iv), claiming that an interpretation in which the overt pronoun (i.e., variable) is bound by *Bill*, and the covert one by *everyone*, is "impossible":

(iv) Bill believes that Sally will marry him, but everyone knows that she won't

That this sort of interpretation is in fact possible is shown by (v):

(v)   Bill still believes that Sally will marry him, but every other eligible bachelor already knows that she won't

(v) shows that the problem with (iv) has nothing to do with whether the binding into ellipsis is proper or not. The problem here appears to stem from the fact that since everyone includes Bill, the truth of the second clause on the sloppy reading entails the falsity of the first. When this is removed, as in (v)—*every other eligible bachelor* pointedly excludes Bill—a sloppy reading (as well as a strict one) is possible. Lappin (1984) proposes a condition on binding in on which this is allowed just in case the bound variables "have the same intended range of possible values" (p. 276). Example (v) is obviously inconsistent with this condition, as is (vi):

(vi) Every sailor thinks Sally loves him, while every soldier thinks that Mary does

Cases such as (38), (v) and (vi) make it abundantly clear that we do not want a theory that structurally excludes sloppy readings with partial ellipsis, but rather one that permits it subject to conditions on discourse coherence that give good cause for taking a partial ellipsis when a full one would be available as a structural option.

which the pronoun is c-commanded by its antecedent; this is the position taken by Reinhart (1983). Examples such as the following, which admit a sloppy reading, show that this is not correct:

(39) a. Max's mother loves him, and Oscar's mother does, too

     b. Everybody in Tokyo rides its subways, but nobody in New York does

Although in each of these cases the pronoun can be dependent upon its antecedent, in neither case does the antecedent c-command the pronoun. However, these facts are consistent with a somewhat different hypothesis, initially mentioned by Lasnik (1976), that sloppy identity tracks the distribution of bound variable anaphora. That is, only if the antecedent of the pronoun occurs in a position from which a quantifier can bind the pronoun, can the pronoun be construed sloppily under ellipsis. As observed by May (1985), the examples in (39) conform to this generalization: both *Everyone's mother loves him* and *Everybody in some Japanese city rides its subways*, with bound variable anaphora, are possible. The question, then, is whether there are contexts that admit sloppy identity, but not bound variable anaphora. There appear to be two such types of contexts.

First, there are contexts that simply do not allow quantifiers, such as partitive phrases: *all of Jane's colleagues* contrasts with **all of nobody's/ everybody's colleagues*. However, (40) is possible, with the meaning that none of Brenda's students admires Brenda—that is, with a sloppy (as well as strict) reading:

(40) All of Jane's colleagues admire her, but none of Brenda's students do

Second, there are contexts in which quantifiers can occur, but from which they cannot bind pronouns in certain positions. The examples in (41) show this (adapted from examples due to M. Wescoat, cited in Dalrymple, Shieber, and Pereira 1991):[12]

---

12. Somewhat more complex cases show the same effect as (41):

(i) The policeman who arrested John said Chief Gates read him his rights, but the one who arrested Bill didn't

If we take the pronouns as sloppy, then it is the VP *said Chief Gates read him his rights* that is elided. In contrast, (ii) allows ellipsis of the smaller VP *read him his rights*:

(ii) The policeman who arrested John said he read him his rights, but the one who arrested Bill didn't

(41) a. The policeman who arrested John read him his rights, and the one who arrested Bill did, too

    b. The person who introduced Mary to John would not give her his phone number, nor would the person who introduced Sue to Bill

In these examples the antecedent NP is within a relative clause, a scope island out of which a quantifier cannot bind a pronoun (see May 1977). But again, sloppy identity is quite natural in the ellipsis. We thus conclude that the conditions on bound variable anaphora are not coextensive with those on sloppy identity.[13] There are cases, however, that appear to support the generalization that sloppy identity tracks binding (i.e., c-command). Thus, (42) has only a strict reading:

(42) Mary's picture of John amused him, and Mary's picture of Bill did, too

---

(ii) differs from (i) in that the definite NP *Chief Gates* has been replaced by a pronoun dependent on the subject NP. Similar observations can be made when PRO is in this position:

(iii) The policeman who arrested John failed to read him his rights, but the one who arrested Bill didn't

These cases would appear problematic because the elided pronouns can be construed as sloppy, even though their dependencies do not appear to be *i*-copies, as they are in (i). Intuitively, what is going on here is that the dependencies are being computed as if in some sense the antecedent occupied the position of the dependent pronoun or PRO in (ii) and (iii), a circumstance that is not possible in (i), since this sentence contains an expression, *Chief Gates*, that bears an α-occurrence. Understood in this way, the dependencies in (ii) and (iii) are *i*-copies, since the NP *John* is "next to" the verb *read*. This proposal has various consequences for our notions of phrase structure and dependencies; we leave aside its formalization for now. (We would like to thank M. Dalrymple, S. Shieber, and F. Pereira for bringing examples of this nature to our attention.)

13. Notice that focal elements can occur inside partitives, so that *all of even John's friends* is well formed. R. Larson has suggested that it might be argued, following suggestions by Chomsky (1976), that if focused elements are subject to LF movement, then variables could occur inside partitives. But if this were to be the whole story, one would not expect a sloppy reading for (i):

(i) The cop who SALLY said arrested Bill beat him up, but the one who MARY said arrested Sam didn't

Here the focal elements are not involved in the sloppy identity. Also note that if focus were related to sloppy identity, then the claim that sloppy identity tracks bound variable anaphora would be undermined, since any position can be a position of focus.

Before we can fully judge the significance of this example, we must consider other factors. Observe that in fully lexicalized pairs of sentences such as *Max saw his mother, and Oscar saw his mother, too*, where we understand the first pronoun as coreferential with *Max*, there are two stress patterns of interest: one has downstress on the pronouns, the other has pair-stress, which lays emphasis on the pronouns and their antecedents. We annotate the latter pattern as in (43):

(43) Máx săw hís mŏther, Osćar săw hís mŏther, too

There is a marked difference in interpretation between the sentences with these stress patterns. Under the downstress pattern, the right-hand pronoun can be understood with either *Max* or *Oscar* as its antecedent. That is, this pronoun can be understood as either strict or sloppy, exactly like the elided pronoun in *Max saw his mother, and Oscar did, too*. Under the pair-stress pattern, however, the pronoun in the right-hand clause has a more limited interpretation; it can have only the sloppy reading on which *Oscar* is its antecedent.

Dependency Theory is a part of a theory of conditions on ways expressions can be related in parallel connected discourse. Its attendant notion of identity (*i*-copy) generates a notion of anaphoric parallelism in such contexts, and such parallelism is sufficient to allow indices of different values to be nondistinct. The redundancy inherent in such parallel discourse settings can be indicated by forms of phonological reduction, either by eliding the redundant material or by downstressing it. Either way, this material is subject to the conditions on reconstruction; for pronouns in such contexts, this means the conditions of Dependency Theory. From this equation of ellipsis and downstress in the context of parallel discourse, it follows that *Max saw his mother, and Oscar did, too* and the downstressed version of *Max saw his mother, and Oscar saw his mother, too* have the same anaphoric properties. Hence, the distribution of strict and sloppy identity is not specific to ellipsis, although it is naturally expressed in such contexts. On the other hand, pair-stress is not comparable to anything in ellipsis. Indeed, it is filtered out in such constructions, since the emphatic stress it involves cannot find any lexical locus in the elided clause. Now consider the following:

(44) Mary's picture of John amused him, and Mary's picture of Bill
       amused him, too

As above, this sentence can be read either with downstress or with pair-stress. Pair-stress gives just the expected sloppy reading; but with downstress only the strict reading is available. Given the interpretive equivalence of downstress with ellipsis, it now follows that the sloppy reading will be unavailable in the elided counterpart of this sentence, (42). The same observation holds for (45):

(45) A picture of John amused him, and a picture of Bill did, too

This shows that the absence of the sloppy reading does not have to do with bound variable anaphora being blocked because the scope of the antecedent expression is limited by a specified subject. Thus, these sentences only have strict readings, but apparently not for any reasons having to do with the sensitivity of ellipsis to bound variable anaphora or c-command. (Similar comments hold if plural nouns are substituted in (42), which arguably makes the subject noun phrase not a scope island (see May 1985), but which does not alter the possibilities of bound variable anaphora in this context.)[14]

In defending the correlation of bound variable anaphora and sloppy identity, Reinhart (1983) provides a range of supporting examples. Typical of the cases she presents is the contrast in (46), where (46a) allows what she labels a "sloppy" reading, but (46b) does not (see Reinhart 1983: chap. 7, (20)–(27)):

(46) a. Zelda criticized Siegfried after he left the room, and Felix, too

   b. After he left the room, Zelda criticized Siegfried, and Felix, too

---

14. Hardt (1991) points out that examples like (i) allow a sloppy reading:

(i) John thinks Mary likes his work, but in Bill's case, I think she actually does

It might be thought that (i) is a case of sloppy identity in the face of the lack of appropriate structural parallelism. But (i) has the further property of precluding a strict reading, and so appears to be subject to somewhat different constraints on anaphoric resolution. Thus, observe that (ii), which would be a strict reading of (i) without elision, is ill formed:

(ii) *John thinks Mary likes his work, but in Bill's case, I think she actually likes John's work

Moreover, if there is no pronoun in the first clause, the result is also ungrammatical:

(iii) *John thinks Mary likes Sam's work, but in Bill's case, I think she actually does

What appears to be going on here is that constructions of the form in (i) require that there be a (focal) dependency, and that the need for such dependencies may overrule other conditions within Dependency Theory. Thus, such cases, of interest in their own right, are irrelevant to the matters of parallelism under discussion in the text.

Although the former example can be glossed as in (47), the latter cannot be comparably paraphrased:

(47) Zelda criticized Siegfried after Siegfried left the room, and Zelda criticized Felix after Felix left the room

Although we generally agree with Reinhart's judgments, these cases are not comparable to those we have been discussing. This is because examples like (46) do not exhibit verb phrase ellipsis, but a different construction, bare-argument ellipsis (or stripping), marked by the absence of the auxiliary element present in verb phrase ellipsis. Reinhart (1991) has now presented a range of arguments that bare-argument ellipsis is not ellipsis at all, but rather involves LF movement forming a derived conjoined phrase. We concur with this proposal, according to which (46a), with the "sloppy" reading, will have the LF representation shown in (48):

(48) [[Zelda criticized e_1 after he$_1$ left the room] [Siegfried and Felix]$_1$]

May (1991) shows that the derived conjoined NPs in (48) are construed as a distributed plural and hence as a quantified expression. Consequently, the pronoun will be construed as a bound variable: the interpretation of the pronouns in this construction will thus track bound variable anaphora because they *are* bound variable pronouns. In contrast, (46b) has the representation in (49):

(49) [[After he$_1$ left the room, Zelda criticized e_1] [Siegfried and Felix]$_1$]

But here the pronoun is not in a position in which it can be construed as a bound variable, as shown by the contrast in (50), observed by Heim, Lasnik, and May (1991b), where bound variable anaphora is possible only in (50a):

(50) a. Zelda criticized everyone after he left the room

b. After he left the room, Zelda criticized everyone

Although bound variable anaphora is thus precluded in (49), nothing blocks the coindexing of the pronoun with *Siegfried* as an instance of coreference anaphora, giving what Reinhart refers to as a "nonsloppy" reading. Note, however, that on this analysis it is a misnomer to describe the pronominal interpretation of (46a) and (46b) in terms of sloppy identity, in the sense that we have applied this term to actual ellipsis, where sloppy construals cut across the bound variable/coreference anaphora distinction.

In chapter 2 we observed that pronouns that stand as variables bear β-occurrences. In this way, a difference between coreference and bound variable anaphora became apparent—a difference that can be directly observed in ellipsis. Consider (51) on the sloppy reading:

(51) Every bachelor saw his mother, and Oscar/every married man did, too

Here the pronoun is a bound variable, and a structure in which the pronoun bears a β-occurrence is available:

(52) Every bachelor$_1$ [$_{VP}$ saw his$_1^\beta$ mother], and Oscar/every married man$_2$ [$_{VP}$ **saw his$_2^\beta$ mother**]

Observe that this structure will be well formed regardless of whether the elided pronoun is construed as participating in coreference anaphora or bound variable anaphora. This will depend upon the semantic status of the pronoun's antecedent: if it is *Oscar* (*Oscar saw his mother*), then we have coreference anaphora; if it is *every married man* (*Every married man saw his mother*), bound variable anaphora. Fixing of values for β-occurrences relative to indexical dependencies is compatible with either reference or quantification, and hence with either type of anaphoric relation. Not so with α-occurrences, which are only compatible with coreference anaphora (leaving aside the marked cases, discussed in chapter 2). Contrasts such as that between *Max saw his mother, and Oscar did, too* and (51) have been taken as indicating, initially by Lasnik (1976) and more forcefully by Reinhart (1983), that the sloppy reading correlates with bound variable anaphora and the strict reading with coreference anaphora (for Reinhart, a matter of pragmatic reference). On this view, not only does *Every married man saw his mother* involve bound variable anaphora, but so does *Oscar saw his mother*, which is ambiguous between bound variable anaphora and coreference anaphora. Our view of these cases is somewhat different. Although we agree that the former sentence is unequivocally a case of bound variable anaphora, we also hold that the latter sentence is unequivocally a case of coreference anaphora; in this regard, they are cases of different types of anaphora. What they can have in common is that they each can reach these types of construals through dependencies, through a pronoun bearing a β-occurrence. Where they differ is that coreference anaphora, but not bound variable anaphora, can also reach this construal in the absence of a dependency, through a pronoun bearing an α-occurrence. And it is this difference, we maintain, that accounts for the asymmetry in the possibility of strict and sloppy readings, not the difference in type of anaphora.

The correlations between types of indices and types of anaphora shed light on observations that begin with Geach (1962). He observes that (53a) and (53b) do not mean the same thing:

(53) a. Only Satan loves himself

b. Only Satan loves Satan

If John loves himself, (53a) is false, but not (53b); but if John loves Satan, then it is (53b) that is false, and not (53a). Commensurate with Binding Theory, we capture this difference by the indexings in (54):[15]

(54) a. [Only Satan$_1$]$_2$ loves himself$_2$

b. [Only Satan$_1$]$_2$ loves Satan$_1$

Evans (1977) extends the observation, pointing out that the sorts of readings exhibited by the sentences in (53) can be collapsed into an ambiguity:

(55) Only Satan loves his mother

On one reading, this sentence would be falsified if John loves his own mother; on the other, if John loves Satan's mother. This follows from whether the pronoun is coindexed with *only Satan* or with *Satan*, and hence is a difference that turns on whether there is bound variable or coreference anaphora. However, this distinction is not sufficient to characterize the anaphora in (55), as can be discerned when it is placed in an ellipsis context:

(56) Only Satan loves his mother, and only Job does, too

This sentence has three readings, not two. First, there is a contradictory reading; if no one but Satan loves his own mother, then certainly Job does not. There is also a second contradictory reading; it says of Satan's mother both that no one but Satan loves her and that no one but Job loves her, too. Interestingly, there is also a third reading, which, unlike the other two,

---

15. This approach was initially suggested by Higginbotham (1980a), developing ideas of Evans (1977) that the difference here turns on whether the pronoun is dependent upon the whole phrase or just upon the constituent phrase. It is not altogether clear whether the coindexing in (54b) is possible because of lack of c-command—the occurrence of *Satan* contained within the subject NP not c-commanding outside of that NP—or because this sentence is part of the "mathematical" metafragment discussed in chapter 1. Indications are that the latter is the case, given the apparent not-coreference effect observed for *Only Satan loves him,* which we would want to account for via Principle B of Binding Theory. Note that under neither treatment does (54b) violate Principle C, as has been claimed, for instance, by Roberts (1987).

is noncontradictory. On this reading, the sentence is true if and only if nobody but Satan loves Satan's mother and nobody but Job loves Job's mother. Of the contradictory readings, the first one is sloppy, the second one, strict. The third, noncontradictory reading is also sloppy, since the elided pronoun refers to Job, not Satan.

That (56) has this three-way ambiguity follows directly from the distribution of indexical types in the following representations:

(57) a. [Only Satan$_1$]$_2$ loves his$_2^\beta$ mother, and [only Job$_3$]$_4$ **loves his$_4^\beta$ mother**

b. [Only Satan$_1$]$_2$ loves his$_1^\alpha$ mother, and [only Job$_3$]$_4$ **loves his$_1^\alpha$ mother**

c. [Only Satan$_1$]$_2$ loves his$_1^\beta$ mother, and [only Job$_3$]$_4$ **loves his$_3^\beta$ mother**

These represent the sloppy contradictory, strict contradictory, and sloppy noncontradictory readings, respectively. We can have the representations in (57b) and (57c) because, since the overt pronouns are coindexed with *Satan*, they can bear either an α- or β-occurrence, and we can have the representation in (57a), in which the pronoun is coindexed with *only Satan* and bears a β-occurrence. What these considerations show, then, is that no approach that distinguishes sentences such as (55) only in terms of which NP is the antecedent will be sufficient. What also must be taken into account is the pronoun's relation—dependent or independent—to that antecedent.

In contrast to the representations in (57), we cannot have the one in (58), which is like (57a), except that the pronoun bears an α-occurrence:

(58) *[Only Satan$_1$]$_2$ loves his$_2^\alpha$ mother, and [only Job$_3$]$_4$ **loves his$_2^\alpha$ mother**

This structure is ill formed because the α-occurrence-bearing pronoun is coindexed with a quantified phrase whose scope it doesn't fall within. This is a salutary result, since the structure's (contradictory) reading that nobody but Satan loves his own mother, whereas Job is the sole lover of Satan's mother, is clearly excluded. Recall from chapter 2, however, that under certain circumstances a pronoun can be anaphoric to a quantifier phrase and bear an α-occurrence; these are E-type occurrences. When we introduce the possibility of an E-type reading, we can in fact observe a full four-way ambiguity. Consider this sentence:

(59) Most of the plumbers love their mothers

Suppose, to be concrete, that there are four plumbers, W, X, Y, and Z. Then, on one way of understanding this sentence, it is true if each of X,

Y, and Z love X, Y, and Z's mothers. This is the E-type reading. It is to be distinguished from a bound variable reading on which X loves X's mother, Y loves Y's mother, and Z loves Z's mother. The anaphora on the E-type reading is to the "descriptive content" associated with the quantifier phrase, to wit, the plumbers who constitute most of them.[16] Thus, (59) is false if W, X, and Y love X, Y, and Z's mothers. Even though we have placed a trio of plumbers in the positions of the quantifier phrase and the pronoun, on the E-type reading it must be that the *same* trio is in both positions. Taking the E-type reading to complete the paradigm of anaphoric relations, being an α-occurrence coindexed with a quantified phrase, consider the effect of placing (59) in an ellipsis context:

(60) Most of the plumbers love their mothers, and most of the carpenters do, too

When we understand the overt occurrence of the pronoun as E-type, the construal that results is that not only do most of the plumbers love those plumbers' mothers, but so do most of the carpenters love those plumbers' mothers. That is, with the E-type pronoun, the interpretation of the elliptical pronoun is *strict*. This is as we would expect, if such E-type pronouns bear independent, and not dependent, occurrences of indices.[17]

Thus, (60) now has the following well-formed representations:

(61) a. [Most of the plumbers$_1$]$_2$ love their$_2^\beta$ mothers, and [most of the carpenters$_3$]$_4$ **love their$_4^\beta$ mothers**

---

16. These cases fall together with the E-type pronouns discussed in chapter 2 if we assume that *most* falls within the descriptive content that determines the value of the pronoun. Thus, the pronoun in (59) refers to all of the plumbers who constitute most of the plumbers. This appears to hold only for the partitive, since there is a contrast between (59) and *Most plumbers love their mothers,* in which on the E-type reading of the pronoun it refers to all the plumbers. We leave aside the formal details of how descriptive content is to be isolated; see Evans 1977, Neale 1990. Notice also that examples like (59) and the one just mentioned show that Evans's claim that E-type pronouns are only possible when the quantified antecedent does not c-command the pronoun is incorrect.

17. Our view of E-type pronouns stands in contrast to that of Higginbotham (1989), who holds that such pronouns are dependent directly upon quantifier phrases (and not on the variables they bind). Although Higginbotham does not present an application of this theory to ellipsis, it would appear that he would have to maintain that sloppy identity is possible whenever there is a dependency (a "link" in his terminology), and hence with E-type pronouns as well. The problem for Higginbotham arises from his only allowing anaphoric connections to be indicated via dependencies, which replace indices (following Evans), so that his theory does not allow for fine enough distinctions. See discussion in chapter 2.

b. [Most of the plumbers$_1$]$_2$ love their$_2^\alpha$ mothers, and [most of the carpenters$_3$]$_4$ **love their$_2^\alpha$ mothers**

c. [Most of the plumbers$_1$]$_2$ love their$_1^\beta$ mothers, and [most of the carpenters$_3$]$_4$ **love their$_3^\beta$ mothers**

d. [Most of the plumbers$_1$]$_2$ love their$_1^\alpha$ mothers, and [most of the carpenters$_3$]$_4$ **love their$_1^\alpha$ mothers**

(61a) represents a sloppy reading, where the pronouns are taken in each clause as bound variables, and (61b) represents the strict E-type reading just described. In these cases anaphora is to be traced back to the quantifier phrase. The truth conditions of (61c) may be sketched as follows. Suppose that the carpenters are A, B, C, and D. Then, for (61c) to be true, most of W, X, Y, and Z (at least any three) love W, X, Y, and Z's mothers, and most of A, B, C, and D love A, B, C, and D's mothers. In contrast, for (61d) to be true, most of A, B, C, and D must love W, X, Y, and Z's mothers, that is, the plumbers' mothers. Note that both of these cases exhibit coreference anaphora. The difference is that in the former this is dependent anaphora, leading to a sloppy reading, whereas in the latter it is independent anaphora, leading to the concomitant strict reading.

To summarize, through the analysis of strict and sloppy readings in elliptical environments we have been able to explore the identity conditions on indices provided by Dependency Theory. This has shed light not only on more general notions of syntactic identity (reconstruction), but also on the representation of coreference, bound variable, and E-type anaphora. Although elliptical environments provide a very sensitive probe into these matters, for the remainder of this chapter we will leave them to one side, in order to explore other phenomena that can be characterized as strict versus sloppy.

3.3   Strict and Sloppy Inference

Strict and sloppy readings are not limited to elliptical contexts. They are also found in focus constructions, adapting an example of Higginbotham (1992):

(62) We only asked whether Mary said JOHN expected he would win, not whether Mary said Bill expected he would win

Here the pronoun in the continuation clause can be understood as referring to John or Bill. In our terms, this ambiguity is a result of whether the initial pronoun bears an α- or a β-occurrence:

(63) a. We only asked whether Mary said JOHN$_1$ expected he$_1^\alpha$ would
        win, not whether Mary said Bill$_2$ expected he$_1^\alpha$ would win

     b. We only asked whether Mary said JOHN$_1$ expected he$_1^\beta$ would
        win, not whether Mary said Bill$_2$ expected he$_2^\beta$ would win

In each case the continuation clause is an *i*-copy of the initial focus-
containing clause. Higginbotham further observes that (62) contrasts with
(64), where the lexical pronoun has been replaced by an occurrence of
PRO, as the understood subject of the infinitive:

(64) We only asked whether Mary said JOHN expected to win, not
     whether Mary said Bill expected to win

Here only a sloppy reading is possible. The reason for this turns on control
PRO, the understood subject of the infinitive, bearing a β-occurrence; in
a sense, we take it as the lexically null counterpart of the pronoun in
(63b).[18] It then follows that (64) will have a reading comparable to (63b),
but not (63a).[19]

Chierchia (1984) has observed cases such as (65), which we can think of
as a sloppy inference, in the sense that what holds of Jane in the premise—
wanting to solve Fermat's theorem—also holds of Mary in the conclusion:

(65) Jane wants to solve Fermat's last theorem
     Mary wants whatever Jane wants
     Therefore, Mary wants to solve Fermat's last theorem

---

18. For a more explicit discussion of the status of PRO, and its relation to personal
and reflexive pronouns, see chapter 5. Note that we do not exclude occurrences of
PRO that bear α-occurrences. For instance, we take it that noncontrol PRO, as in
John said [PRO to leave] or *PRO to win an election is gratifying*, is of this type.

19. A reviewer points to a similar example, in which the focused NP is a bound
pronoun:

(i) Each boy$_1$'s mother only asked whether Mary said HE$_1$ expected he$_1$ would
    win, not whether Mary said Bill expected he would win

The observation is that the pronoun in the second clause can be understood either
as bound by *each boy* or as referring to *Bill*—in essence, as strict or sloppy. The
focused pronoun, however, being a bound variable, presumably can only be a
β-occurrence. Notice, though, that (i) contains conjoined complement clauses, so
the quantifier *each boy* has scope over both clauses. Thus, it can bind the occurrence of the pronoun in the second clause as a bound variable. This will be what
we have labeled the strict reading. The sloppy reading will result as in the cases
discussed in the text. Note, however, that (i) will differ from those examples, since
under either reading the pronoun will be a β-occurrence.

In contrast are strict inferences such as the following:

(66) Jane wants Sally to solve Fermat's last theorem
       Mary wants whatever Jane wants
       Therefore, Mary wants Sally to solve Fermat's last theorem

Chierchia points out that there is a minimal difference between the first premises in these cases; in (65) the subject is "understood," yielding sloppy validity, and in the latter it is lexically overt, yielding strict validity. Starting with an understood subject, however, we cannot make a strict inference. Thus, the inference in (67) is invalid:

(67) Jane wants to solve Fermat's last theorem
       Mary wants whatever Jane wants
       Therefore, Mary wants Jane to solve Fermat's last theorem

Nor, conversely, can we make a sloppy inference starting with a lexical subject:

(68) Mary wants Jane to solve Fermat's last theorem
       Jane wants whatever Mary wants
       Therefore, Jane wants to solve Fermat's last theorem

This is also invalid.

Our analysis is as follows. We represent (65) as in (69), again assuming that control PRO is a β-occurrence:

(69) Jane$_1$ wants [PRO$_1^\beta$ to solve Fermat's last theorem]
       Mary wants whatever Jane wants
       Therefore, Mary$_2$ wants [PRO$_2^\beta$ to solve Fermat's last theorem]

This inference is of the form in (70), where the quantifier ranges over linguistic expressions of the appropriate type as objects (here, clauses):[20]

20. Note that our quantifier here is not substitutional, since its values are linguistic expressions, not names of those expressions. We thus allow first-order quantifiers over individuals of the usual sort as well as over linguistic objects. This obviates the need for second-order quantifiers over properties, as assumed in Chierchia's (1984) analysis; see discussion below. However, it is still an open question whether there are other sorts of second-order quantifiers over nonlinguistic entities. One case might be branching quantification, which requires quantification over whatever sorts of things plurals denote; see Barwise 1979, May 1989, Sher 1991. But it is at least debatable that pluralities might be treated as individuals of a special sort, rather than as sets; for discussion, see Heim, Lasnik, and May 1991b, Link 1987, and Schein 1994.

(70) NP_i wants x

$\quad\forall x(NP_i \text{ wants } x \to NP_j \text{ wants } x)$

$\quad\therefore NP_j$ wants x

(69) is a valid instance of (70) because the complement clause in the first premise is the same as that in the conclusion. This is the case even though they contain elements that bear occurrences of different indices. These elements bear β-occurrences of these indices, and the dependencies in which these occurrences figure are i-copies and hence are nondistinct. Because of this, the numerical values of the indices are irrelevant to determining the identity of the clauses. Thus, the critical aspect of structure for the validity of this sort of inference is indexical *type*; this is true not only of the sloppy inference, but also of the strict one. Thus, (71) also counts as a valid instance of (70), since both the premise and conclusion clauses contain α-occurrences:

(71) Jane$_1$ wants [Sally$_1^\alpha$ to solve Fermat's last theorem]

$\quad$Mary wants whatever Jane wants

$\quad$Therefore, Mary$_2$ wants [Sally$_1^\alpha$ to solve Fermat's last theorem]

But since these are α-occurrences, for the clauses to be identical, they both must be realized as occurrences of a single index. Hence, here it is the strict inference that is valid. What is invalid is (72), corresponding to (67):

(72) Jane$_1$ wants [PRO$_1^\beta$ to solve Fermat's last theorem]

$\quad$Mary wants whatever Jane wants

$\quad$Therefore, Mary$_2$ wants [Jane$_1^\alpha$ to solve Fermat's last theorem]

Here, the complement clause of the conclusion is not identical to that of the initial premise. Since they contain elements of different indexical type, there obviously isn't a dependency in the conclusion that is an i-copy of the dependency in the premise. Thus, (72) is not an instance of (70).

The examples of inferential failure we have observed thus far have all turned on elements bearing different indexical types in a premise and the conclusion. Inference can also fail when indexical type is preserved. Thus, consider the invalid inference in (73), pointed out by Ladusaw (1987):

(73) John persuaded Mary to solve Fermat's last theorem

$\quad$Max promised Sally whatever John persuaded Mary of

$\quad$Therefore, Max promised Sally to solve Fermat's last theorem

Equally invalid is (74), where controlled subjects are replaced by lexical pronouns:

(74) John persuaded Mary that she would solve Fermat's last theorem
Max promised Sally whatever John persuaded Mary of
Therefore, Max promised Sally that he would solve Fermat's last theorem

Using the control case to illustrate the reason for the failure of the inference, we represent (73) as in (75):

(75) John persuaded Mary$_1$ [PRO$_1^\beta$ to solve Fermat's last theorem]
Max promised Sally whatever John persuaded Mary of
Therefore, Max$_2$ promised Sally [PRO$_2^\beta$ to solve Fermat's last theorem]

Because of the difference in control properties displayed by *promise* and *persuade*, which are mirrored for the pronouns in (74), the expressions bearing the β-occurrences are not in parallel structural relations to their antecedents. In the premise PRO is dependent on the matrix object, and in the conclusion it is dependent on the subject, yielding the dependencies in (76):

(76) a. $\langle(\text{Mary, PRO}), 1, \langle\text{NP, C, NP}\rangle\rangle$

b. $\langle(\text{Max, PRO}), 2, \langle\text{NP, V, NP, C, NP}\rangle\rangle$

Thus, the dependency in the conclusion is not an *i*-copy of that in the premise; but crucial to the validity of such inferences is that the anaphoric relation in the conclusion must be an *i*-copy of that in the initial premise. Hence, the inferences in (74) and (75) fail.[21]

Strict and sloppy anaphoric relations have been used to argue for the need to assume a richer semantic structure, encompassing a notion of

---

21. There are certain cases in which strict inferences with control are possible:

(i) Mary wants to solve Fermat's last theorem
Her mother wants whatever Mary wants
Therefore, Mary's mother wants her to solve Fermat's last theorem

We return to this inference in chapter 5, and to the (perhaps surprising) strict inference in (ii), which is valid with *her* in the conclusion referring to Jane:

(ii) Jane believes herself to have solved Fermat's last theorem
Mary believes whatever Jane believes
Therefore, Mary believes her to have solved Fermat's last theorem

We propose in chapter 5 that reflexive pronouns are composites of a pronoun and the element *self*, and we argue that this pronominal part, like other pronouns, can bear either an α- or a β-occurrence, giving rise to strict and sloppy inferences, respectively.

property expressed or denoted. For example, it has been a common view, since the work of Sag (1976) and Williams (1977), that to account for the sloppy reading in verb phrase ellipsis, it is necessary to employ a notion of identity of predication. The reasoning behind this view is that a sloppy reading can be inferred for the elided phrase because it can be taken as expressing the same property as the overt antecedent. Thus, one would gloss *John saw his mother, and Max did, too* as the same property, that of loving one's own mother, holding of both John and Max. Formally, this is captured on this theory by predicate-abstraction:

(77) $\lambda x(x$ saw x's mother)(John), and $\lambda x(x$ saw x's mother)(Max)

In his presentation of strict and sloppy inference, Chierchia (1984) argues in a similar vein, proposing that understood-subject infinitives are verb phrases that denote properties. The validity of a sloppy inference then turns on a property holding, as in verb phrase ellipsis, of different individuals, so that the inference in (65) from *Jane wants to solve Fermat's last theorem* to *Mary wants to solve Fermat's last theorem* is of the form (78):

(78) NP_i wants $\mathscr{P}$
$\quad$ $\forall x(NP_i$ wants $x \rightarrow NP_j$ wants $x)$
$\quad$ $\therefore$ NP_j wants $\mathscr{P}$

Infinitives with overt subjects, on the other hand, are clauses, and they denote propositions. But if a proposition, rather than a property, meets the call of the variable, then the inference must be strict, since propositions have no "open" position that allows them to hold of different individuals at different occurrences, as in the inference in (68). What ought not to be possible are "mixed" inferences, from a property to a proposition, or vice versa, since they are of different types and cannot simultaneously satisfy the variable in the second premise.

Ladusaw (1987) observes, however, that this is not sufficient to rule out invalid inferences of the sort in (67) and (68); we repeat the former here:

(67) Jane wants to solve Fermat's last theorem
$\quad$ Mary wants whatever Jane wants
$\quad$ Therefore, Mary wants Jane to solve Fermat's last theorem

Ladusaw points out that any theory of control that assumes that infinitives denote properties must allow the following equivalence,

$want(x, \mathscr{P}) \leftrightarrow want(x, \mathscr{P}(x))$

since it must follow from *Jane wants to solve Fermat's last theorem* that it is Jane who is to solve the theorem. But the control entailment then allows for inferences of the form (79):

(79) NP_i wants $\mathscr{P}$
       NP_i wants $\mathscr{P}(NP_i)$
       $\forall x(NP_i$ wants $x \rightarrow NP_j$ wants $x)$
       $\therefore$ NP_j wants $\mathscr{P}(NP_i)$

But this would yield, incorrectly, that (67) is valid.

In contrast, on our view, both types of complements are clauses, and both have sentential meanings (truth-values). They differ in that one type contains a lexically null subject, so that the determination of the value of the clause is subject to the resolution of a dependency, whereas the other contains a lexically nonnull subject, a name, and is independent of such resolution. Since the inferences generated from these two types of sentences depend solely on their form—α-occurrence to α-occurrence; β-occurrence to β-occurrence—no mixed inferences are possible. Although it certainly does follow on our theory that *Jane wants to solve Fermat's last theorem* implies that it is Jane who is to solve the theorem, this is by means of resolving the dependency of PRO upon *Jane*. However, this fact is irrelevant to the analysis of inferences that turn on the syntactic characterization of dependencies. Thus, on our view, the possibility of strict and sloppy anaphora depends upon *formal* aspects of expressions, without appeal to notions of a semantic nature such as properties or propositions. We return in chapter 4 to discussion of the relevance of predication in the context of verb phrase ellipsis, the most extensively investigated application of the appeal to properties.

3.4 Belief *De Se* and Indexical Types

Chierchia (1989) extends his previous observations to strict and sloppy inferences turning on the presence of pronouns, as in (80):

(80) Jane believes she solved Fermat's last theorem
       Mary believes whatever Jane believes
       Therefore, Mary believes she solved Fermat's last theorem

Chierchia discerns that the conclusion of (80) can be understood in different ways, given that there is coreference in the initial premise. Either Mary believes that Jane solved the theorem, or Mary believes that she herself solved it. Relative to the initial premise, these constitute valid strict and sloppy inferences. In our terms, this is because they can be represented as follows, that is, as inferences of the same general form as (70), with *believe* substituted for *want*:

(81) Jane$_1$ believes [she$_1^\alpha$ solved Fermat's last theorem]
      Mary believes whatever Jane believes
      Therefore, Mary$_2$ believes [she$_1^\alpha$ solved Fermat's last theorem]

(82) Jane$_1$ believes [she$_1^\beta$ solved Fermat's last theorem]
      Mary believes whatever Jane believes
      Therefore, Mary$_2$ believes [she$_2^\beta$ solved Fermat's last theorem]

Chierchia makes another claim regarding the strict and sloppy inferences
in (81) and (82), namely, that which conclusion is drawn correlates with
different characters of belief. With strict inference, the belief attributions
are understood *de re*. If, on the other hand, the sloppy inference is drawn,
Chierchia argues that the attribution may be understood in another way.
On this understanding, what is attributed is not only that Jane has a belief
about Jane, but a stronger attribution that she has a certain belief about
herself. Similarly for Mary. However, the possibility of understanding the
conclusion of the strict inference in (81) as such a *de se*, or self-ascriptive,
belief is precluded. Thus, to have a report of a *de se* belief, there must be
an anaphoric connection into the belief context. In the context of Dependency Theory, this correlation of type of belief with strict and sloppy
inference invites an association of β-occurrences with *de se* belief, and
α-occurrences with belief *de re*. On this view, we would have *de se* belief
when there is a dependency on the agent of the belief, and *de re* belief when
there is no such dependency. Although this line of reasoning is attractive,
it turns out that the linguistic basis of this difference in belief is of a
somewhat different nature.

To see this, consider the following puzzle, which stems from the work
of Castañeda (1966, 1968). Suppose that John is reading a book describing
the acts of some individual but that John does not realize the person he is
reading about is himself. Suppose further that John has no very high
opinion of his own heroism, but considers the acts of the person he is
reading about heroic indeed. On the basis of John's reading, *we* would
affirm (83), but John would affirm (84):

(83) John believes that he is heroic

(84) I do not believe that I am heroic

It would appear that something more than mere coreference must be at
work in these examples, since otherwise a contradiction is readily derived.
What is that extra something? Notice that although (84) is certainly an
ascription of a belief concerning one's self (i.e., a *de se* belief ascription),
(83), in the context of the puzzle, is not. In the context of the puzzle, (83)

is *de re*, but not *de se*. Furthermore, there would appear to be a *de se* understanding of (83), false in the context of the puzzle, and hence consistent with (84). If the correlation mentioned in the previous paragraph were to hold, then we could account for these observations in terms of indices and dependencies, on the assumption that since the pronouns differ in indexical type, (83) and (84) are not of the form P and $\neg P$.

Let us consider, then, the proposition that sentences such as (83) are understood *de se* if and only if the pronoun is a β-occurrence. There is evidence showing that this generalization cannot be right in either direction. Consider (85):

(85) John thinks that he is heroic, and Bill does, too

The ellipsis in (85) can be understood sloppily, yet Bill, like John, could be ignorant of the fact that the person he is reading about is himself. For a pronoun to be sloppy, it must bear a β-occurrence; yet the interpretation is not *de se*. (85) also shows that there are *de se* readings with α-occurrences. Thus, observe that the ellipsis in (85) can be construed as strict with the initial clause understood *de se*. On this way of understanding the sentence, John has a belief about himself that Bill has about John *de re*. Notice that a *de se* ascription for the initial clause is all that is normally available in (86):

(86) I think I am heroic, and you do, too

(86) is also ambiguous between strict and sloppy readings; hence, the embedded first person pronoun can bear either an α- or a β-occurrence.

Further observations amplify the independence of *de se* readings from matters of indices and dependencies. Thus, consider the following example, devised by Higginbotham (1990), in which the pronoun, being a bound variable, bears a β-occurrence:

(87) Each of these men thinks that he is heroic, but none thinks he himself is heroic

By (87), we take it that each of the men suffers from the relevant ignorance. From this we conclude that β-occurrences can support non–*de se* construals. On the other hand, there are *de se* readings with α-occurrences, as can be seen from the interpretation of (88):

(88) John doesn't believe that John is heroic

The two instances of *John* in (88) are α-occurrences in the relation of not-coreference, due to Principle C, but this essentially irrelevant fact can be controlled for. As has already been discussed, this indexical pattern is

consistent with coreference in a variety of contexts. Suppose that we
select such a context. It would appear that (88), although it contains an
α-occurrence, can be used to ascribe a *de se* belief, the one John would
report via (84). Thus, there are pronouns bearing β-occurrences that are
not *de se* and names and pronouns bearing α-occurrences that are *de se*.
These considerations, along with those of the previous paragraph, eliminate the possibility that β-occurrences are either necessary or sufficient to
de se belief ascription. Since there are both *de se* and *de re* α-occurrences,
it is clear that no very simple generalization along these lines can be
hoped for.

What these considerations show, then, is that the expressive power of
language, at least as determined by indices and dependencies, is not cru-
cially implicated in the *de re/de se* distinction. The speaker may wish to
ascribe *de se* belief, and there are many periphrastic routes to this that can
succeed unambiguously. But there is no unambiguous route solely in terms
of indices and dependencies; this is beyond their descriptive power. Rather, what appears to distinguish sentences such as (83) and (84) is the fact
that in (84) the speaker and the agent of belief are the same. It is possible
to test this more directly.

Consider (89), a sentence of the form *Bill believes that P*:

(89) Bill believes that every man believes that he is heroic

The pronoun in *P* is a β-occurrence bound by *every man* that may be
understood either *de re*, as in the puzzle, or *de se*. There is no difference
between the two readings with regard to indices or dependencies. Suppose
the speaker thinks that Bill believes that every man has a *de se* belief. Then
the speaker will wish the pronoun to be understood *de se*. This will be so
even if the speaker thinks that every man has a *de re* belief. Contrast (90):

(90) I believe that every man believes that he is heroic

Suppose the speaker thinks that every man has a *de se* belief. It must then
be true that the referent of the matrix subject *I* thinks every man has a *de
se* belief. This follows from the fact that the agent of belief is the speaker.
In such sentences the *de re/de se* distinction is transparent. This can be seen
more simply by considering the contrast between (91) and (92):

(91) John believes that he is heroic, but he doesn't realize it

(92) I believe that I am heroic, but I don't realize it

In the context of the puzzle, (91) may be appropriately uttered, but (92)
remains strange. Note that the point we are making here is not limited to

personal pronouns; it also holds for emphatic pronouns like *he himself* and, as the following paradigm illustrates, for reflexives:

(93) a. I believe myself to be heroic, but I don't realize it

    b. You believe yourself to be heroic, but you don't realize it

    c. He believes himself to be heroic, but he doesn't realize it

(93a) is anomalous, since the initial clause expresses belief *de se*; in contrast, (93b) and (93c) are coherent, since they express just belief *de re*.

The situation just described contrasts with the interpretation of indices. Coindexing in general enforces a grammatical requirement of covaluation —for the case at hand, coreference. But the indices are invariably the speaker's indices. Consider again sentence (89). In (89) *every man* and *he* are coindexed, as shown in (94):

(94) Bill believes that every man$_1$ believes that he$_1$ is heroic

But, in the context of the puzzle, Bill would never affirm (95), since he holds himself to be nonheroic:

(95) Every man$_1$ believes that he$_1$ is heroic

Our original account of the power of indices and dependencies seems to be correct; that power cannot be extended to include the distinction between *de re* and *de se* belief ascription.

Returning to the inferences (81) and (82), we now conclude that they both give rise to conclusions that are *de re*, as far as language per se is concerned—that is, regardless of whether the inference is strict or sloppy.[22] Only the inference on the β-occurrence, however, could be used to

---

22. We are thus disclaiming that linguistically there are two distinct *senses* of belief, *de re* and *de se*, as held, for instance, by Chierchia (1989), Lewis (1979), and Richard (1983). Rather, in agreement with arguments by Higginbotham (1990, 1991a), we assume that there is only one sense of belief, which can have different objects individuated by indices; we now take this to mean that they can be individuated not only in terms of indexical value (see chapter 1, section 2) but also by indexical type. Thus, although the sentences in (i) attribute different token beliefs to John and Max, they do attribute the same *type* of belief, in which there is a pronoun dependent on an expression that denotes the agent of the belief:

(i) a. John$_1$ believes he$_1^\beta$ is smart

    b. Max$_2$ believes he$_2^\beta$ is smart

However, these are different particular beliefs, since one implies a belief in John's being smart, the other a belief in Max's being smart. Similar comments obtain when the pronouns are replaced with ones bearing α-occurrences. In this way we derive a conclusion that a speaker could use in context to attribute a belief *de se*. This is because the inference on the α-occurrence leads to a conclusion in which Mary has a belief about Jane, and hence it could never be about herself. However, this fact arises from Dependency Theory, and how it determines the possibilities of strict and sloppy inference, and is independent of whether belief contexts containing pronouns bearing α-occurrences can express *de se* belief, or those bearing β-occurrences belief *de re*. The only grammatical way to unequivocally express *de se* belief is by the use of first person pronouns. This is because by the use of such pronouns, the agent of the belief will be the speaker, and only he is in a position to speak authoritatively about his own beliefs. The *de se* nature of first person belief ascriptions does not arise from indexical structure, however, since first person and third person are the same in this regard, yet third person belief ascriptions do not unequivocally express *de se* belief. Thus, the linguistic determinants of the character of belief ascriptions are independent of Dependency Theory, although they will interact with it in the sorts of cases we have been considering.[23]

---

capture what Perry (1979) describes as a difference between belief and belief state. Thus, relative to (i), John and Max are in the same belief state, but have different beliefs.

23. Higginbotham (1992) draws essentially the same conclusion. Chierchia (1989) proposes that the *de re*/*de se* distinction turns on whether the object of belief is a proposition or a self-ascriptive property, representing the readings as follows (after Lewis 1979; see also Richard 1983):

(i) a. λx[believe $(x, x$ solved Fermat's last theorem)] (Jane)

    b. believe (Jane, $\lambda x[x$ solved Fermat's last theorem])

In the former, *de re* representation, *believe* is a relation between an individual, who is Jane, and the proposition that Jane solved Fermat's theorem. In the latter, *de se* representation, *believe* holds between Jane and the self-ascriptive property of being someone who solved the theorem, although it is not clear what it is about (ib) that makes it self-ascriptive. Chierchia further proposes that (ib) has a syntactic reflex in which an empty operator links the pronoun to the agent of the belief, as in (ii):

(ii) Jane$_i$ believes [O_i [she$_i$ is smart]]

As Chierchia notes, such connection is possible from a pronoun in a syntactic island; he gives example (iii):

(iii) John thinks that Mary is still wondering whether to marry him

This behavior contrasts with that of other empty operators in syntax, and with that of other logical operators, such as quantifiers. On the proposal made here, however, these facts are unexceptional, since pronominal binding is not subject to the island constraints that limit movement.

Chapter 4
Eliminative Puzzles of Ellipsis

4.1 Eliminative Puzzles of Ellipsis

Discussions of anaphora in ellipsis usually begin with the observation that the elided occurrence of the pronoun in a string such as (1) is understood ambiguously:

(1) Max saw his mother, and Oscar did, too

Fixing the overt pronoun as anaphoric to the NP *Max*, (1) can be understood as saying either that Oscar saw Max's mother—the *strict* reading—or that Oscar saw Oscar's mother—the *sloppy* reading. Our initial discussion of this phenomenon in chapter 2 has not broken this mold, since an ability to account for this observation is assuredly a baseline requirement for any adequate theory of ellipsis and anaphora. This fact is in certain ways uninteresting, however, since the anaphoric construals of (1) are no different from those of the string in (2), without ellipsis:

(2) Max saw his mother, and Oscar saw his mother, too

That is, the second occurrence of *his* can be understood as anaphorically related either to *Max* or to *Oscar*; it can find its antecedent either in its own clause or in another. Eliding the VP in (1) therefore raises no questions about the possibilities of anaphora above and beyond those raised by (2). On the basis of this observation, the relevant question is why ellipsis should leave anaphora unaffected, yet limit deixis—although the pronouns in (2) can refer to different individuals (who are neither Max nor Oscar), in (1) there is reference to only one other individual. This way of stating the issue is misleading, however, since there are a number of puzzles of strict and sloppy identity that show the effect of ellipsis on anaphora to be not conserving, but eliminative. These puzzles arise when we increase the complexity of the data, either by increasing the number of pronouns contained in the ellipsis or by increasing the number of clauses that contain ellipses.

The first puzzle pertains to strings such as (3), due to Dahl (1974):

(3) Max said he saw his mother, and Oscar did, too

Taking both overt pronouns in (3) as anaphorically related to *Max*, the natural readings of this string are those where the elided pronouns are read "across-the-board": either both are understood strictly (... *and Oscar said Max saw Max's mother*), or both are understood sloppily (... *and Oscar said that Oscar saw Oscar's mother*). In addition to these, there is a third reading, under which the first pronoun is understood as sloppy and the second as strict (... *and Oscar said that Oscar saw Max's mother*). This reading is usually perceived as marginal and somewhat marked relative to the across-the-board readings. However, this "mixed" reading sharply contrasts with another, in which the pronouns would be understood in the opposite manner: the first as strict and the second as sloppy. This reading is precluded for all speakers. It is not precluded, however, in (4), which can be taken to mean that Oscar said that Max saw Oscar's mother:

(4) Max said he saw his mother, and Oscar said he saw his mother

In this string, all four readings are available; although stress may be a factor in sorting them out, none appears marked relative to others. The issue, then, is that there is some way of saying the fully lexicalized (4) such that all four readings are possible, but there is no way of saying the elliptical (3) for which this is so. For that case, only three readings are possible. The effect of ellipsis here is thus *eliminative*. Ellipsis no longer preserves anaphoric possibilities; rather, it restricts their realization. We will refer to this as the *many-pronouns puzzle*.[1]

The filtering effect of ellipsis can be observed in a second puzzle, the *many-clauses puzzle*. Rather than increasing the number of pronouns rela-

---

1. Let us be clear here about the role of stress in giving prominence to readings of (4). We take it that (4) is one *string* corresponding to four *sentences*, in the technical sense of phrase markers individuated in terms of their indexical structure. In uttering (4), however, a speaker may place emphasis on one or the other of the pronouns in the string in order to bring out which of the sentences the string corresponds to; doing so, however, does not transform (4) into a different string in terms of anaphoric possibilities. This sort of emphasis can have this effect because, as we argued in chapter 3, it can indicate a pronoun bearing a β-occurrence, hence pointing out a sloppy reading for the pronoun. Of course, such indication is not required, and will not be possible if the pronoun is elided.

tive to a single ellipsis, we can increase the number of ellipses relative to one pronoun:

(5) Max saw his mother, Oscar did, too, but Sam didn't

This string also displays an "across-the-board" effect for the elided pronouns: (5) can be understood to mean either that Max saw Max's mother, and Oscar saw Max's mother, but Sam didn't see Max's mother—the across-the-board strict reading—or that Max saw Max's mother, and Oscar saw Oscar's mother, but Sam didn't see Sam's mother—the across-the-board sloppy reading. Completely missing, however, are any mixed readings, where one ellipsis is understood strictly and the other sloppily; for instance, (5) cannot mean that Max saw Max's mother, and Oscar saw Oscar's mother, but Sam didn't see Max's mother. Such readings are possible where there is no ellipsis:

(6) Max saw his mother, Oscar saw his mother, but Sam didn't see his mother

However, this filtering effect is not quite so severe in strings very similar to (5):

(7) Max thinks he is strong, Oscar does, too, but his father doesn't

What is curious about this string is that it allows, in addition to the across-the-board readings, a reading under which the elided pronoun in the medial clause is interpreted as sloppy, whereas the one in the final clause is interpreted strictly relative to the medial elided pronoun. Thus, roughly, (7) can mean what (8) does:

(8) Max thinks that Max is strong, Oscar thinks that Oscar is strong, but Oscar's father doesn't think that Oscar is strong

The occurrence of this particular reading of the final clause of (7) is quite restricted, being possible only if the pronoun *his* is taken as referring to Oscar. If it refers to someone else, or is replaced by a name with a different reference, then the relevant intuition vanishes. Also not possible are readings where *his* is anaphoric to *Oscar* but the elided pronoun in the final clause is anaphoric to *Max*, or where *his* is anaphoric to *Max* and the pronoun to *Oscar*. That is, the readings described in (9) are not available:

(9) a. Max thinks that Max is strong, Oscar thinks that Oscar is strong, but Oscar's father doesn't think that Max is strong

   b. Max thinks that Max is strong, Oscar thinks that Oscar is strong, but Max's father doesn't think that Oscar is strong

In contrast, when all three clauses are lexically realized, all of the readings we have described, including (8) and especially those in (9), are available:

(10) Max thinks he is strong, Oscar thinks he is strong, too, but his father doesn't think that he is strong

We will refer to this last puzzle as the *Dahl puzzle*, after its discoverer (Ö. Dahl (1973), who adapts examples from Schiebe 1971). As a group, we will call these puzzles the *eliminative puzzles* of ellipsis.

The problems posed by the eliminative puzzles for an understanding of anaphora in elliptical contexts, both conceptually and empirically, should not be underestimated: *no current theory of ellipsis can account for them.* To see why, let us examine the assumptions underlying the influential analysis jointly due to Sag (1976) and Williams (1977). The basic premise of this approach is that ellipsis is licensed by a notion of identity of predication. The roots of the strict/sloppy distinction are to be traced back to the assumption that sentences with bound pronouns can be taken to express formally distinct predications, depending upon whether the pronoun is treated as an (indexed) pronoun or as the (indexed) variable the pronoun expresses—*Max saw his mother* can be taken as roughly expressing either the property of seeing Max's mother or the property of seeing one's own mother.[2] Formally, this is the difference between (11) and (12), which represent the strict and sloppy readings, respectively:

(11) $\text{Max}_i \, \lambda x(x \text{ saw his}_i \text{ mother})$, and $\text{Oscar}_j \, \lambda y(y \text{ saw his}_i \text{ mother})$

(12) $\text{Max}_i \, \lambda x(x \text{ saw } x\text{'s mother})$, and $\text{Oscar}_j \, \lambda y(y \text{ saw } y\text{'s mother})$

In both (11) and (12), what is predicated of *Max* is also predicated of *Oscar*, with the allowance that the λ-expressions expressing the elided

---

2. Although, as we discussed in chapter 2 in regard to comments by Evans (1977), there is nothing inherent in the repeated occurrence of variables that gives a reflexive meaning to the latter predicate. Rather, this must be an additional condition. Notice that the predication theory carries with it the idea that on the sloppy, as well as the strict, reading, the same predication (property) is attributed in each clause. We hold, on the contrary, that there are different predications; for example, in *Max saw his mother, and Oscar did, too,* what is predicated is "seeing Max's mother" and "seeing Oscar's mother," respectively, the truth of each sentence entailing that each man saw his own mother. It is unclear what turns on this difference, empirically, since the same truth conditions will be obtained regardless of what is assumed to be predicated. This is not to say, however, that there is nothing in common on the sloppy reading. The commonality is that both clauses will encode the same indexical dependency.

predicates can differ from their antecedents only in the *alphabetic* values of their variables.[3] Identity of predication thus warrants ellipsis just in case this formal aspect of the semantic structure of predication is respected.

This "predication theory" of ellipsis has the property that it independently permits each *occurrence* of a pronoun to be realized "strictly" in its syntactic guise, or "sloppily" in its semantic form as a variable. When a sentence contains just one pronoun, this will result in a simple strict/sloppy ambiguity in pronominal interpretation. With the addition of another pronoun, however, the possibilities grow. Thus, for the sentence *Max said he saw his mother* the following four representations should be possible:

(13) a. $\text{Max}_i \, \lambda x(x \text{ said he}_i \text{ saw his}_i \text{ mother})$

b. $\text{Max}_i \, \lambda x(x \text{ said } x \text{ saw } x\text{'s mother})$

c. $\text{Max}_i \, \lambda x(x \text{ said } x \text{ saw his}_i \text{ mother})$

d. $\text{Max}_i \, \lambda x(x \text{ said he}_i \text{ saw } x\text{'s mother})$

The first eliminative puzzle of ellipsis, the many-pronouns puzzle, now emerges. When (13) is placed in an ellipsis context—*Max said he saw his mother, and Oscar did, too*—a four-way ambiguity should arise, corresponding to an alphabetic variant of each of these predicates:

(14) a. $\text{Max}_i \, \lambda x(x \text{ said he}_i \text{ saw his}_i \text{ mother})$, and $\text{Oscar}_j \, \lambda y(y \text{ said he}_i$ saw his$_i$ mother)

b. $\text{Max}_i \, \lambda x(x \text{ said } x \text{ saw } x\text{'s mother})$, and $\text{Oscar}_j \, \lambda y(y \text{ said } y \text{ saw}$ y's mother)

c. $\text{Max}_i \, \lambda x(x \text{ said } x \text{ saw his}_i \text{ mother})$, and $\text{Oscar}_j \, \lambda y(y \text{ said } y \text{ saw}$ his$_i$ mother)

d. $\text{Max}_i \, \lambda x(x \text{ said he}_i \text{ saw } x\text{'s mother})$, and $\text{Oscar}_j \, \lambda y(y \text{ said he}_i$ saw y's mother)

Therefore, the predication theory can tell us neither why the available

---

3. Sag (1976:104) states the condition as follows:

For two λ-expressions, $\lambda x(A)$ and $\lambda y(B)$, to be alphabetic variants, every occurrence of x in A must have a corresponding occurrence of y in B, and vice versa. Also, any quantifier in A that binds variables (in A) must have a corresponding (identical) quantifier in B that binds variables in all the corresponding positions (in B). However, if there are any variables in A that are bound by some quantifier outside of $\lambda x(A)$, then the corresponding variable in $\lambda y(B)$ must be bound by the same operator in order for alphabetic variance to obtain.

As Sag observes, the last clause excludes as alphabetic variants λ-expressions in which variables are bound from outside the expression by different operators. We return to this aspect of the alphabetic variance condition in chapter 5.

mixed reading—the sloppy/strict reading given by (14c)—is marked relative to the across-the-board readings (14a) and (14b), nor, more seriously, why the other mixed reading—the strict/sloppy reading given by (14d)—is missing.[4]

Recall that the many-pronouns puzzle arises because a filtering effect comes into play when a sentence contains more than a single pronoun. Thus, for two pronouns, there are three possible readings, not four. Increasing to three pronouns—*Max said he thinks he saw his mother, and Oscar did, too*—increases the available readings by one, to four. In addition to the strict and sloppy across-the-board readings, either the final pronoun or the final two pronouns can be strict (... *and Oscar said Oscar thinks Oscar saw Max's mother*; ... *and Oscar said Oscar thinks Max saw Max's mother*), although, as above, these mixed construals are more marginal and marked. Abstractly, we can characterize the filtering function imposed by adding pronouns as follows. Suppose that we let α stand for a strictly read pronoun, and β for one read sloppily. If there is one pronoun, then we have the following matrix:

α

β

This matrix is unfiltered—ellipsis does not eliminate any readings when there is just one pronoun. For two pronouns, where a reading is filtered, we have:

$\alpha \quad \alpha$

$\beta \quad \alpha$

$\beta \quad \beta$

This matrix can be expanded into its successor matrix by the following rules:

(15) a. If a row begins with a β, form a new row by adding a β to its left.

b. If a row ends with an α, form a new row by adding an α to its right.

---

4. Sag (1976) suggests that (14d) could be ruled out in the same way as *Who did he think left*, as strong crossover. Presumably, this is because the most deeply embedded variable is not free in the antecedent, being bound by the pronoun *he*. But then (14b) would also be ruled out, since the variable is also bound, comparably to an improper movement violation (May 1979). Sag offers no suggestions about the status of (14c).

Thus, the following matrix characterizes the readings available when there are three pronouns:

$$\alpha \quad \alpha \quad \alpha$$
$$\beta \quad \alpha \quad \alpha$$
$$\beta \quad \beta \quad \alpha$$
$$\beta \quad \beta \quad \beta$$

From this, the rules in (15) can generate the following matrix for the four-pronoun case:

$$\alpha \quad \alpha \quad \alpha \quad \alpha$$
$$\beta \quad \alpha \quad \alpha \quad \alpha$$
$$\beta \quad \beta \quad \alpha \quad \alpha$$
$$\beta \quad \beta \quad \beta \quad \alpha$$
$$\beta \quad \beta \quad \beta \quad \beta$$

The problem faced by the predication theory is that although the derivable representations grow exponentially, the number of actual readings expands only linearly: for n-many pronouns, 2^n readings are predicted, but $n + 1$ readings are observed. For example, for three pronouns, eight readings are predicted, but only four are observed; for four pronouns, sixteen are predicted, but five are observed; and so on. In a sense, the root of the problem for the predication theory is that there is no "crosstalk" in the realization of each pronoun—each may independently be realized as a variable or not, with the resulting combinatoric possibilities.

Although predication-based theories fare poorly in solving the many-pronouns puzzle, they apparently do much better on the many-clauses puzzle. This is because they take the difference between strict and sloppy readings of anaphora in ellipsis to be an ambiguity, turning on the mode of representation of the pronoun(s). Every replication of a predicate must preserve the initial representation of the pronoun: $\lambda x(\ldots x \ldots he_i \ldots)$ is not an alphabetic variant of $\lambda x(\ldots x \ldots x \ldots)$; instead, they are formally distinct predications. Thus, although the representations in (16) are possible for *Max saw his mother, Oscar did, too, but Sam didn't*, no mixing is allowed:

(16) a. $Max_i \; \lambda x(x$ saw his_i mother), $Oscar_j \; \lambda y(y$ saw his_i mother), but $Sam_k \; \lambda z(z$ didn't see his_i mother)

   b. $Max_i \; \lambda x(x$ saw x's mother), $Oscar_j, \; \lambda y(y$ saw y's mother), but $Sam_k \; \lambda z(z$ didn't see z's mother)

The ambiguity aspect of the predication theory, although useful in accounting for the many-clauses puzzle, becomes detrimental when turned on the Dahl puzzle. If the pronoun is left as a pronoun, then all variants of it must give strict readings; if it is a variable, then all must give sloppy readings. This is just as much true for the Dahl puzzle as for those we have just discussed. In this theory, there is no way to change to a strict construal once the pronoun in the antecedent is taken as a variable, as would have to be the case to account for the Dahl examples. Consequently, all that is available for these examples are the across-the-board strict and sloppy readings—that is, exactly the types of readings that are made available for the many-clauses sentences.[5]

There are other predication-based theories that do at least permit a description of the reading available in the Dahl puzzle. Dalrymple, Shieber, and Pereira (1991) present an analysis under which once a reconstructed property is established for one elided clause, λ-conversion is possible, followed by further λ-abstraction. Thus, for the analysis of the Dahl puzzle, the following property would give the sloppy reading of the medial clause of *Max thinks he is strong, Oscar does, too, but his father doesn't*:

(17) Oscar, $\lambda x(x$ thinks that x is strong)

λ-conversion results in (18), which can then be abstracted to give the strict property for the third clause as in (19), where *his* has been replaced by its antecedent NP *Oscar*:

(18) Oscar thinks that Oscar is strong

(19) Oscar's father, $\lambda x(x$ doesn't think that Oscar is strong)

The failing of this treatment is that although the available reading of the Dahl sentence can be derived, representations of the nonavailable readings given in (9), and repeated here, can be derived as well:

(9) a. Max thinks that Max is strong, Oscar thinks that Oscar is strong, but Oscar's father doesn't think that Max is strong

   b. Max thinks that Max is strong, Oscar thinks that Oscar is strong, but Max's father doesn't think that Oscar is strong

---

5. As with the many-pronouns puzzle, these problems were not unknown to Sag (1976) (although apparently they were to Williams (1977), who does not cite Dahl 1973). Faced with the problem, Sag seeks to cast doubt on the data, but our intuitions, as well as those of all other commentators on this topic, are in accord with Dahl's.

(9a) would be derived by converting the property expressed by the first clause of (7), rather than the second, then reabstracting and applying the resulting abstract to the subject of the third clause, with the pronoun taken, as in (19), as anaphoric to *Oscar*:

(20) a. Max, $\lambda x(x$ thinks that x is strong)

    b. Max thinks that Max is strong

    c. Oscar's father, $\lambda x(x$ doesn't think that Max is strong)

To derive (9b), the converted property would again be that of the second clause, with the derivation proceeding as in (17) through (19), except that instead of the pronoun being anaphoric to *Oscar*, it is anaphoric to *Max*. The result is (21):

(21) Max's father, $\lambda x(x$ doesn't think that Oscar is strong)

Notice further that the mechanism employed by Dalrymple, Shieber, and Pereira to describe the Dahl sentence also undermines the account of the many-clauses puzzle otherwise afforded by predication theories. Thus, although the available across-the-board readings are derivable, so are the unavailable mixed readings of *Max thinks he is strong, Oscar does, too, but Sam doesn't*. For instance, we can form up the property $\lambda x(x$ *thinks Oscar is strong*) as we did in (17) through (19), and then apply it to the NP *Sam*. But this simply is not a reading of this sentence. Apparently, then, although under this version of the predication theory we may avoid some of the vices of Sag's and Williams's version—but not all, since for essentially the same reasons, Dalrymple, Shieber, and Pereira are also unable to account for the many-pronouns puzzle—we also lose its virtues.

The predication theories of Sag and Williams, with their attendant problems regarding the eliminative puzzles, are what we might call *ambiguity theories* of ellipsis. This is because the strict/sloppy distinction is to be traced back to an ambiguity in the representation of the antecedent clause of the ellipsis. Such theories are to be contrasted with another type of theory, which we will refer to as *condition theories* of ellipsis. An example is the account proposed by Klein (1987), which is framed in discourse representation theory. The idea here is that ellipsis turns not on identity of predication, but on identity of *conditioned* predications. Suppose that *Max saw his mother* has the predicate in (22), with a free position:

(22) $\lambda x(x$ saw y's mother)

This predicate could then be closed relative to one of two conditions: (i) $y = x$ or (ii) $y =$ Max. An elided predicate would then be identified with

(22), relative to either (i) or (ii). If (i), the sloppy reading ensues; if (ii), the strict. This theory differs from the previous ones in that no ambiguity is involved; all that is available as an antecedent for the ellipsis is a single predication as in (22).

Now, what of the puzzles? For the many-pronouns case, the predicate in (23) would be available for the analysis of *Max said he saw his mother, and Oscar did, too*:

(23) $\lambda x(x$ said y saw z's mother)

Although we could certainly have the conditions $y = x$ & $z = x$ (the across-the-board sloppy reading) and $y = $ Max & $z = $ Max (the across-the-board strict reading), we can also have the conditions $y = x$ & $z = $ Max and $y = $ Max & $z = x$ (the mixed readings). The availability of too many choices also undermines an account of the many-clauses puzzle.[6] For *Max saw his mother, Oscar did, too, but Sam didn't*, not only can we take both elisions relative to condition (i) or both relative to condition (ii)—the occurring across-the-board readings—we can also take one of them relative to condition (i) and the other relative to condition (ii). This derives the nonoccurring mixed readings. Finally, for the Dahl puzzle, recall that the first elision is taken as sloppy, and then the second is taken as strict relative to the first. On Klein's version of the predication theory, to obtain the initial sloppy reading for *Max thinks he is strong, Oscar does, too, but his father doesn't*, the first elided predicate must be taken as identical to the predicate expressed by the antecedent predicate relative to condition (i), that is, as functional. If we are then to identify the second elided predicate with the first, we must do so respecting this condition. But the reading that will result is not the one we are after, since condition (i) is the *sloppy* condition. A solution to the Dahl puzzle is therefore unattainable, since here again the relevant reading cannot be described.

6. One could cut down on the number of many-pronoun readings by requiring that both pronouns be tied to the same discourse referent, perhaps by taking them as occurrences of one pronominal expression, rather than as independent expressions. But then it would only be possible to derive the two-way ambiguity of the across-the-board readings. Additionally, it is not clear how in a discourse representation theory the pronouns could be required to be occurrences, and not independent elements anchored to the same discourse referent, and if they were required to be occurrences, what would constrain their distribution. That is, what would then be the binding theory, and would it have to make reference to syntactic structure independently of the discourse representation structure?

The problems we are observing are quite general and pervasive, and are to be found regardless of the particulars of the theory in which the account is couched. They are to be found in all sorts of frameworks, and not just under the initial assumptions of Sag and Williams.[7] A common inability to account for the many-pronouns puzzle and the Dahl puzzle (as opposed to the many-clauses puzzle) also afflicts approaches stated in terms of Extended Standard Theory (Reinhart 1983), Extended Montague Grammar (Partee and Bach 1984),[8] Discourse Representation Theory (Roberts 1987, Sells, Zaenen, and Zec 1986, Sells 1986), Combinatory Categorial Grammar (Szabolcsi 1990), and Situation Semantics (Gawron and Peters 1990a).[9] We have already seen the failings of theories stated in terms of

---

7. Sag and Williams place their accounts in somewhat different technical contexts. These differences in formulation are relatively trivial, however, compared to the more fundamental problems accruing to predication-based theories that lead us to reject them as a class. For some discussion of differences between Sag's and Williams's approaches, see Rooth 1981.

8. Partee and Bach (1984) analyze both strict and sloppy pronouns as variables, the former as free variables, the latter as bound. This engenders certain complications in the analysis of the strict reading; since one free variable, qua variable, is the same as the next, this would in itself allow a reading of *Max saw him, and Oscar did, too* where Max and Oscar saw different people. This leads Partee and Bach to propose that free pronouns express not free variables, but free variables relative to their assignments (technically, in their system, functions from assignments to intensions). This differs from Sag's and Williams's theory, in which what is copied on the strict reading is a *syntactic* pronoun, and not a variable that it purportedly semantically expresses.

9. Gawron and Peters's (1990a) analysis has the additional problem that although it can account for the sloppy reading of (i), it cannot account for the sloppy reading of (ii):

(i) Max washed his car, and Oscar did, too

(ii) Max's mother saw him, and Oscar's mother did, too

They observe that on the sloppy reading, (i) does not require that Max and Oscar washed the same car, as it does on the strict. Their account is based on the idea that if the object NP contains an occurrence of an abstracted variable, then the object NP itself must also be abstracted. This is achieved by what Gawron and Peters call the Absorption Principle; in essence, "Bind by an abstraction operator any variable that depends on another abstracted variable." This gives (iii); we have used a more familiar notation than Gawron and Peters and have also simplified their representations, but only with respect to matters that are irrelevant to the issues at hand:

(iii) $\lambda x \lambda y(x$ washed y, y a car x owns)(Max) $\wedge$ $\lambda x \lambda y(x$ washed y, y a car x owns) (Oscar)

Unification Grammar (Dalrymple, Shieber, and Pereira 1991) and another approach in the context of Discourse Representation Theory (Klein 1987).[10] Although these accounts may have various problems inherent to their particular assumptions—for instance, Reinhart (1983) predicts that the distribution of strict and sloppy readings will differ depending on whether a single speaker utters both the antecedent and the ellipsis or

---

Since x is abstracted, y must be also; hence, (iii) is true independently of whether Max and Oscar washed the same car. Thus, for Gawron and Peters, the sloppy reading involves a relation, not a predicate. (Note that Gawron and Peters are incorrect in describing (iii) as "... not a property of washers of their own cars, but a relation between car owners and the cars they wash" (p. 94), since (i) could then be true if Max and Oscar, car owners, washed cars they do not own.) In contrast, in the derivation for (ii), the Absorption Principle cannot apply, since y, which in this case would correspond to the overt and elided pronouns, does not contain any occurrence of x:

(iv) $\lambda x(x$'s mother saw $y)$(Max) $\wedge$ $\lambda x(x$'s mother saw $y)$(Oscar)

This would leave both occurrences of y free, subject to later existential closure. But then it follows that Max's mother and Oscar's mother saw the same person, a strict construal. Gawron and Peters (1990a:sec. 7.3.1) in fact note this; they point to the contrast between (v) and (vi), citing the lack of a sloppy reading for the latter:

(v) John's mother loves him, and Bill's mother does, too

(vi) John's mother loves him, and Bill's father does, too

The reason for this distinction, we believe, is that (vi) is not a case of same-saying, as required by the presence of *too*; see discussion in chapter 3, footnote 4. Note that when *too* can be omitted, a sloppy reading becomes available:

(vii) John's mother loves him, but I'm not sure that Bill's father does

Here there is no assumption of same-saying, so either sloppy or strict identity is possible. For discussion of the issues surrounding (i), see chapter 5.

10. The approach taken by Roberts (1987) differs from that of Klein (1987) in assuming that there is an ambiguity of predication. Following Reinhart (1983) (see footnote 11), Roberts assumes that an overt pronoun can be read anaphorically whether it is coindexed or not (bound anaphora versus pragmatic coreference). Since this approach incorporates an ambiguity assumption, unlike Klein's, it falters on the many-pronouns and Dahl puzzles, but not on the many clauses puzzle. (Gawron and Peters (1990a) point to other problems with Roberts's approach relative to cases discussed in section 4.3.) Sells, Zaenen, and Zec (1986) also propose an ambiguity theory, distinguishing two kinds of anaphoric relations between discourse referents: a bound relation, which identifies arguments and gives the sloppy reading, and a cospecificational link to an antecedent NP, which gives the strict reading. This approach falters in the same way as Roberts's, in that it cannot account for the many-pronouns and Dahl puzzles.

whether they are shared between interlocutors[11]—we should emphasize that failure to account for the eliminative puzzles of ellipsis is endemic to all predication-based approaches to ellipsis of which we are aware. In chapter 2, we expressed our conceptual reservations to appealing to predicate-abstraction, and the notion of predication it involves. We now add further empirical reservations.

It is a unifying mark of predication-based theories that they assume that identity of *semantic* structure must be brought into play to reveal the identity involved in sloppy (if not strict) identity. This is because to obtain a representation of the sloppy reading, the pronoun must be realized as a variable in order for there to be identity of predication. However, the considerations of this chapter make it appear unlikely that such a theory can properly state the nexus of dependencies found in anaphora in cases of ellipsis, and that any semantically unified theory of ellipsis will be forthcoming on these assumptions. Notice further that the semantic structure assumed under predication-based theories is one that expresses a *property*. But it can be seen that expressions that would be of other semantic types are also subject to verb phrase ellipsis. A case due to Baltin (1991) is revealing:

(24) *Speaker A*: It seems that Mary is smart

     Speaker B: It certainly does

---

11. This is pointed out by Lasnik (1989:fn.1). The idea behind Reinhart's theory is that the use of bound anaphora indicates that the speaker intends coreference, and the hearer will assume that this is so, but if there is no such intention, then the speaker will avoid bound anaphora, and the hearer will again assume likewise. In *Max saw his mother, and Oscar did, too* the speaker may employ bound anaphora, expressed by taking the pronoun as a variable under predicate-abstraction, giving the sloppy reading. The speaker may also avoid this option, if he intends to say that Oscar saw Max's, not his own, mother—that is, if he does not intend bound anaphora in the elided clause. Then the overt anaphora is an instance of pragmatic coreference, and the reading of the elision is strict. Lasnik then observes that there is a problem with the following discourse, since only a sloppy reading should be available:

(i) *Speaker A*: Max saw his mother
    Speaker B: Oscar did, too

In uttering his sentence, Speaker A intends coreference, and has no reason to avoid it. The interlocutor, Speaker B, will assume likewise, and hence, assuming bound anaphora, will employ it in the ellipsis. This will give the sloppy reading, but to the exclusion of the obviously available strict reading.

Here the elided material would be the type of a proposition, not a property. Further examples due to S. Lappin extend the point:

(25) a. John thinks there will be a performance tonight, but Mary thinks there won't

   b. Max said it would rain today, and Lucy said it would, too

What these examples have in common with those we have been discussing is that a verb phrase has been elided, independently of its semantic type. In striving for unification, therefore, we might look at alternatives that place the causes of the strict/sloppy distinction in the syntax. The natural place to look for such a syntactically unified theory would be relative to the constraints fixing possible anaphoric connections. We are aware of two such theories, one placed in the context of Binding Theory, the other in the context of Linking Theory. However, each of these theories suffers from one of the previously described problems in dealing with the eliminative puzzles.

Kitagawa (1991b) presents a theory within the context of Binding Theory. The central idea is that elided verb phrases are categorially and lexically empty at S-Structure (i.e., $[_{VP} e]$), but that a copy of an antecedent verb phrase fills such phrases at LF. Any nominal elements within the copied VP must satisfy the appropriate conditions of Binding Theory. On this way of looking at things, *Max saw his mother, and Oscar did, too* could be syntactically represented in the two ways shown in (26), since either way the pronoun is free in its governing category; the italics represent the VPs copied into the ellipses:

(26) a. Max_1 saw his_1 mother, and Oscar_2 *saw his_1 mother*

   b. Max_1 saw his_1 mother, and Oscar_2 *saw his_2 mother*

The structures in (26) correspond to the strict and sloppy readings, respectively. Although this account is initially attractive, if on no grounds other than simplicity of description, it too has problems with the eliminative puzzles of a now familiar sort.

Concerning the many-pronouns puzzle, Kitagawa's account shares with predication-based theories the problem that representations of both the across-the-board and mixed readings of *Max said he saw his mother, and Oscar did, too* are available. (27a) through (27d) are all compatible with Binding Theory:[12]

---

12. Notice that since pronouns are not realized as variables on this theory, appeal to crossover, following Sag (1976), would not be an option. See footnote 4.

(27) a. Max_1 said he_1 saw his_1 mother, and $Oscar_2$ *said he_1 saw his_1 mother*

b. Max_1 said he_1 saw his_1 mother, and $Oscar_2$ *said he_2 saw his_2 mother*

c. Max_1 said he_1 saw his_1 mother, and $Oscar_2$ *said he_2 saw his_1 mother*

d. Max_1 said he_1 saw his_1 mother, and $Oscar_2$ *said he_1 saw his_2 mother*

These failings extend to the many-clauses puzzle, since representations of the mixed readings are just as consistent with Binding Theory as representations of the across-the-board readings. Nothing distinguishes the representations in (28) for *Max saw his mother, Oscar did, too, but Sam didn't*:

(28) a. Max_1 saw his_1 mother, $Oscar_2$ *saw his_1 mother*, but Sam_3 didn't *see his_1 mother*

b. Max_1 saw his_1 mother, $Oscar_2$ *saw his_2 mother*, but Sam_3 didn't *see his_3 mother*

c. Max_1 saw his_1 mother, $Oscar_2$ *saw his_1 mother*, but Sam_3 didn't see *his_3 mother*

d. Max_1 saw his_1 mother, $Oscar_2$ *saw his_2 mother*, but Sam_3 didn't *see his_1 mother*

Indeed, even more representations are possible, for example, ones in which the pronoun in the final clause is coindexed with *Oscar*. But these also would not represent available readings. And although this approach can describe the extant reading in the Dahl puzzle, since it allows the representation in (29), this seems small solace, for the representations in (30) are also well formed:

(29) Max_1 thinks he_1 is strong, $Oscar_2$ *thinks he_2 is strong*, but his_2 father doesn't *think he_2 is strong*

(30) a. Max_1 thinks he_1 is strong, $Oscar_2$ *thinks he_2 is strong*, but his_2 father doesn't *think he_1 is strong*

b. Max_1 thinks he_1 is strong, $Oscar_2$ *thinks he_2 is strong*, but his_1 father doesn't *think he_2 is strong*

These latter structures, however, represent the readings described in (9).

For coverage of the data, therefore, we seem no better off with this syntactic alternative.[13]

There is one additional and important problem with Kitagawa's proposal. Although Binding Theory can account for the absence of a sloppy reading of *Max's mother saw him, and Oscar did, too*, since (31b) contravenes Principle B,

(31) a. Max_1's mother saw him_1, and $Oscar_2$ *saw him_1*

b.   *Max_1's mother saw him_1, and $Oscar_2$ *saw him_2*

it predicts that sloppy construals will only be absent in contexts where binding is not possible. This leads to the expectation that *Max's mother saw him, and Oscar said Mary did, too* should be ambiguous. This is because (32) is consistent with Binding Theory, since the pronoun is free in its governing category:

(32) Max_1's mother saw him_1, and $Oscar_2$ said Mary *saw him_2*

13. Thus, the empirical failings of Kitagawa's theory are comparable to those afflicting the proposal of Dalrymple, Shieber, and Pereira (1991). Notice that the approach as described must be augmented by some further principle(s), since if the only constraints are those placed by Binding Theory, then (i) can be derived alongside (26):

(i) Max_1 saw his_1 mother, and $Oscar_2$ *saw his_3 mother*

This would presumably mean that whereas Max saw Max's mother, Oscar saw some third party's mother. But this patently is not a possible construal of *Max saw his mother, and Oscar did, too*. Because of such problems, Kitagawa maintains that there is a rule of coindexing that can apply either prior to copying of the VP, to give the strict reading, or after copying, to give the sloppy reading. (i) would then be excluded because a coindexing is not copied. In a sense, then, Kitagawa must assume that there is a pronominalization rule in the grammar. Kitagawa himself points out that such a rule would have to be extrinsically ordered with the rule of "VP-copy." The problem arises from examples such as (ii) (= Kitagawa's (50)):

(ii) The friends of $John_1$ told him_2 to leave, but the friends of $Bill_2$ didn't

Although this sentence can have a sloppy reading, so that Bill's friends didn't tell Bill to leave, it cannot have a reading to the effect that Bill's friends didn't tell John to leave. That is, the indexing in (iii) is excluded:

(iii) The friends of $John_1$ told him_2 to leave, but the friends of $Bill_2$ *didn't tell him_1 to leave*

This should be allowed, since coindexing of *John* and the reconstructed occurrence of *him* is possible relative to Binding Theory. Kitagawa suggests that for this case the rule of coindexing must be extrinsically ordered prior to VP-copy, whereas for other cases it can be freely ordered. Why this should be so is not explained.

The fact is that here, only a strict reading is possible. Thus, some sort of "parallelism" constraint must be built into this theory, above and beyond Binding Theory. We turn to the nature of this constraint in the next section.[14]

Ristad (1990) presents an account in the context of Linking Theory (Higginbotham 1983, 1985). Ristad assumes that the theory of anaphora allows for the relation of two sorts of elements: arguments and the argument, or thematic, positions they occupy. There are two sorts of relations, *link* and *obviate*, which can hold between pairs of arguments or pairs of positions. The anaphoric construal of *Max saw his mother* can then be established relative to linking either the arguments *Max* and *his* or their thematic positions. We can (roughly) represent this by associating (33a) with the linking conditions in (33b) and (33c), where θ^2 and θ^3 are the thematic positions of V and N—occupied by *his mother* and *his*, respectively—and θ^1 is the thematic position of VP, occupied by *Max*:

(33) a. Max_1 [saw, θ^2[his_2 mother, θ^3], θ^1]

   b. **link** (2, 1)

   c. **link** (θ^3, θ^1)

The analysis of ellipsis proceeds from the assumption that the elided verb phrase shares the thematic structure of its antecedent. Thus, in *Max saw his mother, and Oscar did, too* the elided VP will be associated with the actor role (and perhaps others) of the overt VP, but not with the arguments or thematic positions of its constituents. No "copying" is involved. We thus have the following representation:

---

14. An inability to account for parallelism effects (as well as the eliminative puzzles) is also found in the predication-based proposal of Hardt (1991), which shares with Kitagawa's approach the idea that pronouns in each clause are independently evaluated. Hardt's account differs from Kitagawa's in that he assumes that pronominal reference is a function of contextual salience; a pronoun's referent will be some individual "evoked (either directly or indirectly) in the current or most recent utterance" (sec. 4). On this basis, Hardt rules out a reading of *Max saw his mother, and Oscar did, too* in which Oscar saw some third party's mother, since the elided pronoun's referent would not be appropriately salient. But observe that the same sort of referential failure is found in the conversation in (i) (supposing that the overt pronoun refers to Max):

(i) *Speaker A*: I saw Sam
    Speaker B: Max saw his mother, and Oscar did, too

The elided pronoun still cannot refer to Sam here, even though this individual has been evoked, and hence raised to salience, in the most recent utterance.

(34) Max_1 [saw, θ^2[his_2 mother, θ^3],θ^1], and Oscar did,θ^1

(34) continues to respect the linking conditions in (33). If it is taken with respect to (33b), then the strict reading ensues—the linking of *his* to *Max* now holds constantly over the entire conjunction. If it is taken with respect to (33c), then the sloppy reading results. This is because there are now two occurrences of θ^1, and by (33c), each is linked with θ^3, the thematic position of the overt pronoun. Thus, whoever satisfies the actor role in each case will also satisfy the possessor role.

It should be clear that Ristad's theory is a type of condition theory, with all the attendant empirical problems. For the many-pronouns puzzle, it too predicts a four-way ambiguity, corresponding to the linkings in (35) (we suppress the roles assigned by the verbs):[15]

(35) a. Max_1 [said he_2 [saw [his_3 mother, θ^3], θ^2], θ^1], and $Oscar_4$ did, θ^1

    b. **link** (2, 1) & **link** (3, 1)

    c. **link** (θ^2, θ^1) & **link** (θ^3, θ^1)

    d. **link** (θ^2, θ^1) & **link** (3, 1)

    e. **link** (2, 1) & **link** (θ^3, θ^1)

In the case of the many-clauses puzzle, we have the two linking conditions indicated in (33), but again not only can we take both elisions in *Max saw his mother, Oscar did, too, but Sam didn't* relative to one or the other condition, we can also take one elision relative to one condition and the other elision relative to the other. We thus derive both the across-the-board and mixed readings. And finally, the Dahl puzzle cannot be described. Suppose we take the medial clause in *Max thinks he's strong, Oscar does, too, but his father doesn't* as sloppy. The options for the final clause remain the same; it can be taken relative to argument linking (strict) or thematic linking (sloppy). But neither of these is the desired Dahl-type reading. The problem is that on Ristad's theory both elisions must be understood relative to the linking conditions established for the overt clause; there is no copying. But if there is no copying, then there can be no linking within the elided material, and hence there can be no anaphoric connections between elided pronouns. In particular, an elided pronoun

15. Ristad (1990) follows Sag (1976) in appealing to crossover to account for the absence of the linkage in (35e); see footnote 4.

cannot be understood strictly relative to another sloppy elided pronoun, as in the Dahl-type reading.[16]

To summarize, we have dwelled on the eliminative puzzles of ellipsis in order to show how pervasive the failings of current theories of ellipsis are. The overall problem is that the underlying question of anaphora in ellipsis has been improperly stated. It is not "Why does ellipsis preserve interpretation?" but "Why does it filter possible interpretations?" In other words, the issue to be faced is why ellipsis is eliminative. In what follows we will examine the results of this reorientation.

4.2 The Many-Pronouns Puzzle

Verb phrase ellipsis is possible only if the elided verb phrase is a *reconstruction* of some other verb phrase.[17] As we defined this notion, such verb

16. In the context of Linking Theory, Higginbotham (1992) intimates a theory of ellipsis. For a sentence such as (i), he distinguishes between an "invariant" reading and a "covariant" one:

(i) It was John who expects he will win

The invariant reading is to be represented by a link from the pronoun to the NP *John*; the covariant reading is to be represented by a link to the variable bound by the *wh*-phrase. In ellipsis, the idea would run, strict and sloppy construals will correspond to invariant and covariant links. There appear to be a number of problems with this suggestion. First, this approach will take on the problems associated with the eliminative puzzles. In the many-pronouns puzzle, it would be possible to invariantly link one pronoun and covariantly link another. Since this is an ambiguity theory, it will be able to account for the many-clauses puzzle, but not for the Dahl puzzle, for reasons parallel to those discussed in the text for other ambiguity theories. Second, there are also unresolved issues specific to Higginbotham's approach. For instance, it is clearly possible to obtain both strict and sloppy readings without overt movement, as in *John expects he will win, and Bill does, too,* so if covariance is to be represented by linking to a variable, movement of all NPs, and not only *wh*, must be allowed. Moreover, if linking is to represent the covariant (sloppy) reading, then there must be some identity condition on links, given the parallelism effects. But it is unclear how this is to be formulated (at least in some way distinct from the formulation we have given for indexical dependencies), so that it applies only to covariant links, and not invariant ones. This will be a nontrivial task, given that both sorts of links are formally arrows. Invariant links in ellipsis might be distinguished in that they link an elided pronoun across sentences in discourse to its antecedent. But that raises issues concerning the domains of links, and the relation of Linking Theory to Binding Theory.

17. Reconstruction is necessary, but not sufficient, for ellipsis. One apparent further condition is that the elided VP must be properly governed by verbal

phrases will be reconstructions if and only if they are occurrences of some one sub–phrase marker over a given terminal vocabulary; hence, only if elided structure is an occurrence in this sense can it count as syntactically projected.[18] Hence, in the representation of *Max saw Sally, and Oscar did, too* there are two occurrences of [$_{VP}$ *saw Sally*], one audible, the other not; elliptical contexts are categorially fully specified, lacking only phonetic expression of the lexical content of the categories. (Thus, in saying that an elided verb phrase is a reconstruction, we do not mean to be taken as presuming that there is some literal derivational operation that builds categorial and lexical structure into an empty verb phrase, that is, [$_{VP}$ *e*].) In what follows we will speak of the unelided verb phrase as the "anteced-ent" of the ellipsis as a means of identifying the verb phrase of which we are considering occurrences, using this term only to distinguish between those occurrences of the verb phrase that are elided and those that are not. We will conventionally represent ellipsis by boldface, now understood simply as inaudibilia—that is, as material that is syntactically, but not phonetically, represented.

The identity required for structures to qualify as reconstructions goes down to the fine structure of whatever indices may occur; this follows from the fact that indices, inclusive of indexical type and indexical value, are formal parts of phrase markers. The operant generalization linking recon-

---

inflection, as discussed by Lobeck (1986, 1987, 1992) and Zagona (1988). Whereas in English this is satisfied because the auxiliary elements count as verbal, in other languages inflection only becomes verbal through raising of the verb to the inflec-tion. Typologically, this gives rise to a second sort of verb phrase ellipsis in which the raised verb is "stranded," since it is moved out of the VP. This sort of ellipsis has been pointed out by Doron (1990) for Hebrew, McCloskey (1991) for Irish, and Otani and Whitman (1991) for Chinese, Japanese, and Korean. In English this type of verb phrase ellipsis is found in *John is happy, and Bill is, too*, where *have/be* raising takes place. Further typological differences are to be found depending upon the position of the subject. Hebrew and the East Asian languages are like English in that the subject is (ultimately) outside the complement to the verbal inflection, whereas in Irish it remains inside, so that the subject is part of the elided material. However, insofar as the government condition is satisfied, the nature of recon-struction does not vary from language to language, as we would expect of a condition on syntactic identity.

18. We will need to make more precise what is meant by "given terminal vocabu-lary," since ellipsis is well known to be insensitive, for instance, to the values of agreement features: *I think I'm smart, and you do, too*. We leave this matter aside for the time being, returning to it, in the context of what we call "vehicle change," in chapter 5.

struction and the possibilities of indexical realization is informally as follows: If an occurrence of an index is independent, an α-occurrence, "copy" the occurrence itself; if the occurrence is dependent, a β-occurrence, "copy" the dependency. We thus have the following ambiguity of representation for the string *Max saw his mother, and Oscar did, too*, where the pronoun is anaphoric, representing the strict and sloppy readings, respectively:

(36) a. Max_1 [$_{VP}$ saw his_1^α mother], and Oscar_2 [$_{VP}$ **saw his_1^α mother**]

b. Max_1 [$_{VP}$ saw his_1^β mother], and Oscar_2 [$_{VP}$ **saw his_2^β mother**]

α-occurrences of indices are the same if and only if they are occurrences of a given index. Thus, for (36a), the identity conditions are no different than in cases where there are no pronominal elements; reconstruction requires a repeated occurrence of the antecedent verb phrase up to and including indexical value. Notice that this holds for α-occurrences regardless of whether there are other occurrences of that index or not. Thus, if we take the pronoun in the string above nonanaphorically, it will also only have a strict interpretation, as represented by (37):

(37) Max_1 [$_{VP}$ saw his_3^α mother], and Oscar_2 [$_{VP}$ **saw his_3^α mother**]

For β-occurrences, on the other hand, there is a criterion deriving from Dependency Theory by which they are nondistinct even if they have different indexical values—namely, just in case they occur in indexical dependencies that are *i*-copies. This allows verb phrases containing β-occurrences to be reconstructions if those verb phrases differ in only the indexical values of the β-occurrences. Therefore, the VPs in (36b) are reconstructions in virtue of the indexical dependencies in (38):

(38) a. $\langle ([_{NP} \text{Max}]^\alpha, [_{NP} \text{his}]^\beta), 1, \langle NP, V, NP \rangle \rangle$

b. $\langle ([_{NP} \text{Oscar}]^\alpha, [_{NP} \text{his}]^\beta), 2, \langle NP, V, NP \rangle \rangle$

In the terms of Dependency Theory as developed in chapter 2, these indexical dependencies are *realized* in the conjoined phrase markers of (36b). This is because there are parts of proper analyses of each conjunct that satisfy the structural descriptions of the dependencies, such that the elements of the dependencies are terms, and there are no smaller parts of which these elements are terms. Hence, in these structures the β-occurrences are *resolved*. Moreover, these indexical dependencies are *i*-copies, since they differ only in their indices; the elements and the structural descriptions are identical. Hence, the indices borne by the pronouns in each clause count as nondistinct. Since they do not count as different, neither do the VPs that contain them; as a result, these in turn count as reconstructions. Given the constraints imposed by the intersection of the conditions on indexical identity of Dependency Theory with those on structural identity of reconstruction, the assignments of indexical values, given indexical types, in (36) and (37) are the only ones possible.

Now let us apply these notions to the many-pronouns puzzle as found in (3), repeated here:

(3) Max said he saw his mother, and Oscar did, too

Recall that the dominant readings of this sentence, assuming that the overt pronouns are understood as anaphoric to *Max*, are those on which the elided pronouns are either both understood as strict or both understood as sloppy. Now, we have attributed the strict/sloppy distinction to properties of indexical types, that is, to whether an index is taken as dependent or independent. These "across-the-board" readings arise just in case a dependency holds of an index in toto; either all of its occurrences are in the dependency or none of them are. That is, either both the pronouns are α-occurrences, or both are β-occurrences:

(39) Max_1 said he_1^{α} saw his_1^{α} mother, and Oscar_2 **said he_1^{α} saw his_1^{α} mother**

(40) a. Max_1 said he_1^{β} saw his_1^{β} mother, and Oscar_2 **said he_2^{β} saw his_2^{β} mother**

b. $\langle(\text{Max, he, his}), 1, \langle\text{NP, V, NP, V, NP}\rangle\rangle$

c. $\langle(\text{Oscar, he, his}), 2, \langle\text{NP, V, NP, V, NP}\rangle\rangle$

(39) represents the across-the-board strict reading of (3), and (40) represents the sloppy reading, licensed by the dependencies in (40b) and (40c), which are *i*-copies.

As discussed in section 4.1, another reading is also available for (3), a "mixed" reading under which the first elided pronoun is understood as sloppy, the second as strict. This reading is represented by (41), in which a β-occurrence precedes an α-occurrence:

(41) a. Max_1 said he_1^{β} saw his_1^{α} mother, and Oscar_2 **said he_2^{β} saw his_1^{α} mother**

b. $\langle(\text{Max, he}), 1, \langle\text{NP, V, NP}\rangle\rangle$

c. $\langle(\text{Oscar, he}), 2, \langle\text{NP, V, NP}\rangle\rangle$

These indexical dependencies are *i*-copies, licensing a sloppy reading of the first of the two elided pronouns. The other elided pronoun bears an α-occurrence and hence can only have a strict construal. Therefore, this structure represents the available mixed reading. Note that nothing in Dependency Theory requires that all occurrences of an index be in a dependency. Indexical dependencies may relate any number of the occurrences of an index so long as the dependency is properly realized and all β-occurrences are resolved. These two conditions are satisfied by the structure and dependencies in (41).

Now recall that there is an unavailable reading for (3) that is also mixed, but in which the first elided pronoun is construed as strict, the second as sloppy. To represent this reading, the structure in (42), in which the order of the indexical types borne by the pronouns is the opposite of that in (41), would have to be well formed:

(42) *Max_1 said he_1^α saw his_1^β mother, and $Oscar_2$ **said he_1^α saw his_2^β mother**

In order for this to be so, the left-hand clause must encode a dependency that is an i-copy of (43):

(43) $\langle (\text{Oscar, his}), 2, \langle NP, V, NP, V, NP \rangle \rangle$

There are three possibilities to consider:

(44) a. $\langle (\text{he, his}), 1, \langle NP, V, NP \rangle \rangle$ – not an i-copy

b. $\langle (\text{Max, his}), 1, \langle NP, V, NP, V, NP \rangle \rangle$ – not realized

c. $\langle (\text{Max, he, his}), 1, \langle NP, V, NP, V, NP \rangle \rangle$ – not an indexical dependency

As we have indicated, none of these will do the job. (44a) is a realized dependency in the first clause, but it is not an i-copy of (43), since it has a different structural description. (44b) has the same structural description, but it is not realized in the first clause, since among the terms of the proper analysis that satisfies the structural description is one that bears an occurrence of "1" but is not among the elements, namely, the pronoun *he*. Inclusion of this element gives (44c), but this is not a well-formed dependency at all, since it contains two elements, *Max* and *he*, that bear α-occurrences. Thus, there is no way that the two clauses in (42) can encode the dependencies that are i-copies. Consequently, the other mixed reading is excluded.[19]

---

19. There is a way to derive a well-formed structure with the distribution of indexical types as in (42) by taking the pronoun bearing the α-occurrence as the antecedent of the dependency. This gives the representation in (i):

(i) Max_1 said he_1^α saw his_1^β mother, and $Oscar_2$ **said he_1^α saw his_1^β mother**

We observed in section 4.1 that the available mixed reading for a many-pronouns sentence such as (3), where the first pronoun is understood as sloppy and the second as strict, is usually perceived as marginal and somewhat marked relative to the robust across-the-board readings, and sharply contrasts with the strict - sloppy order, which is completely precluded for all speakers. Given that we can now appropriately represent this third reading (and can exclude the fourth), how can we characterize its markedness? Our idea is to formulate a markedness metric in terms of partiality of dependency. Intuitively, the "normal" circumstance is one where a realized dependency is defined relative to all the elements that bear occurrences of the index in the structure. Insofar as a dependency excludes some number of occurrences of the index in the structure in which it is realized, that structure will be marked to some degree. We can formulate this idea as follows:

(45) *Markedness Theory*
Let C be the set of expressions bearing I in a phrase marker P, and let ID be an indexical dependency realized in P with respect to some set of elements c and index I. Then, P is *degree n marked* with respect to ID if and only if $|C| - |c| = n$.

(45) says that a structure is marked to the degree that occurrences of the relevant index are left out of a dependency. Structures are unmarked if they are degree 0 marked or not associated with any dependency at all, that is, if all occurrences are α-occurrences. The accessibility of a reading is inversely related to the degree of markedness: the more marked the structure, the less accessible the relevant reading. By this metric, (39) and (40), the representations of the across-the-board readings, come out as degree 0 marked and are fully accessible. Less accessible is the mixed

---

Because the elided occurrence of *he* bears an α-occurrence, it must bear the same index as the unelided occurrence, as must any elements that are dependent upon it. Thus, in both clauses of (i) the dependency in (ii) ($=$(44a)) will be realized:

(ii) $\langle(\text{he, his}), 1, \langle\text{NP, V, NP}\rangle\rangle$

What this example shows, then, is that if mixed types of occurrences are ordered α, then β, the reading obtained is across-the-board strict. Hence, mixing of occurrence types does not necessarily lead to mixing of values, between strict and sloppy, for the pronouns. This is not to say, however, that (i) and (39) do not differ in meaning, only that insofar as they do this will depend on the difference in indexical type, not on any difference in indexical value. For discussion of differences in meaning that turn on indexical type, see chapter 2. Note also that (i) is a marked structure relative to (39); see discussion below.

reading; its representation in (41) is degree 1 marked, since a realized dependency excludes one element bearing an occurrence of the index. Notice that this markedness accrues to the fully overt first clause of (41); no markedness accrues to the clause containing the ellipsis, since both occurrences of the index "2" are in the dependency. Although the markedness of that clause would be undetectable if it stood in isolation, since the anaphoric relations it represents are the same as in the unmarked structures that stand as the first clauses of (39) and (40), it is unmasked in elliptical contexts, since the interpretations of the elided clauses differ when taken in the context of marked and unmarked structures.

Summarizing to this point, we have shown that the many-pronouns sentence (3) may be associated with the following representations:

(39) Max_1 said he_1^α saw his_1^α mother, and Oscar_2 **said he_1^α saw his_1^α mother**

(40) Max_1 said he_1^β saw his_1^β mother, and Oscar_2 **said he_2^β saw his_2^β mother**

(41) Max_1 said he_1^β saw his_1^α mother, and Oscar_2 **said he_2^β saw his_1^α mother**

(42)   *Max_1 said he_1^α saw his_1^β mother, and Oscar_2 **said he_1^α saw his_2^β mother**

In terms of strict and sloppy identity, these structures represent three readings: across-the-board strict (39), across-the-board sloppy (40), and mixed sloppy/strict (41). (42), which is ill formed, is not a possible structure for (3). Thus, in allowing for more fine-grained discriminations in the calculation of anaphoric possibilities in ellipsis, Dependency Theory leads to a prediction different from that of predication-based theories, which predict a four-way ambiguity here.

In section 4.1 we observed that as pronouns are added in many-pronouns sentences, the number of readings with respect to the strict/sloppy distinction grows linearly, at a rate of $n + 1$. For a sentence such as *Max said he thinks he saw his mother, and Oscar did, too*, with three pronouns, the four available readings are the across-the-board strict reading represented by (46a), the across-the-board sloppy reading given by (46b), and two mixed readings. One, where just the final pronoun is read as strict, is represented by (46c); the other, where the final two pronouns are read as strict, is represented by (46d):

(46) Max_1 said he_1 thinks he_1 saw his_1 mother,
    a. ... and Oscar_2 **said he_1^α thinks he_1^α saw his_1^α mother**
    b. ... and Oscar_2 **said he_2^β thinks he_2^β saw his_2^β mother**
    c. ... and Oscar_2 **said he_2^β thinks he_2^β saw his_1^α mother**
    d. ... and Oscar_2 **said he_2^β thinks he_1^α saw his_1^α mother**

These readings differ by the markedness metric just formulated: the clauses that (46a) and (46b) reconstruct are unmarked, the one reconstructed by (46c) is degree 1 marked, and the one reconstructed by (46d) is degree 2 marked. These markedness values correspond to the accessibility of each of these readings.

In terms of the distribution of α- and β-occurrences, four more representations are in fact possible. None of these, however, is well formed:

(47) Max_1 said he_1 thinks he_1 saw his_1 mother,

　　a. *... and $Oscar_2$ said he_1^α thinks he_1^α saw his_2^β mother

　　b. *... and $Oscar_2$ said he_1^α thinks he_2^β saw his_1^α mother

　　c. *... and $Oscar_2$ said he_1^α thinks he_2^β saw his_2^β mother

　　d. *... and $Oscar_2$ said he_2^β thinks he_1^α saw his_2^β mother

The structures in (47) are ill formed for the same reason as (42). So, for example, for (47a) to be well formed, a dependency would have to be realized in the left-hand clause that is an *i*-copy of (48):

(48) $\langle$(Oscar, his), 2, $\langle$NP, V, NP, V, NP, V, NP$\rangle\rangle$

But any dependency in the left-hand clause that matched the structural description of (48) would not be realized, since it would not contain the occurrences of *he*. If these elements were added, then the result would not be an indexical dependency, since they bear α-occurrences, of which there would be too many. Similar remarks carry over to the other representations in (47).[20] Thus, in terms of strict and sloppy identity, only one

---

20. As discussed in footnote 19, there are assignments of indexical values that render structures with the assignment of indexical types in (47) well formed. However, the readings that result will duplicate readings (with respect to strict and sloppy) that are otherwise available. For example, (i), comparable to (47a), represents an across-the-board strict reading:

(i) ... and $Oscar_2$ said he_1^α thinks he_1^α saw his_1^β mother

Here the β-occurrence is taken to be dependent on the most local α-occurrence; but since this occurrence is strict, its dependent will be, too. Structures with the patterns of indexical types shown in (47b) and (47c) will also yield across-the-board strict readings, whereas the pattern in (47d) will give a reading in which the final two pronouns are strict. We leave it to the reader to work this out. Note further that, as a technical matter, nothing in Dependency Theory as formulated requires that the α-occurrence antecedent in a dependency must be the leftmost element; conceivably, it could be elsewhere. This allows for a structure in which indexical types are distributed as in (46c), for instance, to encode two dependencies —the first β-occurrence dependent upon the NP *Oscar*, and the second β-

additional reading results when the sentence contains three pronouns rather than two. Adding a fourth pronoun, as in *Max is certain he said he thinks he saw his mother, and Oscar did, too*, will give yet another reading. As the reader can verify, following our line of reasoning there will be only five possible readings for this sentence: the two across-the-board readings, and the three readings in which the final, the two final, and the three final pronouns are construed as strict. The last three readings, however, will be at increasing levels of markedness, with increasingly reduced levels of accessibility.

The distribution of readings that we have observed with many-pronouns sentences can be disturbed, since it is sensitive to a number of structural parameters that limit the available interpretations. For instance, embedding the head of a dependency restricts the possible readings:

(49) a. Max said he saw his mother, and Oscar's sister did, too

b. Max's sister said he saw his mother, and Oscar did, too

Both of these cases are unambiguously limited to across-the-board strict readings for the elided pronouns. The reason for this is that *he* in the antecedent clause, if a β-occurrence, must be in a dependency that is headed by *Max*. But this dependency could not be an *i*-copy of the dependency containing the reconstructed pronoun, since they would not be structurally parallel. This will rule out the across-the-board sloppy reading and the mixed reading otherwise available for a sentence such as (3). Also ruled out, taking (49a) as our exemplar, is the representation in (50); here no dependency is realizable in the first clause that is an *i*-copy of the one in the second:

(50) *Max_1 said he_1^α saw his_1^β mother, and Oscar_2's sister **said he_1^α saw his$_2^\beta$ mother**

Consequently, the only representation possible is of the across-the-board strict reading:[21]

---

occurrence dependent upon the final pronoun, which bears an α-occurrence— rather than one, as we have assumed in the text. However, this would not generate any new reading from the strict/sloppy perspective. The result would be (ii), namely, an indexing in which the final two pronouns are strict:

(ii) ... and Oscar_2 **said he_2^β thinks he_1^β saw his_1^α mother**

21. This reading can also be represented by a structure with the pattern of indexical types in (50), except that the dependencies are taken to hold just between the two pronouns in each clause; see footnotes 19 and 20.

(51) Max_1 said he_1^α saw his_1^α mother, and Oscar_2's sister **said he_1^α saw his_1^α mother**

Notice that the examples in (49) contrast with the one in (52), in which structural parallelism has been restored:

(52) Max's sister said he saw his mother, and Oscar's sister did, too

This sentence can support parallel dependencies and hence is comparable in its range of interpretations to (3), our original many-pronouns example.

   Although embedding the antecedent of a dependency can narrow the range of interpretations, embedding a dependent expands the range:

(53) Max said his mother saw him, and Oscar did, too

This sentence has the three types of readings with respect to the strict/sloppy distinction that we have described for (3), *Max said he saw his mother, and Oscar did, too*. It has both across-the-board strict and sloppy readings, and a reading on which the final pronoun is construed as strict. What is of interest is that it also has the sort of reading that is precluded for (3), where the final pronoun is sloppy and the medial pronoun is strict: *Oscar said Max's mother saw Oscar*. This sort of reading is particularly salient in (54):

(54) I thought my tax accountant should do my taxes, and you did, too

To represent this reading, we must have the distribution of occurrence types and values shown in (55), a distribution that has thus far not led to well-formed results:

(55) Max_1 said his_1^α mother saw him_1^β, and Oscar_2 **said his_1^α mother saw him_2^β**

This structure, however, allows for the following dependencies, which are *i*-copies:

(56) a. $\langle (\text{Max, him}), 1, \langle \text{NP, V, NP, V, NP} \rangle \rangle$

   b. $\langle (\text{Oscar, him}), 2, \langle \text{NP, V, NP, V, NP} \rangle \rangle$

The reason it is possible to realize the dependencies in (55) is that there are proper analyses of its clauses in which the NP *his mother* is a term; *his*, the pronoun bearing the α-occurrence, is contained within this term and hence will be invisible to the dependency. This structure should be compared to (42), repeated here, which has the same linear arrangement of occurrences:

(42) *Max_1 said he_1^α saw his_1^β mother, and Oscar_2 **said he_1^α saw his_2^β mother**

For this structure, there is no factorization that mentions the initial NP bearing the α-occurrence and the final pronoun as terms, to the exclusion of the medial pronoun. In this regard, (42) is just like (57), which has no pronouns embedded within an NP, in excluding the fourth reading:

(57) Griswold said he thinks he makes better hollowware, and Wagner did, too

When the pronoun is embedded as in (53), it can be, so to speak, skipped over in a dependency, and can be strict while the other pronoun is sloppy.

A different pattern of readings is found in an example seemingly quite similar to (53), noted by Sag (1976):

(58) Edith said that finding her husband nude upsets her, and Martha did, too

This sentence is just like (53) in displaying the across-the-board readings. It differs, however, in the mixed readings, lacking the one in which the first elided pronoun is read as sloppy and the second as strict. Thus, Sag reports that the ellipsis in (58) can be understood as ... *said that finding Edith's husband nude upsets Martha*, but not as *... said that finding Martha's husband nude upsets Edith*. In this regard, we can contrast (58) not only with (53), but also with (3), of which it is a mirror image with respect to mixed readings.

What differentiates (58) from the other examples we have discussed is that the ellipsis contains not only many pronouns, but also an occurrence of PRO, standing as the subject of the gerund and controlled by the direct object. Recall that control PRO bears a β-occurrence and must be in a dependency with its controller; otherwise, there would be no control. Taking the pronouns as α- or β-occurrences, we then have the following representations:

(59) a. Edith$_1$ said that [PRO$_1^\beta$ finding her$_1^\alpha$ husband nude] upsets her$_1^\alpha$, and Martha$_2$ **said that [PRO$_1^\beta$ finding her$_1^\alpha$ husband nude] upsets her$_1^\alpha$**

b. Edith$_1$ said that [PRO$_1^\beta$ finding her$_1^\beta$ husband nude] upsets her$_1^\beta$, and Martha$_2$ **said that [PRO$_2^\beta$ finding her$_2^\beta$ husband nude] upsets her$_2^\beta$**

c. Edith$_1$ said that [PRO$_1^\beta$ finding her$_1^\alpha$ husband nude] upsets her$_1^\beta$, and Martha$_2$ **said that [PRO$_2^\beta$ finding her$_1^\alpha$ husband nude] upsets her$_2^\beta$**

d. Edith$_1$ said that [PRO$_1^\beta$ finding her$_1^\beta$ husband nude] upsets her$_1^\alpha$, and Martha$_2$ **said that [PRO$_1^\beta$ finding her$_1^\beta$ husband nude] upsets her$_1^\alpha$**

(59a) and (59b) represent the across-the-board readings. In (59a) PRO will be strict. This is because its controller bears an α-occurrence, so that the only dependency in which it can occur, in either clause, is (60):[22]

(60) $\langle(\text{PRO, her}), 1, \langle\text{NP, VP, V, NP}\rangle\rangle$

In (59b), by comparison, PRO, along with the pronouns, will be sloppy. This is licensed by the dependencies in (61); note that there is no bar to other elements occurring in the dependency that joins PRO to its controller:

(61) a. $\langle(\text{Edith, PRO, her, her}), 1, \langle\text{NP, V, C, NP, V, NP, N, A, V, NP}\rangle\rangle$

   b. $\langle(\text{Martha, PRO, her, her}), 2, \langle\text{NP, V, C, NP, V, NP, N, A, V, NP}\rangle\rangle$

The mixed cases are given by (59c) and (59d). The former has the dependencies in (62):

(62) a. $\langle(\text{Edith, PRO, her}), 1, \langle\text{NP, V, C, NP, VP, V, NP}\rangle\rangle$

   b. $\langle(\text{Martha, PRO, her}), 2, \langle\text{NP, V, C, NP, VP, V, NP}\rangle\rangle$

In these dependencies, the structural description does not mention the pronoun *her* bearing the α-occurrence as a term. Rather, this NP is contained within a term (VP) and hence is not part of the dependency. It will be construed as strict and will not interfere with the sloppy construal of the other occurrence of *her*, which bears a β-occurrence and does form part of the dependency. This gives the mixed reading with strict-sloppy order.

22. The existence of indexical dependencies such as that in (59a), in which the β-occurrence precedes the α-occurrence, is allowed by our definitions, as pointed out in footnote 3 of chapter 2. However, this appears to contrast with dependencies involving overt pronouns; in (i) a sloppy reading is difficult to obtain:

(i) That I saw his mother upset Max, and that you did upset Oscar

This suggests that "backward dependencies" are licensed by rule: control in (59a) licenses such a dependency, whereas in (i) there is no rule of grammar to serve that role. The implications of these considerations for weak crossover phenomena are apparent.

The remaining structure, (59d), does not give rise to the other mixed reading, the sloppy - strict order. It can only result in an across-the-board strict reading; since the controlling NP is an α-occurrence, and hence strict, so are its dependents, including the other pronoun:

(63) $\langle(\text{PRO, her, her}), 1, \langle \text{NP, V, NP, N, A, V, NP}\rangle\rangle$

What we cannot have is a representation that is like (59d) with respect to indexical types, but differs in indexical value so that the medial pronoun is sloppy:

(64) *Edith$_1$ said that [PRO$_1^\beta$ finding her$_1^\beta$ husband nude] upsets her$_1^\alpha$, and Martha$_2$ **said that [PRO$_1^\beta$ finding her$_2^\beta$ husband nude] upsets her$_1^\alpha$**

The reason for this is that the relevant dependency in the right-hand clause, namely (65),

(65) $\langle(\text{Martha, her}), 2, \langle \text{NP, V, C, NP, V, NP}\rangle\rangle$

cannot have an i-copy realized in the left-hand clause. A dependency linking *her* and *Edith* would also have to include PRO. It would also have to include the controller of PRO, but the result then would not be a dependency, since it would mention two α-occurrences. Eliminating *Edith* as a term would restore the dependency, but it would obviously not be an i-copy of (65). We thus account for the observed data.

What is of interest about an example such as (58) is how the available readings result from interactions of dependency effects operant in many-pronouns sentences with control relations. Varying these relations will alter the available readings. In (58), what was significant was that dependencies could be headed by two distinct, but coindexed, NPs, one of which was the controlling NP. If the head of the dependency and the controller are the same phrase, however, the interpretive possibilities become more restricted. (58) is a control context in which PRO is locally controlled if the object is present, but open to long-distance control if it is not. (66), where PRO is controlled by the matrix subject, is thus possible:

(66) Edith said that finding her husband nude was weird, and Martha did, too

Unlike (58), this sentence is just two-ways ambiguous, with the elided pronoun understood as strict or sloppy. Because the dependency relation of PRO to its controller is constant, the possible readings depend only upon whether the pronoun is part of this dependency. If it bears an

α-occurrence, it will not be, and a strict reading results; if it bears a β-occurrence, it will be, yielding the sloppy reading. These sorts of phenomena, then, show something quite interesting about control, namely, that such relations must be syntactically represented in the same way as other anaphoric dependencies, that is, through coindexing, since they interact with Dependency Theory. Thus, we see that indices have a certain "reality" as syntactically representing control relations.

In chapter 2, we pointed out that the redundancy inherent in parallel connected discourse settings is indicated by forms of phonological reduction, either by eliding the redundant material or by downstressing it. This material is subject to the conditions on reconstruction; for pronouns in such contexts, this means the identity conditions of Dependency Theory. Thus, the interpretation of the second pronoun in *Max saw his mother, and Oscar saw his mother, too*, with the pronouns downstressed, is exactly the same as the interpretation of the elided pronoun in *Max saw his mother, and Oscar did, too*. As would be expected, mixing downstress and ellipsis is immaterial to available readings; consider (67), with *he* in the right-hand clause downstressed:

(67) Max said he loves his mother, and Oscar said he does, too

Along the strict/sloppy dimension, the interpretations we can discern for this sentence vary depending upon whether the overt pronoun in the right-hand clause is taken as "strict" or "sloppy," where we extend these terms in the obvious fashion to reflect whether the overt pronoun is coindexed with the subject of the left-hand or right-hand clause. If this pronoun is strict, then the elided one must be strict, too. If it is sloppy, however, then the elided pronoun can be sloppy or strict. That is, (67) can be read with across-the-board strict pronouns, with across-the-board sloppy pronouns, or with the sloppy-strict order. But these are precisely the readings possible for (3), in which both pronouns are elided; as with (3), the reading in which the pronouns have the sloppy-strict order is excluded. Concomitantly, the admissible representations of (67) will be exactly the same as those for (3); it will be immaterial whether the pronouns in the right-hand clause are overt or not, since ellipsis and downstress amount to the same thing, equally sensitive to parallelism of dependencies. So, for instance, the readings of (68) are just the same as (49a)—both pronouns must be read as strict—even though here one is overt, but downstressed, and the other is covert, part of an ellipsis:

(68) Max said he saw his mother, and Oscar's sister said he did, too

From the point of view of the representation of indices, this follows from the fact that the structures associated with (68) are the same as those associated with (49a).[23]

Notice that if the pronoun in the right-hand clause of (68) is stressed, then it becomes possible to read it as sloppy, with the elided pronoun read as either sloppy or strict. Why should stress make this difference? The answer lies in the observation that if the pronoun is stressed, then it is no longer comparable to ellipsis and is not itself directly subject to the conditions on reconstruction. Only the elided pronoun is subject to the conditions. Stress, however, can signal independent reference, comparable in function to ostension. Thus, the overt pronoun can only be an α-occurrence. This makes possible the representations in (69), where the pronoun, in being coindexed with *Oscar*, is construed as "sloppy" relative to its counterpart in the initial clause:

23. A case of interest in connection with the many-pronouns puzzle is discussed by McCloskey (1991). McCloskey shows that in Irish, when the verb is raised out of the VP to Infl, giving the VSO word order of that language, the complement of Infl, which includes the subject, can be elided, stranding the verb; see footnote 17. He then points to the example in (i):

(i) Dúirt Ciarán$_1$ go   labharfadh sé$_1$ le-n-a$_1$ mhac agus dúirt
    said Ciarán Comp would-speak he to his son   and said
    Eoghnai go   labharfadh   fosta
    Eoghnai, Comp would-speak also
    'Ciarán said he would talk to his son, and Eoghnai said he would, too'

This example is like (67) in that there are two overt verbs in the right-hand clause; but two pronouns have been elided, as in (3). McCloskey reports that this example is three-ways ambiguous, precisely in the ways we have described for the examples in the text. Interestingly, if the two verbs are elided as in (3), the range of readings is limited to the across-the-board strict interpretation. McCloskey (personal communication) provides the following example:

(ii) Deirtear gur   dúirt Ciarán$_1$ go   labharfadh sé$_1$ le-n-a$_1$ mhac agus
     it-is-said Comp said Ciarán Comp would-speak he to his son   and
     dúirt
     said
     'It is said that Ciarán said that he would speak to his son, and he did'

The reason for this is that the reconstruction will include the subject of the complement clause; since this is a name, it will bear an α-occurrence. Hence, any pronoun dependent on it will have to be construed as strict. Thus, regardless of the distribution of indexical types, the only resulting reading will be across-the-board strict.

(69) a. Max_1 said $\text{he}_1^{\alpha/\beta}$ saw his_1^{α} mother, and Oscar_2's sister said $\text{h\'e}_2^{\alpha}$ **saw his$_1^{\alpha}$ mother**

b. Max_1 said he_1^{α} saw his_1^{β} mother, and Oscar_2's sister said $\text{h\'e}_2^{\alpha}$ **saw his$_2^{\beta}$ mother**

These structures represent a mixed sloppy/strict reading—(69a)—and an across-the-board sloppy reading—(69b). Thus, by stressing the overt pronoun in the right-hand clause, we no longer meet the conditions on connected parallel discourse, and this permits other interpretive possibilities than those found in ellipsis, which obviously precludes heightened stress.

In addition to Sag (1976), whose approach is discussed in footnote 4, both Dahl (1974) and Dalrymple, Shieber, and Pereira (1991) have addressed the many-pronouns puzzle. Both accounts turn on a notion of depth of embedding. For Dahl, the central notion is functional embedding; for Dalrymple, Shieber, and Pereira, it is syntactic embedding. Dahl accounts for the sloppy reading of a simple case like *Max saw his mother, and Oscar did, too* by allowing the derivation from (70a) (where f stands for "saw," g for "is mother of," and m for "Max") to (70b) by substituting o, standing for "Oscar," for m:

(70) a. $f(m, g(m))$

b. $f(o, g(o))$

c. $f(o, g(m))$

Not making this substitution for the second occurrence of m gives the strict reading, as represented by (70c). Dahl notes that given his mode of representation, the substitution rule must somehow be constrained, since in addition to (70a–c), (71) can also be derived:

(71) $f(m, g(o))$

Dahl proposes that "before the substitution operation is performed . . . , we may derive the value of any function 'embedded' in this object" (pp. 8–9). Substitution then applies to any positions that still show. For the case at hand, this means that substitution can apply either to (70a), giving (70b), or to (72a), itself derived by taking the value of $g(m) = j$ (j being Max's mother) in (70a), to give (72b), which is equivalent to (70c):

(72) a. $f(m, j)$

b. $f(o, j)$

(72b) now represents the strict reading. Applied to the many-pronouns case, this ordering of (optional) value taking and (obligatory) substitution will derive from (73a) just the options in (73b) through (73d) for *Max said he saw his mother, and Oscar did, too* where *s* stands for "said":

(73) a. s(m, f(m, g(m)))

    b. s(o, f(m, g(m)))

    c. s(o, f(o, g(m)))

    d. s(o, f(o, g(o)))

(73b) results if the value of *f* is taken, so that only the initial occurrence of *m* is open to substitution; (73c) if the value of *g* is taken, leaving the first two occurrences as substitution positions; (73d) if no values are taken, and all three occurrences are substituted for. What is excluded is (74):

(74) s(o, f(m, g(o)))

This is because in order for the medial position to be strict, the value of its function must be taken. But *f* embeds *g* as an argument, so to take the value of *f* will "close" any argument within *g*. In this way, the excluded mixed reading is accounted for.

    Whatever the independent merits of Dahl's proposal,[24] however, his notion of functional embedding is too coarse. Suppose that we had a case just like (73a), except that the arguments of *f* were inverted:

(75) s(m, f(g(m), m))

The prediction is that again just three readings should be available, with (76) being precluded, since *g* is just as much an embedded function as in (74):

(76) s(m, f(g(o), m))

But examples such as (53), *Max said his mother saw him, and Oscar did, too*, which are of the requisite form, have the reading corresponding to (76), where the medial elided pronoun is sloppy and the final one strict. This sentence is four-ways, not three-ways, ambiguous.

---

24. Particularly problematical for Dahl's analysis are examples like (i):

(i) John's mother loves him, and Bill's does, too

The basic functional structure is (ii):

(ii) f(g(j), j)

We can derive the sloppy reading by substituting for the occurrences of *j*; but how is the strict reading to be derived? Taking the value of the embedded function will just give a reading where John's mother loves Bill, which is obviously impossible.

Dalrymple, Shieber, and Pereira (1991) propose an alternative notion of embedding, stating that the "ordering correlates with depth of syntactic embedding" (p. 448). In the context of the sort of predication-based theory they assume, they propose that "if the position corresponding to a more deeply embedded pronoun is abstracted over, the position corresponding to a less deeply embedded pronoun must also be abstracted over" (p. 448). This is intended to rule out (77) as a meaning of the right-hand clause of *Max said he loves his mother, and Oscar did, too*:

(77) Oscar, $\lambda x(x$ said Max loves x's mother)

Since the position corresponding to the most deeply embedded pronoun is abstracted, but the medial position is not, this case does not fall under the generalization. Dalrymple, Shieber, and Pereira then cite the example from Sag 1976 that we have given as (58), *Edith said that finding her husband nude upsets her, and Martha did, too*, as further support. Recall that this sentence precludes the sloppy – strict mixed reading; the reason is that the medial occurrence of *her* is more deeply embedded than the last one.

In the context of their brief and informal remarks on this matter, Dalrymple, Shieber, and Pereira do not specify how to measure syntactic embeddedness. One possibility would be to count the number of NP and S nodes between the root and the element in question. This would work for the two cases they discuss, but not for *Max said his mother saw him, and Oscar did, too*, since then *his* would be more deeply embedded than *him*, and, as with Dahl's treatment, the strict – sloppy mixed reading would be improperly excluded. Another possibility would be to simply count the number of nodes from the root. This would make the pronouns equally embedded and presumably would allow for both mixed readings. But the problem would resurface in analyzing (78):

(78) Max said his mother saw his father, and Oscar did, too

Here the second occurrence of *his* is again more deeply embedded, but the same range of meanings emerges; this sentence is also four-ways ambiguous. Also, it is by no means clear that an embedding approach properly accounts for example (58) in anything but the coarsest sense. As we have noted, the distribution of strict and sloppy construals of the pronouns is correlated with the control of PRO. This interaction is left unaccounted for on both Dalrymple, Shieber, and Pereira's and Dahl's approaches.[25]

---

25. Dalrymple, Shieber, and Pereira (1991) in fact reject the proposal discussed in the text, citing examples given by Gawron and Peters (1990a) as a determining

The proposals put forth by Dahl and by Dalrymple, Shieber, and Pereira both add ad hoc and apparently inadequate conditions to theories that basically overgenerate. In contrast, the solution to the many-pronouns puzzle afforded by Dependency Theory follows directly from the characterization of dependencies, as they can be realized in phrase markers of various forms. The theory has been applied not only to the basic sort of many-pronouns case, of which (3) has been our exemplar, but also to cases with increasingly more pronouns, to cases with differing structural relations between the pronouns, to cases where there are overt but downstressed pronouns in addition to elided ones, and to cases involving interaction with control relations. With this understanding of Dependency Theory and its relation to reconstruction, we now turn to the other eliminative puzzle, the many-clauses puzzle.

4.3   The Many-Clauses Puzzles

On the theory we have developed, the strict/sloppy distinction reflects a structural ambiguity of indexical type, corresponding to whether α-occurrences or β-occurrences are involved (modulo the resolvability of the latter). Given this formal ambiguity, elliptical reconstruction is itself structurally "strict," in the sense that both the antecedent and the ellipsis are occurrences of a given sub–phrase marker. A reconstruction is thus a structural carbon copy of its antecedent, *up to indexical type*; identity of structural value is not necessary for nondistinctness of occurrences. The particular indexical value—the strict or sloppy value—a pronoun attains is not a consequence of reconstruction per se, but a consequence of the type of occurrence reconstructed, and, if it is a β-occurrence, its structural relations to occurrences of that index. Reconstruction in this sense of occurrences will of course be "strict" in the way described regardless of

---

factor. (See section 4.3 for discussion of these cases.) They give an informal description of their revised proposal as follows:

These various readings can be captured by positing a linking relationship between the semantics of pronouns and that of their antecedents, and generalizing it to include the relation between the semantics of terms induced by ellipsis and that of their source parallel element. Under a suitable definition of this generalized antecedent linking, all of the cases here can be captured by requiring that if an occurrence is abstracted over, so must its generalized antecedent. (p. 448)

The intent of this proposal, with its appeal to the semantics of pronouns, is opaque to us, especially given the absence of any formulation of the "suitable definition" of "generalized antecedent linking." We thus leave evaluation of this proposal in abeyance.

the number of occurrences; there can be any number of elided "copies" of an antecedent phrase. From this, the solution to the many-clauses puzzle for a sentence such as (5)—*Max saw his mother, Oscar did, too, but Sam didn't*—follows directly; depending on the type of the pronoun, just the following representations are possible:

(79) a. Max$_1$ [$_{VP}$ saw his$_1^\alpha$ mother], Oscar$_2$ [$_{VP}$ **saw his$_1^\alpha$ mother**] but Sam$_3$ [$_{VP}$ didn't **see his$_1^\alpha$ mother**]

   b. Max$_1$ [$_{VP}$ saw his$_1^\beta$ mother], Oscar$_2$ [$_{VP}$ **saw his$_2^\beta$ mother**] but Sam$_3$ [$_{VP}$ didn't **see his$_3^\beta$ mother**]

In (79a) the pronoun bears an α-occurrence, and does so in all three occurrences of the VPs; hence, both reconstructed pronouns are construed as strict. On the other hand, in (79b) the pronouns bear β-occurrences, each of which must be resolved in its respective clause in order to be in a well-formed dependency. Hence, both reconstructed pronouns here are read as sloppy. Any mixed readings of the elided pronouns are excluded, since this would require reconstructing an α-occurrence as a β-occurrence, or vice versa. But these would not be reconstructions at all, since the phrases would be distinct.

The many-clauses puzzle shows quite clearly the necessity of taking indexical independence and dependence as *formally represented*—in our terms, as α- and β-occurrences—rather than as just different "ways of taking" coindexed elements. For suppose that the formal structure of indices were encompassed by indexical value, the distinction in question being differentiated in some other way, perhaps through the manners of semantic resolution of pronouns, and not by any formal syntactic representation. Then, since the distinction would not be structurally determinate, in a many-clauses sentence it would be possible to construe the elided pronouns in different ways. This would incorrectly allow for mixed readings, because nothing would require that if one of the elided pronouns is taken a certain way, then all must be taken that way. But even if there were some such condition enforcing this requirement, it would still not be correct, since it would fail to account for the Dahl puzzle, repeated here:

(80) Max thinks he is strong, Oscar does, too, but his father doesn't

This sentence has a mixed reading; it can be understood as in (81):

(81) Max thinks that Max is strong, Oscar thinks that Oscar is strong, but Oscar's father doesn't think that Oscar is strong

That is, (80) can be read so that the elided pronoun in the medial clause is interpreted as sloppy, whereas the one in the final clause is interpreted as strict relative to the prior sloppy pronoun. This conundrum does not arise, however, if indexical type is part of the formal structure of indices. To see why this is so, we must clarify the relation of indexical types to strict and sloppy identity in the context of reconstruction.

From the sorts of cases we have considered thus far, there appears to be a neat correlation between α-occurrences and strict readings on the one hand, and β-occurrences and sloppy readings on the other. This is because reconstruction of α-occurrences tolerates no alteration of indexical value, although reconstruction of β-occurrences does. They tolerate such alteration just in case they are realized in dependencies that are i-copies. In principle, however, there is no reason that β-occurrences cannot be reconstructed with the *same* indexical value. In such a circumstance, the β-occurrences would just be occurrences of a single index, and the verb phrases containing them would be reconstructions in the narrow sense of being the same down to both the types and values of the indices. In this regard, the situation of such β-occurrences would be just like that of α-occurrences. Since there is no alteration of indexical value in either case, the resulting readings would be strict. By the logic of our theory, therefore, we have not only the two possibilities for anaphora in ellipsis cited above (strict readings derived from reconstruction of an independent index and sloppy readings derived from reconstruction of a dependent index) but also a *third* possibility (strict readings derived from reconstruction of a dependent index). This third circumstance of reconstructing β-occurrences without altering their indexical values is unlike reconstructing α-occurrences in one respect: the β-occurrences must be resolved in dependencies. The important point here is that unlike the reconstruction of β-occurrences with altered values, this resolution need not be relative to parallel dependencies that are i-copies. Since occurrences of a given index are already nondistinct, there is no need to call upon any further conditions to establish nondistinctness for reconstruction. Only if we are considering the reconstruction of β-occurrences with altered indexical values is it required that they be resolved in dependencies that are i-copies.

Now, we have already seen ample cases of the first two types of reconstruction; in what contexts do we find the third type? Consider the following sentence:

(82) Oscar thinks he is strong, but his father doesn't

What is of interest is that this sentence allows a reading where it means that Oscar's father doesn't think that Oscar is strong—that is, with the elided pronoun understood as strict. Now the pronoun in the initial clause of (82) can be a β-occurrence, so that we can have the representation in (83):

(83) Oscar$_1$ thinks he$_1^\beta$ is strong, but his$_1$ father doesn't **think he$_1^\beta$ is strong**

This is therefore a structure of the third type. A β-occurrence has been reconstructed that must be resolved in an indexical dependency. It can be because there is independently an anaphoric connection between the pronoun *his* and an antecedent, *Oscar*, in the prior clause. This pronoun will thus bear an occurrence of the same index as the reconstructed pronoun and hence can serve as its antecedent. The resulting dependency need not be parallel to the one in the other clause, however, since there has been no change of indexical value, and we need not appeal to identity of dependencies to ensure proper reconstruction. (83), it should be clear, represents the intended reading.

The third type of reconstruction can also be observed by comparing the examples in (84):

(84) a. Every bachelor thinks he is strong, and every bachelor's mother does, too

    b. Every married man thinks he is strong, and every bachelor's mother does, too

These sentences differ in that only (84a) has a reading on which the elided pronoun can be a bound variable; that is, the second clause can mean something like *for every bachelor x, x's mother thinks x is strong*. The only reading for (84b) is an irrelevant one on which *he* is taken as deictic. The representation of the reading in question for (84a) is shown in (85):

(85) a. Every bachelor$_1$ thinks he$_1^\beta$ is strong, and every bachelor$_1$'s mother **thinks he$_1^\beta$ is strong**

    b. $\langle$(every bachelor, he), 1, $\langle$NP, V, NP$\rangle\rangle$

    c. $\langle$(every bachelor, he), 1, $\langle$NP, N, V, NP$\rangle\rangle$

(We show the dependencies here as extending back to the phrase *every bachelor*. More precisely, they are defined with respect to its trace at LF and the pronoun. This detail is insignificant here.) The dependencies shown are not *i*-copies, but, by hypothesis, this is not an impediment to the well-formedness of (85a), since they are defined with respect to the same index. That the quantifiers bear the same index is permissible because they have the same range of values, that is, the bachelors. The quantifiers in (84b), on the other hand, have distinct ranges, as indicated by the different nouns, so a representation comparable to (85) would realize dependencies defined over distinct indices:

(86) a. *Every married man$_1$ thinks he$_1^\beta$ is strong, and every bachelor$_2$'s mother **thinks he$_2^\beta$ is strong**

   b. $\langle$(every married man, he), 1, $\langle$NP, V, NP$\rangle\rangle$

   c. $\langle$(every bachelor, he), 2, $\langle$NP, N, V, NP$\rangle\rangle$

But these dependencies are not i-copies; hence the unavailability of a bound variable construal of the elided pronoun. Notice that the reading we have isolated for (84a) does not easily fall under either of the rubrics "strict" and "sloppy." Rather, it is the third sort of reading, a type of dependent reading, keyed by what we may think of as an "anaphoric" occurrence of the quantifier phrase *every bachelor*.

Returning now to (82), it is true that there is another representation that expresses the relevant reading, namely, where the pronoun is an α-occurrence rather than a β-occurrence:

(87) Oscar$_1$ thinks he$_1^\alpha$ is strong, but his$_1$ father doesn't **think he$_1^\alpha$ is strong**

However, we can eliminate this possibility of an α-occurrence of an index and hence isolate the third sort of anaphora in ellipsis. Suppose that (82) itself is embedded in an environment in which the overt VP is elided:

(88) Max thinks he is strong, Oscar does, too, but his father doesn't

In this case, if the pronoun in the first elision is read as sloppy, then the pronoun in the second can be construed as strict relative to this sloppy reading. This is, of course, the Dahl puzzle. We can now see that it is an instance of the third sort of anaphora in ellipsis; it involves a strict reading related to a dependent occurrence. Since the pronoun in the first ellipsis is sloppy, it must bear a β-occurrence; hence, any other reconstruction must also bear this type of occurrence. This gives (89) to represent (88); the clauses realize the dependencies indicated in (89b) through (89d), respectively:

(89) a. Max$_1$ thinks he$_1^\beta$ is strong, Oscar$_2$ **thinks he$_2^\beta$ is strong**, but his$_2^\alpha$ father doesn't **think he$_2^\beta$ is strong**

   b. $\langle$(Max, he), 1, $\langle$NP, V, NP$\rangle\rangle$

   c. $\langle$(Oscar, he), 2, $\langle$NP, V, NP$\rangle\rangle$

   d. $\langle$(his, he), 2, $\langle$NP, N,V, NP$\rangle\rangle$

In this structure the first and second VPs are reconstructions (the dependencies are i-copies) and so are the second and third (the dependencies are not i-copies, but they need not be, since the indexical value is undisturbed). Hence, all three VPs are reconstructions, by transitivity. Thus, (89) represents the mixed reading for (88) characteristic of the Dahl puzzle: that Max thinks Max is strong, and Oscar thinks Oscar is strong, but Oscar's father doesn't think Oscar is strong. Of course, the string in (88) can be read in other ways; it also has the readings typical of simple many-clauses sentences.

(90) a. Max_1 thinks he_1^α is strong, Oscar_2 **thinks he_1^α is strong**, but his_2^α father_3 doesn't **think he_1^α is strong**

   b. Max_1 thinks he_1^β is strong, Oscar_2 **thinks he_2^β is strong**, but his_2^α father_3 doesn't **think he_3^β is strong**

These represent the across-the-board strict and across-the-board sloppy readings, respectively.

With respect to the representation of the Dahl-type reading in (89) it is critical to observe that although the β-occurrence in the final clause is legitimately reconstructed as strict without change of its indexical value, it is still resolved in a dependency in that clause. This dependency exists, however, only because it is coindexed with the pronoun *his*, which itself is coindexed with the NP *Oscar* in the previous clause. As noted in section 4.1, it is only if *his* is taken as referring to Oscar that the relevant reading is possible; if this pronoun has some other reference to someone in context, this reading is precluded. This is because the pronoun in (88) would then not bear an index that would make it possible to resolve in an indexical dependency the reconstructed β-occurrence in the final clause, and the resulting structure would be ruled out:

(91) *Max_1 thinks he_1^β is strong, Oscar_2 **thinks he_2^β is strong**, but his_3^α father doesn't **think he_2^β is strong**

What these observations bring to light about the Dahl-type reading in sentences like (88) is that its existence is *anaphora dependent*. The anaphora is needed to provide an antecedent for a dependency, and for this reason the pronoun coindexed with *Oscar* can only be replaced by an NP that is another, coreferential, occurrence of *Oscar*. We thus have the contrast in (92):

(92) a. Max thinks he is strong, Oscar does, too, but Oscar's father doesn't

   b. Max thinks he is strong, Oscar does, too, but Sam's father doesn't

(92a) is just like (88) with respect to the Dahl-type reading, presuming that the two occurrences of *Oscar* corefer and are coindexed. But such a reading is not to be found in (92b); the third clause cannot mean that Sam's father doesn't think that Oscar is strong.

The pronoun that facilitates the Dahl-type reading in (88) can, of course, be coindexed with *Max* (i.e., with the subject of the initial clause), rather than with *Oscar* (the subject of the medial clause). But then the elided pronoun, on the Dahl-type reading, will be understood as referring to Max, and not to Oscar. Similarly, shifting the clauses to give (93) will shift the order of interpretation:

(93) Max thinks he is strong, his father does, too, but Oscar doesn't

Here, on the Dahl-type reading, the medial clause is construed as strict, the final one as sloppy. What connects all of these cases is that the overt facilitating pronoun and the elided pronoun are ultimately linked to the same antecedent. What is excluded, however, are readings in which the facilitating and elided pronouns have different antecedents; for (88), this would be the reading in which one pronoun is coindexed with *Max*, the other with *Oscar*. The excluded readings are the ones we described in section 4.1 as follows:

(94) a. Max thinks that Max is strong, Oscar thinks that Oscar is strong, but Oscar's father doesn't think that Max is strong

     b. Max thinks that Max is strong, Oscar thinks that Oscar is strong, but Max's father doesn't think that Oscar is strong

For these readings, we know that the initial occurrence of the pronoun in (88) must be a β-occurrence, because, in both, the medial clause is understood as sloppy. Consequently, the reconstructed pronoun in the final clause also must be a β-occurrence. Fixing the indexings to represent the readings in (94) yields the representations in (95):

(95) a. *Max_1 thinks he_1^β is strong, $Oscar_2$ **thinks he_2^β is strong**, but his_2^α father doesn't **think he_1^β is strong**

     b. *Max_1 thinks he_1^β is strong, $Oscar_2$ **thinks he_2^β is strong**, but his_1^α father doesn't **think he_2^β is strong**

Both of these are ill formed, because the final β-occurrence is unresolved. We conclude, therefore, that the availability of the "mixed" Dahl-type readings tracks the possibilities of anaphoric connections, since these are determined relative to Dependency Theory.

To summarize what we have learned thus far from exploring the Dahl puzzle: In studies of anaphora in ellipsis, the goal has traditionally been to account for strict and sloppy readings. Insofar as we take these terms as names of intuitions, thinking of matters in terms of this dichotomy is appropriate, but in technical analysis of anaphora in ellipsis it is a too coarse (and ultimately misleading) distinction, since they basically only describe relations of indexical values. The Dahl puzzle shows that a more fine-grained distinction is necessary, one that can represent not only sloppy and strict readings, but in fact two sorts of strict readings. Thus, what is novel in our approach is that by taking into account indexical type, we can discriminate among a strict reading correlated with an independent occurrence of an index, a sloppy reading correlated with a dependent occurrence, and a third type of reading, where a strict reading is correlated with a dependent occurrence. Recognizing this third sort of anaphora in ellipsis is what affords a solution to the Dahl puzzle, which arises when a β-occurrence is reconstructed without altering its indexical value, yet can be properly resolved. This resolution is possible because of an anaphoric connection otherwise established between clauses, although it need not be structurally parallel to that of any other β-occurrence in the discourse. This is because such parallelism is not needed to establish that the elided verb phrases are appropriately identical.

The characteristic anaphoric patterning of the Dahl-type sentence—one elided clause being construed as sloppy, and another as strict relative to it—is also found in another type of case. This case is of interest because it appears to show the Dahl-type reading without the sort of anaphoric connection that facilitates this construal in the previous examples. Examples are given in (96) through (98), the importance of which was brought to our attention by I. Heim:

(96) Max still thinks he is strong, but Oscar only did as long as I did

(97) a. Max thought he was strong, and Oscar would if Sam did

   b. John wouldn't tell if Mary kissed him, but Max would if she had

(98) a. Max recognized his mother, Oscar did, too, but later Sam didn't

   b. Max polished his shoes, Oscar did, too, and Sam will again

In these examples there is no anaphoric connection between the last two clauses other than that of the elided pronoun. Yet, along with the now-familiar across-the-board readings, these sentences can have the Dahl-type reading; (96), for instance, can be understood as follows:

(99) Max still thinks Max is strong, but Oscar only thought Oscar was strong as long as I thought Oscar was strong

Why does the Dahl puzzle arise with sentences of this sort? The key is to observe that in these sentences the final clause is *subordinate* to the medial clause. By contrast, in the other cases we have been considering the clauses have been *coordinate*.

To see why subordination is the key, let us first look at some simpler cases, simpler in that there is only one ellipsis. As established in chapter 2, a sentence such as (100) has only a sloppy reading:

(100) Every bachelor said he was crazy, and Bill did, too

The strict reading is precluded because the pronoun, being a bound variable, does not bear an α-occurrence. Sag (1976) and Williams (1977) have observed, however, that in addition to its sloppy reading a sentence such as (101) does have a strict reading of sorts:

(101) Every bachelor said he was crazy before Bill did

(101) can be understood as *for every bachelor x, x said that x was crazy before Bill said that x was crazy*. Thus, the reading that interests us is strict in that the elided pronoun in the adverbial clause is construed as another occurrence of the overt bound variable pronoun. That a quantifier can bind a pronominal variable in such a subordinated clause can be seen from (102), where the pronoun is not elided:

(102) Every bachelor said he was crazy before he left

Notice further that this sort of strict reading is the only one available for (103):

(103) Every bachelor's mother said he was crazy before Bill did

This sentence is just like (101), except for the structural position of the quantifier phrase; yet it precludes a sloppy reading.

Now, since the pronoun in (101) bears a β-occurrence, one possible representation is (104):

(104) Every bachelor$_1$ said he$_1^\beta$ was crazy before Bill$_2$ **said he$_2^\beta$ was crazy**

(104) represents the sloppy reading. The reconstructed β-occurrence, which has an altered indexical value, is resolved in an indexical dependency that is an i-copy of the occurrence borne by the overt pronoun. Alternatively, there is a representation of (101) in which the index is unaltered in value:

(105) Every bachelor$_1$ said he$_1^\beta$ was crazy before Bill$_2$ **said he$_1^\beta$ was crazy**

This is the representation that interests us. The first thing to notice about it is that the VPs are reconstructions as is, since the indexical values of the β-occurrences are the same. The second thing to notice is that the reconstructed β-occurrence can be resolved, since (105) realizes the dependency in (106a) for the elided pronoun, in addition to the one in (106b) for the overt pronoun:

(106) a. $\langle$(every bachelor, he), 1, $\langle$NP, VP, C, NP, V, NP$\rangle\rangle$

  b. $\langle$(every bachelor, he), 1, $\langle$NP, V, NP$\rangle\rangle$

These dependencies are not i-copies, but they need not be, since the VPs in (105) are otherwise well-formed reconstructions. (101) thus allows the third type of anaphora in ellipsis isolated by our theory, a reading that is strict, but arises from reconstruction of a dependent index. This type of anaphora in ellipsis is not available for (100), since (107), which would represent it, is ill formed:

(107) *Every bachelor$_1$ said he$_1^\beta$ was crazy, and Bill$_2$ **said he$_1^\beta$ was crazy**

Here there is no way to have a dependency that can extend from the reconstructed β-occurrence back to the quantifier, since the scope of the quantifier does not extend to this clause, just as it does not in *Every bachelor said he was crazy, and he left*. Conversely, this sort of reading, represented by (108) with the dependency for the reconstructed pronoun indicated, is the only type available for (103):

(108) a. Every bachelor$_1$'s mother said he$_1^\beta$ was crazy before Bill$_2$ **said he$_1^\beta$ was crazy**

  b. $\langle$(every bachelor, he), 1, $\langle$NP, N, VP, C, NP, V, NP$\rangle\rangle$

Here both pronouns are bound variables; compare *Every bachelor's mother said he was crazy before he left*. What is not possible, however, is (109), which would represent the sloppy reading:

(109) a. *Every bachelor$_1$'s mother said he$_1^\beta$ was crazy before Bill$_2$ **said he$_2^\beta$ was crazy**

  b. $\langle$(every bachelor, he), 1, $\langle$NP, N, V, NP$\rangle\rangle$

  c. $\langle$(Bill, he), 2, $\langle$NP, V, NP$\rangle\rangle$

Even though the binding represented by (109) is well formed, this structure is not, since the dependencies are not i-copies.

These cases show that when one clause is subordinated within another, it is possible to have structures that realize various dependencies *on the same antecedent*. Nothing proscribes dependencies that share an antecedent; a given noun phrase can be the antecedent for any number of dependencies, so long as all of these dependencies are realized in a single phrase marker. In (106), for instance, both dependencies have *every bachelor* as their antecedent. When multiple dependencies share a single antecedent, the resulting readings will be strict, since the indexical values associated with the dependencies will be the same. Now, strict readings with dependent occurrences are the hallmark of the Dahl-type reading. Such readings can arise without facilitating anaphoric connections because the pronoun reconstructed in the subordinated clause can trace a dependency directly back to its antecedent. Thus, consider (110), which represents the Dahl-type reading of (96), *Max still thinks he is strong, but Oscar only did as long as I did*:

(110) a. Max$_1$ still thinks he$_1^\beta$ is strong, [but Oscar$_2$ only **thought he$_2^\beta$ was strong** as long as I **thought he$_2^\beta$ was strong**]

  b. $\langle$(Max, he), 1, $\langle$NP, V, NP$\rangle\rangle$

  c. $\langle$(Oscar, he), 2, $\langle$NP, V, NP$\rangle\rangle$

  d. $\langle$(Oscar, he), 2, $\langle$NP, VP, C, NP, V, NP$\rangle\rangle$

In this structure the first two clauses are coordinated, and the final clause is a subordinated adjunct of the second. Moreover, as with the other Dahl puzzle cases, we are only trafficking in β-occurrences, since the medial clause is to be understood as sloppy. The dependencies realized in the first two clauses, (110b) and (110c), each have their own antecedent and are *i*-copies warranting sloppy identity. (110c) and (110d) are not *i*-copies; but they are compatible because there is no alteration of indexical value for which structural parallelism is necessary. They are, however, dependencies that link the pronouns to the same antecedent, possible just because of the subordinate position of the clause realizing (110d) within that realizing (110c). We have thus shown that there are two (and only two) routes to the Dahl-type reading, depending upon the source of resolution of β-occurrences: either directly to the antecedent noun phrase itself, possible in subordination contexts, or indirectly to a pronoun anaphoric to it, in coordination (or, more generally, list) contexts.

In the cases we have just been considering, the subordination has been within the second clause. Reversing the order of coordination and subordination, so that the subordination is within the first clause, raises some very interesting subtleties. Thus, consider (111), an example of a sort brought to light by Gawron and Peters (1990a):

(111) John said he was crazy before the teacher did, and Bill did, too

We take it that what is elided in the second clause is the entire VP, that headed by *say*, which itself contains an ellipsis. Thus, the ellipsis in the subordinated medial clause forms part of the antecedent for the ellipsis in the coordinated final clause. Given this, there are three ways in which (111) can be understood. First, there is a "double" across-the-board strict reading, as spelled out in (112):

(112) John said that John was crazy before the teacher said that John was crazy, and Bill said that John was crazy before the teacher said that John was crazy

Second, there is an across-the-board sloppy reading, as spelled out in (113):

(113) John said that John was crazy before the teacher said that the teacher was crazy, and Bill said that Bill was crazy before the teacher said that the teacher was crazy

And third, there is the reading expressed in (114):

(114) John said that John was crazy before the teacher said that John was crazy, and Bill said that Bill was crazy before the teacher said that Bill was crazy

The first two readings are unproblematical. The across-the-board strict reading results from analyzing the index of the overt pronoun with an α-occurrence, and the across-the-board sloppy reading results from analyzing it with a β-occurrence. In this regard, these cases are just a variant of the many-clauses case, and they are represented as in (115):

(115) a. John$_1$ said he$_1^\alpha$ was crazy before the teacher$_2$ **said he$_1^\alpha$ was crazy, and Bill$_3$ said he$_1^\alpha$ was crazy before the teacher$_2$ said he$_1^\alpha$ was crazy**

b. John$_1$ said he$_1^\beta$ was crazy before the teacher$_2$ **said he$_2^\beta$ was crazy, and Bill$_3$ said he$_3^\beta$ was crazy before the teacher$_2$ said he$_2^\beta$ was crazy**

The dependencies attendant to (115b) are as follows:

(116) a. $\langle$(John, he), 1, $\langle$NP, V, NP$\rangle\rangle$

b. $\langle$(the teacher, he), 2, $\langle$NP, V, NP$\rangle\rangle$

c. $\langle$(Bill, he), 3, $\langle$NP, V, NP$\rangle\rangle$

What particularly piques our curiosity about (111), however, is the existence of the third reading, that described by (114).

The interesting point about this reading is that with respect to the elision within the first clause we appear to have a strict reading, but with respect to the elision across the two clauses we appear to have a sloppy one. Since in the simple cases the strict reading is associated with an α-occurrence and the sloppy reading is associated with a β-occurrence, and the values are complementary, we appear to derive a contradiction. However, we have seen that there is a third possibility, and it is this mechanism that allows us to derive this third reading. To see this, consider the representation of the first clause of (111), making the assumption that the index of the overt *he* is a β-occurrence:

(117) John$_1$ said he$_1^\beta$ was crazy before the teacher$_2$ **said he$_1^\beta$ was crazy**

Recall that in structures of this form, discussed in relation to (110), the reconstructed instance of *he* may be in a dependency with *John*. This is possible because (117) is an instance of subordination, not coordination; if it were the latter, then no dependency with *John* would be possible. (*The teacher*, note, is in a position structurally parallel to *John*, and, if parallelism *forced* index alteration, (117) would be underivable. But parallelism only *allows* index alteration, so (117) is possible.) We now take (117) itself as the antecedent of ellipsis, deriving the structure in (118), with the indicated dependencies, which are *i*-copies:[26]

(118) a. John$_1$ said he$_1^\beta$ was crazy before the teacher$_2$ **said he$_1^\beta$ was crazy**, and Bill$_3$ **said he$_3^\beta$ was crazy before the teacher$_2$ said he$_3^\beta$ was crazy**

    b. $\langle$(John, he), 1, $\langle$NP, V, NP$\rangle\rangle$

    c. $\langle$(John, he), 1, $\langle$NP, VP, C, NP, V, NP$\rangle\rangle$

    d. $\langle$(Bill, he), 3, $\langle$NP, V, NP$\rangle\rangle$

    e. $\langle$(Bill, he), 3, $\langle$NP, VP, C, NP, V, NP$\rangle\rangle$

This is the representation of the reading given in (114). Given the resources of the theory on which the characterization of this reading turns, we

---

26. Notice that with structures such as (118) there would be no harm in amalgamating the dependencies that are defined with respect to the same antecedent. In that case the dependencies in question would be (i) and (ii):

(i) $\langle$(John, he, he), 1, $\langle$NP, V, NP, VP, C, NP, V, NP$\rangle\rangle$

(ii) $\langle$(Bill, he, he), 3, $\langle$NP, V, NP, VP, C, NP, V, NP$\rangle\rangle$

These dependencies are *i*-copies. For clarity, however, we will continue to give the dependencies in unamalgamated form, as in the text.

classify it with the Dahl-type reading of examples such as (96) through (98), discussed above.

There are other readings that seemingly might be carried by (111). For instance, can (111) have the interpretation given in (119)?

(119) John said that John was crazy before the teacher said that the teacher was crazy, and Bill said that Bill was crazy before the teacher said that Bill was crazy

It seems intuitively clear that the answer is no. This reading would be represented as in (120); note that since the first elision is construed as sloppy, the index of the overt pronoun must be a β-occurrence:

(120) *John$_1$ said he$_1^\beta$ was crazy before the teacher$_2$ **said he$_2^\beta$ was crazy,** **and Bill$_3$ said he$_3^\beta$ was crazy before the teacher$_2$ said he$_3^\beta$ was crazy**

In the medial clause, the occurrence of the reconstructed pronoun can be coindexed with *the teacher*, since it can occur in a dependency that is an *i*-copy of the dependency in which the overt pronoun occurs. In the second conjunct, there are two reconstructed occurrences of the pronoun, both of which would have to be coindexed with *Bill* in order to represent the desired reading. The critical dependency is the one that resolves the second occurrence:

(121) $\langle$(Bill, he), 3, $\langle$NP, VP, C, NP, V, NP$\rangle\rangle$

Since the reconstruction of this pronoun involves alteration of indexical value, its dependency (121) must be an *i*-copy of some other dependency realized by (120). But it is not, as the reader can verify; hence, (120) is ill formed.

Another conceivable interpretation for (111) is the following:

(122) John said that John was crazy before the teacher said that the teacher was crazy, and Bill said that John was crazy before the teacher said that the teacher was crazy

Again it seems to us that this reading is precluded. It would have to be represented as in (123):

(123) *John$_1$ said he$_1^\beta$ was crazy before the teacher$_2$ **said he$_2^\beta$ was crazy,** **and Bill$_3$ said he$_1^\beta$ was crazy before the teacher$_2$ said he$_2^\beta$ was crazy**

Again, the index of the overt pronoun bears a β-occurrence since the reconstructed pronoun in the medial clause is sloppy. The problem is with the reconstructed occurrence of he_1^β in the second conjunct, which is not in a proper dependency. Thus, this representation is precluded, as is a representation of another possible reading:

(124) John said that John was crazy before the teacher said that John was crazy, and Bill said that Bill was crazy before the teacher said that John was crazy

This also does not appear to be a possible construal of (111). Its representation would have to be (125):

(125) *John$_1$ said he$_1^\beta$ was crazy before the teacher$_2$ **said he$_1^\beta$ was crazy, and Bill$_3$ said he$_3^\beta$ was crazy before the teacher$_2$ said he$_1^\beta$ was crazy**

Here the last occurrence of he_1^β also does not occur in any proper dependency. Reflection indicates that no other readings are conceivable.[27]

In discussing examples of this sort, Gawron and Peters (1990a) observe that characterizing the Dahl-type reading is beyond the scope of the analysis proposed by Sag (1976) and Williams (1977). The reason for this is the same one that undermines their account of the initially considered Dahl puzzle cases; that is, since the antecedent predicate is either strict or sloppy itself, each of its copied occurrences must be either strict or sloppy. The modification of this approach that Gawron and Peters supply to account for examples like (111)—their example being (126)—

(126) John revised his paper before the teacher did, and Bill did, too

turns on the observation that there are three options for representing the pronoun in *John revised his paper*. It can be an occurrence either of the variable standing for *John*, or of another variable, or of a constant:[28]

27. Apparently, although no speakers allow (119), for some speakers the readings described by (122) and (124) are marginally available. The reason, we believe, is that these speakers allow a strategy in which they take the third clause in (111) as subordinated as well, and not as coordinated. In that case the β-occurrences that are unresolved in the representations (123) and (125) can be resolved in dependencies whose antecedents are in the initial clause. No such strategy would save (120), however, since in this representation the β-occurrences are resolved within the final clause, and this is so regardless of whether this clause is taken as coordinated or subordinated. (We would like to thank S. Berman and H. Kamp for discussion of this point.)

28. As in footnote 9, we again take Gawron and Peters (1990a:19) up on their invitation to replace the notions of parameters, anchoring, and absorption of Situation Semantics with variables, assignments, and abstraction, respectively. In doing so, we also free ourselves of the (dubious) metaphysics of Situation Semantics, and view the representations garnered as linguistic representations (which apparently Gawron and Peters do not). We also simplify the representations to include only what is essential to matters of strict and sloppy identity.

(127) a. $\lambda x \lambda y(x$ revised y, y a paper by $x)$

   b. $\lambda x(x$ revised y, y a paper by $w)$

   c. $\lambda x(x$ revised y, y a paper by John)

(127a) differs from (127b) and (127c) in that it is a relation, not a property. This is because it brings into play what Gawron and Peters call the Absorption Principle, which mandates the binding of any variable that depends on another abstracted variable (see footnote 9). Thus, in (127a) y depends upon x, the variable that corresponds to the pronoun, and hence it is bound by an abstraction operator. Absorption is not called into play in (127b), however, since w is not abstracted. Nor is it called into play in (127c), since there is a constant, not a variable. The "VP-contents" given in (127) can in turn each serve as an antecedent for an ellipsis, yielding the forms in (128) for *John revised his paper before the teacher did*:

(128) a. $\lambda w[\text{BEFORE } (\lambda x \lambda y(x$ revised y, y a paper by $x))(w)$
      $(\lambda x \lambda y(x$ revised y, y a paper by $x))(\text{the teacher})]$

   b. $\lambda w \lambda y[\text{BEFORE } (\lambda x(x$ revised y, y a paper by $w))(w)$
      $(\lambda x(x$ revised y, y a paper by $w))(\text{the teacher})]$

   c. $\lambda w[\text{BEFORE } (\lambda x(x$ revised y, y a paper by John$))(w)$
      $(\lambda x(x$ revised y, y a paper by John$))(\text{the teacher})]$

Notice that in (128b) there has been a further application of the Absorption Principle, since y is now dependent on w, which has become abstracted in virtue of the composition effected by *before*. In (128c) only y remains free, subject ultimately to existential closure. These three contents, as interpretations of the second ellipsis in (126), will give the following full representations:

(129) a. $\lambda w[\text{BEFORE } (\lambda x \lambda y(x$ revised y, y a paper by $x))(w)$
      $(\lambda x \lambda y(x$ revised y, y a paper by $x))$
      $(\text{the teacher})](\text{John}) \ \&$
      $\lambda w[\text{BEFORE } (\lambda x \lambda y(x$ revised y, y a paper by $x))(w)$
      $(\lambda x \lambda y(x$ revised y, y a paper by $x))$
      $(\text{the teacher})](\text{Bill})$

   b. $\lambda w \lambda y[\text{BEFORE } (\lambda x(x$ revised y, y a paper by $w))(w)$
      $(\lambda x(x$ revised y, y a paper by $w))$
      $(\text{the teacher})](\text{John}) \ \&$
      $\lambda w \lambda y[\text{BEFORE } (\lambda x(x$ revised y, y a paper by $w))(w)$
      $(\lambda x(x$ revised y, y a paper by $w))$
      $(\text{the teacher})](\text{Bill})$

c. $\exists y[\lambda w[\text{BEFORE } (\lambda x(x \text{ revised } y, y \text{ a paper by John}))(w)$
   $(\lambda x(x \text{ revised } y, y \text{ a paper by John}))$
   (the teacher)](John) &
   $\lambda w[\text{BEFORE } (\lambda x(x \text{ revised } y, y \text{ a paper by John}))(w)$
   $(\lambda x(x \text{ revised } y, y \text{ a paper by John}))$
   (the teacher)](Bill)]

These give the three readings: (129a), the across-the-board sloppy, (129b), the mixed sloppy/strict (Dahl-type reading), and (129c), the across-the-board strict.

As Gawron and Peters (1990a:124) themselves observe, there are significant flaws with this account; they point to its inability to account for the anaphora-dependent sentence that introduced the Dahl puzzle. The problem can be seen from (130):

(130) John revised his paper, and Bill should before the teacher does

This sentence is comparable to ones like *Max still loves his mother, but Oscar only did as long as I did* discussed earlier, where the subordinating conjunction follows, rather than precedes, the coordination. Like that sentence, (130) has a Dahl-type reading; it can mean that Bill should revise his own paper before the teacher revises his, that is, Bill's, paper. To obtain this type of reading on Gawron and Peters's assumptions, it would be necessary, as it was for (126), that the overt NP contain a free variable corresponding to the pronoun. Thus, the VP of the first clause of (130) would be (131), parallel to (127b):

(131) $\lambda x(x \text{ revised } y, y \text{ a paper by } w)$

In the derivation of the mixed reading for (126), the variable w comes to be bound under the composition effected by the subordinating element *before*; see (128b). For (130), however, this variable will remain free, since it is outside the scope of *before*. Because in Gawron and Peters's theory such variables are then subject to existential closure, it will not be possible to establish an anaphoric connection with the subject. At best, therefore, (130) will be represented as meaning that John revised someone's paper, it being left open whether it was his paper or not. But this is not an available reading for (130), nor is it the reading we are after, which is unattainable on Gawron and Peters's theory.

To summarize, there are two distinct ways in which the Dahl-type reading can arise, turning on whether conjunction is structurally coordinating or subordinating, that is, on whether there is logical, truth-functional conjunction or the conjunction of sentences describing sequences of temporally, spatially, or causally related events. With coordinating conjunction, because there are distinct dependency domains, to obtain a Dahl-type reading there must be some way of linking to an antecedent in another sentence. This is the function anaphora serves, and if it is absent, no Dahl-type reading is possible. With subordinating conjunction, on the other hand, clauses are bracketed as a single sentence, and there is just one domain of dependency. Exterior linking is unnecessary because the relevant dependencies can be established intrasententially. In the more general context of our understanding of ellipsis, our discussion of the Dahl puzzle and other related curiosities implies that the standard way of looking at the ambiguities of anaphora in ellipsis—the strict/sloppy distinction—is not descriptively adequate, since there is a third type of ambiguity, which is like the strict reading in indexical value, but like the sloppy reading in indexical type. The Dahl-type reading is this third type of reading. Whereas the strict reading has intuitively been thought of as corresponding to a free occurrence of a pronoun (in our parlance, an independent occurrence) and the sloppy reading as corresponding to a bound (to us, dependent) occurrence, we must also countenance a reading that is strict, yet dependent. It is the inability to analytically recognize this three-way distinction, and in particular, the strict, dependent reading, that has undermined other approaches to the many-clauses puzzles.

4.4   Ellipsis and Discourse

Sentences (or, more precisely, phrase markers) may be strung together to form a discourse; a discourse, therefore, is an ordered sequence of sentences. The phrase markers that correspond to *Mary left; Jane came; Sally stayed* can thus form a discourse that is made up of three sentences; it will be a true discourse just in case each of its member sentences is true. Since discourses are finite sets, the truth conditions for a discourse are equivalent to taking the sentences of the discourse as coordinated; the truth conditions for the above discourse are just those of *Mary left and Jane came and Sally stayed.* The phrase markers above can also enter into discourses that are made up of fewer sentences, if, for instance, some of them are joined by means of an appropriate connective. We can therefore also have a discourse consisting of *Mary left* and *Jane came because Sally stayed* in which there are two sentences rather than three. In this case, in one of the sentences of the discourse one phrase marker is subordinated to another. Although the phrase markers that make up the "discourse sentences" in this latter discourse—those that are coordinated as opposed to being subordinated—are made apparent by the subordinating conjunction, there are a range of other factors, some overtly indicated, others not, that determine structural relations in discourse. To take an example, consider (132), noted by Sells (1986). Of interest is that the reconstructed pronoun can be taken as strict, so that the latter clause can mean that the director of each movie thinks that the actress in that movie is the new Monroe:

(132) With each new Hollywood hit, the lead actress thinks she is the new Monroe, and the director does, too

(132) is an example of what has been called "quantificational subordination" (Roberts 1987). What distinguishes it is that the scope of the universal in the preposed phrase covers both clauses, which together form a single discourse sentence. From the point of view of discourse structure, (132) is the same as (133):

(133) With each new Hollywood hit, the lead actress thinks she is the new Monroe because the director does, too

Now it is a central tenet of Dependency Theory that sentences are the domains of indexical dependencies; more precisely, we now take their domain to be discourse sentences. Given this, we can straightforwardly represent the reading of (132) described above by (134):

(134) With each new Hollywood hit, [the lead actress$_1$ thinks she$_1^\beta$ is the new Monroe, and the director **thinks she$_1^\beta$ is the new Monroe**]

Because there is one discourse sentence in this sort of structural context, the reconstructed pronoun can be resolved, without change in the value of its index, back to an antecedent in a nonparallel dependency.[29]

29. We assume, following the discussion in chapter 2, that the pronouns in (134) bear β-occurrences, and not α-occurrences, given markedness considerations for bound variable anaphora. There is a question here whether in quantificational subordination environments, the existence of a dependency is sufficient for bound variable anaphora, since it is insufficient in other contexts that require c-command. The existence of a strict reading in (i) indicates that it is sufficient, since even if the second clause is structurally subordinate to the first, the scope of *the lead actress* will not include the second clause:

(i) With each new Hollywood hit, the producer realizes that the lead actress will think she is the new Monroe, and the director does, too

Sells (1986) proposes that the pronoun in (132) is a sort of E-type pronoun, which is in an anaphoric relation between, rather than within, sentences. Such pronouns pick out sets; but it does not appear to follow from the truth of (132) that any director has more than any one actress in mind. Finally, observe that the quantifier that keys the subordination can do so in terms of its position at LF, since *The lead actress in each new Hollywood movie thinks she is the new Monroe, and the director does, too* has the same sort of reading as (132).

In our discussion of the many-clauses puzzle, we assumed that the sentences were to be understood against a neutral context; for example, in considering *Max saw his mother, Oscar did, too, but Sam didn't*, we assumed that these sentences were just about three people named *Max*, *Oscar*, and *Sam*. It has been observed, in particular by Roberts (1987), that sentences of a discourse are often linked together by a presuppositional structure, a common ground of relevant assumptions, some of which may be explicit, but which more often than not are implicit. Roberts argues that the sentences within the scope of such presuppositions are subordinated within the discourse and form (in our terms) a single discourse sentence.[30] This makes a prediction that in such presuppositional contexts, many-clauses sentences like the one just given will allow a Dahl-type reading. A relevant example is (135), in which the second elided VP can be understood, as predicted, as *... but the coach didn't think Bill should run in the race*:[31]

(135) John thought he should run in the race, Bill did, too, but the coach didn't

The use of a familiar definite expression here indicates that there is a presuppositional basis between the last sentence and the preceding parts of the discourse (see Heim 1982). Thus, we understand this expression as referring to Bill's coach.[32] It now follows that the medial and the final

---

30. We set aside here the issue of how to characterize the effect of such presuppositions on the determination of truth conditions. Here we are instead interested in the consequences of the existence of such presuppositions for structural relations in discourse.

31. Examples of this sort were first brought to our attention by R. Kayne, and subsequently by M. Dalrymple, S. Shieber, and F. Pereira; example (135) is due to M. Rooth.

32. Or perhaps as John and Bill's coach, in which case it is also possible to have a "split" Dahl-type reading: *... but the coach didn't think John and Bill should run in the race*. See discussion of split antecedents and ellipsis in chapter 3. Notice that the facilitating common ground need not have the kind of direct anaphoric characterization found in (135). For example, we find facilitating common ground also in (i), and in (ii):

(i) John thought he should run in the race, Bill did, too, but the opposing team's coach didn't

(ii) John thought he should run in the race, Bill did, too, but Coach Jones didn't

Nevertheless, there is a clear intuitive sense in which the opposing team's coach and Coach Jones are appropriately familiar to the presuppositional basis.

clauses form a discourse sentence, and this will be sufficient to allow for the Dahl-type reading, since (135) can now be represented with the β-occurrence of the reconstructed pronoun resolved in a dependency that has the NP *Bill* as its antecedent. Thus, it will have a representation like that of the cases with subordinating conjunctions considered in section 4.3, as befits its status as involving discourse subordination.

Notice that in contrast to (135) there are cases in which the presuppositional effects on discourse subordination are not to be found. Our initial many-clauses case is one example; (136) is another:

(136) John thought he should run in the race, Bill did, too, but a coach didn't

This example differs from (135) only in the substitution of a novel indefinite expression for the familiar definite; this substitution has the effect of eliminating the Dahl-type reading. The use of the indefinite indicates that there is a lack of presuppositional basis, and hence there are no grounds for the discourse subordination that gives rise to a Dahl-type reading.[33] (137) also lacks this reading:

(137) Max thinks he is strong, Oscar does, too, but the father doesn't

For reasons that are not entirely clear, the definite in this context does not allow for the sort of presuppositional/familiarity reading found in (135); we take it as indicating only that there is one and only one father, and not (or at least not very easily) that he is Oscar's father. Since this case involves not discourse subordination but coordination, the only way to obtain a Dahl-type reading is to substitute a pronoun for the definite:

(138) Max thinks he is strong, Oscar does, too, but his father doesn't

But of course this is our prototypical Dahl puzzle example.

Another sort of discourse subordination is found in (139), brought to our attention by R. Dale:

(139) Max thinks he is strong, Oscar does, too, but Max doesn't

One's initial reaction to this sentence is that the final clause contradicts the first. This will be so presuming that (139) is a many-clauses sentence; taking it as such would mean that it has the representations in (140):

---

33. In construing (136), we must resist the temptation to read *a coach* as *one of the coaches*, since to do so is just to return the familiar definite in another guise, and hence to allow a Dahl-type reading for the reasons just outlined.

(140) a. Max_1 thinks he_1^α is strong, Oscar_2 **thinks he_1^α is strong**, but Max_1
doesn't **think he_1^α is strong**

   b. Max_1 thinks he_1^β is strong, Oscar_2 **thinks he_2^β is strong**, but
Max_1 doesn't **think he_1^β is strong**

As is clear from these representations, a contradiction results regardless of whether the medial clause is understood as strict (140a) or sloppy (140b). Hence, (139) cannot possibly be a true discourse, and consequently, no utterance of (139), under either analysis in (140), could be a felicitous speech act, since it is not possible to speak truthfully: these analyses must violate the Gricean Principle of Quality.

On second thought, however, (139) can be understood in a noncontradictory manner. With the occurrences of *Max* understood as coreferential, it can entail that although Oscar thinks Oscar is strong, Max doesn't think Oscar is strong. That is, this sentence can have a Dahl-type reading, with the elided pronoun in the final clause understood as strict relative to the sloppy construal of the elided pronoun in the medial clause. Now suppose that one were to analyze the conjunction of the second and third clauses as subordinating, rather than coordinating. Then it is possible to comply with the conversational maxim, relative to the representation in (141):

(141) Max_1 thinks he_1^β is strong, [Oscar_2 **thinks he_2^β is strong**, but Max_1
doesn't **think he_2^β is strong**]

This structure has the pattern of indices typical of the subordinated Dahl puzzle examples discussed in section 4.3. Here the reconstructed pronoun in the final clause depends upon the subject of the medial clause. Clearly, there is now no contradiction, and (141) can underlie a felicitous utterance of (139). Notice that if the two occurrences of *Max* are not understood as coreferential in (139), then it allows only the across-the-board readings; the Dahl-type reading is absent. This is because the Principle of Quality will not be contravened, and there is no reason to assume (modulo presuppositional structure) that anything but coordination is involved. Thus, if interlocutors strive to bring their utterances into compliance with conversational maxims, then they will impose a subordinating analysis on (139) so that it can be a usable sentence.

By contrast to (139), observe that a contradiction is inescapable in (142), again taking the occurrences of *Max* as coreferential:

(142) Oscar thinks he is strong, Max does, too, but Max doesn't

Plainly this will be so if we take the conjunction as coordinating, so that it is a many-clauses-type case. However, it will also be so if the conjunction is taken as subordinating, yielding a representation comparable to (141):

(143) $Oscar_1$ thinks he_1^β is strong, [Max_2 **thinks he_2^β is strong**, but Max_2 doesn't **think he_2^β is strong**]

This structure retains the contradiction, regardless of how the conjunction is taken.[34] The contrast between (139) and (142) shows quite clearly that there is a difference between the two types of Dahl puzzle sentences. Where the reading is anaphora-facilitated, the sloppy reading that is picked up as strict can be in any antecedent clause, intersententially. Thus, as discussed earlier, in *Max thinks he is strong, Oscar does, too, but his father doesn't* the antecedent of *his* can be *Max*, with the final clause being strict relative to it. (Since the medial clause is sloppy, the pronoun there must bear a β-occurrence.) Although this type of reading may be somewhat less favored for this example, it is quite easy to obtain for (144), where the second clause is subordinated to the first:

(144) Max thought he was strong before Oscar did, and his father did, too

On the other hand, where the Dahl-type reading results from directly linking a dependency to the antecedent, it can arise only in local, intrasentential contexts. This is because the antecedent must be located within the domain of the dependency, that is, within the discourse sentence. Thus, (142) must be contradictory, since the dependency cannot cross the medial clause to the subject of the initial clause, not being subordinated within the latter. There are, therefore, two types of Dahl puzzle sentences: those whose domain is intersentential, and those whose domain is intrasentential.

Observe that the contrast between (139) and (142) taken as utterances by single speakers is recapitulated when the utterances are spread among speakers in a discourse. Thus, consider the conversations in (145) and (146):

34. In fact, technically this structure cannot be any different, relative to dependencies, than the many-clauses case, since the dependency in which the initial occurrence of *Max* is the antecedent for the second elided pronoun would also have to include the latter occurrence of *Max*. But then the dependency would contain two elements bearing α-occurrences, so that in fact for (143) the dependencies must be limited to the individual clauses.

(145) *Speaker A*: Max thinks that he is strong
    Speaker B: Oscar does, too
    Speaker C: Oh, really. Max doesn't

(146) *Speaker A*: Oscar thinks that he is strong
    Speaker B: Max does, too
    Speaker C: Oh, really. Max doesn't

In (145) a noncontradictory Dahl-type reading is possible; in (146) it is not. This shows that we must have a notion of discourse that is sufficiently general so that it is irrelevant whether utterances come out of a single mouth or out of many. To do so, we must keep distinct issues of the structure of discourse and those of the structure of conversation; one utterance may correspond to many sentences in a discourse, or many utterances may correspond to just one discourse sentence. So, for example, the discourse *Mary left; Jane came; Sally stayed* could enter into a conversation as one, two, or three utterances, which may be spoken by one, two, or three speakers. What a speaker utters, then, may be, and normally will be, just part of a discourse, although from this we should not conclude that the speaker does not represent the entire discourse that has thus far transpired. On the contrary; a discourse may arise for a speaker as a result of his own production, or from a combination of structural representations of his production and perception. Thus, suppose that Speaker A says, "Max thinks he is strong" and Speaker B says, "Oscar does, too." To account for Speaker B's ability to utter "Oscar does, too" with sloppy identity relative to Speaker A's utterance, we must attribute to Speaker B a representation of Speaker A's sentence. In this regard, at the moment of his utterance Speaker B represents (as Speaker A does too after Speaker B's utterance) just what a single speaker who utters *Max thinks he is strong, and Oscar does, too* represents. The difference is that Speaker B does not repeat what Speaker A has said, on pain of redundancy. By extension, in (145) and (146) Speaker C, at the time of utterance, finds himself in exactly the same analytic situation as single speakers of (139) and (142) find themselves. In (145) Speaker C can avoid contradiction by analyzing his contribution to the discourse as subordinate, *in his representation*, to Speaker B's; similarly for Speaker A and Speaker B for their representations. And, Speaker C in (146) utters a contradiction just as much as a speaker of (142); all that differs is that he contradicts someone else rather than himself.

To conclude, in representing a discourse, what a speaker represents is a sequence of phrase markers, which are either coordinated or subordinated, where this structure results in part from structural conditions and in part from various principles of conversation. Those that are coordinated form separate "discourse sentences," and lists of such sentences may form a connected parallel discourse. Those that are subordinated form but one such sentence. We may contrast this notion of discourse as involving relations of linguistic objects with a notion of discourse as a flow of information. On the latter view, the role of language is to contribute to, or modify, this information. Among what can be supplied by an utterance made by someone at some time and place is information about discourse referents, properties and relations that hold of these referents, and their situations and circumstances. But neither sentences nor their utterances themselves form part of the discourse per se; they only serve to specify the information and relate it to its context of use. The considerations of this chapter show this notion of discourse to be problematical, however. If ellipsis is resolved relative to discourse, and a discourse is a flow of information, then ellipsis must be resolved relative to the information—the property—that a verb phrase contributes to the discourse. But as we have shown, notions of identity of properties are insufficient to account for the various eliminative puzzles of ellipsis. Rather, if we are correct, their solution resides in the structure of language, and not of information.

Chapter 5
On Reconstruction

A *reconstruction* is a set of token structures under a syntactic identity condition. When we speak of structures as reconstructions, we mean that they are occurrences in a discourse of a given (sub–)phrase marker over a terminal vocabulary. These occurrences may be one or many, and members of a reconstruction may be overt or not. Typically, the cases we have considered have contained multiple occurrences of verb phrases, some of which have been elided. Although such ellipsis is possible just when there are multiple occurrences in a reconstruction, it is not required; for example, in *Max left, and Oscar left, too* there are two members of the reconstruction of the verb phrase that are overt. Conversely, all occurrences in a reconstruction can be covert, and none overt. Chao (1987) observes that one individual on a precipice could say to another *I will, if you will,* although he could just as well have said *I'll jump, if you will* or *I'll jump, if you'll jump.* From the point of view of the theory of structural representation, these sentences are all the same; they each contain members of a reconstruction of the verb phrase *jump.* The theory encompassing reconstruction does not contain any information about whether its elements are overt; this is a matter immaterial to the theory of structural representation.

In chapters 3 and 4 we have been interested in reconstruction and its relation to ellipsis as it plays a role in characterizing connected parallel discourse. Intuitively, however, the overall analysis of elliptical constructions should be able to specify more information about a sentence such as *Max left, and Oscar did, too* than that it contains a reconstruction in the sense described above. In particular, it should tell us that the overt occurrence of the VP serves as the "antecedent" of the elided one and in some sense identifies the reconstruction. Indeed, most approaches to ellipsis include some form or other of a notion of antecedent of an ellipsis; it has been expressed, for instance, as "deletion under identity" or "copying" into an ellipsis. To be clear on this, our notion of reconstruction does *not* in itself imply any notion of antecedence. Reconstruction, in our terms, is an *identity* condition within the theory of structural representation; it defines what are occurrences of the same phrase marker. In principle, *any* member of a reconstruction can be reduced to inaudibilia; if an utterance has one or more such reductions, then it contains an ellipsis. But, since the members of a reconstruction are related solely in virtue of identity, a symmetrical relation, there can be no dependencies among the occurrences. Therefore, no notion of "antecedent of an ellipsis" can be derived from the theory of structural representation alone. This is not to say, however, that there is no notion of antecedence within a theory of *ellipsis*. On the contrary, an antecedent is apparently necessary for an ellipsis. But this stems, we believe, from the role of ellipsis in the theory of use as a device for the reduction of redundancy. For such reduction to be effective, there must be some token expression with respect to which the elided material would have been redundant. The latter expression is the antecedent of the ellipsis. To be usable for ellipsis, then, a reconstruction must have at least two members (otherwise, there would not be any redundant repetitions); but at least one of its members must not be elided if there is to be redundancy at all. That is, it is a consequence of the conditions on the felicitous utterance of sentences containing ellipsis, and not of the theory of their formal representation, that they have antecedents—as is, ultimately, the issue of which member of a reconstruction can stand as that antecedent. Therefore, the analysis of ellipsis has at least two parts: a structural component, of which reconstruction is the central notion, and a use component, of which antecedence is of primary concern.

That ellipses have antecedents seems plain enough in sentences in which one occurrence of an expression is uttered and the other not. This is the circumstance we find with utterances of *Max left, and Oscar did, too*. The possibility of ellipsis apparently does not depend upon such overt presence, however, as examples like (1) show. Suppose that Max walks into your office and is hesitating about whether to sit down. Then you might say to him:

(1) Please do

(1) is clearly understood with a verb phrase missing; it means, please sit down, and its speaker could just as well have said *Please, do sit down*. But (1) does not appear to have an antecedent; it is the only sentence uttered in the conversation. Thus, such sentences would seem to fly in the face of the claim that there must be an antecedent. But this conclusion is not warranted; all we can conclude is that there need not be an *uttered* anteced-

ent. Therefore, if (1) is to have an antecedent, it must be an unuttered antecedent.

The salient fact about (1) is that its utterance makes sense only if there is a *question* about whether Max should sit down or not. It is this question —*Should I sit down*—that contains the antecedent of the ellipsis. This is so even though this sentence is not uttered in the conversation. Lack of utterance, however, does not bar the speaker or hearer from having a syntactic representation of this question; plainly, utterance is not a prerequisite for linguistic representation. A discourse is a set of linguistic representations (sentences); a conversation, a set of utterances, some of which may have parts elided. Not all of the sentences of a discourse, however, need have corresponding overt utterances in a conversation. (Lack of utterance is not the same thing as ellipsis. An ellipsis is a missing part of an utterance; if there is no utterance, there can be no ellipsis.) Typically, utterances will be made if the speaker believes that the hearer does not represent the corresponding sentence; if the speaker wishes that the hearer represent some sentence, a good way to ensure this result is by making an appropriate utterance. If, however, the speaker believes a sentence is already represented by the hearer, he may refrain from utterance and continue on with the conversation. Thus, the only difference between (1) and (2) is that in the latter both sentences of the discourse have corresponding utterances:

(2) *Question*: Should I sit down
    Answer: Please do

Since this question is represented as part of the discourse, its verb phrase can stand as the antecedent of the elided occurrence in (2). But there seems no reason to think that anything different is going on in (1), especially since the same constraints are obeyed in either sort of conversation. Thus, in the circumstance described for (1), (3) is *not* a possible utterance:

(3) *Please do, too

This sentence is also not possible if the conversation had gone as follows:

(4) *Question*: Should I sit down
    Answer: *Please do, too

To have a proper utterance containing an ellipsis, that ellipsis must have an antecedent. But from this, it does not follow that the antecedent must be uttered as part of a conversation. Nor, from the fact that antecedents do not have to be uttered, does it follow that the antecedent is not represented in the discourse. Rather, the parallel patterns in (3) and (4) show that the antecedent is represented in the discourse whether uttered or not, and that the mode of representation of uttered and unuttered antecedents is the same. The parallel oddness of (3) and the answer in (4) follows because they occur in instances of the same discourse, although the conversational structure is different. Therefore, ellipses must have antecedents, but these antecedents may or may not be overt, depending on conversational context.[1]

These considerations show that determination of elliptical antecedence arises from an interaction between reconstruction in the representation of discourse and the role of ellipsis in conversation. However, ellipsis and reconstruction must be kept conceptually distinct. Although reconstruction is possible without ellipsis, the opposite does not hold; ellipsis requires reconstruction. In saying this, we do not imply that there is a requirement that a single ellipsis correspond to a single reconstruction, although this has been the predominant sort of case we have considered. Rather, it is possible for many ellipses to correspond to one reconstruction (*Max left, Oscar did, too, but Sam didn't*) and for one ellipsis to correspond to many reconstructions—the ellipsis in *Max's mother left, and Oscar's did, too* corresponds to reconstructions of two sub–phrase markers, one nominal, the other verbal. It would make no sense to say that there are two ellipses here as well, since there is no constituency in silence; there is only constituency in the structure that is left unuttered. Notice that the identity of the reconstructions is sufficient to determine what is elided; how the antecedent or elided occurrences are themselves related is immaterial. For example, that together they do not form a constituent in the above example, for which information about dominating constituent structure is needed, does not weigh in the licensing of the ellipsis. How the elided occurrences are structurally related is just a matter of how the overt and covert parts can be exhaustively put together in a well-formed phrase marker. Thus, the answer to "How many reconstructions can a given ellipsis correspond to?" is "As many as the phrase structure of the language allows."

Now consider an elliptical context of the form *NP do* ..., that is, a context of verb phrase ellipsis. How many reconstructions does the phrase

1. In our opinion it would be a mistake to hold that the possibility of ellipsis without an uttered antecedent argues against a structural theory of reconstruction. Any such argument would have to assume (i) that antecedence is part of a structural theory, and (ii) that the antecedent of an ellipsis must be uttered. There seems no reason to accept either of these assumptions, however. For an example of such an argument, see Dalrymple 1991.

structure allow here? Certainly one, but in principle an indefinite number, since there is a way that multiple VP-occurrences can be fit in, namely, by coordinating them. Thus, we can have sentences such as *Max swims and plays tennis, and Oscar does, too*, in which two VPs are conjoined. Here there is one ellipsis—one "string of silence"—but this string of silence corresponds to multiple reconstructions. It might be thought that the ellipsis here is licensed because the pair of antecedent occurrences themselves form a VP-constituent, and this is what is reconstructed. Such coordinating VPs, however, cannot in and of themselves be reconstructions. Reconstructions are defined over terminal vocabulary; but coordinating VPs are not associated with terminal vocabulary of their own, instead being associated with such vocabulary only through the lexical contents of the VPs they coordinate, and that of the coordinating element. Hence, reconstruction of a coordinating VP amounts to just reconstructions of its constituent parts. That they form a constituent, which can only be determined by reference to higher constituent relations, is no more or less germane for licensing ellipsis than that the reconstructions do not form a constituent in *Max's mother left, and Oscar's did, too*. This is instead an artifact of the particular example; indeed, since this sort of structural information is irrelevant to ellipsis of multiple reconstructions, there is nothing that requires that for ellipsis the antecedent and elided occurrences must be related in the same way. Thus, we also find examples like (5):[2]

(5) I did everything that Mary did. Mary swam the English Channel, and Mary climbed Kilimanjaro, and I did, too

In this sentence, what is elided are occurrences of the VPs *swim the English Channel* and *climb Kilimanjaro* (and an occurrence of the conjunction *and*). This is all we need to know to "recover" the ellipsis—that is, that the final clause is *I swam the English Channel and climbed Kilimanjaro*. That the elided occurrences must be conjoined in the representation of (5) just follows from the way they can "fit" into its structure. Again, it doesn't

2. It is a common misconception that examples like (5) are problematic for a structural theory of reconstruction because there is no single constituent composed of the two antecedent VPs; in a recent instance, Hardt (1992) claims that because of this such cases are "clearly beyond the scope of syntactic theories" (p. 12). However, independently of any actual theory of reconstruction, it is merely stipulation to require that the antecedents must make up a constituent. Indeed, if we are correct, ellipsis of a conjoined VP never involves a single syntactic object, but rather a multiplicity of such objects.

matter how the antecedent phrases are related for the licensing of the ellipsis. Whereas in this case the antecedent occurrences do not make up a constituent but the elided ones do, note that we also find the inverse, in which the antecedent occurrences are conjoined but the elided ones are not:[3]

(6) Connors and McEnroe can win the U.S. Open and win Wimbledon, respectively. I predict that Connors will, but that McEnroe won't

From the standpoint of reconstruction, there is no difference between (5) and (6), since reconstruction is a symmetrical notion, a condition on syntactic identity.[4]

Examples like (5) were first observed by Webber (1978). In essence, she proposes that if properties P and Q are predicated of instances of the same argument, then it is possible to form the conjoined property P & Q predicated of that argument. This combined property will then underlie the ellipsis. However, this analysis is falsified by examples such as (7), a variation of (5) in which the antecedent VPs have different, rather than the same, subjects:

(7) I did everything that Mary and Jane did. Mary swam the English Channel, and Jane climbed Kilimanjaro, and I did, too

3. A variation of (6) brings up an interesting matter:

(i) Connors and McEnroe can win the U.S. Open and win Wimbledon, respectively. I predict that one of them will, and that the other won't

The prediction being made here is that either Connors will win the U.S. Open and McEnroe will not win Wimbledon, or McEnroe will win Wimbledon and Connors will not win the U.S. Open. That is, the ellipses here correspond, so to speak, to two simultaneous reconstructions of the verb phrases, as a function of which of Connors and McEnroe is the one, and which is the other. (A similar example is observed by Webber (1978), but to different ends; see discussion immediately below.)

4. That there is reconstruction of conjuncts leads us to expect that where conjoined verb phrases occur, not all of them need be reconstructed. Examples like (i), in which the ellipsis can be understood as just *happily married*, attest to this possibility:

(i) John plays chess and is happily married, but Bill isn't

(ii), however, is not possible:

(ii) *John plays chess and swims, but Bill plays checkers and

The ill-formedness of (ii) stems, we believe, from the requirement mentioned in chapter 3 that the elided phrase must be properly governed by Infl; thus, if there were to be an ellipsis, it would have to encompass an entire conjoined VP.

In this example, as in (5), the elided elements are understood to be *swim the English Channel* and *climb Kilimanjaro*, as is also the case if we substitute plural subjects of the ellipses for the singulars in (5) and (7):

(8) a. You and I did everything that Mary did. Mary swam the English Channel, and Mary climbed Kilimanjaro, and you and I did, too

   b. You and I did everything that Mary and Jane did. Mary swam the English Channel, and Jane climbed Kilimanjaro, and you and I did, too

The last example is comparable in relevant respects to a sort also discussed by Webber (1978):[5]

---

5. In the context of split antecedent ellipsis like (8) and (9), issues can be raised about the relationship of the plural subjects to the conjoined elided verb phrases. For example, although (8a) and (8b) are perhaps most naturally read as saying that you and I can both swim the English Channel and climb Kilimanjaro, they also allow a "respectively" reading in which you do the former and I do the latter. However, this ambiguity is independent of matters of the relation between ellipsis and reconstruction, since it is also found in (i), for instance:

(i) You and I did everything that Mary and Jane did. Mary swam the English Channel, and Jane climbed Kilimanjaro, and you and I swam the English Channel and climbed Kilimanjaro, too

Here too a "collective" reading is favored, but a "respectively" reading is possible. Interestingly, if we alter (8b) by overtly putting in the word *respectively* a "collective" reading is still possible:

(ii) You and I did everything that Mary and Jane did. Mary swam the English Channel, and Jane climbed Kilimanjaro, respectively, and you and I did, too

Of course, this reading is eliminated if *respectively* is placed before the final clause. In contrast to (8), (9) favors a "respectively" reading, but again this is true if we lexicalize the ellipsis:

(iii) Sally wants to sail around the world, and Barbara wants to fly to South America, and they will sail around the world and fly to South America, if money is available

This sort of reading is found in this context even if there are no reconstructions, as in (iv):

(iv) Sally wants to sail around the world, and Barbara wants to fly to South America, but they will visit San Francisco and climb Mt. Everest, instead

Although the "respectively" reading is clearly favored in these cases, the "collective" reading is by no means excluded, as shown by (v):

(v) Sally wants to sail around the world, and Barbara wants to fly to South America, and together they will, if money is available

Lexicalization of this case again makes no difference in how the conjoined VPs are related to the plural subject NP.

(9) Sally wants to sail around the world, and Barbara wants to fly to
     South America, and they will, if money is available

As Webber herself notes, this sort of example does not fall under her
analysis, since the antecedent VPs have different subjects. She thus argues
that examples like (9) show that ellipsis can be licensed by an inferential
process. The analysis, she proposes, proceeds from taking (9) under the
following paraphrase:

(10) What Sally wants to do is to sail around the world, and what
      Barbara wants to do is to fly to South America, and Sally and
      Barbara will, if money is available

From (10) we can infer (11):

(11) Sally wants to do what she wants to do, and Barbara wants to do
      what she wants to do, and Sally and Barbara will, if money is
      available

Now we have the single VP *do what she wants to do*, which can serve as the
antecedent of the ellipsis in (9).[6] This analysis cannot be right, however, as
shown by (12):

(12) Sally thought she would sail around the world, and Barbara
      decided that she would fly to South America, and Sally and
      Barbara will, if money is available

By the route we have followed for (9) we can infer (13), comparable to (11):

(13) Sally thought she would do what she thought she would do, and
      Barbara decided to do what she decided to do, and Sally and
      Barbara will, if money is available

But by this inferential route we cannot recover from (13) any single verb
phrase as the antecedent of the ellipsis. Yet the ellipsis in (12) is perfectly
acceptable, on a par with (9).

The point we wish to emphasize is that there is no reason to think that
ellipsis with "split" antecedents involves any additional mechanisms, or is
inherently any more or less restricted, than ellipsis with single antecedents,
given the existence of conjunction in the language. Although there are no

---

6. Concerning these examples, Dalrymple, Shieber, and Pereira (1991) state that
"Recovery of the pertinent properties ... requires non-linguistic knowledge concerning social norms and economic processes" (p. 442). We are far from sure what
to make of this comment for the analysis of cases of this sort.

further matters of principle that arise in the licensing of ellipsis with many reconstructions rather than one, the multiple case does shed some light on restrictions on the relation between antecedent and ellipsis that are masked in the simpler case. Since the multiple case involves reconstructions of some number of phrases, it might be thought that the antecedent occurrences of these parts might be scattered around the sentences of the discourse, so that split elliptical antecedents could be plucked from anywhere in the discourse. The positions of the antecedents appear to be more narrowly constrained than this, however. To see the nature of the constraint involved, consider the sentence pairs in (14):

(14) a. I play tennis and I swim

     b. I play tennis and you swim

Given no indication to the contrary, our inclination is to construe these cases as being lists of sentences, of the sort that can stand as answers to questions. Thus, (14a) and (14b) can be taken to answer the complex question *Who plays tennis and who swims* (14a) can also be taken as an answer to another question, namely, *Who (both) plays tennis and swims*, as can *I play tennis and swim*; (14b), however, cannot be taken as an answer to this question. Being able to stand as an answer to a singular question, there is a sense in which (14a) can be taken as a single sentence— a single discourse sentence, as defined in chapter 3. (14b), on the other hand, can only be taken as a list of two sentences, which can stand as an answer to a complex question. Now consider what happens when we append to (14a–b) a third clause that contains an ellipsis:

(15) a. I play tennis and I swim, and Max does, too

     b. I play tennis and you swim, and Max does, too

Although a split elliptical reading is possible for (15a)—Max plays tennis and swims—it is precluded for (15b), which is ambiguous between readings on which either Max swims or Max plays tennis. The reason for this can now be stated as follows: the antecedents of an ellipsis must be drawn from a single discourse sentence. The ellipsis in (15a) meets this constraint, but the one in (15b) does not, because here the antecedents occur in distinct sentences of a list. The sentences in (5), (7), and (8) also meet this constraint because they are placed in the context of preambles that establish a presuppositional basis for linking the next two clauses together as a discourse sentence, rather than as two members of a list of sentences. (See discussion in chapter 4.) Compare in this regard (7) and (15b). In both of these the antecedent VPs have different subjects; yet a conjoined reconstruction is possible for the former, since there are grounds for grouping the clauses containing those antecedents as a single discourse sentence.[7] Consideration of split elliptical antecedents, then, demonstrates something about the discourse relations of the occurrences of reconstructions. So long as all the reconstructive parts of an ellipsis have their antecedents in a discourse sentence, it doesn't matter how they are organized in order for the identity conditions governing ellipsis—that is, reconstruction —to be properly satisfied.

Turning away from our concerns with relations in ellipsis between antecedent and elided occurrences of reconstructions, let us return to exploring the identity conditions that constitute reconstruction. As we understand it, a reconstruction is a set of occurrences of a structure, defined over a given terminal vocabulary. This means that the occurrences must be of the same formal structure—modulo the tolerance of variance in indexical value allowed for β-occurrences—and have the same terminal vocabulary. Thus, although *fly an airplane* and *drive a car* are phrases of the same categorial structure, they are not reconstructions, since they contain different terminal vocabulary. Neither, for that matter, are *see Max* and *see Oscar*, or *see the guy that Max knows* and *see the guy that*

---

7. As a general rule, the discourse sentence is also the domain from which the elided coordinating element is drawn. In a case of disjunction, for instance, *or* is reconstructed:

(i) What an inconvenience. Whenever Max uses the fax or Oscar uses the Xerox, I can't

That is, I can't use the fax or use the Xerox. Similarly for other sorts of connectives; for instance, in *I can drink Scotch, and then I can drink beer, but you can't* the whole temporal connective must be reconstructed. Notice that the final clause in (i), the one containing the ellipsis, is understood as *I can't use the fax or I can't use the Xerox*, with the negation, so to speak, spread across the disjunction. If the negation were instead taken as having scope over the entire disjunction, then this clause would be equivalent to *I can't use the fax and I can't use the Xerox*, so that the wrong truth conditions would result. This is so regardless of whether there is ellipsis or not; the same interpretation is found if *I can't use the fax or use the Xerox* is lexically realized in this context. (Parallel comments hold for interactions between conjunctions and negation.) At issue here, therefore, are matters pertaining to the relations between subsentential connectives and other logical operators— such as how to ensure that *Mary and possibly Jane will climb Mt. Everest* comes out to mean *Mary will climb Mt. Everest and possibly Jane will climb Mt. Everest*. Though of significant interest, we set these matters aside, since they are independent of our concerns with ellipsis and reconstruction. (We would like to thank R. Oehrle and R. Larson for bringing these matters to our attention.)

Oscar knows, which differ in the terminal vocabulary of NPs they contain. Nor is *see him*$^\alpha$ identical to *see him*$^\beta$. In this last case the terminals are the same, but they bear different indexical types, and this is sufficient to differentiate them even if they have the same indexical value. Let us identify those NPs that bear indexical occurrences as *arguments*. Reconstruction requires that each token structure in the set have the same set of arguments. Nonarguments, and nonargument parts of NPs, are a different matter, as we will discuss presently.

Consider the sentence in (16), of a sort initially observed by Sag (1976); additional examples from texts are cited by Dalrymple, Shieber, and Pereira (1991):[8]

(16) This law restricting free speech should be repealed by Congress, but I can assure you that it won't

As can be readily determined from the verbal inflection, the elided material here consists of an active verb plus its object argument, so that (16) has the structure in (17):

(17) This law restricting free speech$^\alpha_1$ should be repealed e_1 by Congress, but I can assure you that it won't **repeal this law restricting free speech$^\alpha_1$**

The question arises, Does this structure contain an antecedent occurrence of the elided material, that is, of *repeal this law restricting free speech*? Although with respect to the verb the answer seems straightforwardly affirmative, it is perhaps not so clear with respect to the verb's argument. This is because the putative antecedent VP contains a trace, and not an occurrence of *this law restricting free speech*. The question we are concerned with thus amounts to an inquiry into the status of NP-trace—in particular, whether it can count as an antecedent of the argument of the elided VP.

Arguments, as we understand them, are composite elements. They consist of two parts, neither of which in and of itself constitutes an argument: an argument expression and an argument position. The proper realization of these argument parts as arguments in syntactic structures is the province of θ-theory. Now although an argument expression may occur in an argument position in a structure, this is not necessary; the parts may also

8. Although some speakers find sentences like *Max hit Oscar, but Sam wasn't* readily acceptable, bear in mind that the naturalness of such examples depends upon the appropriateness of switching voice in mid-discourse.

be spread out in a structure. In the latter case we say that the structure contains an *argument chain*. Such argument chains are typically found in raising and passive constructions. Thus, the coindexing of *this law restricting free speech* and the trace in the first clause of (17) indicates an argument chain; observe that such chains, being single arguments, are marked with but a single indexical type.[9] With this in mind, let us ask whether the antecedent verb phrase in (17) has the same argument structure as the elided verb phrase. The answer is clearly yes. Although the two clauses differ by the presence versus the absence of an argument chain, the two verb phrases still count as reconstructions since they are each occurrences of the verb plus the argument. Thus, if we take reconstruction to be sensitive to arguments, then (17) is well formed and allows for ellipsis.

Notice that the mirror image sentence of (16), in the sense that it contains an active antecedent and a passive ellipsis, is also possible:

(18) Congress repealed this law restricting free speech, but I can assure you that this other one won't be

The structure of (18) is (19):

(19) Congress repealed this law restricting free speech$_1^\alpha$, but I can assure you that this other one$_2^\alpha$ won't be **repealed** e_2

By the line of analysis given for (17), (19) should not be well formed, since the elided argument is not the same as that of the antecedent, in virtue of their indices. However, there is another way we could view NP-trace other than as an argument, as in (17)—namely, as just part of an argument. If we take it this way, then what is its status in reconstruction? The answer is that it has no status at all, since reconstruction, by hypothesis, is defined only with respect to arguments. But if the trace is immaterial to reconstruction, then the ellipsis need contain an antecedent only for the verb, not the verb phrase. Since what licenses the ellipsis is V-reconstruction, not VP-reconstruction, that the overt VP contains an argument is irrelevant, just as it is irrelevant if it contains an NP-trace that is in a distinct argument chain:

---

9. The coindexing in (17) indicates not that two distinct arguments are covalued, in which case each indexical occurrence would bear an indexical type, but rather that there is just one argument. Although Binding Theory is arguably sensitive to patterns of indexing among argument parts in a chain, as well as among arguments, Dependency Theory is irrelevant to the internal structure of arguments. Rather, its domain is the possible indexical relations among coindexed arguments only.

(20) This law restricting free speech was repealed, and this other one
      was, too

In a sense, what we are saying then is that ellipsis with respect to (19) is
akin not to cases in which an argument within the VP is reconstructed, but
to cases such as *John left, and Bill did, too*, where nothing but the verb
within the VP is relevant to the reconstruction. Indeed, it is possible for
intransitive and passive verbs to be reconstructions, as examples like (21),
of a sort due to Sag (1976), illustrate:

(21) It should be noted, as Max did, that Fermat's last theorem has not
      yet been proven

Even though (19) involves only verbal reconstruction, the structure of
the second clause will consist of a VP containing a verb and a trace, since
this structure is necessitated by general grammatical principles governing
verbal selection, thematic structure, and categorial projection. But since
it is only the verb that is phonologically missing in such examples, V-
reconstruction will be sufficient to license the ellipsis; the presence of the
trace, although significant to the overall well-formedness of the structure,
is not a function of reconstruction and hence it plays no role in the
licensing of ellipsis. This sort of reconstruction will be severely limited in
its scope, since like any other reconstruction it is defined only with respect
to identity of terminal vocabulary. But the only way a sentence can have
occurrences of the same verb but not of the same verb phrase is by
containing an active/passive pair (or more generally, morphologically
related forms with the same effect on argument structure found with
active/passive).[10]

---

10. Active/passive reconstruction pairs raise certain issues concerning what counts
as morphological nondistinctness. Sentences such as (16) indicate that the passive
morphology can be ignored, and the elided verb taken in its active form. But notice
the contrast in (i):

(i) a. This law restricting free speech should be repealed by Congress, but I can
       assure you that it hasn't yet
    b. This law restricting free speech should be repealed by Congress, but I can
       assure you that it isn't yet

In these sentences the reference of the pronoun *it* differs; in (ia) it refers to
Congress, and in (ib) to the law. This correlates with a difference in construal for
the ellipsis, the former being an active reconstruction, the latter a passive. The
reason for this appears to be that although in (ia) the reconstructed verb can be
taken as bearing perfect inflection, it is not possible to take the verb with progres-

Noun phrases that can stand as arguments are commonly classified with respect to their inherent anaphoric nature. In the standard view, for instance, the typology is projected from the features [±anaphor] and [±pronoun], giving four categories of nominal expressions (see Chomsky 1981). In chapter 2 we suggested a somewhat different conception of nominal categorization, which we gave as follows:

$$NP^\alpha_{[-\text{pronoun}]} \qquad NP^\beta_{[-\text{pronoun}]}$$
$$NP^\alpha_{[+\text{pronoun}]} \qquad NP^\beta_{[+\text{pronoun}]}$$

In our typology, there is only one inherent anaphoric feature, [±pronoun], the matrix being filled out by the distinction in indexical type. Now, in the standard classification, reflexive pronouns occupy the corner of the matrix characterized by [+anaphor, −pronoun]. In ours, reflexives are the odd man out, if we take them as atomic elements. Since this typology includes no feature [±anaphor], there is nothing to distinguish them as a basic nominal type. Morphologically, however, reflexive pronouns appear not to be atomic elements at all, but rather to be composed of two parts: a pronoun and the grammatical formative *self*. Suppose that looks are not deceiving here.[11] Then reflexives are anchored into the nominal typology through their pronominal parts, so that with respect to the typology, pronouns and reflexives are nondistinct. The pronominals are the argument parts of the reflexive and play the same semantic roles as they do when they appear without *self*: they are what bear the indexical occurrences and hence can refer or be bound. Hence, what holds for the semantics of pronouns bearing α- or β-occurrences holds mutatis mutandis for reflexives bearing such occurrences (see chapter 2). The grammatical formative *self*, on the other hand, has only a syntactic status. Its role is to

---

sive inflection in (iib). Hence, the latter verb can only be taken as a passive. A comparable circumstance can be observed with a passive reconstruction of an active, as shown by the contrast in (ii):

(ii) a. John fired Max, although it was Bill who should have been

    b. John was firing Max, although it was Bill who should have been

(iib) can only be understood as a strict ellipsis of *firing Max*; this is so even though the overt parts of the right-hand clauses are the same. Thus, it appears that part of the reason that passive reconstructions are possible is based on the phonological nondistinctness of the past tense and passive participle in these cases. *John saw Max, but it was Bill who should have been* is therefore less grammatical than (iia).

11. This suggestion has been put forth in a number of places. See for instance Pica 1985, 1987 and various contributions in Koster and Reuland 1991.

trigger Principle A of Binding Theory, that is, the grammatical requirement that the element to which it is attached must be bound (in an appropriately local domain). Thus, a reflexive pronoun has the structure in (22):

(22) $[_{NP}[\text{pronoun}_i^{\alpha/\beta}] \text{ self}]$

On the system we envisage, grammatically unmarked elements of the typology only have free occurrences. The value of the feature [±pronoun] indicates whether they are to be free in a domain or not, that is, whether they are subject to Principle B or Principle C. Attachment of the grammatical marker *self* to a [+pronoun] element adds a binding requirement while retaining the domain requirement accruing to that feature value; hence, reflexives are subject to Principle A.[12]

Reconstruction of nominals, we have proposed, is sensitive to identity of arguments. Thus, to have a reconstruction of (22) all that is required is recapitulation of the argument part of the overall expression. Thus, not only could another occurrence of a type-identical reflexive pronoun be a reconstruction, so could a type-identical *pronoun*. Pairs of the form shown in (23) are reconstructions, then, if their pronominal parts are themselves reconstructions:

(23) $[_{NP}[_{NP} \text{ him}] \text{ self}]$ – $[_{NP} \text{ him}]$

For reconstruction, these expressions are nondistinct—they are the same argument. Hence, any difference in their terminal vocabulary is irrelevant. Therefore, the structure of reflexives allows two possibilities for their reconstruction: either with or without *self*.

---

12. We leave open here various issues that the interaction of Dependency Theory and Binding Theory raises for bound anaphors. These include more precise proposals regarding the indexing of reflexives—for instance, whether the index borne by the argument part percolates to the entire reflexive NP—as well as foundational questions pertaining to just why pronouns within reflexives must be locally bound. Besides the general ideas in the text, there are a number of other possibilities that could be explored. For instance, it could be maintained that *self* is the head of the NP, the pronoun occupying some other position within the phrase. Then, the containing NP would be its governing category, and it could be bound by the subject. Another possibility is that *self* is an "argument-identifier" operating on the predicate, inducing coindexing of coarguments. The latter approach is explored in Reinhart and Reuland 1993; see also Szabolcsi 1990. Working out the implications of either of these views would take us beyond the bounds of the present study, especially as it interacts with the treatment of long-distance anaphora and logophoricity. Either, however, could be compatible with the analysis in the text.

That reflexive and personal pronouns can be reconstructions is seen from (24), which can have a reading under which the ellipsis is understood as ... *believes John to be heroic*:

(24) John believes himself to be heroic, and he said that Mary does, too

Now suppose that *John* and *he* are coindexed, and that we have reconstruction of a reflexive pronoun, as shown in (25):

(25) *John$_1$ believes him$_1$ + self to be heroic, and he$_1$ said that Mary **believes him$_1$ + self to be heroic**

This structure violates Principle A, since the reconstructed reflexive is not locally bound. If, on the other hand, just the pronominal part of the reflexive is reconstructed, the result is (26):

(26) John$_1$ believes him$_1$ + self to be heroic, and he$_1$ said that Mary **believes him$_1$ to be heroic**

This structure does conform to Binding Theory, the relevant condition in this case being Principle B, and it therefore represents the strict reflexive reading of (24).

The significance of the distinction in the reconstruction of reflexive pronouns is further displayed by (27):

(27) Max hit himself before Oscar did

What is of interest about this example is that it is ambiguous; not only can it have a sloppy reading (28a), but it can also have a strict reading (28b):

(28) a. Max hit himself before Oscar hit himself

   b. Max hit himself before Oscar hit him

To see how this strict/sloppy ambiguity arises from the possibilities of reconstruction, consider the structures in (29). In (29a) the entire reflexive pronoun is represented; in (29b), just its pronominal argument part:

(29) a. Max$_1$ hit him$_1^\beta$ + self before Oscar$_2$ **hit him$_2^\beta$ + self**

   b. Max$_1$ hit him$_1^\beta$ + self before Oscar$_2$ **hit him$_1^\beta$**

Both of these structures are well formed, the elided VPs being proper occurrences of reconstructions. In (29a) the presence of *self* mandates that the pronoun be locally bound, and indeed it is. In (29b), on the other hand, since here there is no occurrence of *self*, the relevant principle of Binding Theory is not Principle A, but Principle B, which is clearly satisfied here, since the pronoun is locally free. Notice that in the representations in (29) the pronouns are taken to bear β-occurrences. In (29a), which represents the sloppy reading, the β-occurrences borne by the pronouns are of different indexical values, but as required by Dependency Theory they are resolved in dependencies that are i-copies. In (29b), which represents the strict reading, the β-occurrences bear the same value; but since this is a subordination context, the reconstructed occurrence can be resolved in a dependency of which the NP *Max* is the antecedent. (Although Binding Theory allows this pronoun to bear some other indexical value, if it did, there would be an unresolved β-occurrence.) Because of the intersecting demands of Binding Theory and Dependency Theory, therefore, these are the only representations possible.

Our observations show that with respect to reconstruction, reflexive pronouns are treated in precisely the same way as personal pronouns. From this perspective, there is no difference in the treatment of *Max hit himself before Oscar did* and *Max hit his lawyer before Oscar did*. This analytic parallelism leads us to expect that in addition to strict reflexives that turn on dependent β-occurrences of indices, there can also be strict reflexives that turn on independent α-occurrences. (30) is an example of the latter sort:[13]

(30) Bush voted for himself, but Barbara didn't

(30) can be understood with a strict reflexive reading, so that the second clause means that Barbara didn't vote for Bush. Like any other pronouns, the pronouns here can bear α-occurrences, allowing for the representation in (31):

(31) Bush$_1$ voted for him$_1^{\alpha}$ + self, but Barbara$_2$ didn't **vote for him$_1^{\alpha}$**

In this structure, too, the VPs are reconstructions, and this represents the strict reflexive reading.

We can now classify reflexive pronouns just like personal pronouns into two sorts: those bearing α-occurrences and those bearing β-occurrences. There exist both "α-reflexives" and "β-reflexives." That there are reflexives of both types can be seen from the following. Consider the question *Who saw himself*. The sentences *Max saw himself, Oscar saw himself, Sam saw himself* can be a list of answers to this question, the pronoun in each case being construed as sloppy. Comparably, *Max saw Harry, Oscar saw Harry, Sam saw Harry* can be a list of "strict" answers to *Who saw Harry*.

---

13. Examples like (30) derive from Dahl 1973, which is, to our knowledge, the first place where the strict reflexive phenomenon is observed. Subordination cases like (27) are to be found in Sag 1976.

Now suppose that Harry is among those who saw Harry. Then this list could perfectly well be extended with *Harry saw himself* as an answer. Given that the question this sentence is answering is of the form *Who saw NP^α*, its direct answers must preserve this indexical type. Hence, in this context, we have a reflexive pronoun that bears an α-occurrence, whereas in the context of the former question, the reflexives bear β-occurrences.

In this light, consider (32) as an answer to the question *Who slashed the samurai.*

(32) The samurai must have slashed himself. Clearly, the shogun
couldn't have

In (32) a strict interpretation is clearly available; the shogun couldn't have slashed the samurai. Given the structure of questions and answers, and that β-occurrences cannot be resolved in prior sentences, it follows that the reflexive must bear an α-occurrence.[14] (32) will then have the structure (33):

(33) The samurai$_1$ must have slashed him$^\alpha_1$ + self. Clearly, the shogun$_2$
couldn't have **slashed him$^\alpha_1$**

The existence of what we have identified as α-reflexives is further discernible in examples like *Yeats disliked hearing himself read in an English accent*, pointed out by Nunberg (1978). Note the availability of a strict reflexive reading in the following:

(34) Yeats disliked hearing himself read in an English accent, and I did,
too

α-reflexives are also to be found in nonelliptical contexts, so that the same kind of strict reading is observed in the "strict inference" (35), which is valid, taking *her* as referring to Jane:

(35) Jane believes herself to have solved Fermat's last theorem
Mary believes whatever Jane believes
Therefore, Mary believes her to have solved Fermat's last theorem

Speakers for whom this inference holds also find that the second clause in (36) can be understood as meaning that Max believes John is heroic:

14. When α-reflexives are forced in the context of answers to questions, they are most comfortably accompanied by primary stress. This is unlike β-reflexives, which are typically downstressed, as well as occurrences of α-reflexives that are not forced by discourse structure; for the latter, see discussion below of α-reflexives in intensional contexts.

(36) John believes himself to be heroic, and Max does, too

Thus, both the conclusion of (35) and the ellipsis of (36) contain strict reflexives, that is, the reconstruction of the pronominal part of an α-reflexive.

The well-formedness of the reconstruction of pronouns in reflexive expressions either with or without *self* is a result of interactions between Binding Theory and Dependency Theory with reconstruction. These interactions can be seen from comparing the well-formed (31), in which the pronouns bear α-occurrences, with the ill-formed (37):

(37) *Bush$_1$ voted for him$_1^\alpha$ + self, but Barbara$_2$ didn't **vote for him$_1^\alpha$ + self**

This is because the presence of *self* requires local binding, but conditions on the reconstruction of indexical type prevent this. A structure just like (37), except with β-occurrences, is well formed, representing a sloppy reading:

(38) Bush$_1$ voted for him$_1^\beta$ + self, but Barbara$_2$ didn't **vote for her$_2^\beta$ + self**

This is to be contrasted with (39), where the reconstruction is just a pronoun:

(39) *Bush$_1$ voted for him$_1^\beta$ + self, but Barbara$_2$ didn't **vote for her$_2^\beta$**

This structure is ill formed, although it is consistent with Dependency Theory. It violates Principle B of Binding Theory; compare this to the situation in (26), which satisfies this principle. Note that leaving the index of the reconstructed pronoun unchanged would not help matters, since it would then not bear a resolvable index. Thus, in this sort of coordinate context, if an α-occurrence of a reflexive is reconstructed, *self* cannot be present in the ellipsis, but if a β-occurrence is reconstructed, *self* must be present.

The distribution of strict reflexives depends upon whether their pronominal parts are α- or β-occurrences. The distribution of strict reflexives with β-occurrences is limited to those contexts in which such occurrences can occur strict, that is, without change of indexical value relative to their antecedents, and it is a productive construction in those domains. Among these are subordinating contexts, and in such contexts the antecedent of the dependencies can be either referring expressions, as in the cases we have observed, or quantifiers:

(40) Every man mentioned himself before Mary did

(This example is drawn from Gawron and Peters 1990a.) (40) contrasts with (41), in which there is a coordinating context:

(41) Every man voted for himself, and Barbara did, too

At best, the second clause here can be understood as *Barbara voted for herself*. In (40) the reflexive bears a β-occurrence; given the subordination, the reconstructed occurrence can be in a dependency with the trace of the quantifier as the antecedent. No comparable dependency is possible in (41). Strict reflexives also can be found in more complex subordination contexts:

(42) John shaved himself, but Bill didn't because the barber does

This can clearly entail that Bill didn't shave himself because the barber shaves him (Bill). The analysis of this case is just the same as that of the Dahl-type sentences with pronouns that we discussed in chapter 4. Sloppy identity is possible for the first elision because there are parallel dependencies. Strict identity is then possible for the second elision because the reconstructed pronominal part of the reflexive can be in a dependency that reaches back to the subject of the medial clause, in virtue of the subordination. Similarly, (43) also displays the Dahl-type reading:

(43) Max believes himself to be smart, Oscar does, too, but his mother
     doesn't

Here the final clause is coordinated, not subordinated, but as we have shown, this is a context that permits strict β-occurrences licensed by the indexing of the genitive pronoun. On the other hand, in simple coordinations, that is, ones without an anaphoric bridge as in (43), strict reflexive readings cannot arise with β-occurrences; instead, strict reflexives in such contexts can only arise with α-occurrences.[15]

It is quite apparent, however, that compared to subordination contexts, coordination contexts are not fully productive for strict reflexives. Thus, there is a common intuition that in a simple sentence like *Max hit himself, and Oscar did, too* the sloppy reading is dominant over the strict reading, as opposed to *Max hit himself before Oscar did*, which allows both readings equally well. This contrast indicates that in neutral contexts a β-reflexive is favored over an α-reflexive, the strict reading of the latter

---

15. That strict reflexives are productively available in subordination contexts is independently observed by Hestvik (1992). We are grateful to A. Hestvik for much helpful discussion of strict reflexive phenomena.

sentence being a reflection of reconstruction of a β-reflexive as described in the previous paragraph. The question that arises for the distribution of strict reflexives is, then, Under what circumstances are α- or β-reflexives preferred relative to one another?[16]

To answer this question, let us suppose, uncontroversially, that speakers will normally use sentences that express their communicative intentions in the maximally determinate and minimally redundant way, given a discourse context. For instance, consider the context of direct answers to *wh*-questions. In answering *Who hit Oscar*, one can reply, *Oscar hit himself*; but given the constraints on the form of answers, the only option for the reflexive is to bear an α-occurrence. The pronominal part of this reflexive can be reconstructed strictly, so that *Oscar hit himself, I didn't* can stand as a list of answers to the question. Use of an α-reflexive here would obviously satisfy the determinacy and redundancy conditions, since a β-reflexive is incompatible with the discourse context. Notice that the use of α-reflexives in this sort of question-answer context is a function of how sentences are related in discourse as questions and answers, and will be required regardless of the verb involved. There are other cases, however, in which the status of α-reflexives turns on the nature of the verb itself, independently of its sentential surrounds. For example, consider (44):

(44) Aaron Burr defended himself, and Luther Martin did, too

The verb *defend* is ambiguous between senses of physical and legal defense. How we understand (44) depends on which sense we take. If the first clause of (44) depicts Aaron Burr defending himself from a mugging, the elided reflexive is most naturally understood as sloppy. On the other hand, if

---

16. Notice that (i), even though a conjunction, can have a strict reading, although it cannot contain an α-reflexive (lacking, for instance, the criterial contrastive stress):

(i) Max hit himself, and everybody else did, too

It is not implausible to suppose that (i) is in fact doubly elliptical, being a shortened form of (ii):

(ii) Max hit himself, and everybody else other than Max did, too

Here, however, we have a legitimate context for a strict reading with a β-reflexive; (i) is, so to speak, a disguised Dahl-type example; see discussion above. The representation of (ii), and ipso facto of (i), will then be as in (iii):

(iii) Max_1 hit him_1^β + self, and everybody else other than Max_1 **hit** him_1^β

The occurrence of *Max* in the second clause can stand as the antecedent that allows for the resolution of the reconstructed β-occurrence.

defend is taken in the legal sense, then (44) may be readily understood either as saying that Aaron Burr represented himself legally and that Luther Martin represented himself legally, that is, as sloppy, or that they both represented Aaron Burr legally, that is, as strict. The legal sense of *defend* is not alone in naturally allowing α-reflexives along with β-reflexives in neutral discourse contexts; it falls together with predicates such as *vote for, play* (in the sense of act), *write about*, and *look for*. A characteristic of these predicates is that empty names, when they appear as their objects, do not render the sentences in which they occur false:

(45) a. Aaron Burr defended Satan

   b. Barbara voted for Pogo

   c. George Reeves played Superman

The generalization here appears to be that predicates whose complements may be nonextensional, including verbs of propositional attitude and predicates like those above that allow empty names as objects, allow naturally for the occurrence of α-reflexives, and hence strict reflexives.

What underlies this generalization? Consider a verb such as *hit*, whose subject and object argument positions both carry an existential presupposition—hence the necessary falsity of *Satan hit Max* and *Max hit Satan*. Now suppose that both arguments of *hit* are coreferential. Given that the subject position of *hit* itself carries an existential presupposition, it would be redundant to satisfy this presupposition over again for a coreferential object argument. This would lead us to favor a β-reflexive in *Max hit himself* as the unmarked form. This is because expressions bearing β-occurrences have no semantic value in and of themselves; they attain such value only through the valuation of some expression bearing an α-occurrence. Consequently, they cannot stand as presupposed arguments, but they can carry on presuppositions otherwise satisfied by their antecedents. That is, with verbs like *hit*, a presupposition once established need not be reiterated, as it would be with an α-reflexive, which would be independently valued. α-reflexives therefore will be marked in this circumstance relative to β-reflexives, given that speakers use the least redundant forms relative to context. α-reflexives are not redundant in this way with nonextensional predicates like those in (45). Characteristically, argument positions in their scope carry no existential presupposition, so that they allow empty (as well as nonempty) names as their object arguments. But since there is no presupposition to be satisfied, α-reflexives are no more or less redundant in such positions than β-reflexives. It now follows that in neutral contexts nonextensional predicates of this class (now taken to include propositional attitude and perception verbs; cf. (34) and (36)) will allow not only for unmarked β-reflexives, but also for unmarked α-reflexives, and hence will allow strict as well as sloppy reflexive readings. On the other hand, extensional predicates like *hit* in such contexts will only have unmarked β-reflexives, although other discourse contexts show that α-reflexives with such predicates are in no sense absolutely precluded.[17]

Because reconstruction is a symmetrical relation, to say that *him* is a reconstruction of *himself* is to say nothing other than that *himself* is a reconstruction of *him*. This symmetry explains an observation due to Dalrymple (1991). She notes the existence of correlated pairs like those in (46), where the ellipsis is understood in (46a) as *defended him* and in (46b) as *defended himself*, the pronoun in each case referring to Burr:

(46) a. Burr defended himself against the accusations better than Luther Martin could have

    b. Luther Martin defended Burr against the accusations better than he could have

Although (46) involves subordination, the same correlation holds with coordination:

(47) a. Bush voted for himself, but Barbara didn't

    b. Barbara voted for him, but Bush didn't

(48) a. Yeats disliked hearing himself read in an English accent, and I did, too

    b. I disliked hearing him read in an English accent, and Yeats did, too

(49) a. Max believes himself to be heroic, and Mary does, too

    b. Mary believes him to be heroic, and Max does, too

---

17. Our current remarks on markedness hold for expressions bearing α- and β-occurrences just as much in their pronominal form as in their reflexive form. It follows from this that in *Max hit his friend, and Oscar did, too* an α-pronoun is marked relative to a β-pronoun (observe that the subject of a noun phrase is extensional: *Max hit Satan's mother* is false just as *Max hit Satan* is). We argue below that another option is available for characterizing the strict reading, what we call vehicle change. Under vehicle change, the example at hand is comparable to *Max hit his friend, and Oscar hit him, too*. Vehicle change structures are in no sense inherently marked relative to those in which there is no vehicle change; indeed, if anything, in the case at hand it is the unmarked option, since representing the strict reading in this way does not run up against any markedness conditions arising from the determinacy and redundancy conventions. See discussion below.

((49b) was brought to our attention by H. Lasnik.) Or consider the following pair, as answers to the questions *Who slashed the samurai* and *Who
slashed the shogun*, respectively:

(50) a. The samurai must have slashed himself. Clearly, the shogun
          couldn't have

      b. The samurai must have slashed him. Clearly, the shogun
          couldn't have

Notice that the relevant reading is possible in the (b) examples just in case
the subject of the elided VP is coreferential with the object of the antecedent VP.

To see why this correlation holds, consider the pair in (47), comparing
(31), the representation of (47a), with (51), the representation of (47b):

(31) Bush$_1$ voted for him$_1^\alpha$ + self, but Barbara$_2$ didn't **vote for him$_1^\alpha$**

(51) Barbara$_2$ voted for him$_1^\alpha$, but Bush$_1$ didn't **vote for him$_1^\alpha$ + self**

With regard to the reconstruction of the pronoun, there is no difference
between these structures; just as *himself* and *him* are nondistinct in (31), so
too are they nondistinct in (51). In each case, too, Principles A and B of
Binding Theory are called into play, although in different clauses: in (31)
Principle A applies in the first clause, Principle B in the second; in (51) it
is the other way round. In (51) Principle A can be satisfied just because the
overt occurrence of the pronoun and the NP *Bush* are coindexed; hence
the coreference requirement.[18]

The reflexives to which Principle A applies in (31) and (51) are α-
reflexives; this predicts that in contexts that disallow such reflexives, pairs
like those above will not be possible. Thus, compare *John hit himself, and
Mary did, too*, which in an appropriately neutral context does not allow a
strict reflexive reading, with (52):

---

18. Dalrymple (1991) views the correlation of these pairs as one between the
distribution of strict reflexives and the apparent, and curious, inapplicability of
Principle B (and C) of Binding Theory. This presumes, however, that the reconstruction in these cases is a pronoun (or name), so that the elided material in (47b),
for instance, would be *voted for him*, and the resulting structure would violate
Principle B. But although this is a possible reconstruction, it is not the only one;
see below. Notice also that (i) exhibits strong crossover; compare (48b):

(i) I disliked hearing every poet read in an English accent, and he did, too

But if Binding Theory for some reason or other were not applicable in these
contexts, we would not expect to find this effect.

(52) Mary hit him, and John did, too

In this sentence the subject and object of the elided verb cannot be understood as coreferential, nor can the overt occurrences of *him* and *John*, although the overt and elided occurrences of the pronoun must be. The reason for this is that the reconstruction here can only be *hit him$^\alpha$*. Just as an α-reflexive cannot occur in *John hit himself, and Mary did, too* (hence the absence of a strict reflexive reading), so it cannot occur as the object of the elided verb in (52). Thus, the representation of (52) can only be (53):

(53) Mary hit him$_1^\alpha$, and John$_2$ **hit him$_1^\alpha$**

If the NPs in the second clause were coindexed, Principle B would be violated. No such violation is found, however, in (54):

(54) Mary hit him, and John said Sally did, too

Here, coreference is possible between *John* and the occurrences of the pronoun. But whereas in this case the elided element must also be a pronoun, it can be coindexed with the NP *John* consistently with Principle B:

(55) Mary hit him$_1^\alpha$, and John$_1$ said Sally **hit him$_1^\alpha$**

Where α-reflexives are possible, then, Dalrymple's generalization in coordinated constructions follows directly from the nondistinctness of pronouns and reflexives and the symmetry of reconstruction. This allows for structures in which Principle A is applicable in one clause, and Principle B (or C) in the other. Where such reflexives are not possible, it follows that the antecedent and elided occurrences must both be either pronouns or reflexives. Hence, the same principle of Binding Theory will be applicable to both clauses.[19]

Our reflections on strict reflexives now lead to a more precise definition of reconstruction as a set of token structures over a terminal vocabulary of predicates and arguments (along with that of whatever inflectional and adverbial baggage goes with them). Excluded from this terminal vocabulary is *self*, since it is not itself the lexical expression of an argument. This means that *him* and *himself* are nondistinct for reconstruction, provided

---

19. The generalization we have been considering primarily concerns the distribution of α-occurrences, and not of β-occurrences. This is not because of reconstruction, however, but because in the environments we have used to frame the discussion, the pronouns cannot bear β-occurrences, since they could not be resolved in the left-hand clauses.

they are of the same indexical type. From this perspective, they are equivalent lexical expressions of the same cells of the nominal typology, [+pronoun] and either α or β. These pronominal cells can also have nonlexical expression, as PRO: either as control PRO, as in *Max wants to find antiques*, where PRO is a β-occurrence, or as noncontrol PRO, as in *Finding antiques is fun*, where it is an α-occurrence. Notice that since PRO is the null analogue of [+pronoun] expressions, it is the nonlexical counterpart of *both* pronoun and reflexive; it is nondistinct from both. Thus, it is not necessary to stipulate that PRO is a pronominal anaphor, as in Chomsky 1981, in order to derive the "PRO Theorem"—that PRO must occur in an ungoverned position. On Chomsky's reasoning, PRO would be subject to both Principle A and Principle B, a contradiction, unless it is ungoverned. From Dependency Theory, however, it follows that control PRO must be coindexed, that is, controlled, since it is a β-occurrence, whereas for noncontrol PRO, an α-occurrence, this is not required.

The nondistinctness of PRO and the lexical pronominal forms also holds for reconstruction; PRO is nondistinct from any realization in a terminal string of [+pronoun]. To see the significance of this, consider the inference in (56), brought to our attention by M. Rooth:

(56) Max wants to solve Fermat's last theorem
     His mother wants whatever Max wants
     Therefore, Max's mother wants him to solve Fermat's last theorem

This is valid as a strict inference, the conclusion being that Max's mother wants him, Max, to solve the theorem. Now, because the initial premise involves control PRO, (56) must be of the form (57):

(57) Max_1 wants [PRO_1^β to solve Fermat's last theorem]
     His mother wants whatever Max wants
     Therefore, Max_1's mother wants [him_1^β to solve Fermat's last
     theorem]

We proposed in chapter 3 that in order for such inferences to be valid, the embedded sentences in the first premise and in the conclusion—the complements of *want*—must be reconstructions; it is in this sense that they must be the same sentence. This is the case in (57), since given the nondistinctness of PRO and pronoun, *PRO_1^β to solve Fermat's last theorem* and *him_1^β to solve Fermat's last theorem* are reconstructions. However, because the latter sentence contains a pronoun, it is not constrained with respect to where it can find its antecedent, as PRO is, and so can be coindexed with *Max*. But this is not problematic, since the β-occurrences in these two sentences, being of the same indexical value, need not be resolved in dependencies that are *i*-copies. Similar reasoning would seem to hold for (58), with ellipsis:

(58) Max wants to solve Fermat's last theorem, and his mother does, too

As B. Bevington brings to our attention, our analysis would now appear to allow (59) as a representation of (58):

(59) Max_1 wants [PRO_1^β to solve Fermat's last theorem], and his_1 mother **wants [him_1^β to solve Fermat's last theorem]**

But the second clause of (58) clearly cannot mean what is represented by (59), that Max's mother wants Max to solve the theorem. In this structure, however, the elided material is not a reconstruction—the VPs *wants PRO to solve Fermat's last theorem* and *wants him to solve Fermat's last theorem* are not the same VP, since if they were, they would have the same government relations. They are no more reconstructions than *believes himself to have solved Fermat's last theorem* and *believes he solved Fermat's last theorem* are, even though *he* and *himself* are nondistinct, just as PRO and *him* are. Thus, the difference between the strict inference and the ellipsis is that the former turns on the reconstruction of a sentence, the latter on the reconstruction of a VP. Note that what (58) does mean is represented by (60):

(60) Max_1 wants [PRO_1^β to solve Fermat's last theorem], and his mother$_2$ **wants [PRO_2^β to solve Fermat's last theorem]**

Here we have reconstructions and, since PRO is a β-occurrence, sloppy identity.[20]

From our scrutiny of pronouns, reflexives, and PRO, we can conclude that for reconstruction, certain aspects of syntactic structure cannot be distinguished. Even though they vary in aspects of their syntactic

---

20. Control PRO is to be contrasted with noncontrol PRO, which bears an α-occurrence. This predicts that whereas the former will give rise just to sloppy readings in elliptical contexts, presence of the latter will give rise only to strict:

(i) Griswold said that finding antiques is fun, and Wagner did, too

Although (i) can be read with control, its more natural reading is the noncontrol version, with PRO read in the arbitrary sense of *one*. This is true of PRO in both the elliptical and overt clauses; PRO cannot be understood as arbitrary in the left-hand clause, but as controlled in the right-hand (or vice versa).

realization, these elements are nondistinct as arguments and hence are nondistinct for reconstruction, provided that they agree properly in indexical terms. In the context of ellipsis, the realization of the [+pronoun] expression that occurs will be whichever is compatible with the overall syntactic context that otherwise satisfies the structural identity conditions. Notice that when a [+pronoun] element is lexical, the contextual effect will extend to the particular inflectional form it takes. Thus, consider (61), on its sloppy reading:

(61) I turned in my assignment, but most of the other students didn't

In the context of (61), we understand that the elided pronoun, if overt, would be third person plural, as opposed to the antecedent occurrence, which is first person singular. Similarly, consider the sloppy reading of *I've never heard myself sing, but you have*.[21] But whereas the correlation of agreement features may be syntactically significant, it is irrelevant for reconstruction. In order to determine the representation of (61), all we need know is that it contains [+pronoun] expressions bearing β-occurrences in a certain verb phrase context, and that they are resolved in appropriately identical dependencies. This information will be sufficient to fully determine the indexing of the elided pronoun. If reconstruction were to require identity of agreement features, then we would expect, counterfactually, only a strict reading for (61); the first person singular pronoun would be reconstructed as a first person singular pronoun and hence could not possibly agree in the second clause. Rather, it doesn't matter if the reconstruction of a pronoun is in the guise of a plural, rather than a singular, so long as its essential indexical characteristics are constant.

Let us call this aspect of reconstruction, where the syntactic form that expresses a given argument is in some sense altered among the tokens of the reconstruction, *vehicle change*. What is the domain of vehicle change? Simply put, vehicle change is closed under invariance of indices. That is, in a reconstruction, a nominal can take any syntactic form so long as its indexical structure (type and value) is unchanged (modulo identity for β-occurrences). From the discussion in the previous paragraph, we can discern two sorts of vehicle change that fall within these parameters.

---

21. We find that when there is variation in gender, as in *Mary turned in her assignment, but Bill didn't*, sloppy identity is possible, although judgments here are less robust than with the examples in the text. See Kitagawa 1991b for some discussion.

The first sort of vehicle change occurs when there are various ways of realizing one sort of expression—for example, the indiscernibility of pronoun, reflexive, and PRO with respect to the nominal typology. This indiscernibility of lexical and null forms of a cell extends to vehicle change between a name and a variable (trace). An example of this is found in (62):

(62) Dulles suspected Philby, who Angleton did, too

It has been suggested in various forms by Emonds (1979), McCawley (1982), and Safir (1986) that in nonrestrictive relatives, as opposed to restrictives, the head and the clause form, not a constituent, but what is referred to as a discontinuous constituent.[22] On this view, (62) can be represented as in (63):

(63) Dulles suspected Philby$_1^z$, who Angleton **suspected** e_1^z

Because names and variables are nondistinct as expressions of a cell of the typology, they are nondistinct for reconstruction just in case the identity conditions applicable to their indices are observed. This is what we find in (63), where the name and the trace, which is properly bound by the *wh*-word, have identical indexical structure, as required for α-occurrences. A similar vehicle change is involved in accounting for examples like (64), as pointed out by Wyngaerd and Zwart (1991):

(64) John kissed Mary, but I wonder who Harry did

22. Support for this view can be obtained by noting that the distribution of *too* in ellipsis with nonrestrictives is parallel to its distribution in ellipsis with conjunction. Thus, *Dulles suspected Philby, who Angleton did* is comparable in grammaticality to *Dulles suspected Philby, and Angleton did*, and just as *too* is left off in *Dulles suspected Philby, who Angleton didn't*, so it is left off in *Dulles suspected Philby, but Angleton didn't*. In May 1985, it was claimed that examples like (62) are ungrammatical as a result of regressive reconstruction; see chapter 6. However, this observation and its analysis were based on an example in which *too* was absent, and which was therefore not representative of the full class of facts. The analysis there was also based on the assumption that in nonrestrictive relatives the head and the clause form a constituent. We do follow May 1985, however, in maintaining that LF movement is inapplicable here, although some care is needed in stating this. Thus, it is argued in May 1991, developing observations by Reinhart (1991), that LF movement itself, being unrestricted, can apply to such phrases, but that the resulting derived structure must be one of quantification. This is possible, for instance, if what is derived is a distributive plural conjunction, as in bare-argument ellipsis, or a complex quantifier, as in exception ellipsis, but not with movement of simple names, as would occur with appositives.

The representation in (65) contains a well-formed reconstruction for the ellipsis:

(65) John kissed Mary$_1^\alpha$, but I wonder who$_1$ Harry **kissed** e_1^α

Since the NP *Mary* and the trace are indexically identical, they count as nondistinct cell members for the purposes of reconstruction; moreover, the reconstructed trace is properly bound by the *wh*-word. Note that semantically there is no problem with the variable reusing the index borne by the NP *Mary*; all that will follow is that in the context sequence g, $g(1) =$ Mary. What is critical to the evaluation of the *wh*-clause are *variants* of the context sequence, those that differ in the assignment to i. But it does not matter whether the initial sequence has an assignment of a value to i, as in this case, or not.

The second sort of vehicle change is indiscernibility of values within syntactic feature paradigms. We have shown one case of this above, with agreement features. Another case (brought to our attention by W. Ladusaw) is suppletive paradigms, such as the *some/any* alternation. For example:

(66) a. Max talked to someone, but Oscar didn't

   b. Max didn't talk to anyone, but Oscar did

Since reconstruction is nondistinct with respect to the elements of the paradigm, which element occurs in the ellipsis is a function of the licensing context. Perhaps the most interesting case, however, arises from the interaction of this sort of featural vehicle change with Binding Theory. Recall that the nominal typology that we have proposed is partially constructed from such a paradigm, being generated from the feature [±pronoun]: the distinction between pronominal and nonpronominal elements. The effect of vehicle change on this feature can be seen from the puzzle posed by the following sentence:

(67) Mary loves John, and he thinks that Sally does, too

Suppose that *John* and *he* are coreferential. Then, quite clearly, (67) can mean that John thinks that Sally loves him, John. However, it would seem that the representation of (67) would be as in (68), with the VP *loves John* reconstructed:

(68) Mary loves John$_1$, and he$_1$ thinks that Sally **loves John$_1$**

But this is ill formed, since it violates Principle C. To get the reading we want for (67), it should instead have the structure of the sentence in (69), understood with coreference all around:

(69) Mary loves John, and he thinks that Sally loves him, too

If we allow for vehicle change, this result will follow. Proper names have the feature [−pronoun]. By hypothesis, reconstruction is insensitive to the value of this feature; it can just as well be realized as [+pronoun]. Let us call this product of vehicle change the *pronominal correlate* of the name. As a diacritic, we annotate pronominal correlates as $^P NP$, so that (67) has the structure in (70):[23]

(70) Mary loves John$_1$, and he$_1$ thinks that Sally **loves ^{P}John$_1^\alpha$**

So long as indices remain constant, proper names and their pronominal correlates must have the same reference (given that there has been prior assignment to the indices). What does change, however, is the applicability of Binding Theory. Because the reconstructed NP is a pronominal, it is now subject to Principle B, and not Principle C. With respect to the former principle, (70) is well formed, since the correlate is free in its governing category.[24] Thus, nonfeatural vehicle change as we found it with the nondistinctness of pronouns and reflexives affected the applicability of Principles A and B; with featural vehicle change what is affected are Principles B and C.

Let us say that A is a *pronominal correlate* of B if and only if A and B differ only in that where B has the feature [−pronoun], A has the feature [+pronoun]. We refer to B as the *correspondent* of A. Being pronouns, pronominal correlates will be evaluated like other pronouns relative to Binding Theory, as falling under Principle B, whereas their correspondents are subject to Principle C. We thus expect to find locality effects for pronominal correlates:

23. Bear in mind that this diacritic is not part of the syntactic structure of pronominal correlates. In this regard, it is only notational, as opposed to the markings for pronominal feature and indexical type (α- versus β-occurrence).

24. Notice that vehicle change is operative in both sentential and nominal domains; thus, coreference is possible in (i):

(i) Mary saw that picture of Bill, and he did, too

In this case the effect of vehicle change will be to give a representation parallel to that for *Mary saw that picture of Bill, and he saw that picture of him, too*, except that in the elided case the pronoun will be the pronominal correlate of the NP *Bill*:

(ii) Mary saw that picture of Bill$_1$, and he$_1$ **saw that picture of ^{P}Bill$_1^\alpha$**

Here the correlate is free in its governing category, the containing NP.

(71) a. Mary hit John, and he did, too

b. Mary introduced John to everyone, and he did, too

These cases show not-coreference effects with respect to *John* and *he*. The reason for this can be discerned from inspection of (72a) and (72b):

(72) a. *Mary introduced John$_1$ to everyone, and he$_1$ **introduced John$_1$ to everyone**

b. *Mary introduced John$_1$ to everyone, and he$_1$ **introduced ^{P}John$_1$ to everyone**

(72a), the reconstruction of the name, violates Principle C; (72b), the reconstruction of the pronominal correlate, violates Principle B, since the correlate is bound in its governing category. A similar observation holds for (73a), but not for (73b):

(73) a. Mary fired Max, although he shouldn't have

b. Mary fired Max, although he shouldn't have been

In (73a) either the VP *fired Max* or the VP *fired ^{P}Max* can be reconstructed; either way, Binding Theory is contravened if the overt occurrence of *Max* and the pronoun *he* are otherwise coindexed. (73b) differs from (73a) in that the elided VP is passive, not active, so that it has the structure in (74) (cf. example (18) for discussion of v-reconstruction):

(74) Mary fired Max$_1^\alpha$, although he$_1^\alpha$ shouldn't have been **fired e_1**

In this structure the coindexing of the pronoun with the trace violates no grammatical principle, so that coreference is possible as the indices show.

The effects of pronominal correlation can explain an interesting observation due to Gawron and Peters (1990a). They note that if *she* in (75) has *her mother* as its antecedent, then it can only follow that Mary's mother corrected her own mistakes, not that she corrected Mary's grandmother's mistakes:

(75) Mary corrected her mother's mistakes before she did

(Note that the subordination is immaterial here, since the construal of *Mary corrected her mother's mistakes, and she did, too* is parallel to that of (75).) The reason for the absence of the "grandmother" reading is straightforward, since its representation, given in (76), violates Principle C:

(76) *Mary$_1$ [$_{VP}$ corrected her$_1^\beta$ mother$_2^\alpha$'s mistakes] before she$_2$
      [$_{VP}$ **corrected her$_2^\beta$ mother$_2^\alpha$'s mistakes**]

The offense occurs in the second clause, where the elided occurrence of *her mother* is c-commanded by *she*, with which it is coindexed. (Of course, no such violation occurs in *Mary corrected her mother's mistakes before Sally did*, and this sentence allows the standard sort of sloppy construal.) Although we have now accounted for the nonexistence of the "grandmother" reading, notice that the account also rules out (77), which would represent the extant reading of (75), again as a violation of Principle C:

(77) *Mary$_1$ [$_{VP}$ corrected her$_1^\alpha$ mother$_2^\alpha$'s mistakes] before she$_2$
    [$_{VP}$ **corrected her$_1^\alpha$ mother$_2^\alpha$'s mistakes**]

There is an alternative to (77), however, a structure in which the pronominal correlate of the elided occurrence of *her mother* is reconstructed, which gives, keeping indexical structure constant, (78):

(78) Mary$_1$ [$_{VP}$ corrected her$_1^\alpha$ mother$_2^\alpha$'s mistakes] before she$_2$
    [$_{VP}$ **corrected ^{p}her$_2^\alpha$ mistakes**]

This structure is consistent with Binding Theory, but can only mean that Mary's mother corrected her own mistakes—that is, the reading observed for (75).[25]

---

25. These "grandmother" readings are possible if the context is strongly priming:

(i) In Mary's family, cookware has been handed down from generation to generation. Mary inherited her mother's cast iron, just as she had years before

The sort of reading we find for (75) is precluded here; (i) cannot mean that Mary's mother inherited her own cookware. We conjecture that such examples are acceptable because they have a structure in which *her mother* and *she* are not coindexed, but the context is such that it strongly indicates coreference. The existence of this sort of reading does not depend on *her mother* being embedded within another NP, as (ii) shows:

(ii) In Mary's family, the art of cooking has been handed down from generation to generation. Mary learned to cook from her mother, just as she had years before

In pointing out (75), Gawron and Peters (1990a, b) offer only the sketchiest comments indicating that the missing reading results from being unable to take the pronoun *she* as a bound variable. However, they allow that this pronoun can function as a referential element, by their REFREL function; what they do not indicate are the conditions of context and use that would be applicable so that this function would distinguish (75) from (i) and (ii). In regard to (75), Gawron and Peters state, "These data show that one cannot determine from syntactic structure supplemented by information about what NP is the antecedent of an anaphoric pronoun (if that is not indicated by coindexing in syntax) whether a sentence will have only one or more than one anaphoric reading" (1990b:39). The above analysis suggests that this conclusion is incorrect.

Featural and nonfeatural vehicle change can interact, as can be seen from examples like those in (79) ((79a) is due to Cormack (1984), who initially observed the significance of such examples for reconstruction):

(79) a. I shaved John because he wouldn't

    b. I disliked hearing Yeats read in an English accent, and he did, too

    c. Mary believes Max to be heroic, and he does, too

These sentences are comparable to those discussed earlier in connection with Dalrymple's generalization in that they allow a reflexive reading for the clause containing the ellipsis. (79a), for example, can mean that I shaved John because he, John, wouldn't shave himself. This reading is possible because the elided NP can be the reflexive form of the pronominal correlate of the overt NP *John*, yielding the representation in (80):

(80) I shaved John$_1$ because he$_1$ wouldn't **shave** ^{P}**John$_1$ + self**

The properties of examples like (79) are just those of their counterparts that contain pronouns rather than names; see (46) through (50) and surrounding discussion. The only difference is that vehicle change to the reflexive form avoids the consequences of Principle C, rather than Principle B.

The conception of vehicle change we are articulating allows for free adjustment of feature values, with indexical type held constant. We have been discussing the change of value of the pronominal feature from negative to positive. What of the change from positive to negative: Can there be nonpronominal correlates, feature change from [+ pronoun] to [− pronoun]? In large part, this type of correlation will be unobservable. This is because the class of Principle B violations is properly included within the violations of Principle C, so that the effect of vehicle change would be to change a structure that is consistent with Binding Theory into one that is not. Thus, consider (81a), represented as in (81b):

(81) a. Mary loves him, and John thinks that Sally does, too

    b. Mary loves him$_1^\alpha$, and John$_1$ thinks that Sally **loves him$_1^\alpha$**

The nonpronominal correlate of the reconstructed pronoun, an α-occurrence, would be a name. The resulting structure would then be ill formed, as a Principle C violation, but unnoticeable, since there is a well-formed structure in which *him* remains a pronoun. Notice that if there is no c-command, then nonpronominal correlation of a pronoun to a name will always be unobservable, since coindexing will be unconstrained by Binding Theory regardless of which form the expression takes. The latter consideration obtains, however, only if the correlation is to a name. If the vehicle change is to a variable, the nonpronominal correlation can be detected, as an example brought to our attention by I. Heim shows:

(82) Which paper did the student who was supposed to read it refuse to

The *wh*-phrase in this structure would bind no trace under the reconstruction of *read it*. But if we vehicle change the pronoun, then we can derive (83), where "$\bar{p}$" indicates a nonpronominal correlate:

(83) Which paper$_1$ did the student who was supposed to read it$_1^\alpha$ refuse to **read** $\bar{p}e_1^\alpha$

Thus, these cases bring out the symmetry of vehicle change.[26]

The case we have just discussed shows not only that correlation can hold freely between feature values, but also that there can be correlation between any manner of expressing the correlated cells. Although the previous case showed nonpronominal correlation from a pronoun to a variable, we can also show pronominal correlation from a variable to a pronoun by considering (84) (adapting an example from Webber 1978):

(84) John named a country which he wants to visit, and given the amount of traveling he does, I'm sure that he will

If what is reconstructed here is *visit e*—that is, with the trace of the *wh*-phrase taken qua variable—the resulting structure will be ill formed, since the reconstructed variable will not be bound by any operator:

(85) *John named a country which$_1$ [he wants to visit e_1^α], and ..., I'm sure that he will **visit** e_1^α

This problem is obviated, however, if we take the pronominal correlate of the variable:

---

26. (83) appears to contain a weak crossover violation with respect to the pronoun in the relative clause. However, with these sorts of *wh*-phrases it is known that certain effects are ameliorated (Pesetsky 1987); compare *What did the student who was supposed to read it refuse to*, which seems considerably worse. Also, notice that the corresponding case to (83) with an unbound pronoun—*The student who was supposed to read it refused to*—would not tell us much, since reconstruction of the pronoun as a name or demonstrative would be the same with respect to binding conditions as reconstruction of the pronoun itself.

(86) John named a country which$_1$ [he wants to visit e_1^α], and ..., I'm
　　　sure that he will **visit** $^Pe_1^\alpha$

The resulting structure will be interpreted the same way as (87), in which
the VP containing the pronoun is overt:

(87) John named a country which he wants to visit, and given the
　　　amount of traveling he does, I'm sure that he will visit it

Similar considerations hold for the analysis of (88):

(88) Who did Mary see, and does he think Sally did, too

Here, if the trace is taken as a variable, then the resulting structure will
violate Principle C, as well as containing a variable that is not bound by
any operator:

(89) *Who$_1$ [did Mary see e_1^α], and does he$_1^\alpha$ think Sally **saw** e_1^α

Such problems do not affect the structure that results from taking the
pronominal correlate of the variable:

(90) Who$_1$ did Mary see e_1^α, and does he$_1^\alpha$ think Sally **saw** $^Pe_1^\alpha$

The resulting structure will have just the status of the sentence *Who did
Mary see, and does he think that Sally saw him, too.*

　　　Vehicle change from a variable to a pronoun can ameliorate the effects
of grammatical conditions other than Binding Theory. To see this, consider (91a), which ought to have the representation in (91b):

(91) a. John saw everyone before Bill did

　　　b. everyone$_1$ [John saw e_1^α before Bill **saw** e_1^α]

The environment in which the reconstructed trace occurs, an adjunct, is a
strong syntactic island. *Wh*-movement from this context is ill formed,
presumably violating proper government; see Huang's (1982) Condition
on Extraction Domains (CED):

(92) *Who did John see everyone before Bill saw

We would thus expect (91b) to be ill formed as well, since its adjunct also
contains a trace. But observe that (93) is well formed:

(93) Who did John see before Bill saw him

Taking the pronominal correlate of the variable in (91) gives a representation essentially parallel to the one that would result for (93):

(94) everyone$_1$ [John saw e_1^α before Bill **saw** $^Pe_1^\alpha$]

But this contains no proper government violation, since a bound pronoun, not a trace, occurs within the island.[27] The theory of vehicle change, observe, allows the reconstructed pronominal correlate to be either singular or plural, since, as pointed out above, this is also a fluctuation in a feature paradigm. Thus, (94) actually bifurcates into two representations, corresponding to the sentences in (95):

(95) a. John saw everyone before Bill saw him

    b. John saw everyone before Bill saw them

That is, the pronominal correlate can have the interpretation of either a bound variable or an E-type pronoun. This will characterize just the ambiguity observed in (91), between readings where each person is such that John saw him before Bill saw him and where John saw the entire group before Bill saw that group.

The account of examples like (91), in which there is a quantifier within the antecedent of the ellipsis, cannot be the whole story for such cases. If it were, then we would expect (96a) to have only the interpretation of (96b):

(96) a. Max saw someone, and Oscar did, too

    b. Max saw someone, and Oscar saw him, too

Although (96a) can certainly be understood in the manner of (96b), the truth of (96a) is compatible with Max and Oscar having seen different people, a circumstance incompatible with the truth of (96b). Rather, the interpretation of (96a) is comparable to that of (97):

(97) Max saw someone, and Oscar saw someone, too

A representation of (96a) identical to that of (97) is directly derivable:

(98) Max [$_{VP}$ someone$_1$ [$_{VP}$ saw e_1^α]], and Oscar [$_{VP}$ **someone**$_1$ [$_{VP}$ **saw** e_1^α]]

Here the VPs are nondistinct and are reconstructions. Notice that since the variables (and the quantifiers that bind them) bear α-occurrences, the reconstruction is, on our terms, strict, so that the indexical occurrences in both the antecedent and the ellipsis are of the same indexical value. But

---

27. Notice that the bound element in the adjunct would not be a variable, since it does not bear a β-occurrence. Having an α-pronoun fill a variable role is usually a marked circumstance, we have argued. But in (94) this is the only possibility for a bound element, given reconstruction. Thus, considerations of markedness are irrelevant to this case, as well as to (83) and (91), in which options are grammatically limited.

from this, it does not follow that the variables are covalued in the sense that coindexed names, for instance, are. Rather, it follows only that (98) is a logical structure of the form $\exists x P(x) \wedge \exists x Q(x)$, and the truth of this does not require that Max and Oscar have seen the same person, although it is compatible with this circumstance. Thus, variables need not employ novel indices in discourse, and for them, sameness of indexical value allows for a sort of "quantificational sloppy" reading, which arises by virtue of quantification theory. Because of the source of the quantificational reading, its existence will depend on the particular quantifier involved. So, for instance, *Max saw everyone, and Oscar did, too* has only a "quantificational strict" reading. But the reason for this simply derives from the meaning of *everyone*, just as does the possibility of a quantificational sloppy reading for *Max saw everyone that he loves, and Oscar did, too*, with the pronouns construed as sloppy, or for *Max saw the woman he loves, and Oscar did, too*, in which the definite determiner is construed as a universal (Chomsky 1975, Neale 1990).[28]

In representing quantificational structure at LF, we assume that there are two possible positions for the quantified phrase: adjoined to VP and adjoined to S, as proposed by Sag (1976), Williams (1977), and May (1985). From this assumption, it follows that there are two possibilities for the reconstruction of verb phrases that contain quantified expressions. The reconstruction may be either of the VP with the adjoined quantifier phrase it contains or of the VP without the adjoined quantifier phrase, which itself would be adjoined outside the VP. We have already observed examples of these two cases, in (98) and (94), respectively.[29] A further

---

28. The quantificational sloppy reading is possible even under variation in the meanings of the overt and covert quantifiers, as an example taken from Sag 1976 (and attributed to G. Nunberg) shows:

(i) They caned a student severely when I was a child, but not like Miss Grundy did yesterday

Although the overt occurrence of *a student* may be construed as generic, the covert occurrence is construed as specific. This is compatible with our theory, which requires only that there be a reconstruction, that is, appropriate identity of phrase markers relative to a terminal vocabulary. The overall contexts in which the reconstructions occur, however, may lead to their being interpreted with differential quantificational force, as in (i).

29. The question arises whether a quantifier that is adjoined to VP can count as "outside" the VP, so that just the inner VP to which it is adjoined is reconstructed. See Larson 1987 for a suggestion along these lines. We leave this possibility open, since we see little that turns on it at this point, given that the entire outer VP, with an adjoined quantifier, can be reconstructed.

example of the latter sort of reconstruction, with a VP that contains a free trace, is found in the following examples:[30]

(99) a. I know which book Max read, and which book Oscar didn't

    b. I know who Mary promised to see, and who Sally promised not to

    c. This is the book of which Bill approves, and this is the one of which he doesn't

    d. Philby, who Angleton suspected, but who Dulles didn't, was a mole

    e. What John knows is minimal, and what he doesn't is vast

The analysis here proceeds relative to the structure in (100):

(100) I know [which book$_1$ [Max read e_1^a]] and [which book$_1$ [Oscar didn't **read** e_1^a]]

(100) has what we have called the quantificational sloppy reading, since its truth is consistent with Max's having read, and Oscar's not having read, different books.[31] However, this reading, vis-à-vis indices, is strict, so we predict that there need not be any parallelism in the material between the *wh*-phrase and the trace in each clause. This is what we find:

(101) I know which book Max read, and which book Oscar thinks that Sally did

Thus, with regard to structural parallelism, (101) is the same as *Max read*

---

30. Sag (1976) and Williams (1977) report examples such as those in (99) to be ungrammatical. The significance of this claim pertains to their theories' predictions on binding into elided VPs; see discussion below. We disagree with their rendition of the facts; for instance, we find Williams's (1977) examples (94) and (98a) to be grammatical. Lappin (1984), who gives the example shown in (99c), reports examples of this sort to be grammatical. It does appear, however, that factors pertaining to appropriate contrastiveness must be controlled in order for such cases to be fully well formed, a fact itself in need of explanation.

31. It might be thought that what is involved with these sorts of cases is not verb phrase ellipsis, but what has been called pseudogapping, which elides a verb, but not its complements, which in this case would be a trace. Examples like (i) show that this would not be a possible account, in general:

(i) I know which book Max thinks Mary read, and which book Bill doesn't

The unexpressed material can be understood as ... *thinks Mary read*. But this is not a verb; it is, however, with the addition of the trace, a verb phrase.

his book, and Oscar thinks that Sally did, which can only have a strict reading.[32]

It is not possible to have a representation just like (100) except that a pronominal correlate of the trace is reconstructed, since this would be a structure in which a *wh*-phrase did not properly bind a variable—namely, a structure comparable to that of *Which book did Oscar read it*. However, there are cases in which just such reconstruction is efficacious, as examples like (102), of a sort due to Lappin (1992), show:

(102) A guide accompanies every tour of the Eiffel Tower, and Jeanne does, too

(102) is ambiguous, as a matter of the scope of the quantifiers in the initial clause, although regardless of the scope of the quantifiers, Jeanne accompanies each of the tours. We can represent one of these readings, on which *a guide* has wider scope, as follows:

(103) a guide$_1$ [$_S$ e_1^α [$_{VP}$ every tour of the Eiffel Tower$_2$ [$_{VP}$ accompanies e_2^α]]], and Jeanne [$_{VP}$ **every tour of the Eiffel Tower$_2$** [$_{VP}$ **accompanies e_2^α**]]

The reading on which *every tour of the Eiffel Tower* has wider scope is represented in (104):

(104) every tour of the Eiffel Tower$_2$ [$_S$ a guide$_1$ [$_S$ e_1^α [$_{VP}$ accompanies e_2^α]]], and Jeanne [$_{VP}$ **accompanies $^Pe_2^\alpha$**]

In this structure the reconstruction can only be the VP, exclusive of the quantified phrase. Thus, the reconstruction must contain the pronominal correlate of the trace; otherwise, the structure itself would contain an unbound trace. This structure has the same meaning as (105):

32. Many of the current considerations come home to roost in the following example:

(i) John kissed somebody yesterday, but nobody would allow him to today

Its representation is as follows:

(ii) somebody$_1$ [John kissed e_1^α yesterday], but nobody$_1$ [e_1^α would allow him to **kiss $^Pe_1^\alpha$ today**]

(ii) exhibits vehicle change from a variable to a pronoun, pursuant to Principle C; see the discussion of (86) and (90). Moreover, (ii) represents a quantificational sloppy reading, and it does so in a nonparallel structural environment. The same comments hold for *John kissed Mary yesterday, but nobody would allow him to today*; that this case is comparable follows from names and variables being nondistinct as members of the nonpronominal/α-occurrence cell of the nominal typology.

(105) A guide accompanies every tour of the Eiffel Tower, and Jeanne accompanies them, too

That is, the pronominal correlate in (104) is an E-type pronoun, and just as (105) allows a reading in which *every tour of the Eiffel Tower* has wide scope, and the pronoun refers to the tours, so does (104).[33]

Our thesis, then, is that sentences like (102) will have a meaning corresponding to that of a counterpart containing an E-type pronoun. In some cases the E-type counterpart will have a more restricted range of possible construals. Thus, compare the sentences in (106):

(106) a. Some student hit everyone, and Max hit them, too

    b. Some student hit everyone, and some professor hit them, too

The interpretation of these sentences appears to be parallel to that of those in (107):

(107) a. Some student hit everyone, and Max did, too

    b. Some student hit everyone, and some professor did, too

Sag (1976) and Williams (1977) have observed that (107a) can only be read with the existential quantifier taking broader scope than the universal; in common parlance, (107a) has only a "specific" reading. (107b), of a type brought to light by Hirschbühler (1982), can be read in a way comparable to (107a); but it also has a reading on which the universal quantifier has broader scope. On this reading, its truth is compatible with each person's having been hit by a student and a professor. The account is as follows. (107a) can have two representations, one in which the universal phrase is

---

33. Although it is not critical to our analysis, on the theory proposed by May (1985), (104) would also be compatible with *a guide* having broader scope than *every tour of the Eiffel Tower*. However, it is consistent with that theory that only (104) can be construed with the latter phrase having broader scope. Note also that structures containing an E-type pronoun will not always represent readings that are discriminable from those represented by structures in which the quantifier phrase is part of the reconstruction. Thus, there is a representation for *Max saw someone, and Oscar did, too* in which the reconstruction is a pronominal correlate:

(i) Max $[_{VP}$ someone$_1$ $[_{VP}$ saw $e_1^\alpha]]$, and Oscar $[_{VP}$ **saw** $^P e_1^\alpha]$

Although this representation is well formed, and certainly characterizes a way of understanding the sentence in question, the circumstances under which it is true are also circumstances under which (98) is true. Thus, (i) provides nothing semantically that is not otherwise characterized through other logical structures. This is not so, however, for (104).

attached to VP and one in which it is attached to S. In the former representation, the reconstruction of the ellipsis will include the universal and will represent the specific reading for the sentence. In the latter representation, the reconstruction will exclude the universal, but it will contain a pronominal correlate. But for whatever reason, this representation will only be compatible with the specific construal, on which the existential has broader scope, comparable to (106a), in which the E-type pronoun is overt. The same remarks hold for the representation of (107b), save the last one, since its overt counterpart (106b) does allow for a reading on which the universal phrase has broader scope. Thus, (107b) is just like (102).[34]

These observations regarding multiple quantification sentences apparently carry over to cases in which the quantifiers are found in embedded contexts. Thus, compare the examples in (108); the former is due to Sag (1976) and Sag and Hankamer (1984):

(108) a. Sandy thinks someone loves everyone, and Chris thinks someone does, too

     b. Sandy thinks that some man loves everyone, and Chris thinks that some woman does, too

These examples appear to differ in that in (108a) an interpretation in which the overt existential quantifier has broader scope than the elided universal is favored, whereas in (108b) either scope order is possible, and in particular, the universal can quite clearly have broader scope. It is the latter circumstance that appears to be indicative, since examples like (108b) can easily be reproduced:[35]

34. It has been suggested by Cormack (1984) and Diesing (1992), although without analysis, that the difference between cases like (107a) and (107b) turns on whether the subject of the elided VP is a quantifier or not. Examples like (102) show that this is not the correct generalization. Note also that the order of the quantifiers in (107b) is inconsequential. *Every student hit someone, and every professor did, too* permits a reading in which the existential has broad scope, but under which different people were hit. Our judgments here coincide with those of Ludlow and Neale (1991) and differ from those of Fodor and Sag (1982).

35. Observe the contrast between (ia) and (ib), which differ only with respect to the presence of *too*:

(i) a. John believes an American flag is flying in front of every embassy, and Bill believes a Canadian flag is

     b. John believes an American flag is flying in front of every embassy, and Bill believes a Canadian flag is, too

(109) a. Max thinks that a Canadian flag is hanging in front of every window, and Max thinks that an American flag is, too

   b. Sally thinks that a guide accompanies every tour of the Eiffel Tower, and Jane thinks that a guide does, too

Now notice that the range of possible construals of the sentences in (108) matches that of the sentences in (110):

(110) a. Sandy thinks someone loves everyone, and Chris thinks someone loves them, too

   b. Sandy thinks that some man loves everyone, and Chris thinks that some woman loves them, too

The account, then, proceeds in exactly the manner described above: the reconstruction of the ellipses in (108) will contain E-type pronouns, pronominal correlates of the variables bound by the overt universal quantifiers. Hence, these sentences will be interpreted in just the same way as those in which the E-type pronoun is overt, as in (110).

If we are right, the limitations on our understanding of (107a) and (108a) have nothing to do with ellipsis and reconstruction aside from the phenomenon of vehicle change, and everything to do with how E-type pronouns are construed in these particular sentences. In this regard, our theory contrasts with predication-based theories like those of Sag (1976) and Williams (1977). In their theories, variables attached to quantifiers interact with those arising from predicate-forming abstractors (λ-operators). (See Sag 1976:104ff.) This is a result of the conditions that characterize alphabetic variance of predications; there are conditions that depend upon whether a variable contained in a λ-expression is bound within the λ-expression or from outside. Suppose we have two predications, $\lambda x(\phi)$ and $\lambda x(\psi)$. If a variable is bound inside ϕ, then there must be a variable bound in a corresponding fashion inside ψ. If a variable is bound from outside ϕ, then there must be a variable in ψ that is bound from outside by the same operator. From this constraint, it follows, as Sag and Williams observe, that in *Someone saw everyone, and Max did, too* the quantifier *someone* must have wider scope, since if *everyone* has wider scope, then the

---

In (ia) both John and Bill believe that there is one flag flying in front the embassies; they disagree over which flag it is. In (ib), however, Bill's belief is in addition to John's; they agree about the American flag, but Bill thinks another flag is flying as well. The function of *too* here is loosely to add a belief to the one already established; its absence indicates a contrast between the two beliefs.

λ-expressions in (111a) are not alphabetic variants, although those in (111b) are:

(111) a. $\forall z \exists x[x, \lambda y(y$ saw $z)]$, and Max, $\lambda w(\forall v[w$ saw $v])$

　　　 b. $\exists x[x, \lambda y(\forall z[y$ saw $z])]$, and Max, $\lambda w(\forall v[w$ saw $v])$

The λ-expressions in (111a) fail to be alphabetic variants because there is a variable, z, bound from outside one of the λ-expressions, for which there is no corresponding occurrence in the other λ-expression also bound from outside by the same operator. The expressions in (111b), on the other hand, are alphabetic variants because the corresponding quantificational variables are bound within the λ-expressions, and in this representation it is *someone* that has broader scope. Hirschbühler's (1982) case—his example is (112), which can be true if there are two flags hanging in front of each window—is problematic for this analysis:

(112) A Canadian flag was hanging in front of each window, and an American flag was, too

Although the proper truth conditions can be derived for (112) by taking the universal quantifier to have broader scope in each clause, as Hirschbühler points out this can also be achieved by allowing the universal quantifier to bind into the λ-expressions that would occur on either side of the conjunction. This would give a representation such as (113), in which the λ-expressions are alphabetic variants, since the variables bound from outside are bound by the same quantifier:

(113) $\forall z$: z a window $\{\exists x$: x a Canadian flag $[x, \lambda y(y$ is hanging in front of $z)]$ and $\exists w$: w an American flag $[w, \lambda v(v$ is hanging in front of $z)]\}$

What cannot be accommodated in this way, Hirschbühler observes, are sentences like the following:

(114) A Canadian flag was hanging in front of many windows, and an American flag was, too

On the reading that concerns us, the truth of (114) does not require that there be any window at all in front of which both American and Canadian flags fly; they may be disjoint sets. To obtain this reading, therefore, we would need to have the representation in (115):

(115) **MANY**z: z a window $\{\exists x$: x a Canadian flag $[x, \lambda y(y$ is hanging in front of $z)]\}$ and **MANY**v: v a window $\{\exists w$: w an American flag $[w, \lambda u(u$ is hanging in front of $v)]\}$

Here, however, the λ-expressions are not alphabetic variants, since the variables that are bound from outside are bound by different quantifiers.

The alphabetic variance conditions pertaining to binding into λ-expressions is intended to be one of the central entailments of the predication theory of ellipsis: that the only element that can bind into the elided VP is the subject of that VP. This is because it is the argument of the λ-expression. Elements in other positions outside the VP cannot (modulo a single element binding into both abstracts). It is this generalization that is falsified by Hirschbühler's example; by *wh*-constructions such as those enumerated in (99), where there is binding by distinct operators extracted from VP; by the above-mentioned "partial" ellipses in complex clauses with quantifiers; and by those with pronouns discussed in chapter 3. Partial ellipses are also possible where the elided VP contains an element bound, perhaps through the intermediation of an empty operator (Chomsky 1977), by the matrix subject:[36]

(116) a. Frank is easy for Mary to like, but tough for Sally to

     b. It is easy for Mary to like Frank, but tough for Sally to

Here both (116a) and its "unmoved" counterpart (116b) are well formed, the former comparable to (117), where there is overt *wh*-movement:

(117) I know who Max promised to see, and who Oscar promised not to

These examples are all cases of separate operators binding into λ-expressions, stranding the infinitival *to*. This overall nexus of facts, however, is just what we would expect to find if the governing conditions for anaphora in ellipsis derive not from identity of predication, but from the conditions of Dependency Theory and reconstruction.

---

36. Sag (1976) points to the contrast in (i) as an example of the ill-formedness of partial ellipsis with *easy*-type predicates:

(i) a. The chicken is ready to eat, and the steak is, too

     b. *The chicken is ready to eat, and the steak is ready to, as well

The judgments we report are Sag's; we find the contrast real, but of a significantly smaller magnitude. We doubt, however, that (ib) should be accounted for as an improper ellipsis; if it were, (ii) would have the status of (ia), rather than of (ib), since here too the binder of the object would be external:

(ii) The chicken is ready to eat, and the steak is ready, too

Although it is not clear to us what leads to the degraded acceptability of (ib)—perhaps it is related to the possibility of null complement anaphora, which is not possible for other *easy*-type constructions—it does not appear to be connected to failure of conditions on identity of predication.

This concludes our discussion of the foundations of reconstruction. To summarize what we have shown: A reconstruction is a set of occurrences of a (sub–)phrase marker over a given terminal vocabulary. When a sentence contains a reconstruction, it is possible to dispense with the phonetic realization of otherwise present syntactic structure of some of the occurrences. The central question regarding reconstruction and ellipsis is, When can we say that some bit of inaudible syntactic structure is sufficiently similar to some other audible bit? (There is thus no substantive issue, on our view, about whether there is a rule of copy or deletion, or some other operation, that effects this process.) However, ellipsis and reconstruction are distinct notions, and their relation may be complex. The former is part of the use of language and incorporates an asymmetrical relation between antecedent and ellipsis; the latter is part of the structure of language and incorporates a symmetrical relation between members of a reconstruction. Since reconstruction is an identity relation over phrase markers, all token occurrences, whether they be uttered or unuttered, overt or elided, preserve grammatical category, as well as linear, domination, and government relations; all occurrences are structurally composed in the same way. Reconstruction also preserves indexical type, but indexical value may vary among the occurrences in accordance with Dependency Theory. It also preserves lexical content, where this matters, for instance, with predicates. With nominal expressions, reconstruction cares about just those aspects of their structure that contribute to their status as arguments; it preserves the integrity of arguments. It is neutral, however, on other aspects of nominal structure: whether the expression is pronominal or not, and, if pronominal, what form the pronominal takes. In an elliptical context, then, a nominal may be taken in any way allowed within these boundaries of vehicle change, so long as the result is a well-formed structure. In this chapter we have examined cases of well-formedness turning on Binding Theory; in chapter 6 we will return to further vehicle change effects with these conditions and others. Reconstruction, then, is syntactic identity, up to vehicle change and indexical variation under Dependency Theory.

Chapter 6
Logical Form and Reconstruction

6.1 Antecedent-Contained Deletion

Reconstruction is an identity condition on structure. At what level of structural articulation is the definition of identity that reconstruction affords fully expressed? In our discussions thus far this issue has not been of any great concern, since the cases we have considered have not, for the most part, critically differed structurally at the various levels of grammatical representation. In this chapter, however, we will give a concrete answer to this question—namely, that reconstruction can be fully characterized only at the grammatical level of Logical Form (LF). It will turn out that there are constructions for which it is only with respect to the syntactic structure of LF that the appropriate structural identity holds. These constructions fall under the rubric of *antecedent-contained deletion*.[1]

Sentence (1) is an elementary example of antecedent-contained deletion:

(1) Dulles suspected everyone that Angleton did

---

1. That having the same logical form is crucial to the characterization of ellipsis has been a central thesis in virtually all contemporary discussions of ellipsis. Thus, Sag (1976) entitled his doctoral dissertation "Deletion and Logical Form," and Williams (1977) called his article "Discourse and Logical Form." The idea that logical form was implicated arose from the view that to capture sloppy readings, pronouns had to be replaced by variables, which could be bound under predicate-abstraction. This in turn facilitated the definition of the identity condition relative to alphabetic variance among functional expressions. We have rejected this approach, and along with it the notion that reference need be made to the structure of predication (either syntactically or semantically represented); see chapter 4. Rather, our appeal to logical form turns on formal aspects of overt logical terms, such as quantifiers, *as this is syntactically represented at the grammatical level of LF*; see May 1985, 1991.

We want to account for (1) in such a way out that it has just the same structure as *Dulles suspected everyone that Angleton suspected*, in which the VP that is elided in (1) is overt. That is, (1) ought to have the structure in (2), where, following our usual convention, the ellipsis is indicated by boldface:

(2) Dulles [$_{VP}$ suspected everyone that Angleton [$_{VP}$ **suspected** e]]

In order for (2) to be well formed, there must be an antecedent occurrence of the VP reconstruction, that is, of [$_{VP}$ *suspected e*]. There is, however, no such antecedent occurrence; all that occurs is a VP of which the overt occurrence of *suspect* is the head and which contains a complement relative clause, which in turn contains the ellipsis. Thus, in these constructions, since the ellipsis is contained within its putative antecedent, it is not possible to satisfy the identity condition for proper reconstruction, and (2) as it stands is not well formed.[2]

The fundamental insight that shows the way out of this conundrum is due to Sag (1976). He observes that the key to understanding antecedent-contained deletion is to recognize that the deletion site is contained within a *quantificational expression*—in (1) the universally quantified restrictive relative. May (1985) shows that this insight can be captured intuitively and straightforwardly in the context of the theory of Logical Form. As observed there, once Quantifier Raising (QR) has applied, the ellipsis site is no longer contained within its antecedent, so that the locus of reconstruction is not the S-Structure form of (1), but its structure at LF. Thus, the structural identity condition is evaluated relative to the structure in (3):[3]

(3) [$_{IP}$[$_{NP}$ everyone [$_{CP}$ O_1 that [$_{IP}$ Angleton [$_{VP}$ **suspected** e_1^α]]]]]$_1$ [$_{IP}$ Dulles [$_{VP}$ suspected e_1^α]]]

In this structure, unlike in (2), the elided VP is identical to the unelided

---

2. It might be thought that (2) could be taken as well formed if the reconstruction were a result of vehicle change of the relative clause. But as pointed out in chapter 5, vehicle change is sensitive only to the full class of arguments as defined by the nominal typology; thus, it is applicable to variables but not the operators that bind them. Thus, (2) cannot be interpreted as the result of vehicle change.

3. If we follow the assumption made in chapter 5 that a quantified phrase adjoined to a VP is within the reconstruction of the VP, then in order to obtain a proper reconstruction, antecedent-contained deletion must involve adjunction to S.

occurrence, giving, as desired, a representation at LF identical to that of *Dulles suspected everyone that Angleton suspected.*[4]

In contrast, there is no way to meet the structural identity conditions for (4):

(4) *Dulles suspected that Angleton did

Here, although the ellipsis is contained within its antecedent, it is not also contained within an NP subject to QR. Thus, any reconstruction of the ellipsis on the basis of the overt VP will be regressive: *Dulles suspected that Angleton suspected that Angleton suspected that....* Of course, if (4) is in a context in which it can find an antecedent in some other sentence of the discourse, it will be perfectly acceptable:

(5) Dulles suspected Philby, and he thought that Angleton did, too

External antecedents are also possible in contexts that otherwise license antecedent-contained deletion:

(6) Dulles suspected everyone that Philby recruited, and Angleton
    suspected everyone that Burgess did

Here we can take the elided VP to be that headed by *recruited*. Therefore, antecedent-contained deletion is not some special sort of ellipsis; instead, it is just that case in which structural conditions as represented at LF allow an elliptical VP to take an intrasentential antecedent. At this level of

---

4. The initial discussion of antecedent-contained deletion is to be found in Bouton 1970. Williams (1977:fn. 4) notices the problem posed by this construction, but offers no analysis. In May 1985 the issue raised by antecedent-contained deletion is posed in a different light as a "reconstructive regress." The idea is based on the assumption that an elided VP is of the form $[_{VP}\ e]$ and that reconstruction of this VP necessarily includes a copy of the ellipsis site within it. This in turn also needs to be reconstructed, but again contains an ellipsis site; and this process would continue ad infinitum. Given the current context, this manner of describing the problem raised by antecedent-contained deletion is no longer appropriate. Baltin (1987) argues against an analysis of the sort outlined in the text, proposing that antecedent-contained deletion is an instance of vacuous extraposition of the relative clause. Larson and May (1990) enumerate problems with Baltin's account. (See also Diesing 1992.) Among them are the inability to account for non-right-peripheral antecedent containment, for the interactions of the scopes of quantification and reconstruction, and for limitations on complementizer choice. These authors also point out that the structures Baltin gives do not in fact do away with the regressive nature of antecedent-contained structures. For detailed discussion of these matters, see Larson and May 1990, as well as the text below.

analysis the properties of antecedent-contained deletion, qua ellipsis, will
be fundamentally the same as those of the "standard" sorts of non-
antecedent-contained ellipsis we have considered thus far. For instance,
they exhibit the ambiguity of strict and sloppy identity for pronouns, as
shown in (7), in which Max can be introduced either to Oscar's mother
(strict) or to his own (sloppy):

(7) Oscar introduced his mother to everyone that Max did

This is because both of the representations in (8) are well formed:

(8) a. everyone that Max$_2$ [$_{VP}$ **introduced his$_1^\alpha$ mother to** t] [Oscar$_1$
       [$_{VP}$ introduced his$_1^\alpha$ mother to t]]

    b. everyone that Max$_2$ [$_{VP}$ **introduced his$_2^\beta$ mother to** t] [Oscar$_1$
       [$_{VP}$ introduced his$_1^\beta$ mother to t]]

In this regard, (7) is the same as *Oscar introduced his mother to Sally,
and Max did, too.* Various complexities can be added to these examples,
and in this way the eliminative puzzles of ellipsis can be recreated in
antecedent-contained contexts. So, to take one example, the many-
pronouns puzzle reasserts itself in *Oscar said he introduced his mother to
everyone that Max did.*

Our thesis, then, is that there can be proper reconstruction in
antecedent-contained deletion because of syntactic structure that is represented at the level of LF, and only at this level. This structure arises
through the agency of QR. That is, the derivation of antecedent-contained
deletion constructions gives a representation of the logical aspects of quantification, namely, scope and binding, and in doing so gives rise to structure
that meets the requisite identity conditions licensing ellipsis. The necessity
of representation at LF will hold whenever the ellipsis is superficially contained within its own antecedent, although the position of the ellipsis
within the antecedent may vary. Thus, whereas in (1) the ellipsis is contained within a verbal argument and right-peripheral, it may be within a
verbal adjunct, as shown in (9), or internal and non-right-peripheral, as
shown in (10a–g), pointed out by Larson and May (1990):[5]

---

5. Although we will limit our attention to antecedent-contained deletion with
relative clauses, it is also found with adverbials (*Max succeeded more frequently
than Oscar did*) and with comparative clauses, either nominal (*Max ate more caviar
than Oscar did*) or adjectival (*Dulles is more suspicious than Angleton is*), as discussed by Larson (1987). Larson observes that in the latter case, after movement
of the comparative clause, there is reconstruction of the AP, as opposed to the VP

(9) Max doesn't love Sally the way that Oscar does

(10) a. I gave everyone that you did two dollars

    b. Tommy put everything he could in his mouth

    c. Dulles believed everybody that Hoover did to be a spy

    d. Max considers everyone that you do smart

    e. Alice painted every barn that you did red

    f. I persuaded everyone you did to be polite

    g. Sally told everyone you did that Fermat's last theorem had been proven

(10) displays a variety of constructions that admit internal antecedent-contained deletion; in each case the elided VP is construed with the matrix VP as the antecedent. So, for example, (10d) can be paraphrased as *everyone that you consider smart, Max considers smart as well*. This reading is represented roughly as follows:

(11) everyone that you [$_{VP}$ **consider** e_1^{α} **smart**]$_1$ [Max [$_{VP}$ considers e_1^{α} smart]]

Such structures for antecedent-contained deletion are possible, therefore, just *because* the grammar encompasses this way of representing the logical structure of quantification. This observation is quite general, so that this construction is possible with relative clauses in which the head is modified by all sorts of determiners:

---

in other cases. In this comparative ellipsis construction, the auxiliary verb is optional prior to the site of the ellipsis, so that *Dulles is more suspicious than Angleton* is an option. Larson (1987) argues that this is also a case of antecedent containment, but containment of an I′ constituent—that is, of [$_{I'}$ *is t*]. That ellipsis is involved here can be garnered from observations by Sells, Zaenen, and Zec (1986), who note that *John defended his mother better than Peter* shows a strict/sloppy ambiguity, just like *John defended his mother better than Peter did*. The treatment proceeds as described for (7). Sells, Zaenen, and Zec also observe that this sentence has a third reading, where it means that John defended his mother better than his mother defended Peter. This reading arises, we believe, not from ellipsis, but from taking the phrase *than Peter* as a PP, as suggested initially by Hankamer (1973). It is no surprise that this sort of reading is absent when the auxiliary verb is present: *John defended his mother better than Peter did* has only the strict/sloppy ambiguity. Larson (1987) argues for other extensions of the antecedent-contained paradigm, including applications to missing subcategorized prepositions, as in *I've lived in every city that Max has lived*, proposing that these are cases of antecedent-contained PP-ellipsis, so that after LF movement of the quantified phrase, the PP *in e* can be reconstructed.

(12) a. Dulles suspected some spy that Angleton did

    b. Dulles suspected the spy that Angleton did

    c. Dulles suspected many spies that Angleton did

    d. Dulles suspected five spies that Angleton did

    e. Which spy-master suspected which spy that Angleton did

Notice, given the dependence of antecedent-contained deletion on the logical form of quantification, that the construction can be taken as a diagnostic for quantification. As such, it can shed light on certain well-known controversies. Consider, for example, the nature of definite descriptions. Here the evidence decides for the Russellian view, given the grammaticality of (12b). The hallmark of the Russellian analysis is that definite descriptions are quantificational. And (12b) shows that definite descriptions have a property in common with other overtly quantificational expressions: they permit antecedent-contained deletion.[6]

One constraint on antecedent-contained deletion has been proposed by Carlson (1977:527–29), who argues that such ellipsis is found only with what he calls "amount relatives." (13) is an example:[7]

6. Diesing (1992) observes that although determiners such as *many* and numerals are ambiguous between weak and strong interpretations, when they appear in antecedent containment contexts they can only be understood as strong. (Diesing, following Carlson (1977), holds that examples like (12c) and (12d) are ungrammatical; we disagree with these judgments.) Diesing argues that the reason for this is that because of the reconstruction problem, antecedent-contained deletion requires LF movement, which, she maintains, is limited to strong determiners. She then employs this construction as a diagnostic for occurrence of strong determiners. However, the undeleted counterparts are also unambiguously strong: *Dulles suspected many spies that Angleton suspected* is construed in just the same way as (12c), with *many* read as strong. Thus, that such determiners are strong is a function of their appearance in relative clauses, quite independently of whether the clause contains an ellipsis. Diesing's thesis is that weak determiners are interpreted as cardinality predicates, occurring in contexts subject to existential closure; in her terms, they occur within the "nuclear scope" and do not take restrictive clauses (cf. Heim 1982). In contrast, true (strong) quantifiers occur with both a nuclear scope and a restrictive clause. We conjecture that with restrictive relatives, the relative clause must form part of this restrictive clause. This will force the determiner of the head noun to be strong, but it will do so regardless of whether the relative clause is lexically fully specified or not. Thus, it seems to us that the effects Diesing observes stem from semantic properties of relative clauses, and not from antecedent-contained deletion.

7. Carlson argues that antecedent-contained deletion is incompatible with certain characteristics of restrictive relatives, such as *wh*-complementizers (as discussed

(13) Max ate all that he could eat

Typically, amount relatives are understood comparably to a paired comparative clause, so that (13) is taken in the manner of *Max ate as much as he could eat*. According to Carlson, the amount reading is to be contrasted with the restrictive or individual reading standardly found in relative clauses. (14) is an example that is ambiguous between these construals:

(14) Max ate everything that he could eat

(14) can mean what (13) means, that Max ate to satiation. This is the amount reading. On the other hand, suppose that Max keeps kosher. Then the truth of (14) is compatible with Max's remaining quite hungry, even though he partook of all of the allowable foods. This is the restrictive reading. Now, Carlson claims that antecedent-contained deletion is possible only with amount relatives and is not found with restrictive relatives; thus, as a counterpart to (13) we have *Max ate all that he could*. But we also have (15), as a counterpart to (14):

(15) Max ate everything that he could

However, (15) is ambiguous in precisely the same way as (14), between amount and restrictive readings, counter to Carlson's thesis.

Antecedent-contained deletion remains possible when we juggle the examples so as to eliminate the amount reading altogether. The hallmark of amount relatives is that they are subject to a maximality condition—the amount involved must be, in some sense, the totality of the universe. Thus, the amount reading is possible with universal expressions like *all* and *everything* (and their *wh* counterparts, *what* and *whatever*), but examples like *Max ate those things that he could eat* and *Max ate many things that he could eat* are unambiguously understood with the restrictive reading. The amount reading is also excluded in the following sentences:

(16) a. Max ate everything that Oscar could eat

    b. Max ate everything that he couldn't eat

    c. Max ate everything that he should eat

---

above) and head occurrences of determiners such as *many* or *three*, which are also incompatible with amount relatives. From this, Carlson concludes that antecedent-contained deletion is only possible with amount relatives, and not with restrictive relatives, although, as he says, this is "for reasons unknown at this time" (p. 528). Although we agree with Carlson regarding amount relatives, we are doubtful about his factual claims regarding antecedent-contained deletion. See discussion in the text.

In these examples no amount is specified; thus, (16a) can only mean that Max partook of those things allowed to Oscar, even though an amount reading, that expressed by *Max ate as much as Oscar could eat*, is a perfectly sensible meaning. The amount reading is therefore anaphora dependent. It is also affirmation/negation dependent: (16b) can only mean that Max ate things normally prohibited to him. In (16c) a modal with only a root meaning has been substituted for *could*, which can also have an epistemic reading; it means that Max ate those things he ought, amount again unspecified. Now observe that the examples above have antecedent-contained deletion counterparts:

(17) a. Max ate those things that he could

   b. Max ate everything that Oscar could

   c. Max ate everything that he couldn't

   d. Max ate everything that he should

These are all well formed and unambiguously understood with restrictive readings. Thus, although we agree with Carlson that fully lexical relative clauses can be ambiguous in the way described, we do not agree with him that antecedent-contained deletion is limited to amount relatives. The fact appears to be that antecedent-contained deletion is possible in all of the following conditions: with unambiguous restrictive relatives (*Dulles suspected everyone that Angleton did*), with unambiguous amount relatives (*Max ate all that he could*), and with relatives that are ambiguous between the two (*Max ate everything that he could*).[8]

In the LF representation of antecedent-contained deletion structures, the structure corresponding to the ellipsis includes a trace that is bound by

8. It is Carlson's (1977) view that amount relatives and restrictive relatives are two distinct *types* of relative clauses, and that antecedent-contained deletion is diagnostic for the two types. On our view, "amount" and "restrictive" are descriptions of different *readings* of relative clauses, amount readings being possible subject to the constraints described above. Among the conditioning factors for amount readings is that *everything* (and its kin) is lexically ambiguous between two types of quantificational meanings. In addition to its standard meaning, it can also mean something like "the entire amount," comparable to the otherwise available meaning displayed by the comparative (13). (That is, *every* is lexically ambiguous between two quantifiers, and not between a quantifier and some sort of "group" reading, presumably interpreted in place. See Williams 1988 and May 1988 for some discussion.) The ambiguity of (14)/(15) thus merely reflects the lexical ambiguity found in even the simplest type of sentence: *John ate everything* is compatible either with John's having consumed the entirety of the food, or with his just having tasted it all.

the relative operator. This trace is licensed by being an occurrence of the trace in the antecedent VP, the trace that arises through the agency of QR. There are certain contexts, however, in which the ellipsis-contained trace is not properly reconstructed. Consider the ill-formedness of (18), due to May (1985):

(18) *Dulles suspected everyone who knew Philby, who Angleton didn't

We cannot take the ellipsis in (18) as being resolved with respect to the VP headed by *suspect* (although it can be understood with ellipsis of the VP headed by *know*). However, the reading that is absent from (18) is present in (19):

(19) Dulles suspected everyone who knew Philby, but Angleton didn't

(20) is the logical form we associate with (18):

(20) *[everyone who$_1$ [e_1 knew Philby$_2$, who$_2$ Angleton didn't **suspect** e_1]]$_1$ [Dulles suspected e_1]

The problem here is that the index of the reconstructed trace is not that of *who* in the nonrestrictive relative, but rather that of the entire containing relative clause, which has undergone QR. These cannot be of the same value, since otherwise Principle C would be violated: the trace of *who* of the restrictive c-commands the NP *Philby*, with which it would be coindexed. The nonrestrictive *wh*-phrase is therefore vacuous, since it binds no trace/variable, accounting for the ungrammaticality of (18).[9]

Let us refer to the sort of case we have been considering thus far as *vacuous* antecedent-contained deletion. The reason for doing so is that relative to surface structures of sentences such as *Dulles suspected everyone that Angleton did*, there is no apparent trace bound by the relative operator, since it occurs within the elided material. At LF, however, there *is* a trace bound by the relative operator, one whose presence is licensed by reconstruction with respect to the trace resulting from QR. This can be seen by inspecting (3), repeated here:

(3) [$_{NP}$ everyone [$_{CP}$ O_1 that [$_{IP}$ Angleton [$_{VP}$ **suspected** e_1^α]]]]$_1$ [$_{IP}$ Dulles [$_{VP}$ suspected e_1^α]]

9. Note that such an account would be necessary even if one were to assume an alphabetic variance principle along the lines proposed by Sag (1976) and Williams (1977). This is because the two predicates that would be involved, $\lambda y(y$ *suspected* $x)$ and $\lambda z(z$ *suspected* $x)$ are alphabetic variants, since each occurrence of x would be bound by the same operator—the universal quantifier—from outside its λ-expression.

Vacuous antecedent-contained deletion is to be contrasted with nonvacuous antecedent-contained deletion, an example of which is found in (21):

(21) Max talked to everyone who wanted him to

In this sentence the *wh*-phrase binds a trace in the overt material—the subject position of *want*—and as a result QR and reconstruction are not called upon to establish proper variable binding for the relative operator. Therefore, the structure of (21) is as follows:[10]

(22) everyone [who$_1$ [e_1 wanted him to [$_{VP}$ **talk to** e_1]]]$_1$ [Max [$_{VP}$ talked to e_1]]

Thus, vacuous and nonvacuous antecedent-contained deletion differ in that only in the former is the availability of a trace bound by the relative operator dependent on reconstruction.[11]

---

10. Observe that (22) appears to display an improper movement configuration, since the reconstructed trace is c-commanded by the overt *wh*-trace. That is, at LF it is comparable to **Who wanted him to talk to*. We return to this matter in section 6.5, where we argue that (22) is akin not to this sentence, but to *Who wanted him to talk to them*.

11. Vacuous and nonvacuous antecedent-contained deletion also differ with respect to complementizer selection. Carlson (1977) initially observed that many speakers find a contrast between the examples in (i):

(i) a.   Dulles suspected everyone that/∅ Angleton did

   b. *?Dulles suspected everyone who Angleton did

(ib) is taken to contrast with *Dulles suspected everyone who Angleton suspected*. With nonvacuous cases, on the other hand, the *wh*-alternative becomes perfectly acceptable and is perhaps slightly preferred to the *that*-form:

(ii) a.   ?Dulles talked to everyone that wanted him to

   b.   Dulles talked to everyone who wanted him to

(Of course, the null option is unavailable here, with short-subject relativization.) Presumably, the difference between (i) and (ii) arises because *wh*-phrases must bind traces that are overtly identifiable as *wh*-traces; this obtains in (iib), but not in (ib). Lacking *wh*-content, lexically empty operators and *that* are not so restricted and may occur in either type of antecedent-contained deletion. Carlson additionally observes that *wh* is incompatible with amount relative readings: **?Max ate all which he could eat* versus *Max ate all that/∅ he could eat*. This contrast follows if we assume that although *wh* is limited to ranging over individuals, *that/∅* are semantically neutral and may occur with amount or restrictive relatives. The complementizer restriction carries over to antecedent-contained deletion with amount relatives:

Given that vacuous and nonvacuous antecedent-contained deletion differ in the levels at which a trace is available, it follows that if no trace can become available at LF in the reconstruction, then examples of the former type should be ungrammatical, but not those of the latter type. This is borne out by the contrast in (23):[12]

(23) a. *Max talked to everyone that Bill did it

    b. Max talked to everyone who wanted him to do it

Instead of ellipsis, these sentences exhibit the VP-anaphor *do it*. The ungrammaticality of (23a) as compared to its counterpart with ellipsis falls under a generalization that *do it* is not possible where the corresponding VP would contain a trace; thus, we also find a contrast between (24a) and (24b), which are not antecedent-contained deletion structures:

(24) a. I know which book Mary read, and which book Bill didn't

    b. *I know which book Mary read, and which book Bill didn't do it

Compare (24b) to *I know that Mary would read* Portrait of a Lady, *but that Bill wouldn't do it*. (23b), on the other hand, is well formed (if a bit stilted), just like (21) with ellipsis. Now suppose that *do it* lexically exhausts the VP, as opposed to ellipsis, in which there is lexically null structure. (We can see from *Bill didn't do it* that *do* is main verb *do*, with *it* presumably the object.) It then follows that (23a) and (24b) contain an operator that does not bind a trace, and hence these examples are ungrammatical. (23b), which is nonvacuous, is grammatical, since the *wh*-phrase otherwise binds a variable. The moral of this is that ellipsis cannot be just a type of anaphora, picking out some VP (or VP meaning) as a referent. That is, we cannot take it as the covert form of the overt anaphora in (23); for if we did, then (23a) ought to be just like *Max talked to everyone that Bill did*. Instead, ellipsis requires structural representation of members of a

---

(iii) a. Max ate all that/∅ he could

    b. *Max ate all which he could

Note that the deviance of (iiib) is exacerbated relative to its nonelided counterpart. This is because (iiib) is both an amount relative and a vacuous antecedent containment structure. Speakers who find examples such as (ib) marginal find it, as we would expect, considerably better than (iiib).

12. Carlson (1977:fn. 6) and Haïk (1987) observe that examples like (23a) are ill formed; their cases use *do so* rather than *do it* anaphora. They do not observe the contrast with (23b), however, which is also acceptable with *do so*: *Max talked to everyone who wanted him to do so*.

reconstruction; what the contrast in (23) shows is that the full realization of such representations is to be had at LF.[13]

Haïk (1985, 1987) points out another way in which nonvacuous antecedent-contained deletion appears to differ from vacuous antecedent containment. She observes that for (21), a reading on which the pronoun *him* is coreferential with the subject NP *Max* is strongly preferred. On our approach, this would follow if in this context the pronoun bears a β-occurrence; that it does is confirmed by observing that a sloppy reading is dominant for (25):

(25) Max talked to everyone who wanted him to, and Oscar did, too

If *him* bears a β-occurrence, then it must be in a dependency, hence coindexed. It cannot be coindexed with the trace of *who*, since this would violate Binding Theory (Principle B). The only other alternative is the

---

13. We should perhaps temper these comments somewhat by observing that certain properties of verb phrase ellipsis can also be observed with comparable examples involving *do it* and *do so*. Thus, *Max hit his friend, and Oscar did it, too* can have both strict and sloppy readings, presumably a consequence of Dependency Theory, and *Max* and *he* are just as much not-coreferential in *Oscar hit Max, and he did it, too* as in *Oscar hit Max, and he did, too*, presumably in both cases a consequence of Binding Theory. Although this parallelism of verb phrase ellipsis and verb phrase anaphora with respect to properties of indices might be taken as indicating the need for a more abstract relation between reconstruction and structural projection than we have envisaged so as to unify verb phrase anaphora and verb phrase ellipsis over these properties, any such development would have to countenance the difference between them shown by the cases in the text. One would also have to bear in mind that verb phrase ellipsis and verb phrase anaphora have different distributions, as do the different forms of verb phrase anaphora. For instance, although verb phrase ellipsis is possible with any verb whatsoever, with statives *do it* is not possible and *do so* only marginal. Thus, *Max knows French, and Oscar does, too* contrasts with the ungrammatical **Max knows French, and Oscar does it, too*, whereas ?*Max knows French, and Oscar does so, too* has an intermediate status. Moreover, *do so*, unlike *do it*, can participate in movement paradigms. Thus, in addition to *Max read a book, and Oscar did so, too*, we find *Max read a book, and so did Oscar, too* and *Max read a book, and so Oscar did, too*. When placed in more complex structural contexts, the latter difference corresponds to a difference in the scope of reconstruction. Thus, compare *Max wants to read a book, and so did he* with *Max wants to read a book, so he did*. In the former sentence the understood VP is *wants to read a book*; in the latter, it is just *read a book*. (Also observe the change in the anaphoric possibilities of the pronoun in the two cases.) These brief remarks are meant to indicate the complexity of verb phrase anaphora phenomena. To do them full justice would take us far afield, so we leave these matters for another time.

matrix subject NP. In discussing these examples, Haïk seeks to relate the bound anaphora effect to the possibility of ellipsis.[14] However, the requirement on the indexical type of this pronoun does not appear to be related to the possibility of antecedent-contained deletion, either vacuous or not. Thus, consider the contrast in (26):

(26) a. John talked to everyone who would have preferred that he had

   b. John talked to everyone who would have preferred that he hadn't

Our intuition here is that (26a) is a case of not-coreference, as opposed to (26b), which is just like (21). This means that in (26a) the pronoun is an α-occurrence, so that it can be nonanaphoric, as opposed to the β-occurrence in (26b). Note that these examples are of the same structure,

---

14. Haïk (1985) offers two accounts of (21). The first assumes that if a predication applies to an individual, then it must apply to that individual at all of its occurrences. Thus, (21) would have the logical form shown in (i):

(i) everyone who [t wanted him$_1$ to **talk to** t][Max$_1$ talked to t]

Only if *him* denotes the same individual as *Max* can the appropriate parallelism of predication be established; if it applied to any other individual (that is, if the pronoun had some other index), then there would be no parallelism. This assumption is too strong, however. It would rule out vacuous antecedent-contained deletion cases such as *Dulles suspected everyone that Philby did*, since here the predication holds of distinct individuals at each occurrence of the predicate in logical form. The assumption behind Haïk's second analysis is that bound elements, and in particular bound pronouns, move at LF, and in doing so pied-pipe their c-command domains. This gives (ii) as an LF representation, where the entire clause *him to talk to t* has been moved:

(ii) everyone who [[him$_1$ to **talk to** t]$_2$ t wanted e_2] [Max$_1$ talked to t]

After movement of the clause at LF, neither occurrence of t c-commands the other; in a sense, the reconstructed trace is now very much like a parasitic gap. If the pronoun were not bound, then there would be no clause movement, and then the subject trace would c-command the reconstructed trace. But as is well known, such configurations are illicit, comparable to the improper movement configuration found in *Who t wanted him to talk to t*. Although the mechanics of this analysis strike us as independently implausible, examples such as (iii), pointed out to us by B. Schein, cast further doubt on it:

(iii) a. *An official who, after telling lies about e, t committed suicide ...

   b. An official who, after telling lies about himself, t committed suicide ...

These examples show that insofar as a structure such as (ii) can be recreated overtly, the pattern of gaps it displays is not possible.

modulo the tensed complement clause, as (21). In particular, they are cases of nonvacuous antecedent-contained deletion. However, just the same contrast in anaphora is found in cases of vacuous antecedent-contained deletion:

(27) a. John talked to everyone who Sally would have preferred that he had

   b. John talked to everyone who Sally would have preferred that he hadn't

The cause of the bound anaphora effect that Haïk observes therefore seems to be a matter of context and plausibility of particular sentences, rather than of grammar per se. Thus, when such matters are favorable, α-occurrences are possible in the contexts Haïk discusses. In (28) cross-sentential anaphora is allowed:

(28) Mary didn't talk to anyone who wanted Bill$_1$ to leave, but Max talked to everyone who wanted him$_1$ to

Although the pronoun (pronounced with downstress) may assuredly corefer with *Max* here, it may also refer to Bill. Moreover, examples such as (29), brought to our attention by T. Reinhart, show that vacuous antecedent-contained deletion does not require any anaphoric connection at all:

(29) a. The secretary of state wrote to everyone who would have rather the president did

   b. The president of the company personally fired everyone who didn't want the personnel manager to

A pronoun is also not needed in the following sentences, although again these are nonvacuous:

(30) a. John fired everyone who should have been

   b. John fired everyone who said Max should have been

That ellipsis, and the matter of vacuity, should not be relevant here is not too surprising. Where it does make a difference is always with respect to reconstruction—whether the reconstructed material includes a trace to bind or not. But what is involved here is independent of matters of reconstruction; in cases of anaphora, the issues revolve just around matters of anaphora resolution.[15]

---

15. The sorts of cases considered in this section pose serious problems for a view of antecedent-contained deletion proposed by Cormack (1984) and echoed by

Summarizing to this point, in this section we have established the basic analysis of antecedent-contained deletion. The significance of this construction is that it shows that a full characterization of reconstruction in a discourse must include representation at LF. This is not a stipulation for this construction; rather, the nature of its structure and independent considerations of logical form lead to this conclusion. We have isolated some elementary properties of antecedent-contained deletion, distinguishing right-peripheral and non-right-peripheral, vacuous and nonvacuous ellipsis, since they will be significant in our discussion of reconstruction and logical form to follow.

Jacobson (1991). These authors wish to eschew empty categories in the grammar, and hence movement, including LF movement. This leads them to the view that what is elided in antecedent-contained deletion is just a transitive verb. The proposed account is placed in the context of categorial grammar. A few details. In categorial grammars, the construction of relative clauses such as *that Angleton suspects* proceeds by taking the subject NP to be of a categorial type that can compose only with a transitive verb, in turn giving a constituent that can be an argument of the relative pronoun (or perhaps the head of the relative) to form the relative clause. This will give the bracketing in (i):

(i)   (Dulles (suspected (everyone (that (Angleton (suspected))))))

With ellipsis, the construction is no different. Thus, what is reconstructed is just the transitive verb, since there is no object position, and not the verb phrase, as in verb phrase ellipsis, or as we have it, in antecedent-contained deletion. Although the treatment just analyzed might seem plausible for vacuous antecedent-contained deletion, it is less appealing for nonvacuous antecedent-contained deletion. Thus, *John talked to everyone who wanted him to* cannot involve just the reconstruction of a transitive verb. (This is observed by Cormack (1984).) The problem is that what is needed here is a full VP-meaning, and not just a transitive verb meaning. This is because the argument for the relative clause is already supplied by the subject slot of *want*, so no further argument can be supplied by another transitive verb. Hence, the reconstruction must be of an "intransitive" verb, that is, of a verb phrase. Difficulties are also posed by *John fired everyone who should have been*, if active and passive verbs differ in type; and it is unclear how the proposal would rule out *John believed that Max did that Harry is heroic*. Appeal to some analogue of an anti-c-command condition would not appear to be possible for the latter case, since that would undermine the analysis as originally proposed for antecedent-contained deletion. Note that these criticisms are over and above those that arise from the eliminative puzzles discussed in chapter 4 (both Cormack and Jacobson assume predication-based theories of ellipsis), from problems with accounting for the anaphora effects in ellipsis discussed in the subsequent sections of this chapter, and from strong reservations we have regarding categorial frameworks in general.

6.2 Scope of Quantification and Scope of Reconstruction

Given the dependence of reconstruction on quantification and LF movement, our analysis predicts that there should be an interaction between the scope of quantification and the "scope" of reconstruction. The greater the "distance" of LF movement and hence the broader the scope, the greater the number of VPs that can serve as the antecedent for the elided VP. This is because as QR effects movement farther up a complex structure with multiple VPs, when these VPs are "crossed" the elided phrase is no longer antecedent-contained, and further possibilities of antecedence arise. We thus expect to find a correlation between scope and reconstruction.

Observations by Larson and May (1990) show that the predicted interaction does occur. Consider (31), which exhibits sentence-internal antecedent-contained deletion:

(31) Dulles believed everyone that Hoover did to be a spy

Here, the elided VP is understood as having the matrix VP, headed by *believe*, as its antecedent. For this to be so, the relative NP must have scope over the entire sentence; that is, it must have broad scope. That broad scope is possible from this position was established by May (1985) on the basis of the following case:

(32) Dulles believed nobody to be a spy before Angleton did

This sentence is ambiguous, between a narrow scope reading (Dulles came to have a belief in a particular proposition, that nobody is a spy, prior to Angleton's coming to have that belief) and a broad scope reading (there is nobody of whom Dulles formed a belief in his spyhood prior to Angleton's coming to have that belief; that is, Angleton's beliefs are all prior to Dulles's). It is possible to clearly distinguish the readings in this context because they differ with respect to who had the beliefs first: on the narrow reading it is Dulles, on the broad reading it is Angleton. In (31) the NP containing the ellipsis site can only have broad scope (because only then is reconstruction possible), so the sentence can only have a broad reading. This is made clear by (33):

(33) Dulles believed nobody that Hoover did to be a spy before
      Angleton did

This sentence only has the construal that involves temporal switching of beliefs, comparable to the broad scope reading of (32).

In (31) through (33), the quantified relative NP occurs in an exceptional Case-marking environment, as the infinitival complement subject of *believe*. May (1985) points out that intuitions markedly differ when the complement clause is changed from infinitive to finite:

(34) Dulles believed nobody is a spy before Angleton did

Here, the temporal switching indicative of the broad reading is absent; the most natural reading of (34) is narrow, on which Dulles's belief is prior to Angleton's. Thus, there is some constraint on quantification, perhaps related to the ECP and other general constraints on movement, that limits the scope of the quantified NP to the embedded clause in the finite context (May 1985, Aoun 1985, Hornstein and Weinberg 1990). That is, QR is admissible only within the complement clause. If this is so, then it predicts that antecedent-contained deletion should be impossible in this context, since for there to be a well-formed reconstruction, movement must be to the upper clause at LF. This prediction is confirmed:

(35) *Dulles believed everyone that Hoover did is a spy

It is clear that the distribution of antecedent-contained deletion is tied to that of quantifier scope, that is, to the syntax of LF movement.

Further evidence of the scope/reconstruction interaction arises from considering antecedent-contained deletion in contexts such as that illustrated by (36), which also displays a well-known ambiguity between narrow and broad construals:

(36) John wants to visit every city in Italy

The two readings here correspond to the possible scopes the quantified phrase may take relative to the verb *want*, where attachment to the embedded clause gives the former, narrow reading, attachment to the higher clause the latter, broad reading. Relative to this distinction, Larson and May (1990), developing observations by Sag (1976), contrast the sentences in (37), where the first is a case of antecedent-contained deletion:

(37) a. John wants to visit every city you do

 b. John wants to visit every city you visit

 c. John wants to visit every city you want to visit

They observe that (37a) is ambiguous between the interpretations displayed by (37b) and (37c). On the narrow reading, comparable to (37b), the elided VP is understood to be the embedded VP, the one headed by *visit*, as it must be, since if the NP *every city that you do* is attached to the complement clause, it is still contained within the matrix VP. On the broad scope reading, corresponding to (37c), the elided VP is understood as the matrix VP, the one headed by *want*. Here movement is to the matrix clause, with reconstruction of the matrix VP.[16]

Larson and May make a further observation regarding (37a). They point out that this sentence displays a sort of intermediate reading, one on which the quantifier is read with broad scope, but it is the embedded VP that is reconstructed. So although the quantifier has broad scope, reconstruction, so to speak, has narrow scope. In contrast, under the broad scope reading described in the previous paragraph, the scope of reconstruction is broad as well. Thus, QR can be to the embedded clause, in which case the embedded VP must be reconstructed, or QR can be to the higher clause, in which case either the lower or the upper VP can be reconstructed. The possibility of the mixed scope case can be made clearer by utilizing contexts that force a broad reading of the quantifier, to the exclusion of the narrow. The presence of *certain* gives the desired result, as Larson and May point out:

(38) a. John wants to visit a certain city that you do

   b. John wants to visit a certain city that you did

---

16. Jacobson (1991) also remarks on these cases, observing the ambiguity of *His father said he read every book that his teacher did*. Her proposal is that the composition of *said he read* is of the same category as *read* and hence a possible antecedent for the ellipsis. She notes a contrast between this example and (i), in that the latter disfavors a reading on which the ellipsis is understood as ... *said Mary put on the shelf*:

(i) John said Mary put every book that Bill also did on the shelf

She poses this as a difficulty for our sort of approach, which should treat this example as it does others, allowing broad or narrow reconstruction (leaving aside here the correlation with quantifier scope). Jacobson's account is based on the idea that *said Mary put on the shelf* cannot be composed in a manner that makes it available as an elliptical antecedent, since it would not be of a category that allows the NP containing the ellipsis to be "wrapped" in as a constituent. This is because of conflicting requirements of *say* as the head of the constituent, and the syntactic position of the wrapped NP. We think that the judgments on this sort of sentence are less secure than Jacobson's analysis would suggest. Consider (ii), in which it seems possible to understand the longer ellipsis:

(ii) John claims that Mary introduced everyone that Bill does to Max

Also, (iii) seems to us to easily permit the broad reconstruction, and it is identical in the relevant respects to (i):

(iii) John requires that Mary put every book that Bill does on the shelf

We feel that no very strong theoretical conclusions can be drawn from these data.

Varying just the tense of the final auxiliary element skews these sentences so as to illustrate clearly the desired distinction: in (38a) the elided VP is most naturally (although not exclusively) construed as that headed by *want*; in (38b), as that headed by *visit*. That is, the higher and lower VPs, respectively, are reconstructions, so that (38a–b) are understood in a manner parallel to (39a–b):

(39) a. John wants to visit a certain city that you want to visit

     b. John wants to visit a certain city that you visited

These facts are recapitulated in other contexts requiring broad scope of embedded elements. Larson and May point to multiple *wh* constructions:

(40) a. Which student wants to visit which city that you do

     b. Which student wants to visit which city that you did

Following the standard assumptions about this construction, the embedded "*wh*-in-situ" moves to the matrix (specifier-of-) Comp position in LF and hence must have broad scope, a movement that allows for the possibility of antecedent-contained deletion. But although the LF position of the phrase containing the elided VP is constant over both examples, they differ in interpretation in the same way as the sentences in (38). (40a), with present tense *do*, reconstructs the higher VP; (40b), with past tense *did*, reconstructs the lower VP.

In the above examples we have taken advantage of properties of the verb *visit* as it occurs in infinitival contexts to show our point clearly. Present tense *visit*, as in *John visits Mary*, has a repetitive or habitual sense; in the past tense, as in *John visited Mary*, it is punctual. In the particular sentences above the infinitival *visit* has the latter reading, so that use of a past tense trailing auxiliary will be most natural with reconstruction of the embedded VP ((38b)/(40b)), whereas use of a present tense auxiliary will accompany reconstruction of the matrix VP ((38a)/(40a)). Although a full account of these skewing effects is quite complex, our manipulation of them above allows us to illustrate a more basic point, namely, that it is *structurally possible* to reconstruct any verb phrase that resides within the scope of the phrase containing the elision site at LF, a point Larson and May stress.[17] Thus, any verb phrase that LF movement passes in a

---

17. A number of factors influence the skewing effect. For instance, the skewing can be altered by adjusting the examples so that the infinitival *visit* is understood most naturally with the repetitive "present" sense. Compare (38a) with (i):

(i) John wants to visit every woman that you do

derivation becomes a possible antecedent for reconstruction. The correlation of broad scopes for quantification and reconstruction also manifests

---

In contrast to *visit*, the verb *want* shows no comparable variation in meaning depending upon tense, so that the same skewing effect emerges when the tense of the matrix verb is changed to past:

(ii) a. ?John wanted to visit a certain city that you do

    b. John wanted to visit a certain city that you did

Whereas (iia) has the same favored broad reconstruction as (38a)/(40a), (iib) shares the favored narrow reconstruction of (38b)/(40b), although, as above, the other reconstructions are available, though more marginally. However, we do find (iia) somewhat less acceptable, as indicated. This we believe is because, although reconstruction is insensitive to inflectional markings such as number, gender, and presumably tense, so that there is no bar to reconstruction in (iia), the superficial mismatch in tense does give this sentence an air of markedness. It is clear that this markedness is a feature of reconstruction, since (iii) shows no comparable degradation of acceptability:

(iii) John wanted to visit a certain city that you want to visit

If what were involved here were some general notion of sequence of tense, we would expect these cases to be comparably marginal. Shifting attention to cases in which the embedded clause is finite expands the class of possible cases, but skewing effects can still be observed:

(iv) a. John believes Max visited a certain city that you do

    b. John believes Max visited a certain city that you did

(v) a. John believed Max visits a certain city that you do

    b. John believed Max visits a certain city that you did

(vi) a. John believes Max visits a certain city that you do

    b. John believed Max visited a certain city that you did

(vii) a. John believes Max visits a certain city that you did

    b. John believed Max visited a certain city that you do

Although judgments are subtle, our understanding of the most natural construals is as follows. (iva) and (ivb) contrast in that the former shows reconstruction of the matrix VP, the latter of the embedded VP; that is, these cases are comparable to the infinitival cases in (38). In (v), where the tenses of the matrix and embedded verbs have been flipped, their natural construals are flipped as well: (va) skews toward an embedded VP reconstruction, (vb) toward a matrix reconstruction. In (vi) the trailing auxiliary is compatible with the tense of either verb, so that the skewing effect is the same relative to either verb. These cases seem to us fully ambiguous. On the other hand, in (vii), where the auxiliary is compatible with the tense of neither verb, there can be no skewing effect at all, and in this case there appears to be a preference for an embedded reconstruction, with appropriate adjustment of the meaning of *visit*. We are indebted to J. Huang for discussion of these points.

itself in cases of infinitivals with lexical subjects and finite complements:[18]

(41) a. Betsy's father wants her to read everything her boss does

b. His father said he read every book that his teacher did

c. Mary thinks that Jane wrote more books than Barbara does

d. Bertie thought the yacht was longer than I did

To conclude, then, there is a correlation between scope of quantification and scope of reconstruction. This correlation applies to the absolute scope of quantifiers, and not to their relative scope. Thus, (42) is well formed with the appropriate understanding of the elided VP regardless of the relative scopes of the quantifiers:[19]

---

18. Example (41a) is from Sag 1976; (41b) from Jacobson 1991. (41c) is to be contrasted with another sort of ellipsis found productively in comparative clauses but not elsewhere—namely, pseudogapping, which elides just a verb, as in *Jane writes more books than Barbara does articles*. Although there is much to learn about pseudogapping and its relation to gapping and verb phrase ellipsis, one apparent distinguishing characteristic is that it shows a locality effect in contexts in which antecedent-contained deletion does not. Thus, (ia), in which the elided verb is understood as *write*, contrasts with (ib), in which the elided material would be *thought that Jane writes*, which is not a verb:

(i) a. Mary thought that Jane writes more books than Barbara does articles

b. *Mary thought that Jane writes more books than Barbara did articles

Lappin and McCord (1990) claim that a proper account should treat pseudogapping and antecedent-contained deletion as the same, and fault an account of the sort presented here for not doing so. But given the difference between (i) and (41c), it is by no means clear that these constructions should not be distinguished.

19. Lappin (1991) claims that (i) is unambiguous, having only a construal on which Mary has a rate of success that is less than that of some other particular person:

(i) Someone succeeded more frequently than Mary did

According to Lappin, this example lacks a "nonspecific" reading: for any given event, it is more frequent that Mary fails, and that some other person, who may be different for each event, succeeds. But, the argument runs, if the adverbial (which is presumably within the VP) moves at LF, the latter reading should be allowed. The force of this argument is unclear, however. First, there are sentences that, if anything, appear to favor the nonspecific interpretation that Lappin claims ought to be impossible:

(ii) In this game, someone else (usually) succeeds more frequently than Mary does

(42) Someone suspected everyone that Angleton did

All that matters in the analysis of (42) is that the quantified expression superficially in the VP occurs outside this phrase at some level of representation. By hypothesis, that level is LF; it is at this level that reconstruction is fully expressed.

6.3   The Uniformity Thesis and Grammatical Constraints

In contemporary syntax, it is taken that there is an intimate relationship among lexical projection, the licensing of categorial structure, the transformational extension of this structure, and the application of grammatical constraints. The notion that ties these aspects of syntax together is that of level of linguistic representation, characterized most generally through the specification of a vocabulary of primitives and a set of well-formedness conditions governing concatenations over that vocabulary. For basic syntactic structure, the class of categorial concatenates is determined through lexical projection, respecting the selectional properties determined by lexical entries. This structure is then transformed into an extended class of levels of representation, the derivation of which gives rise to structures containing, among their other elements, various empty categories. Syntactic well-formedness conditions applicable to these derived levels, in particular those governing bounding and binding, are, at least in part, sensitive to the distribution of these empty categories.

There are syntactic structures, however, that contain phonetically unrealized elements whose genesis is not derivational in the sense just described. Such is the case with ellipsis. Underlying our view of elliptical structure is that in order for it to count as *projected* structure, it must be reconstructed, that is, satisfy structural identity conditions. In this regard, elliptical structure differs from those structures for which projection is lexically licensed. A question arises at this point. If elliptical and non-elliptical structure differ in the way they are projected, are grammatical constraints applicable to the former also applicable to the latter? Our answer will be yes. Note that this means that once projected grammatically, these two types of structure are indistinguishable, so that re-

---

Second, insofar as the observations regarding the particular example (i) are valid, they do not pertain to antecedent-contained deletion, since (iii) does not differ in interpretation:

(iii) Someone succeeded more frequently than Mary succeeded

For further discussion, see May 1991.

constructed structure will be the same as "constructed" structure. This identification amounts to a *uniformity thesis*, a thesis we have assumed throughout our investigations.

The significance of antecedent-contained deletion with respect to the uniformity thesis is that it allows us to explore a special version of the thesis: At what levels of representation are elliptical and nonelliptical structure fully projected, so that the full generality of the applicability of grammatical constraints can be determined? The specifics of our discussion will pertain to conditions of two sorts: those of bounding and government usually thought to constrain syntactic movement, which we address in this section, and those of binding and anaphora, stemming from Binding Theory, to which we turn in the next. When we ask at what level these constraints apply, we have a range of answers open to us, from "at one particular level" to "at all levels" (or even, we imagine, "at no level," for instance, if they in some sense apply in the lexicon). Moreover, the answer could conceivably vary from level to level: certain constraints or parts of constraints could apply at one level and not at others. In fact, we will answer that the special version of the uniformity thesis holds of LF. It is at this level that overt syntactic structure is sufficiently articulated to support the identity conditions required for a full characterization of reconstruction. In this regard, ellipsis provides a probe into the nature of logical form, as well as affording a very restricted conception of reconstruction as parasitic on structure otherwise lexically licensed.

Our starting point is Haïk's (1987) observation that examples such as (43a) are ungrammatical, in contrast to (43b):

(43) a. *Dulles suspected everyone that Angleton wondered why Philby did

b. Dulles suspected everyone that Angleton believed that Philby did

This contrast parallels the one in (44), where (44a) violates the *Wh*-Island Constraint:

(44) a. *Who did Angleton wonder why Philby suspected

b. Who did Angleton believe that Philby suspected

And just as (45a) is a "weak" *Wh*-Island violation, so is (45b):

(45) a. ?Who did Angleton wonder whether Philby suspected

b. ?Dulles suspected everyone that Angleton wondered whether Philby did

These observations can be extended directly to other bounding effects. (46a), for instance, displays a reconstructed Complex NP Constraint violation:

(46) a. *Dulles suspected everyone that Angleton made the claim that Philby did

   b. Dulles suspected everyone that Angleton claimed that Philby did

Again, these examples contrast to just the same degree as their counterparts without antecedent-contained deletion:

(47) a. *Who did Angleton make the claim that Hoover suspected

   b. Who did Angleton claim that Hoover suspected

Examples of this sort show quite clearly that when the locus of the violation is within the VP, we will find island effects in ellipsis.

   That the data should pattern as just described becomes quite apparent once LF representations are considered. To see this, observe (48), the structure of (43a):[20]

(48) everyone [O_1 that Angleton wondered why Philby **suspected** e_1] [Dulles suspected e_1]

Plainly, this is exactly the structural configuration that gives rise to the strong bounding violation for (44a), except that here the violation arises only relative to reconstructed structure. Similar considerations carry over directly to the weak *Wh*-Island violations in (45) and the Complex NP violations in (46a)/(47a). In contrast, (43b) has the structure in (49):

(49) everyone [O_1 that Angleton believed [e_1 that Philby **suspected** e_1]] [Dulles suspected e_1]

This structure is consistent with the bounding conditions, since the complement clause no longer constitutes an island domain.

   The reconstructed island violations we have been observing all have the structural property that in their surface structure, the ellipsis contains the island context. We can also construct cases with the inverse embedding, that is, with the island containing the ellipsis. Thus, consider the examples in (50), where the ellipsis is contained within a *wh*-island:

20. Our comments here are modulo vehicle change of traces into their pronominal correlates. See section 6.5 for discussion.

(50) a. John wondered who visited every city that Bill did

     b. John wondered why Max visited every city that Bill did

These sentences are inverses of examples such as (43a). In contrast to that example, however, (50a–b) are both grammatical, comparable to (51a–b), which contain no island context:

(51) a. John wondered whether to visit every city that Bill did

     b. John expected to visit every city that Bill did

These sentences do differ in a significant way, however: whereas (51a–b) are ambiguous, (50a–b) are unambiguous. As discussed earlier, sentences like (51a–b) are ambiguous in that the elided material can be understood as being either the matrix or the complement VP. Thus, (51a) admits the readings expressed by the sentences in (52):

(52) a. John wondered whether to visit every city that Bill visited

     b. John wondered whether to visit every city that Bill wondered whether to visit

By contrast, (50a) cannot be understood in the manner of (52b). Its meaning is comparable to that of (53):

(53) John wondered who visited every city that Bill visited

This sentence has no reading on which the ellipsis has matrix "scope." Why should this be? Suppose that the ellipsis in (50a) had matrix scope; then its representation would be (54):

(54) *every city [O_1 that Bill **wondered who visited** e_1] [John wondered who visited e_1]

But this structure is ill formed, since there is an island violation in the relative clause: the trace bound by the relative operator is within a (reconstructed) wh-island. No island context, however, will be reconstructed in the examples in (51), so that for them both broad and narrow reconstructions are possible.

    Parallel examples can be constructed for other islands such as complex NPs and adjuncts; particularly interesting is the specificity island, illustrated in (55):

(55) a. *John bought the picture of every city that Bill did

     b. John bought a picture of every city that Bill did

Here the introduction of an island leads to ungrammaticality, since—

there being only one VP—(56) is the only possible representation for (55a):

(56) *every city [O_1 that Bill **bought the picture of** e_1] [John bought the picture of e_1]

Again, note that the ill-formedness stems from an island violation involving the reconstruction within the relative clause. In this regard, we are saying that the island effects are a result of the bounding patterns associated with *wh*-movement. One might suppose, on the contrary, that this is not the cause of the observed effects—that instead, they result from the extraction, via QR, of the relative clause from the overt island. This would be incorrect, however, since the contexts we have examined are *not* scope islands. For example, *wh*-complements are known not to be LF movement islands, since, for instance, the embedded *wh*-phrase can be associated with the matrix *wh* in multiple questions:

(57) Who remembered when John visited which city

In (58), however, the ellipsis can only be understood with narrow scope, as *visited*:

(58) Who remembered when John visited which city that Max did

The effects we observe, therefore, are keyed by LF movement, through whose agency the reconstructed trace becomes available. And it is this trace, with respect to its occurrence bound by the relative operator, that directly gives the island violation.

Constraints on bounding (Subjacency) are not the only sort of constraint whose effects can be detected in antecedent-contained deletion. Consider (59a), with its accompanying reconstructed LF representation (59b):

(59) a. *Oscar talked to everyone who did

b.   everyone who$_1$ [e_1 **talked to** e_1]$_1$ [Oscar talked to e_1]

Here *wh*-movement has taken place from the subject position of the relative clause, outside the ellipsis site. Upon reconstruction, we arrive at a configuration in which the reconstructed trace is not free, since it is c-commanded by this other trace. Thus, this is an "improper movement" configuration (May 1979, 1981), variously thought to run afoul of either Principle C of Binding Theory (Chomsky 1981), or the θ-Criterion/chain formation (Rizzi 1986). (59a) is to be compared with the well-formed (60):

(60) Oscar talked to everyone whose mother did

Inspection of its logical form reveals the reason for this difference:

(61) everyone$_1$ [$_{CP}$ whose$_1$ mother$_2$ [$_{IP}$ e_2 **talked to** e_1]]$_1$ [Oscar talked to e_1]

We follow Safir (1986) regarding the indexing of relatives with pied-piped heads, so that the *wh*-phrase and its containing phrase have different indices. It then follows that in this structure the trace of *wh*-movement does not have the same index as the reconstructed trace. Rather, it bears the index of the embedded *wh*-phrase, which in turn is the index of the head of the relative as well as the entire NP, and consequently of its trace under QR. Since the two traces in the relative clause have different indices, (60) is not a case of improper movement, and the requisite contrast is derived.[21]

Examples such as (62a), with the LF structure indicated in (62b), would appear to indicate that antecedent-contained deletion can also be used to show that the ECP is in effect at LF:

(62) a. *Dulles suspected everyone Angleton believed that did

b. everyone [O_1 Angleton believed that e_1 [**suspected** e_1]] [Dulles suspected e_1]

Here we find the classic "*that*-trace" configuration, hence an ECP effect. Unfortunately, it is not apparent that we can draw this conclusion so facilely, given that (63) is just as ill formed as (62a):

(63) *Dulles suspected everyone Angleton believed did

One possible account would be that, for some reason, verb phrase ellipsis is just excluded contiguous to an empty category. But the grammaticality of (60) shows that this is not the right approach. A more promising line of analysis arises when we observe that (62b), besides violating the ECP, is also a configuration in which a trace in an argument position is c-commanded by a coindexed trace also occurring in an argument position: the reconstructed trace is c-commanded by the trace following *that*. Thus, here too we have reconstructed an "improper movement" configuration. If this is the reason for the ungrammaticality of (62a), it then follows that (64) should also be ungrammatical, since improper movement violations are not complementizer sensitive:

21. In (60) e_1 is apparently not in a position of proper binding; but this case must be considered in the context of vehicle change. See section 6.5, where we argue that at LF it is comparable to *Oscar talked to everyone whose mother talked to him.*

(64) a. *Who did Angleton believe that suspected

     b. *Who did Angleton believe suspected

Thus, although the ECP may very well be in effect here, and in fact may cause (62a) to be slightly worse than (64), its effects will be essentially masked by the more general constraints limiting coindexing of argument positions. We return to ECP effects in section 6.5.

We can see from these observations regarding the uniformity thesis that various constraints on movement are satisfied or violated in elliptical as well as nonelliptical contexts. These conditions apply regardless of whether the structural configurations to which they are sensitive are licensed directly by lexical projection, or indirectly through reconstruction. This shows directly that ellipsis must have a structural representation no different from that of comparable unelided forms. Notice that this result does not turn on whether *wh*-movement has applied in the antecedent-contained deletion cases. For all intents and purposes, we can assume it has applied in exactly the same fashion as in their unelided counterparts, and so we may assume that whatever formulation of the constraints applies to the unelided forms applies equally well to the elided ones.[22] Given that there is structural and derivational uniformity, the issue still remains, At what level of representation is the *projected* structure of the elided and unelided forms the same; that is, at what level is reconstruction fully defined? The importance of this issue is that grammatical conditions are only applicable to structure whose presence is projected or licensed; with antecedent-contained deletion constructions, structure is only fully licensed at LF. Insofar as we can give a general account of the proper level of structural projection, we will shed light on a fundamental theoretical issue: the role of grammatical conditions in the characterization of linguistic levels. In the next section our task will be to extend this account to Binding Theory, and to its interaction with reconstruction and logical form.

6.4 Logical Form and Binding Theory

In this section we turn our attention to Binding Theory. We will show that all of its clauses are in effect in antecedent-contained deletion. However,

---

22. In this regard, we thus remain agnostic concerning the approach to bounding and proper government effects, be it Subjacency/ECP (Chomsky 1981), barriers (Chomsky 1986a), Relativized Minimality (Rizzi 1990), or others formulated in other grammatical approaches, and concerning whether the conditions hold of rule application or derived representations.

the application of these clauses will be quite surprising, at least superficially. We consider the clauses individually, starting with Principle C.

6.4.1 Principle C

Observe the properties of the sentences in (65), to be understood (as are all examples to follow unless specifically noted) under anaphoric interpretations of the pronouns:

(65) a. Dulles suspected everyone that he did

   b. Dulles suspected nobody that he did

These sentences are grammatical, but semantically trivial: (65a) is a tautology, (65b) a contradiction. Importantly, from the viewpoint of Binding Theory, there is apparently nothing out of the ordinary about these sentences. Since the pronoun in either case is free in its governing category, the embedded relative clause, it is unproblematic to take the higher subject NP *Dulles* as the pronoun's antecedent. Turning to a slightly different construction, we also find examples that exhibit the same semantic triviality:

(66) a. Mary introduced John to everyone that she did

   b. Mary introduced John to nobody that she did

And for exactly the reasons just adumbrated, there is nothing to bar the possibility of the pronoun taking *Mary* as its antecedent, since the latter NP stands outside the governing category of the pronoun.

At first glance, then, nothing very surprising seems to be going on here: Principle B is apparently satisfied in the usual ways, and the sentences have the sorts of readings we would expect them to have if the pronouns are read anaphorically. But if these cases seem rather mundane, a simple change reveals a surprise. Consider the result of substituting a masculine pronoun for the feminine one in (66a):

(67) *Mary introduced John to everyone that he did

This sentence displays a not-coreference effect; standardly, we understand it with the NP *John* and the pronoun denoting different people. But clearly, from the perspective of Binding Theory, (67) ought to be just like (66). The pronouns in all these sentences are just as much in anaphorically transparent positions as the pronoun in *Mary introduced John to everyone he met at the party*, which allows coreference perfectly well. In all cases, Principle B is equally well satisfied. Further small changes return things to what we would expect. Thus, replacing the pronoun in (67) with one embedded in an NP restores the possibility of an anaphoric construal:

(68) Mary introduced John to everyone that his mother did

Again this is quite normal in Binding Theory terms, since the pronoun is properly free. Note, however, that the anaphoric reading here does not occasion a trivial interpretation of the sort observed above.

If we are to view the cases we have been describing from the perspective of S-Structure constituency, then these observations are, to say the least, problematic for Binding Theory. It is far from clear what modifications one would have to make in either Binding Theory or the assigned constituency in order to bring these cases under the theory. This would be a useless exercise, however, since it is based on an incorrect assumption, namely, that only constituency at S-Structure is relevant to Binding Theory— that is, that its clauses are applicable only at S-Structure. Once we shift our gaze to their structure at LF, the properties of the data come into crisp focus. If Binding Theory holds of this level, then our observations no longer fall into the categories of "normal" and "weird"—all of them are straightforward consequences of Binding Theory, and there is nothing strange about them.

To see this, consider first example (65a), which under the analysis developed above will have the LF structure (informally) given as (69):

(69) everyone that he$_1$ [$_{VP}$ **suspected** t] [Dulles$_1$ [$_{VP}$ suspected t]]

Between this LF representation and the S-Structure form from which it is derived, there is a significant structural difference with respect to the position of the pronoun and its antecedent, the subject NP *Dulles*. Whereas at S-Structure the pronoun will be c-commanded by this NP, not so at LF, where there is no c-command relation. This difference, however, makes no difference in the possibilities of anaphora; the pronoun is equally free of its antecedent (in its governing category) in (69). This difference that implicates no change holds for the LF representation of (66a):

(70) everyone that she$_1$ [$_{VP}$ **introduced John to** t] [Mary$_1$ [$_{VP}$ introduced John to t]]

Once again the pronoun is free, as it must be, and may take the NP *Mary* as its antecedent. These LF structures will, for obvious reasons, lead directly to the trivial interpretations that we so clearly intuit for the corresponding strings.

The two cases we have looked at so far have the property that although LF movement affects the structural relationship between the pronoun and its antecedent, reconstruction does not. That is, both the pronoun and its antecedent reside outside the elision site. When we look at our "weird" case, (67), we find a situation in which part of the pronoun-antecedent pairing is within the reconstruction. Thus, consider the derivation of the LF structure of (67), given as (71):

(71) *everyone that he₁ [_VP **introduced John₁ to** *t*] [Mary [_VP introduced John₁ to *t*]]

Here an occurrence of the NP *John* has been reconstructed. Although the occurrence of this NP in the antecedent VP neither c-commands nor is c-commanded by the pronoun, and hence is in a structurally comparable position to the antecedent NPs in (69) and (70), the reconstructed occurrence does stand in a c-command relation to the pronoun: *the pronoun, with which it is coindexed, c-commands it*. We thus arrive at the heart of the matter: at LF (71) violates Principle C of Binding Theory, which requires that names be free: the reconstructed occurrence of *John* is not free of the pronoun. We thus account for the not-coreference effect observed in (67).

Reorienting ourselves to Binding Theory applying at LF relative to "post-reconstructive" structure, we turn to (68), where coreference is perfectly permissible. That this is as it should be is clear from (68)'s LF representation:

(72) everyone that his₁ mother [_VP **introduced John₁ to** *t*] [Mary [_VP introduced John₁ to *t*]]

In this structure, in which, comparable to (71), an occurrence of *John* has been reconstructed, the pronoun *his* is equally well free. Since the pronoun is embedded in an NP, it does not c-command the contents of the reconstructed VP, so that both occurrences of the NP *John* are free of the pronoun (and of each other). Coreference thus remains a viable possibility, since Principle C is not brought into play in this structure.

Now clearly, from the perspective of their superficial structure, it would appear that all the examples just considered should satisfy Binding Theory; in every case a pronoun is free in its governing category. For certain cases, however, the derivation onto LF had the effect of *feeding* Principle C. Thus, in virtue of its LF representation (71), (67) is now rightly seen as violating Binding Theory. Derivations also exist that *bleed* Binding Theory. Thus, consider the examples in (73), all of which we would categorize as "weird," since anaphoric interpretations are possible:

(73) a. Mary always buys him whatever John's other friends do

 b. Mary gave him for his birthday the same thing that John's mother did

 c. Mary introduced him to everyone that John's mother wanted her to

These all violate Principle C at S-Structure, but not at LF. As a case in point, consider (74), the LF representation of (73c):

(74) everyone that John$_1$'s mother wanted her to [$_{VP}$ **introduce him$_1$ to** t]
     [Mary introduced him$_1$ to t]

Here Principle C is no longer contravened, since the NP *John* is now free, as it must be, but was not at S-Structure. Moreover, both occurrences of the pronoun are properly free; thus, *John* can serve as their antecedent.[23]

These cases show that LF movement can both feed and bleed Binding Theory. This talk of feeding or bleeding Binding Theory should not be taken, however, as suggesting that Binding Theory applies to both S-Structure and LF. The evidence we have reviewed thus far indicates that at least as far as antecedent-contained deletion is concerned, LF is the sole locus of application of the structural conditions on anaphora. The reason for this, we believe, stems from the nature of reconstruction: since all the relevant structure is not "visible" prior to LF, Binding Theory cannot yet come into play. We return to this matter in section 6.6. For now, we simply note that as expected, we find a uniformity between our antecedent containment cases and the following structurally analogous cases:

(75) a. *After he introduced John to everyone, Mary introduced John
          to everyone

     b.   After she introduced John to everyone, Mary introduced John
          to everyone

     c.   After his mother introduced John to everyone, Mary introduced
          John to everyone

     d.   After John's mother introduced him to everyone, Mary
          introduced him to everyone

Whereas these examples illustrate these anaphoric patterns in base-generated structures, the antecedent-contained deletion examples illustrate them in derived structure. It is the derived structure as it occurs at LF that is crucial for Binding Theory.

The examples we have considered thus far pertain to the application of Principle C. The question immediately arises whether the claim that Bind-

---

23. The cases under discussion should be kept distinct from ones like *He suspected everyone that Angleton did*, which show not-coreference effects arising from a Principle C violation. In this regard, this example is no different from a circumstance in which ellipsis has not occurred: *He suspected everyone that Angleton investigated*. See section 6.6 for implications of such observations.

ing Theory applies at LF extends to Principles A and B. Does Binding
Theory in its full generality apply at LF? The answer, quite clearly, is yes.

6.4.2 Principle A

Principle A first. (76) is the relevant example:

(76) Max introduced himself to everyone that Oscar did

This sentence has a sloppy reading; to wit, Max introduced himself and
Oscar introduced himself. Now, if we again focus on S-Structure, that this
construal should exist is quite puzzling, since it would require what we
know to be impossible, namely, that the NP *Oscar* can be the antecedent
of a reflexive pronoun that c-commands it. But focusing on LF once more
changes matters for the better:

(77) [everyone that Oscar$_2$ [$_{VP}$ **introduced him$_2$ + self to t**]] [Max$_1$
introduced him$_1$ + self to t]

After reconstruction, there are two occurrences of the reflexive *himself*.
Their positions are such that the reconstructed occurrence can have *Oscar*
as its antecedent, and the other can have *Max*; they can have different
indices because their pronominal parts will bear β-occurrences. This structure is in strict accordance with Principle A, since the reflexives are properly bound in their governing categories. Evidence exists, therefore, that
Principle A as well applies at LF.

These observations carry over to reciprocal pronouns:

(78) The men introduced each other to everyone that the women did

This sentence has a sloppy reading in which the reciprocal applies to both
the men and *the women*. On this reading, it means something like *Each
person the women introduced each other to, the men introduced each other
to that person as well*. As with reflexives, this follows directly from the
sentence's representation at LF:

(79) everyone that the women [$_{VP}$ **introduced each other to t**] [the men
introduced each other to t]

Here, the reciprocals can each be related to their antecedents in accordance with Principle A. Notice that the following slight variant of (78)
contrasts markedly with it in grammaticality:

(80) *The men introduced each other to everyone that the women each
did

If what is going on here is based on reconstruction to a form like (79), then the deviance of (80) can be reduced to that of *The men each introduced each other to Max*. For reasons discussed by Heim, Lasnik, and May (1991b), the distributor element *each* is incompatible with the reciprocal *each*. It is just this incompatibility that we observe in (81), the proposed LF structure for (80):

(81) *everyone that the women each [$_{VP}$ **introduced each other to** *t*] [the men introduced each other to *t*]

Here again the properties of overt structures are seen surfacing in their elided counterparts.

Before proceeding, we should point out that the reciprocal sentence (78) also has a strict reading alongside the sloppy reading we have described. On this construal, the women, rather than introducing other women, introduced the men, so that every man was introduced by (at least) a man and a woman. (The existence of this sort of reading is noted independently by Kitagawa (1991a).) To show why this is, we need to be more specific about our theory of reciprocals. The essentials of the treatment, which we draw from the analysis of Heim, Lasnik, and May (1991b), is that *each* bears a β-occurrence and is subject to Principle A, and the overall expression *each other* bears an α-occurrence and is subject to Principle C. Thus, the structure of (78) can be fleshed out somewhat more as in (82):[24]

(82) everyone that the women$_3$ [$_{VP}$ **introduced each$_3^\beta$ other$_2^\alpha$ to** *t*] [the men$_1$ introduced each$_1^\beta$ other$_2^\alpha$ to *t*]

---

24. More precisely, Heim, Lasnik, and May (1991b) assume that it is the trace of *each* and the trace of *other* at LF that are subject to Binding Theory. Thus, *Max and Oscar saw each other*, for instance, would have the representation in (i):

(i) [$_{IP}$[[Max and Oscar$_1$] each$_2$] [$_{IP}$ e_2^α [$_{VP}$[e_2^β other]$_3$ [$_{VP}$ saw e_3^α]]]]

In (i) *each* is moved and attached to the "antecedent" NP, and its trace is subject to Principle A. (Or, under an alternative suggested in Heim, Lasnik, and May 1991a, *each* is unmoved but is bound by a covert distribution operator attached to the antecedent NP.) Moreover, *e other* (*e* the trace of *each*) is moved and attached to VP, and its trace is subject to Principle C. As shown in the semantics given in Heim, Lasnik, and May 1991b, the complex phrase with *each* attached and the *other*-phrase correspond to quantificational conditions. (ii) is the semantics given there for (i), where "$\cdot \Pi$" is glossed as "is-an-atomic-part-of":

(ii) $\forall x_2 (x_2 \cdot \Pi \text{ Max and Oscar}_1) \forall x_3 (x_3 \cdot \Pi \text{ Max and Oscar}_1 \wedge x_2 \neq x_3) x_2 \text{ saw } x_3$

The representation in (82) glosses over the movements involved in the LF representation of reciprocal sentences in the service of clarity to the point at hand.

(82) represents the sloppy reading of (78), given the β-occurrences borne by the occurrences of *each*. The *other*-phrases do not bear novel indices, even though one ranges over the men, the other over the women. This is unproblematic, however, since this is a quantificational sloppy reading— semantically, an *other*-phrase is a quantifier, so that the (simplified) semantics of *The men introduced each other to Max* will be something like *Each of the men introduced each man different from himself to Max*. Now observe that the *other*-phrase can have a pronominal correlate, so that (78) has not only the representation in (82), but also the one in (83):[25]

(83) everyone that the women$_3$ [$_{VP}$ **introduced** $^{\bar{P}}$**them**$_2^z$ **to** *t*] [the men$_1$ introduced each$_1^\beta$ other$_2^z$ to *t*]

The pronominal correlate will be an E-type pronoun; given its indexing, its reference will be the men, since this is what the *other*-phrase with which it is coindexed ranges over. Hence, (83) represents the strict reading of (78), comparable to *The men introduced each other to everyone that the women introduced them to*.

   In being ambiguous between strict and sloppy readings, (78) interestingly contrasts with its fully lexical counterpart, which has only a sloppy reading:

(84) The men introduced each other to everyone that the women introduced each other to

This is because this sentence is already, so to speak, "constructed" to a form equivalent to (79), and no reconstruction is involved in arriving at its LF representation. It is just when we add reconstructive effects in ellipsis that the other reading, the strict one, becomes possible, given the indeterminacy of ellipsis with respect to vehicle change.

6.4.3 Principle B

We now turn to the remaining clause of Binding Theory, Principle B, which determines the anaphoric domains of personal pronouns. The first case we consider is (85):

(85) *Mary introduced him to everyone that he did

25. More precisely, the pronominal correlate will be of the trace of the *other*-phrase, given the movement that this expression undergoes in virtue of its quantificational status; see footnote 24. For clarity, however, we have represented the correlate as *them*.

This sentence rates as a "weird" example. Although both pronouns meet the condition of being free in their respective governing categories, they cannot be construed anaphorically: not-coreference is required. Once again, the sentence's representation at LF tells the story:

(86) *everyone that he$_1$ [$_{VP}$ **introduced him$_1$ to t**] [Mary introduced him$_1$ to t]

In the LF representation the reconstructed occurrence of the pronoun must be free in its governing category. But it patently is not. For well-formedness to obtain, it must not be coindexed with the pronoun *he* with which it is a clause-mate. We thus must have the following representation, which is one of not-coreference:

(87) everyone that he$_2$ [$_{VP}$ **introduced him$_1$ to t**] [Mary introduced him$_1$ to t]

In this structure both occurrences of *him* bear the same index, so that the reconstructed pronoun corefers with the antecedent pronoun. On the other hand, it follows from Binding Theory at LF that both of these pronouns not be coindexed with the other pronoun *he*.

It is revealing in this context to contrast (85) with (88), brought to our attention by I. Sag, which seems considerably better with coreference:

(88) Mary introduced me to everyone that I did

In terms of indices, (85) and (88) are identical, since Binding Theory is blind to the person of the pronoun. The point to notice here is that the contrast is echoed by the contrast in (89):

(89) a. Mary introduced me to everyone that I introduced me to

  b. Mary introduced him to everyone that he introduced him to

Similar observations hold in (90):

(90) a. Mary introduced me to everyone, and I introduced me to everyone, too

  b. Mary introduced him to everyone, and he introduced him to everyone, too

In our view, these considerations show the following. (88) *does* obey Binding Theory and is a context of not-coreference in virtue of noncoindexing. Such contexts do not necessarily preclude coreference, however, and in fact may allow it under certain linguistic or pragmatic conditions. (88) is such a case. Coreference is allowed in virtue of the lexical meaning of first person pronouns, but not in virtue of the lexical meaning of third person pronouns, as in (85). Thus, given this line of reasoning, the contrast between (85) and (88) is just what we would expect.[26]

(85) contrasts with the "normal" cases in (91) and (92):

(91) a. Mary introduced him to everyone that his mother did

     b. Mary introduced his mother to everyone that he did

     c. Mary introduced his mother to everyone that John did

(92) *Mary introduced him to everyone that John did

These examples count as "normal" in the sense that their anaphoric properties can be determined from their S-Structure form: whereas the examples in (91) are consistent with Binding Theory at this level, so that coreference is perfectly well possible, (92) is not, since it violates Principle C, and not-coreference is required. From the standpoint of LF the results are effectively no different. For (91) this is because the derived constituent structure remains consistent with Binding Theory:

(93) a. everyone that his$_1$ mother [$_{VP}$ **introduced him$_1$ to** t] [Mary introduced him$_1$ to t]

     b. everyone that he$_1$ [$_{VP}$ **introduced his$_1$ mother to** t] [Mary introduced his$_1$ mother to t]

     c. everyone that John$_1$ [$_{VP}$ **introduced his$_1$ mother to** t] [Mary introduced his$_1$ mother to t]

In these structures all the pronouns are free in their governing categories, so that no violations, particularly Principle B violations, can ensue. Turning to the LF representation of (92), its derivation has the interesting property of *bleeding* Principle C, since QR will remove the NP *John* from the c-command domain of the pronoun:

(94) [everyone that John$_1$ [$_{VP}$ **introduced him$_1$ to** t]] [Mary introduced him$_1$ to t]

However, this derivation also has the effect of *feeding* Principle B, which requires that the pronoun not be coindexed with the c-commanding proper name. If it were, it would be bound in its governing category. Thus, the facts follow here as well.

---

26. Another possibility is that (88) involves vehicle change, so that the personal pronoun is realized under reconstruction as reflexive. We disfavor this account because the context under consideration is not one that would normally admit reflexives bearing α-occurrences; hence the absence of the reflexive reading for *Mary introduced him to everyone that he did.*

The examples in (95) illustrate Specified Subject Condition (SSC) effects falling under Principle B:

(95) a.   Mary introduced him to everyone that John wanted her to

     b.   *Mary introduced him to everyone that she wanted John to

We have here a clear and surprising contrast, surprising because expectations are that (95a) should be just as much a not-coreference case as (95b), since in both cases the pronoun c-commands its antecedent at S-Structure, and hence both violate Principle C. But quite counter to our expectations, (95a) does allow coreference. Thus, although we classify (95b) as normal, (95a) is weird. Both cases normalize, however, when we shift our focus away from their superficial structure to their logical forms. Consider the representations in (96):

(96) a.   everyone that John$_1$ [$_{VP}$ wanted her to **introduce him$_1$ to** t]
          [Mary introduced him$_1$ to t]

     b.   *everyone that she [$_{VP}$ wanted John$_1$ to **introduce him$_1$ to** t]
          [Mary introduced him$_1$ to t]

These structures conform to Binding Theory as expected. In (96a) both occurrences of *him* are locally free of the antecedent NP *John* and hence may be coreferential with it. In (96b), on the other hand, the reconstructed occurrence of the pronoun is *not* locally free; *John* is the subject of its clause. What we have reconstructed, therefore, is a Specified Subject Condition effect at LF. Note that these cases also involve the feeding/bleeding relation among the clauses of Binding Theory. QR bleeds Principle C, but reconstruction feeds Principle B and causes (96b) to violate this clause. Consequently, (96b) must be replaced with (97):

(97) everyone that she [$_{VP}$ wanted John$_2$ to **introduce him$_1$ to** t] [Mary introduced him$_1$ to t]

This can only be construed as a structure of not-coreference.[27]

---

27. There is also an interaction between Principle B and quantifier scope, as shown by (i):

(i) John proved Max had slandered her to everyone he thought she hadn't yet

Understanding the ellipsis as broad, that is, as *proved* ..., the pronouns can be taken as coreferential. This is because the reconstructed occurrence of *her* is free in its governing category, in particular, free of the pronoun *she*. If the reconstruction is narrow, on the other hand, then this case is just like those discussed in the text.

In the context of Principle B effects, the contrast in (98), involving control and antecedent-contained deletion, is of particular interest:

(98) a. Bill promised John to introduce her to everyone that Sally did

     b. Bill persuaded John to introduce her to everyone that Sally did

Understanding the elided VPs to have the higher VPs as their antecedents —that is, with *promise* or *persuade* as their heads—we judge that although an anaphoric interpretation of the pronoun is completely excluded in the former, it is not in the latter. The relevant LF representations are as follows:

(99) a. *everyone that Sally$_3$ [$_{VP}$ **promised John$_2$ PRO$_3$ to introduce her$_3$ to** t] [Bill$_1$ promised John$_2$ PRO$_1$ to introduce her$_3$ to t]

     b. everyone that Sally$_3$ [$_{VP}$ **persuaded John$_2$ PRO$_2$ to introduce her$_3$ to** t] [Bill$_1$ persuaded John$_2$ PRO$_2$ to introduce her$_3$ to t]

The difference between these examples is that in (99a) the controller of the reconstructed PRO is *Sally*, and the reconstructed occurrence of the pronoun is therefore bound in its governing category, by PRO. In (99b), on the other hand, PRO is reconstructed along with its controller. This then allows the pronoun to be free in its governing category, and take *Sally*, in this case not the controller of PRO, legitimately as its antecedent. (We are grateful to M. den Dikken for bringing these examples to our attention.)

We conclude that Principle B holds at LF, and more generally that Binding Theory in toto holds of this level of representation.

6.5 Vehicle Change

In the previous section we were concerned with the relation between antecedent-contained deletion and Binding Theory. We observed cases indicating that the various principles are applicable at LF. In this light, consider the rather puzzling contrast in (100) (cf. (95)):

(100) a. Mary introduced John$_1$ to everyone that he$_1$ wanted her to

      b. *Mary introduced John$_1$ to everyone that she wanted him$_1$ to

Under the indicated indexing, only (100a) is acceptable; (100b) displays a not-coreference effect. Now, of course, if we calculate the effects of Binding Theory relative to the superficial structure of these examples, we get the wrong results, since this would predict that (100a) and (100b) are the same. But as we have seen, in this context we must consider their relevant structure at LF:

(101) a.   everyone that he₁ wanted her to **introduce John₁ to** *t* [Mary introduced John₁ to *t*]

 b.   *everyone that she wanted him₁ to **introduce John₁ to** *t* [Mary introduced John₁ to *t*]

Given the discussion in the previous section, this result is rather surprising. This is because both of these cases run afoul of Principle C; in neither does the reconstructed NP *John* have the requisite freedom. However, there is another option here: vehicle change. Since the sentences contain a proper name, we can realize it alternatively as its pronominal correlate, allowing for the representations in (102):

(102) a.   everyone that he₁ wanted her to **introduce ᴾJohn₁ to** *t* [Mary introduced John₁ to *t*]

 b.   *everyone that she wanted him₁ to **introduce ᴾJohn₁ to** *t* [Mary introduced John₁ to *t*]

Since the reconstructed NP is pronominal, rather than being subject to Principle C, it is subject to Principle B. But then the structures in (102) correctly characterize the data: in (102a) the pronominal correlate is properly free in its governing category, and the structure is well formed; but in (102b) the correlate is bound in this domain and hence contravenes Binding Theory.

   A consequence of the theory of vehicle change is that elements that are otherwise subject to Principle C will have the option of being submitted to Principle B, but only under reconstruction. Note that for the cases discussed in the previous section with reference to Principle C, vehicle change will have no impact. For instance, reconsider the analysis of (67):

(67) *Mary introduced John to everyone that he did

In addition to the representation given in (71), we now also have (103):

(103) *everyone that he₁ [ᵥₚ **introduced ᴾJohn₁ to** *t*] [Mary introduced John₁ to *t*]

But this structure is no better than its predecessor. Rather than violating Principle C, it violates Principle B. Conversely, the correlated LF representation of (68)

(68) Mary introduced John to everyone that his mother did

(104) everyone that his$_1$ mother [$_{VP}$ **introduced** ^{P}**John**$_1$ **to** t] [Mary
       introduced John$_1$ to t]

satisfies Principle B for just the same reason that (72) satisfied Principle C,
since none of the coindexed elements c-command any of the others. Here
again, any empirical effects of vehicle change will be unobservable. They
will not go unnoticed for (105), however:

(105) Mary introduced John's mother to everyone that he did

Under simple reconstruction, we would expect this case to violate Principle C, since the reconstructed occurrence of *John* would be c-commanded
by the pronoun. But this is not a case of not-coreference. On the contrary,
coreference is possible, just as in (68).[28] This is because we can derive for
(105) the LF representation in (106), with vehicle change:

(106) everyone that he$_1$ [$_{VP}$ **introduced** ^{P}**John**$_1$**'s mother to** t] [Mary
       introduced John$_1$'s mother to t]

Thus, the analysis of (105) at LF is in effect identical to that of (107):

(107) Mary introduced his mother to everyone that he did

The only difference is that in the latter case the pronoun occurs overtly.

Thus far we have considered cases that involve possible anaphoric
pairings of names and pronouns. But what of examples that contain two
proper names, also known to be subject to not-coreference effects? (108)
gives the significant paradigm:

(108) a. Mary gave John whatever John's mother did

       b. Mary gave John's mother whatever John did

       c. *Mary gave John whatever John did

       d. Mary gave John whatever John wanted her to

Now, if we were going by superficial constituency, we would be led to
classify (108a) and (108d) as weird, and (108b) and (108c) as normal—the
apparent c-command relations indicate that the former should display the
sort of not-coreference effects characteristic of pairings of proper names.
(See chapter 1.) But this is not what we observe; rather, coreference is
possible in these two cases. Turning to their LF representations, our
classification changes: (108b) and (108d) are now judged "weird." This is

28. The intended reading is perhaps highlighted by adding an emphatic reflexive:
Mary introduced John's mother to everyone that he himself did. A similar facilitation
can be obtained via stress as well.

because for these two cases reconstructed occurrences of the object NP will be c-commanded by the subject of the relative clause. But again, this violates our intuitions. Representations consistent with our intuitions arise, however, in those LF representations with vehicle change:

(109) a.   whatever John$_1$'s mother **gave ᴾJohn$_1$** t [Mary gave John$_1$ t]

   b.   whatever John$_1$ **gave ᴾJohn$_1$'s mother** t [Mary gave John$_1$'s mother t]

   c.   *whatever John$_1$ **gave ᴾJohn$_1$** t [Mary gave John$_1$ t]

   d.   whatever John$_1$ wanted her to **give ᴾJohn$_1$** t [Mary gave John$_1$ t]

In (109a), (109b), and (109d) the pronominal correlate is properly free. In (109a) it is not c-commanded by a coindexed element, in (109b) it is free in NP, and in (109d) it is free in the embedded clause. Since all are free in their governing categories, they satisfy the requisite condition of Binding Theory, Principle B. (109c), on the other hand, contains a pronominal correlate that is *bound* in its governing category; hence, this case exhibits the not-coreference effect, in just the same way that such effects are found overtly with pairs of proper names.

The observations of this section lead to a rather surprising conclusion: *no Principle C effects are observable at LF under reconstruction.* Given vehicle change, the various cases of Principle C effects will collapse into Principle B effects. Hence, if the pronominal correlate is appropriately local to its antecedent, then the consequences of the two conditions will be indistinguishable, but if it is distant, then they will diverge. Since Principle B makes available as well formed structures that would be proscribed under Principle C, with vehicle change any effects of the latter clause will be rendered invisible. The residue of Principle C effects will be reducible to Principle B. All that will be seen at LF under reconstruction are Principle B and Principle A.

6.5.1   Crossover

Now we know that pronouns bearing α-occurrences of their indices can play two roles in the grammar: their normal role as referring expressions or, where markedness conditions permit when no alternative with a β-occurrence is available, the role of variables. In the cases of vehicle change above, we observed pronominal correlation of a name in antecedent-contained deletion; we can also observe the effects of pronominal correlation of a variable.

Consider (110):

(110) *Mary introduced every boy to someone he did

This is a case of strong crossover—the pronoun cannot be construed as a variable bound by the quantifier *every boy*. (111) reveals the reason:

(111) every boy$_1$ [someone he$_1$ **introduced** e_1 **to** t [Mary introduced e_1 to t]]

This representation violates Principle C, since the reconstructed variable is not free—a standard crossover violation. But by hypothesis, we have the option of taking the pronominal correlate of the trace:

(112) every boy$_1$ [someone he$_1$ **introduced** $^P e_1$ **to** t [Mary introduced e_1 to t]]

The result here is a Principle B violation. However, an interesting prediction is lurking here: strong crossover under reconstruction should show SSC (Principle B) effects. The critical examples are just the quantificational counterparts of the sentences in (100):

(113) a.   Mary introduced every guy to every woman he wanted her to

   b.   *Mary introduced every guy to every woman she wanted him to

Although a bound variable construal is impossible in (113b)—in other words, it is a case of crossover—this construal is perfectly possible in (113a). The same observations hold for the slightly varying cases in (114):

(114) a.   Mary introduced every boy to someone he thought Sally was going to

   b.   *Mary introduced every boy to someone Sally thought he was going to

Taking the examples in (113), we again have two possibilities: one where the variable is reconstructed, the other where the pronominal correlate is reconstructed. These are shown in (115) and (116), respectively:

(115) a. every guy$_1$ [every woman he$_1$ wanted her to **introduce** e_1 **to** t [Mary introduced e_1 to t]]

   b. every guy$_1$ [every woman she wanted him$_1$ to **introduce** e_1 **to** t [Mary introduced e_1 to t]]

(116) a. every guy$_1$ [every woman he$_1$ wanted her to **introduce** $^P e_1$ **to** t
[Mary introduced e_1 to t]]

b. every guy$_1$ [every woman she wanted him$_1$ to **introduce** $^P e_1$ **to** t
[Mary introduced e_1 to t]]

Following our line of reasoning, (115a), (115b), and (116b) are all ill formed: the first two violate Principle C, the latter violates Principle B. (116a), however, is well formed. Since this structure contains a pronominal correlate, and it is free in its governing category, this structure is consistent with Binding Theory. In this configuration strong crossover is ameliorated under reconstruction.

Weak crossover is also ameliorated. Consider (117):

(117) Mary introduced every boy to someone his mother did

Despite the fact that its LF representation (118)

(118) every boy$_1$ [someone his$_1$ mother **introduced** e_1 **to** t [Mary introduced e_1 to t]]

seems to directly display the structural configuration giving rise to this effect, our intuition is clear that the pronoun *can* be anaphorically connected to the quantifier phrase *every boy*. There is no weak crossover. However, we have the option of vehicle change, so that the pronominal correlate of the trace can be substituted:

(119) every boy$_1$ [someone his$_1$ mother **introduced** $^P e_1$ **to** t [Mary introduced e_1 to t]]

This configuration, however, is *not* a weak crossover configuration, as initially pointed out by Safir (1984). Examples like (120), cited by May (1985), adapting examples of Safir's, show no crossover effects:

(120) Every student whom Mary was wondering whether or not his professor failed him is sitting over there

Once the possibility of vehicle change in reconstruction is taken into account, the lack of weak crossover in antecedent-contained deletion becomes explicable.[29]

29. There is a more general problem lurking in the analysis of weak crossover: Why doesn't a weak crossover violation arise from the relation of the quantifier, the pronoun, and the nonreconstructed trace of QR in (119)? Although the answer is not altogether clear, it is worth noting that the problem is endemic to the account of bound variable anaphora: Why shouldn't the LF representation of *Someone saw everyone he loves* also be a crossover violation?

6.5.2 Crossed Anaphora

Given the possibility of internal antecedent-contained deletion, there can be double antecedent containment, that is, two instances of ellipsis within one verb phrase. (121) illustrates this possibility:

(121) Max promised everything that Oscar did to everyone that Sally did

The LF representation of this sentence is (122); we indicate the presence of pronominal correlates:

(122) everything O_1 that Oscar [**promised** e_1 **to** $^P e_2$]$_1$ [everyone O_2 that Sally [**promised** $^P e_1$ **to** e_2]$_2$ [Max promised e_1 to e_2]]

By contrast, a structure in which there was no vehicle change would incorporate two sorts of violations. If it contained an occurrence of e_2 rather than its pronominal correlate, this trace would be free, and if it contained an occurrence of e_1, it would violate Subjacency. (122) suffers from neither of these problems. Notice that the binding properties of (122) are not unique; they are the same as those found in the logical form of Bach-Peters sentences such as *Every pilot who shot at it hit some MIG which chased him*:

(123) [every pilot who$_1$ e_1 shot at it$_2$]$_1$ [[some MIG which$_2$ e_2 chased him$_1$]$_2$ [e_2 hit e_1]]

As discussed in May 1985, since adjuncts of a single category c-command one another, it follows that the occurrence of e_1 contained within NP$_2$ is bound by NP$_1$, and the occurrence of e_2 contained within NP$_1$ is bound by NP$_2$. As such, this structure is subject to interpretation by the semantics of absorbed quantification developed in Higginbotham and May 1981b, and placed in the context of the scope analysis of May 1985 in May 1989.

6.5.3 Improper "Movement"

The amelioration effects that we have observed extend to other grammatical constraints that turn on the distribution of variables. They can also be shown to obtain, for instance, in improper movement configurations (May 1979). Thus, consider (124), the case of nonvacuous antecedent-contained deletion discussed by Haïk (1985, 1987):

(124) Oscar talked to everyone who wanted him to

As discussed above, in (124) the relative *wh*-operator is not superficially vacuous, since it has an overt source—the subject position of *want*. LF movement gives the following representation:

(125) everyone who$_1$ e_1 wanted him to **talk to** e_1 [Oscar talked to e_1]

This structure contains a trace—the reconstructed one—that is c-commanded by another coindexed trace. This configuration is the familiar one of improper movement, a violation of Principle C (or perhaps the θ-Criterion). Hence, the grammatical status of (124) should be the same as that of (126):

(126) *Who$_1$ [e_1 wanted him to talk to e_1]

Once again, however, we can conclude that these results are only prima facie, for we have not factored in the effect of vehicle change, and the realization of the reconstructed variable as its pronominal correlate. Thus, we have the additional representation (127):

(127) everyone who$_1$ e_1 wanted him to **talk to** $^P e_1$ [Oscar talked to e_1]

This structure comes under the purview of Binding Theory with respect to Principle B, not Principle C. But with respect to this principle, (127) is well formed, since the pronoun is properly free in its governing category. The plausibility of this account of (124) is bolstered by observing that its most natural paraphrase contains an overt pronoun: *Oscar talked to everyone who wanted him to talk to him*. Although (126) is a case of improper movement, we conclude that (124) is a case of *proper* reconstruction.

Cases comparable to nonvacuous antecedent-contained deletion can be constructed with nonrestrictive relative clauses:

(128) a. Dulles suspected Philby, who didn't really want him to

b. John proposed to Mary, who thought that Bill would have ages ago

In chapter 5, we considered simpler cases of this construction such as *Dulles suspected Philby, who Angleton did, too*, which, extending our terminology, would be a case of vacuous ellipsis, since it contains no overt trace bound by the *wh*-phrase. On the analysis given there, the reconstructed trace results from a nonfeatural vehicle change of a name to its null counterpart. In cases like (128), on the other hand, featural vehicle change is at work, so that (129) contains a pronominal correlate of a name:

(129) Dulles suspected Philby$_1$, who$_1$ e_1 didn't really want him to **suspect ^{P}Philby$_1$**

This structure is well formed, conforming to Binding Theory by satisfying Principle B. If we had reconstructed without taking the pronominal correlate, the result would not have conformed to Binding Theory; it would have violated Principle C.

Vehicle change will not be able to save examples like the following, which repeats (59a):

(130) *Oscar talked to everyone who did

Like the Haïk examples, (130) is nonvacuous; it differs in that the source of *wh*-movement is contiguous to the elided VP. Its LF representation, with vehicle change, is (131):

(131) *everyone who$_1$ e_1 **talked to** $^P e_1$ [Oscar talked to e_1]

This structure violates Principle B, since the pronominal correlate is bound in its governing category. Recall that (130) contrasts with (132); (132b) ($=61$)) is the representation we gave for this sentence:

(132) a. Oscar talked to everyone whose mother did

      b. everyone$_1$ [whose$_1$ mother$_2$ [$_{IP}$ e_2 **talked to** e_1]]$_1$ [Oscar talked to e_1]

As it stands, it is not apparent that this structure is well formed, since the reconstructed trace is not properly bound. However, if we take its pronominal correlate, the resulting structure definitely is well formed:

(133) everyone$_1$ [whose$_1$ mother$_2$ [$_{IP}$ e_2 **talked to** $^P e_1$]]$_1$ [Oscar talked to e_1]

Given this structure, the construal of (132a) will be just that of *Oscar talked to everyone whose mother talked to him*, with the pronoun bound by the quantifier.

Principle B is also at work in accounting for the curious pair given earlier as (62a) and (63):

(134) a. *Dulles suspected everyone Angleton believed that did

      b. *Dulles suspected everyone Angleton believed did

Like (130), these examples involve movement from an immediately pre-ellipsis position. Our expectation is that they should contrast as ECP effects, which are standardly sensitive to the lexical presence of the complementizer with movement from this position. ECP effects, however, will be masked here by Binding Theory. Thus, the LF structures in (135) violate Principle B, even if the vehicle change option is taken, since neither of the pronominal correlates is appropriately free:

(135) a. *everyone [O_1 Angleton believed that e_1 [**suspected** $^Pe_1$]] [Dulles
          suspected e_1]

   b. *everyone [O_1 Angleton believed e_1 [**suspected** $^Pe_1$]] [Dulles
          suspected e_1]

ECP effects can be unmasked, however, by constructing contexts in which
the pronominal correlate is free, erasing the improper movement (Principle B) violation. Consider the contrast in (136):

(136) a.   Dulles suspected everyone Angleton believed wanted him to

   b. *Dulles suspected everyone Angleton believed that wanted
          him to

These examples show a straightforward *that*-trace effect; they have the LF
representations in (137):

(137) a.   everyone [O_1 Angleton believed e_1 wanted him to [**suspect** $^Pe_1$]]
          [Dulles suspected e_1]

   b. *everyone [O_1 Angleton believed that e_1 wanted him to [**suspect**
          $^Pe_1$]] [Dulles suspected e_1]

If we had reconstructed without vehicle change, the resulting structures
would have been ill formed, cases of improper movement (Principle C).
But, with vehicle change, the pronominal correlates are properly free in
the embedded clauses, and the structures are differentiated with respect to
proper government and the ECP.

6.5.4 Subjacency Effects
In section 6.3 we pointed to the presence of Subjacency effects under
reconstruction, observing contrasts such as the following:

(138) a. *Dulles suspected everyone who Angleton wondered why
          Philby did

   b.   Dulles suspected everyone who Angleton believed that Philby
          did

The account is straightforward, since the postreconstruction LF representation will violate the *Wh*-Island Constraint:

(139) *everyone [who$_1$ Angleton wondered why Philby [**suspected** e_1]]
          [Dulles suspected e_1]

It might be thought that since trace/variables can be reconstructed as their
pronominal correlates, and since it is well known that pronominal binding

is not subject to bounding constraints, bounding effects such as these ought not be observable. That is, (138a) will have an alternative LF representation with vehicle change:

(140) everyone [who$_1$ Angleton wondered why Philby **suspected** $^P e_1$]
      [Dulles suspected e_1]

However, this case has a different status than other cases of vehicle change of variables, since it is only through the reconstruction of the pronominal correlate that the vacuity of the *wh*-phrase is relieved. In just these sorts of cases, therefore, the pronominal correlate would be functioning as a resumptive pronoun. But English does not allow resumptive pronouns in this context, so that on this analysis the ungrammaticality of (138a) is comparable to that of (141):

(141) *Who did Angleton wonder why Philby suspected him

In contrast, examples such as (142), brought to our attention by M. Rooth, are markedly better than (138a):

(142) Dulles suspected everyone who wondered why Philby did

This sentence has the following LF representation, with vehicle change:

(143) everyone [who$_1$ e_1 wondered why Philby **suspected** $^P e_1$] [Dulles
      suspected e_1]

The pronominal correlate here is free in its governing category and bound by the occurrence of the variable outside its governing category. Obviously, if we had not chosen the vehicle change option, the resulting structure would have been ill formed, a case of improper movement. Thus, just as (138a) is to be compared (with respect to its logical form) with (141), (142) is to be compared with (144), which has an overt pronoun in place of the pronominal correlate:

(144) Dulles suspected everyone who wondered why Philby suspected
      him

6.5.5 Parasitic Gaps

One of the functions of resumptive pronouns, where they can occur, is to allow operator binding into island configurations that do not otherwise allow binding of traces. The considerations of the previous section turn in part on the limitations on such resumptive pronouns in English. There are, however, environments in which empty pronominal categories can occur in syntactic islands without leading to violations. These are parasitic gaps.

It turns out that the existence of this type of element can also be shown under reconstruction. The example to consider is (145):

(145) Who did John introduce to everyone that Max did

Here the *wh*-phrase has been extracted from the direct object position, so that its trace will be part of the VP that is reconstructed into the ellipsis site, after LF movement. The resulting structure is (146):

(146) who$_1$ [everyone that Max **introduced** e_1 **to** t [John introduced e_1 to t]]

On initial inspection, we would expect (146) to violate Subjacency, since the reconstructed trace, bound by the *wh*-phrase, is contained within a relative clause. However, we have the option of deriving a structure with vehicle change:

(147) who$_1$ [everyone that Max **introduced** $^Pe_1$ **to** t [John introduced e_1 to t]]

Our claim is that the pronominal correlate in (147) is an occurrence of a (derived) parasitic gap as found in examples like (148a), shown with its counterparts with overt pronominals:

(148) a.   Which book did John file without reading

b.   Which book did John file without reading it

c.   *Which book did John file it without reading

The occurrence of the pronominal correlate in (147) bears certain basic similarities to other parasitic gaps. Like them, it neither c-commands nor is c-commanded by the "real" gap, nor is it subject to bounding conditions, if licensed. Also like other parasitic gaps, it cannot be further embedded in a second island (Contreras 1984). Thus, we find the contrasts illustrated in the complex NP examples in (149) and the *wh*-island examples in (150):

(149) a.   Which book did John file without reading the blurb that Bill wrote about it

b.   *Which book did John file without reading the blurb that Bill wrote about

(150) a.   Which book did John read without wondering why the author wrote it

b.   *Which book did John read without wondering why the author wrote

And similar contrasts are found with antecedent-contained deletion. Observe example (151) and the contrast in (152):

(151) *Who did John introduce to everyone that Bill knows someone that Max did

(152) a. *Who did John introduce to everyone that Bill wondered why Max did

b. Who did John introduce to everyone that Bill believed that Max did

(153) is the LF structure of (152a):

(153) *who$_1$ [everyone that Bill wondered why Max **introduced** $^P e_1$ **to** t [John introduced e_1 to t]]

Here we see plainly that the reconstructed category—a reconstructed parasitic gap—resides in a position that is illicit for such a category.[30]

Although we have framed our discussion of parasitic gaps in terms of *wh*-constructions, directly comparable examples can be given with quantifiers:

(154) John introduced someone to everyone that Max did

This shows the same interaction with islands that we have just observed:

(155) a. *John introduced someone to everyone that Bill wondered why Max did

b. John introduced someone to everyone that Bill believed that Max did

(154) has the representation in (156):

(156) someone$_1$ [everyone that Max **introduced** $^P e_1$ **to** t [John introduced e_1 to t]]

Aside from the lexical identity of the operator, this structure is identical to (147) for all intents and purposes.

These observations advance our understanding of parasitic gaps. Because of the contrast between *John filed every book without reading* and

---

30. Rooth (1981) observes sentences like *Which document did someone who shouldn't have see*, which although not a case of antecedent-contained deletion, is a case of a reconstructed parasitic gap. Here the VP *see t* is reconstructed into the relative clause, with the trace, in our terms, being realized as its pronominal correlate.

(148a), it is usually maintained that parasitic gaps are an S-Structure phenomenon and that they cannot be generated by LF operations (Chomsky 1982). The examples above falsify this view, since LF movement and reconstruction play a vital role in deriving syntactic environments that can license parasitic gaps. Interestingly, these cases of LF parasitic gaps involve both *wh* gaps and QR gaps. Thus, it appears to be the case that the occurrence of these parasitic gaps is constrained only by the conditions that determine well-formedness at LF as this interacts with reconstruction.

6.6 What Is Reconstruction?

We have now arrived at a more comprehensive characterization of reconstruction: a reconstruction is a set of token structures, closed under identity of syntactic structure up to variance in indexical value and vehicle change. Now, insofar as ellipsis is licensed by reconstruction, it follows that ellipses are syntactically specified. Since elided constructions share this syntactic specification with their unelided counterparts, grammatical principles apply equally well to elided and unelided structures. Our observations regarding the applicability of these principles in antecedent-contained deletion lead us to conclude that the full class of structures falling within reconstructions is to be found with respect to representations at LF.

One can imagine alternatives to our perspective on reconstruction. Let us consider two, one syntactic and the other semantic. Although the syntactic alternative agrees that what is reconstructed is the form of the verb phrase, it differs in denying that this is its *logical* form. By contrast, the semantic alternative denies that it is the form of the verb phrase that is reconstructed and claims instead that it is its *meaning*. Although these alternatives indicate very different lines of analysis, they agree that reconstruction does not depend upon logical form. What content is there to these alternatives?

What makes the argument for the role of LF in reconstruction, we have claimed, is the necessity of referring to the logical form of quantification in accounting for antecedent-contained deletion. This is what has taken us beyond mere superficial structure. That quantification plays a role in the description of antecedent-contained deletion is perhaps unarguable; but one could still take exception to the claim that it is the *logical form* of quantification that is relevant. For suppose that there were some mechanism within the semantics that is functionally equivalent to QR in assigning an analogue of scope to quantifiers. In taking on this role, it might be argued, this mechanism would create contexts that are not antecedent-contained, just as QR does, and that could be reconstructed. Reconstruction would be semantic, since it could only occur after this quantifier operation defined on meanings had applied. The results we have observed, and claimed to be matters of logical form, would then carry over to the ways in which meanings are composed out of other meanings. This would then be a form of the semantic alternative.

Such semantic analogues for quantification have indeed been advanced in the form of the "quantifier-stores" proposed by Cooper (1983). Informally, the idea is that if a quantifier is encountered in the course of interpreting a sentential structure, its meaning, a function of a particular type, can be "stored," while a pronoun-meaning is composed in its place. When the level of the clause is reached, the quantifier is retrieved, and quantified in, the pronoun-meaning serving as the variable it binds. This treatment of quantification differs from ours in the requisite sense, in that the scope analogue affects *meanings* (functions), storing and retrieving them, as opposed to QR, which affects syntactic entities. In this context, Rooth (1981) offers a precise answer to our question about reconstruction. He proposes that along with NPs, VPs can also be stored, their place in the composition being taken by a variable of the appropriate type. An elided VP (actually the stranded auxiliary element) also translates as a VP-type variable. Reconstruction is the quantifying in, via λ-conversion, of a previously stored VP-meaning into the positions of the occurrences of the VP variable. It is an arguable virtue of this approach that reconstruction is not any kind of special operation, but rather just another case of λ-conversion.[31]

When applied to a sentence such as *John talked to everyone Max did*, that is, to antecedent-contained deletion, the composition would proceed by first building up and storing an NP-meaning containing a VP variable, then building up and storing a VP-meaning, leaving appropriate variables in their places, and then retrieving the NP- and VP-meanings in turn. After this retrieval the sentence would have, informally, the following translation, where Φ is a variable over VP-meanings:

(157) $\lambda\Phi(\forall x(\lambda x_i[\Phi(\text{Max}')](x) \rightarrow \lambda x_i[\Phi(\text{John}')](x)))(\text{talk-to}'(x_i))$

31. Bear in mind that we consider this analysis in the context of our rejection, in the face of the eliminative puzzles, of predication-based theories of ellipsis, of which this proposal is an instance. That is, in assuming that ellipsis is based on identity of λ-expressions—here, occurrences that are quantified in—it takes on the empirical shortcomings associated with this general approach.

Reconstruction via λ-conversion then yields (158), which is equivalent to (159):

(158) $\forall x(\lambda x_i[\text{talk-to}'(x_i)(\text{Max}')](x) \rightarrow \lambda x_i[\text{talk-to}'(x_i)(\text{John}')](x))$

(159) $\forall x(\text{talk-to}'(x)(\text{Max}') \rightarrow \text{talk-to}'(x)(\text{John}'))$

Placing this in a more formal context, and following the line of analysis suggested by Rooth, the treatment would proceed as follows, where each line is a 4-tuple consisting of a syntactic phrase, its category, its translation, and a store; for perspicuity, we have ignored intensionality and dispensed with taking names as generalized quantifiers:

1. did, VP, Φ_1, $\varnothing$
2. Max did, IP, $\Phi_1(\text{Max}')$, $\varnothing$
3. Max did, CP, $\lambda x_2 [\Phi_1(\text{Max}')](x)$, $\varnothing$
4. everyone Max did, NP, x_2, $\{\langle \lambda\text{P everyone}' (\lambda x_2 [\Phi_1(\text{Max}')](x), \text{P}), 2\rangle\}$ (STORE NP)
5. talk to everyone Max did, VP, Φ_1, $\{\langle \lambda\text{P everyone}' (\lambda x_2 [\Phi_1(\text{Max}')](x), \text{P}), 2\rangle, \langle\text{talk-to}' (x_2), 1\rangle\}$ (STORE VP)
6. John talked to everyone Max did, IP, $\Phi_1(\text{John}')$, $\{\langle \lambda\text{P everyone}' (\lambda x_2 [\Phi_1(\text{Max}')(x)], \text{P}), 2\rangle, \langle\text{talk-to}' (x_2), 1\rangle\}$
7. John talked to everyone Max did, IP, $\lambda\text{P everyone}' (\lambda x_2 [\Phi_1(\text{Max}')] (x), \text{P})$ $\lambda x_2 [\Phi_1(\text{John}')](x)$, $\{\langle\text{talk-to}' (x_2), 1\rangle\}$ (RETRIEVE NP)
8. John talked to everyone Max did, IP, $\text{everyone}' (\lambda x_2 [\Phi_1(\text{Max}')](x), \lambda x_2 [\Phi_1(\text{John}')](x))$, $\{\langle\text{talk-to}' (x_2), 1\rangle\}$ (λ-CONVERSION)
9. John talked to everyone Max did, IP, $\lambda\Phi_1 (\text{everyone}' (\lambda x_2 [\Phi_1(\text{Max}')] (x), \lambda x_2 [\Phi_1(\text{John}')](x)))(\text{talk-to}' (x_2))$, $\varnothing$ (RETRIEVE VP)
10. John talked to everyone Max did, IP, $\text{everyone}' (\lambda x_2 [\text{talk-to}' (x_2)(\text{Max}')](x), \lambda x_2 [\text{talk-to}' (x_2)(\text{John}')](x))$, $\varnothing$ (λ-CONVERSION)
11. John talked to everyone Max did, IP, $\text{everyone}' (\text{talk-to}' (x)(\text{Max}'), \text{talk-to}' (x)(\text{John}'))$, $\varnothing$ (λ-CONVERSION)

The last three lines of this derivation correspond to (157) through (159). Although such a derivation would yield the correct result, Larson (1986) points out that it involves the illicit capture of a free variable within the λ-expressions in the step from (157) to (158). That is, the λ-conversion that brings the VP-meaning inside improperly involves the variable x_i being captured within the scope of λx_i [...]. Larson locates the root of the problem in the idea that ellipsis involves VP-meanings and suggests a departure from this assumption. He suggests replacing the variable over VP-meanings with a variable over transitive verbs, that is, over functions from individuals to VP-meanings. In a sense, what is being reconstructed is just the (meaning of the) verb *talk to*, and not that of the entire VP that it heads. Then rather than (157), we would have (160), which by proper λ-conversion/reconstruction would lead to (161), and then to (162), the desired interpretation:

(160) $\lambda\Phi(\forall x(\Phi(x)(\text{Max}') \rightarrow \Phi(x)(\text{John}')))(\lambda x_i[\text{talk-to}'(x_i)])$

(161) $\forall x(\lambda x_i[\text{talk-to}'(x_i)](x)(\text{Max}') \rightarrow \lambda x_i[\text{talk-to}'(x_i)](x)(\text{John}'))$

(162) $\forall x(\text{talk-to}'(x)(\text{Max}') \rightarrow \text{talk-to}'(x)(\text{John}'))$

The trick involved here is to provide for a prior encoding of a to-be-resolved dependency (regardless of the adicity of the predicate), which would subsequently allow for proper λ-conversion, resulting in a circumstance, as Larson observes, where although reconstruction has been made semantically explicit, this is done at the cost of abandoning the notion that reconstruction is defined relative to VP-meanings per se. Antecedent-contained deletion would therefore not be of a piece with other forms of verb phrase ellipsis, where a VP-meaning, not a transitive VP-meaning, is reconstructed.[32]

Setting aside general problems afflicting this approach (e.g., those of the eliminative puzzles), it is of some interest to consider how the meaning reconstruction/storage approach fares with the previously discussed cases of interaction between antecedent-contained deletion and anaphora. After all, we have made a virtue of the manner in which an LF-based approach allows for proper application of Binding Theory. The needed extensions are provided by Partee and Bach (1984), and assumed by Rooth (1981). The idea is that there is an additional store, the Local Pronoun Store (LPST), into which the indices of pronouns are entered; their anaphoric possibilities are then derived from conditions on the stores. So, for instance, the not-coreference of the NPs in *He saw him* follows from requiring that the NP pronoun store, which contains the index of the subject NP, and VP pronoun store, which contains the index of the object NP, have no members in common: if these NPs are coindexed, then the stores will have a nonnull intersection. The conjointness in *He believes Max saw him* arises from conditions requiring that the LPST of S be null, so that the indices of the pronouns will not be passed up to the pronoun store of the

32. In requiring that a transitive verb phrase be reconstructed, the storage approach is like the approach of Cormack (1984) and Jacobson (1991) stated in terms of categorial grammar. For problems endemic to this class of treatments, see footnote 15.

higher VP. With this much in mind, consider the analysis of (85), repeated here:

(85) Mary introduced him to everyone that he did

In giving its composition, the elided VP would be translated as a VP variable, which would then combine with the pronoun, the index of which would be placed in the LPST. This index would then be discharged from the store, at the point of composition of the relative clause, just as it would in the analysis of *Mary introduced him to everyone he likes*. The translation in (163a) would be built up, via storage and retrieval, and (163a) would in turn be converted into (163b):

(163) a. $\lambda\Phi[\forall x(\Phi(x)(\text{he}') \rightarrow \Phi(x)(\text{Mary}'))](\lambda x_1[\text{introduce}'\ (\text{him}')(x_1)])$

       b. $\forall x(\text{introduce}(\text{him}')(x)(\text{he}') \rightarrow \text{introduce}(\text{him}')(x)(\text{Mary}'))$

In this translation, however, there is nothing that blocks the pronouns from being coindexed and hence coreferential. But the pronouns in (85), as discussed, must be not-coreferential. Thus, the approach fails here, just as it fails to characterize the difference between (164a) and (164b):

(164) a. Mary introduced him to everyone that he wanted her to

       b. *Mary introduced him to everyone that she wanted him to

This is because in general the indices of embedded pronouns are not retained in the LPST associated with the meanings of higher constituents.

It might be argued that a way to circumvent this problem could be constructed, based on the observation that after reconstruction (λ-conversion) in (163b), the two pronouns are coarguments of a predicate. The LPST could then be recalculated at this point to account for the observed facts. This would be a rather curious direction to take, however. First, it would mean that to get the right result, we would have to map one semantically equivalent translation into another—λ-conversion, so to speak, is "meaning preserving." Second, in a storage system meanings are calculated over syntactic representations; hence, if there is to be a recalculation, there must be a new syntactic representation. But this is not what (163b) is; rather, it is a translation, a meaning, associated with exactly the same syntactic structure as (163a). And finally, and perhaps most egregiously, allowing such a recalculation would undermine the very notion of compositionality that the storage approach seeks to implement: once the meanings of the parts are composed, one doesn't want to have to go back and compose those very sentence parts again. In contrast, the theory of ellipsis we are espousing does not violate even the spirit of compositionality. This is because reconstruction is syntactic, and is accomplished prior to interpretation, in deriving LF. Once such structures are obtained, the calculation of anaphora and the determination of meaning can proceed, in a strictly compositional manner.

These considerations lead us to dismiss the semantic alternative to logical form. What of the syntactic alternative, which also eschews this notion? On one form of this view, the elided VP, although lexically unspecified at S-Structure (and perhaps also D-Structure), is *not* categorially unspecified, so that the structure of *Dulles suspected everyone that Angleton did* would be exactly the same as that of the nonelliptical *Dulles suspected everyone that Angleton suspected*. The two would differ only in their lexical realizations. One apparent advantage of this approach is that antecedent-contained deletion would be a misnomer, and any matter of reconstruction turning on LF or LF movement would be moot. A treatment that makes reconstruction explicit in this fashion has been broached by Lappin (1991) and Lappin and McCord (1990).[33]

A number of problems arise on this approach. First, since it disassociates quantifier scope and reconstruction scope, it cannot account for their interactions. For instance, there would seem to be no reason that we could not have narrow quantifier scope with broad reconstruction, a circumstance that is not possible (recall section 6.2). Second, since the structure of elided VPs would be all there is at S-Structure, it ought to be possible to define Binding Theory at this level. If getting the binding facts "right" requires looking at "reconstructed" structure, then since this structure is present at least at S-Structure, representations at this level should be equal to the task. For many cases this is indeed so. To take but one example, recall (67):

(67) *Mary introduced John to everyone that he did

---

33. Lappin (1991) takes the view that whereas antecedent-contained deletion involves categorial specification, standard ellipsis does not, the elided VP being empty in this construction at LF. He bases this on a putative contrast between *I know which book John read and Mary didn't* and *I know which book John read and which book Mary didn't*, finding the latter marginal relative to the former. The reason for this, according to Lappin, is that since the VP is empty in the latter case, there is no trace for the second *wh*-phrase to bind. Operator vacuity, however, standardly gives rise to strong ungrammaticality, and at best the case in question is only marginally ill formed, if ill formed at all. Lappin proposes that this sentence can be "repaired" by copying at another level, presumably LF. But if such copying is available for this type of ellipsis, why not for antecedent-contained deletion? See May 1991.

Its hypothesized S-Structure representation would be something like (165):

(165) $[_{IP}$ Mary $[_{VP}[_V$ introduced] $[_{NP}$ John]$_1$ $[_{PP}[_P$ to] $[_{NP}$ everyone $[_{CP}$ that $[_{IP}$ he$_1$ $[_{VP}[_V$ $e]$ $[_{NP}$ $e]_1$ $[_{PP}[_P$ $e]]$ $[_{NP}$ $e]]]]]]]]]$

Since the layered trace contains a category corresponding to the NP *John*, and since this category is c-commanded by the pronoun, a Principle C violation ensues. This line of reasoning can be extended to many of the other cases we have explored, although notice that it will have to incorporate vehicle change to accommodate sentences such as *Mary introduced John to everyone that he wanted her to* ($= (100a)$), which allow coreference. One should not be led astray by such demonstrations, however. This is because, with respect to Binding Theory, S-Structure and LF are in a feeding/bleeding relation. Any case in which S-Structure Binding Theory violations are *bled* through the derivation onto LF will remain unaccounted for. Recall the following examples:

(73c) Mary introduced him to everyone that John's mother wanted her to

(95)   a.   Mary introduced him to everyone that John wanted her to

       b. *Mary introduced him to everyone that she wanted John to

Each of these, as it stands, violates Principle C; amelioration is afforded, as described, via the derivation to LF. But if only S-Structure is available —with or without elided structure specified—then these should all display not-coreference effects. Thus, (166) contrasts minimally with (73c), and (167) with (95a), where (166) and (167) lack the readings indicated by the indices:

(166) *Mary introduced him$_1$ to everyone that John$_1$'s mother introduced him$_1$ to

(167) *Mary introduced him$_1$ to everyone that John$_1$ wanted her to introduce him$_1$ to

On the approach under consideration, there should be no difference between the elided and nonelided sentences. Similarly, there should be no difference between (78) and (84), repeated here:

(78) The men introduced each other to everyone that the women did

(84) The men introduced each other to everyone that the women introduced each other to

There is no apparent reason why there should be an additional strict reading created by ellipsis in (78), since here too the elided and nonelided

forms should be indistinguishable for Binding Theory. These considerations therefore lead us to reject this syntactic alternative as well.

The view of reconstruction we have defended is one in which elliptical
material is syntactically specified at LF and, we have assumed, at other
levels as well. Standardly, syntactic structure is lexically projected, licensed
by the selectional and thematic information encoded in lexical entries. But
this is precisely what does *not* happen in ellipsis: ellipsis is the *absence of
lexical projection*. But from this it does not follow that ellipsis also involves
absence of structure, only that this structure has not been licensed lexically.
Projection of elliptical material is instead determined *structurally*, by conditions that determine structural identity. That is, elliptical structure is
licensed by its relation to other, lexically projected, structure. This difference between structural and lexical projection is just the difference between
elided and nonelided material. It is only at the point in a derivation at
which the identity condition is satisfied that a structure containing ellipsis
can be said to be projected, and the elided material reconstructed. Prior to
its projection, then, elided structure although syntactically present is, to all
intents and purposes, invisible. Only when it is projected can it fall under
the purview of grammatical principles.

Antecedent-contained deletion is of special interest here. This is because
the elided structure it contains can only be projected at LF. Prior to QR,
the antecedence condition for the elided VP simply is not satisfied; no
noncircular structural projection can be established without LF movement. For antecedent-contained deletion, QR is tantamount to reconstruction; it is a reflex of this operation. Once such movement occurs, the
antecedence condition is satisfied, and the structure projects, that is, becomes visible. At prior levels the structure, although present, would be
dysfunctional, since it is unprojected. Syntactic constraints become applicable at the point of projection, since constraints apply only to projected
structure. Thus, conditions that involve the elided material in antecedent-
contained circumstances will become applicable only at LF, and not at
prior structural levels.

Consider the case of Binding Theory. It applies to indices borne by
various elements: it is with respect to occurrences of indices that the crucial
notions of bound and free are defined. For Binding Theory to be applicable to an element, then, its index must be structurally projected. An index
is projected, let us say, just in case *all* of its occurrences appear within the
projected structure. The indices in (168a) and (168b) will count as projected by this definition:

(168) a. *He$_1$ suspected everyone that Angleton$_1$ investigated

    b. *He$_1$ suspected everyone that Angleton$_1$ did

Binding Theory will be applicable to both, making them cases of not-coreference. This is so, even though these cases differ in that only in (168a) does the projected structure exhaust the phrase marker; (168b), in containing elliptical material, is only partially projected at S-Structure. The unprojected structure contains no occurrence of the relevant index. This is not the case, however, in (169), the S-Structure representation of *You introduced him to everyone that John wanted you to*, which allows coreference:

(169) You introduced him$_1$ to everyone that John$_1$ wanted you to
    introduce him$_1$ to *t*

Here there are occurrences of the index that fall outside the projected structure; hence, the well-formedness of this index cannot yet be evaluated. This will become possible after reconstruction. Therefore, Binding Theory will become applicable just at LF, with respect to the fully projected structure (170):

(170) everyone that John$_1$ wanted you to **introduce him$_1$ to *t*** [you introduced him$_1$ to *t*]

Now all occurrences of the index are within the projected material; hence, the index itself is projected and may be evaluated by Binding Theory. On the other hand, the index will be projected in the S-Structure representation of *You introduced him to everyone that John likes*, correctly occasioning a Principle C violation. A Principle C violation also ensues in (171), where we take the ellipsis as non-antecedent-contained:

(171) I introduced him to everyone that John wanted me to meet, and you introduced him to everyone that John wanted you to

Although the second clause is string identical to (169), where the ellipsis is antecedent-contained, it differs in that the index is projected (since here the ellipsis corresponds to *meet t*).[34]

The view we are advancing is that strings must be associated with well-formed phrase markers at every level of representation, up to projectability; that is, whatever *part* of a string's structure is projected must be well formed. Full projectability, required at LF, is the syntactic face of

---

34. We would like to thank K. Johnson for bringing these considerations to our attention.

full interpretation. Antecedent-contained deletion is a case in point where there will be structures that are fully projected at certain levels (LF), but only partially projected at others (D-Structure, S-Structure). Because of this, antecedent-contained deletion allows us to isolate phenomena peculiar to LF; but with other types of ellipsis, matters can be determined at other levels, since the conditions determining projection can be satisfied at other levels. The approach to reconstruction we are advocating thus partially answers a central question raised by our observations regarding Binding Theory and other grammatical conditions: At what level of representation do they apply? The answer is, with respect to indices, the level at which those indices are projected. Clearly, our view has wide-ranging consequences for the theory of grammar, for it says that a sentence need not be projected at all levels to have a well-formed syntactic structure. Exploring these implications, however, will have to wait for future research.

References

Aoun, J. (1985). *A grammar of anaphora*. MIT Press, Cambridge, Mass.

Aoun, J., and D. Sportiche (1983). On the formal theory of government. *The Linguistic Review* 2:211–36.

Baltin, M. (1987). Do antecedent-contained deletions exist? *Linguistic Inquiry* 18:579–95.

Baltin, M. (1991). VP-ellipsis as non-lambda predicate ellipsis. Ms., New York University.

Barwise, J. (1979). On branching quantifiers in English. *Journal of Philosophical Logic* 8:47–80.

Barwise, J. (1987). Noun phrases, generalized quantifiers and anaphora. In P. Gärdenfors, ed., *Generalized quantifiers: Linguistic and logical approaches*. Reidel, Dordrecht.

Bevington, B. (1993). Dependencies among variable indices: An extension of Dependency Theory. Ms., The Graduate Center, City University of New York.

Bouton, L. (1970). Antecedent contained pro-forms. In M. Campbell et al., eds., *CLS 6: Papers from the Sixth Regional Meeting of the Chicago Linguistic Society*. University of Chicago, Chicago, Ill.

Brody, M. (1982). On circular readings. In N. V. Smith, ed., *Mutual knowledge*. Academic Press, New York.

Carlson, G. (1977). Amount relatives. *Language* 53:520–42

Castañeda, H. (1966). "He": A study in the logic of self-conciousness. *Ratio* 8:130–57

Castañeda, H. (1968). On the logic of attribution of self-knowledge to others. *Journal of Philosophy* 65:439–56.

Chao, W. (1987). On ellipsis. Doctoral dissertation, University of Massachusetts, Amherst.

Chierchia, G. (1984). Topics in the syntax and semantics of infinitives and gerunds. Doctoral dissertation, University of Massacusetts, Amherst.

Chierchia, G. (1989). Anaphora and attitudes *de se*. In R. Bartsch, J. van Benthem, and P. van Emde Boas, eds., *Semantics and contextual expression*. Foris, Dordrecht.

Chomsky, N. (1955/1975). *The logical structure of linguistic theory*. Plenum Press, New York.

Chomsky, N. (1975). Questions of form and interpretation. In R. Austerlitz, ed., *The scope of American linguistics*. The Peter de Ridder Press, Lisse. Also appears in *Essays on form and interpretation*, North-Holland, New York (1977).

Chomsky, N. (1976). Conditions on rules of grammar. *Linguistic Analysis* 2:303–51. Also appears in *Essays on form and interpretation*, North-Holland, New York (1977).

Chomsky, N. (1977). On *wh*-movement, In P. Culicover, T. Wasow, and A. Akmajian, eds., *Formal syntax*. Academic Press, New York.

Chomsky, N. (1981). *Lectures on government and binding*. Foris, Dordrecht.

Chomsky, N. (1982). *Some concepts and consequences of the theory of government and binding*. MIT Press, Cambridge, Mass.

Chomsky, N. (1986a). *Barriers*. MIT Press, Cambridge, Mass.

Chomsky, N. (1986b). *Knowledge of language: Its nature, origin, and use*. Praeger, New York.

Chomsky, N. (1993). A minimalist program for linguistic theory. In K. Hale and S. J. Keyser, eds., *The view from Building 20: Essays in linguistics in honor of Sylvain Bromberger*. MIT Press, Cambridge, Mass.

Contreras, H. (1984). A note on parasitic gaps. *Linguistic Inquiry* 15:704–13.

Cooper, R. (1983). *Quantification and syntactic theory*. Reidel, Dordrecht.

Cormack, A. (1984). VP anaphora: Variables and scope. In F. Landman and F. Veltman, eds., *Varieties of formal semantics*. Foris, Dordrecht.

Dahl, Ö. (1973). On so-called "sloppy identity." *Synthese* 26:81–112.

Dahl, Ö. (1974). How to open a sentence: Abstraction in natural language. In *Logical grammar reports*, no. 12. University of Göteberg.

Dalrymple, M. (1991). Against reconstruction in ellipsis. Xerox Technical Report, Xerox-PARC, Palo Alto, Calif.

Dalrymple, M., S. Shieber, and F. Pereira (1991). Ellipsis and higher-order unification. *Linguistics and Philosophy* 14:399–452.

Diesing, M. (1992). *Indefinites*. MIT Press, Cambridge, Mass.

Doron, E. (1990). V-movement and VP-ellipsis. Ms., The Hebrew University of Jerusalem.

Emonds, J. (1979). Appositive relatives have no properties. *Linguistic Inquiry* 10:211–43.

Enç, M. (1989). Pronouns, licensing, and binding. *Natural Language & Linguistic Theory* 7:51–92.

Evans, G. (1977). Pronouns, quantifiers, and relative clauses (I). *The Canadian Journal of Philosophy* 7:467–536.

Evans, G. (1980). Pronouns. *Linguistic Inquiry* 11:337–62.

Fodor, J. D., and I. Sag (1982). Referential and quantificational indefinites. *Linguistics and Philosophy* 5:355–98.

Gawron, J. M., and S. Peters (1990a). *Anaphora and quantification in situation semantics*. Center for the Study of Language and Information, Stanford, Calif.

Gawron, J. M., and S. Peters (1990b). Some puzzles about pronouns. In R. Cooper, K. Mukai, and J. Perry, eds., *Situation theory and its applications*. Center for the Study of Language and Information, Stanford, Calif.

Geach, P. (1962). *Reference and generality*. Cornell University Press, Ithaca, N.Y.

Grodzinsky, Y., and T. Reinhart (1993). The innateness of binding and coreference. *Linguistic Inquiry* 24:69–101.

Haïk, I. (1983). Indirect binding and referential circularity. *The Linguistic Review* 2:313–30.

Haïk, I. (1985). The syntax of operators. Doctoral dissertation, MIT.

Haïk, I. (1987). Bound VPs that need to be. *Linguistics and Philosophy* 10:503–30.

Hankamer, J. (1973). Why there are two *than*'s in English. In C. Corum, T. C. Smith-Stark, and A. Weiser, eds., *Papers from the Ninth Regional Meeting of the Chicago Linguistic Society*. University of Chicago, Chicago, Ill.

Hardt, D. (1991). A discourse model approach to VP-ellipsis. In *Proceedings of the AAAI Symposium on Discourse Structure in Natural Language Understanding and Generation*. Asilomar, Calif.

Hardt, D. (1992). VP ellipsis and semantic identity. In S. Berman and A. Hestvik, eds., *Proceedings of the Stuttgart Ellipsis Workshop*. Arbeitspapiere des Sonderforschungsbereichs 340, Bericht Nr. 29. IBM Germany, Heidelberg.

Heim, I. (1982). The semantics of definite and indefinite noun phrases. Doctoral dissertation, University of Massachusetts, Amherst.

Heim, I. (1990). E-type pronouns and donkey anaphora. *Linguistics and Philosophy* 13:137–78.

Heim, I., H. Lasnik, and R. May (1991a). On "Reciprocal Scope." *Linguistic Inquiry* 22:173–92.

Heim, I., H. Lasnik, and R. May (1991b). Reciprocity and plurality. *Linguistic Inquiry* 22:63–102.

Hestvik, A. (1992). Strict reflexives and the subordination effect. In S. Berman and A. Hestvik, eds., *Proceedings of the Stuttgart Ellipsis Workshop*. Arbeitspapiere des Sonderforschungsbereichs 340, Bericht Nr. 29. IBM Germany, Heidelberg.

Higginbotham, J. (1980a). Anaphora and GB. In J. Jensen, ed., *Proceedings of the Tenth Annual Meeting of NELS Cahiers linguistiques d'Ottawa* 9. Department of Linguistics, University of Ottawa.

Higginbotham, J. (1980b). Pronouns and bound variables. *Linguistic Inquiry* 11:679–708.

Higginbotham, J. (1983). Logical Form, binding, and nominals. *Linguistic Inquiry* 14:395–420.

Higginbotham, J. (1985). On semantics. *Linguistic Inquiry* 16:547–94.

Higginbotham, J. (1989). Varieties of cross-reference. In A. Cardinaletti et al., eds., *Annali di Ca'Foscari, 27: Papers from the 1987 GLOW Conference.* Foris, Dordrecht.

Higginbotham, J. (1990). Anaphoric intentions. Ms., MIT.

Higginbotham, J. (1991a). Belief and Logical Form. *Mind and Language* 6:344–69.

Higginbotham, J. (1991b). Interrogatives I. Ms., MIT.

Higginbotham, J. (1992). Reference and control. In R. Larson, S. Iatridou, U. Lahiri, and J. Higginbotham, eds., *Control and grammar.* Kluwer, Dordrecht.

Higginbotham, J. (1993). Anaphoric reference and common reference. Ms., MIT.

Higginbotham, J., and R. May (1981a). Crossing, markedness, pragmatics. In A. Belletti, L. Brandi, and L. Rizzi, eds., *Theory of markedness in generative grammar.* Scuola Normale Superiore, Pisa.

Higginbotham, J., and R. May (1981b). Questions, quantifiers and crossing. *The Linguistic Review* 1:41–79.

Hirschbühler, P. (1982). VP-deletion and across-the-board quantifier scope. In J. Pustejovsky and P. Sells, eds., *Proceedings of NELS 12.* GLSA, University of Massachusetts, Amherst.

Hoeksema, J., and D. J. Napoli (1990). A condition on circular chains: A restatement of i-within-i. *Journal of Linguistics* 26:403–24

Hornstein, N., and A. Weinberg (1990). The necessity of LF. *The Linguistic Review* 7:129–68.

Huang, C.-T. J. (1982). Logical relations in chinese and the theory of grammar. Doctoral dissertation, MIT.

Jacobson, P. (1977). The syntax of crossing coreference sentences. Doctoral dissertation, University of California, Berkeley.

Jacobson, P. (1991). Flexible categorial grammars: Questions and prospects. In R. Levine, ed., *Formal linguistics: Theory and implementation.* Vancouver Studies in Cognitive Science. University of British Columbia Press, Vancouver.

Kamp, H. (1984). A theory of truth and semantic representation. In J. Groenendijk, T. M. V. Janssen, and M. Stokhof, eds., *Truth, interpretation and information.* Foris, Dordrecht.

Kimball, J. (1970). Categories of meaning. Doctoral dissertation, MIT.

Kitagawa, Y. (1991a). Binding under the internal subject hypothesis. In H. Nakajima, ed., *Trends in linguistics: State of the art report 16*. Mouton de Gruyter.

Kitagawa, Y. (1991b). Copying identity. *Natural Language & Linguistic Theory* 9:497–536.

Klein, E. (1987). VP ellipsis in DR Theory. In J. Groenendijk, D. de Jongh, and M. Stokhof, eds., *Studies in Discourse Representation Theory and the theory of generalized quantifiers*. Foris, Dordrecht.

Koopman, H., and D. Sportiche (1982). Variables and the Bijection Principle. *The Linguistic Review* 2:139–61.

Koster, J., and E. Reuland, eds. (1991). *Long-distance anaphora*. Cambridge University Press, Cambridge.

Kripke, S. (1979). Speaker's reference and semantic reference. In P. French, T. E. Uehling, Jr., and H. K. Wettstein, eds., *Contemporary perspectives in the philosophy of language*. University of Minnesota Press, Minneapolis.

Ladusaw, W. (1987). Inference patterns from infinitival complements. In M. Crowhurst, ed., *Proceedings of the Sixth West Coast Conference on Formal Linguistics*. Stanford Linguistics Association, Stanford University, Stanford, Calif.

Lahiri, U. (1991). Embedded interrogatives and predicates that embed them. Doctoral dissertation, MIT.

Landman, F. (1989). Groups, I. *Linguistics and Philosophy* 12:559–605.

Lappin, S. (1984). VP anaphora, quantifier scope, and Logical Form. *Linguistic Analysis* 13:273–315.

Lappin, S. (1991). Concepts of Logical Form in linguistics and philosophy. In A. Kasher, ed., *The Chomskyan turn*. Blackwell, Oxford.

Lappin, S. (1992). The syntactic basis of ellipsis resolution. In S. Berman and A. Hestvik, eds., *Proceedings of the Stuttgart Ellipsis Workshop*. Arbeitspapiere des Sonderforschungsbereichs 340, Bericht Nr. 29. IBM Germany, Heidelberg.

Lappin, S., and M. McCord (1990). Anaphora resolution in Slot Grammar. *Computational Linguistics* 16:197–212.

Larson, R. (1986). Lambda conversion and antecedent-contained deletion. Ms., MIT.

Larson, R. (1987). "Missing prepositions" and the analysis of English free relative clauses. *Linguistic Inquiry* 18:239–66.

Larson, R. (1988). On the double object construction. *Linguistic Inquiry* 19:335–91.

Larson, R., and P. Ludlow (1993). Interpreted Logical Form. To appear in *Synthese*.

Larson, R., and R. May (1990). Antecedent containment or vacuous movement: Reply to Baltin. *Linguistic Inquiry* 21:103–22.

Larson, R., and G. Segal (forthcoming). *Knowledge of meaning: Semantic value and Logical Form.* MIT Press, Cambridge, Mass.

Lasnik, H. (1976). Remarks on coreference. *Linguistic Analysis* 2:1–22.

Lasnik, H. (1981). On two recent treatments of disjoint reference. *Journal of Linguistic Research* 1.4:48–58.

Lasnik, H. (1989). On the necessity of binding conditions. In *Essays on anaphora.* Kluwer, Dordrecht.

Lasnik, H., and J. Uriagereka (1988). *A course in GB syntax.* MIT Press, Cambridge, Mass.

Lewis, D. (1979). Attitudes *de dicto* and *de se. The Philosophical Review* 88:513–43.

Link, G. (1983). The logical analysis of plurals and mass terms: A lattice-theoretical approach. In R. Bauerle et al., eds., *Meaning, use and interpretation of language.* de Gruyter, Berlin.

Link, G. (1987). Generalized quantifiers and plurals. In P. Gärdenfors, ed., *Generalized quantifiers: Linguistic and logical approaches.* Reidel, Dordrecht.

Lobeck, A. (1986). Syntactic constraints on VP anaphora. Doctoral dissertation, University of Washington, Seattle.

Lobeck, A (1987). VP ellipsis in infinitives: INFL as a proper governor. In J. M. McDonough and B. Plunkett, eds., *Proceedings of NELS 17.* GLSA, University of Massachusetts, Amherst.

Lobeck, A. (1992). Licensing and identification of ellipted categories in English. In S. Berman and A. Hestvik, eds., *Proceedings of the Stuttgart Ellipsis Workshop.* Arbeitspapiere des Sonderforschungsbereichs 340, Bericht Nr. 29. IBM Germany, Heidelberg.

Ludlow, P., and S. Neale (1991). Indefinite descriptions: In defense of Russell. *Linguistics and Philosophy* 14:171–202.

McCawley, J. (1982). Parentheticals and discontinuous constituents. *Linguistic Inquiry* 13:91–106.

McCloskey, J. (1991). Clause structure, ellipsis and proper government. *Lingua* 85:259–302.

May, R. (1977). The grammar of quantification. Doctoral dissertation, MIT.

May, R. (1979). Must Comp-to-Comp movement be stipulated? *Linguistic Inquiry* 10:719–25.

May, R. (1981). Movement and binding. *Linguistic Inquiry* 12:215–43.

May, R. (1985). *Logical Form: Its structure and derivation.* MIT Press, Cambridge, Mass.

May, R. (1988). Ambiguities of quantification and *wh*: A reply to Williams. *Linguistic Inquiry* 19:118–35.

May, R. (1989). Interpreting Logical Form. *Linguistics and Philosophy* 12:387–435.

May, R. (1991). Syntax, semantics, and Logical Form. In A. Kasher, ed., *The Chomskyan turn*. Blackwell, Oxford.

Neale, S. (1990). *Descriptions*. MIT Press, Cambridge, Mass.

Nunberg, G. (1978). The pragmatics of reference. Doctoral dissertation, The Graduate Center, City University of New York. (Distributed by Indiana University Linguistics Club, Bloomington.)

Otani, K., and J. Whitman (1991). V-raising and VP-ellipsis. *Linguistic Inquiry* 22:345–58.

Partee, B., and E. Bach (1984). Quantification, pronouns, and VP anaphora. In J. Groenendijk, T. M. V. Janssen, and M. Stokhof, eds., *Truth, interpretation and information*. Foris, Dordrecht.

Perry, J. (1977). Frege on demonstratives. *The Philosophical Review* 86:474–97.

Perry, J. (1979). The problem of the essential indexical. *Nous* 13:3–21.

Pesetsky, D. (1987). *Wh*-in-situ: Movement and unselective binding. In E. Reuland and A. ter Meulen, eds., *The representation of (in)definiteness*. MIT Press, Cambridge, Mass.

Pica, P. (1985). Subject, tense and truth: Towards a modular approach to binding. In J. Guéron, H.-G. Obenauer, and J.-Y. Pollock, eds., *Grammatical representation*. Foris, Dordrecht.

Pica, P. (1987). On the nature of the reflexivization cycle. In J. M. McDonough and B. Plunkett, eds., *Proceedings of NELS 17*. GLSA, University of Massachusetts, Amherst.

Reinhart, T. (1976). The syntactic domain of anaphora. Doctoral dissertation, MIT.

Reinhart, T. (1983). *Anaphora and semantic interpretation*. Croom Heim, London.

Reinhart, T. (1991). Non-quantificational LF. In A. Kasher, ed., *The Chomskyan turn*. Blackwell, Oxford.

Reinhart, T., and E. Reuland (1993). Reflexivity. *Linguistic Inquiry* 24:657–720.

Richard, M. (1983). Direct reference and ascriptions of belief. *Journal of Philosophical Logic* 12:425–52.

Richard, M. (1990). *Propositional attitudes*. Cambridge University Press, Cambridge.

Ristad, E. (1990). A constructive complexity thesis for human language. Ms., Princeton University.

Rizzi, L. (1986). On chain formation. In H. Borer, ed., *The syntax of pronominal clitics. Syntax and semantics, vol. 19.* Academic Press, Orlando, Fla.

Rizzi, L. (1990). *Relativized minimality.* MIT Press, Cambridge, Mass.

Roberts, C. (1987). Modal subordination, anaphora and distributivity. Doctoral dissertation, University of Massachusetts, Amherst.

Rooth, M. (1981). A comparison of three theories of verb phrase ellipsis. In W. Chao and D. Wheeler, eds., *University of Massachusetts occasional papers in linguistics 7.* GLSA, University of Massachusetts, Amherst.

Rooth, M. (1987). NP interpretation in Montague Grammar, File Change Semantics, and Situation Semantics. In P. Gärdenfors, ed., *Generalized quantifiers: Linguistic and logical approaches.* Reidel, Dordrecht.

Rooth, M. (1992). Ellipsis redundancy and reduction redundancy. In S. Berman and A. Hestvik, eds., *Proceedings of the Stuttgart Ellipsis Workshop.* Arbeitspapiere des Sonderforschungsbereichs 340, Bericht Nr. 29. IBM Germany, Heidelberg.

Safir, K. (1984). Multiple variable binding. *Linguistic Inquiry* 15:603–38.

Safir, K. (1986). Relative clauses in a theory of binding and levels. *Linguistic Inquiry* 17:663–90.

Sag, I. (1976). Deletion and Logical Form. Doctoral dissertation, MIT.

Sag, I., and J. Hankamer (1984). Toward a theory of anaphoric processing. *Linguistics and Philosophy* 7:325–45.

Saito, M., and H. Hoji (1983). Weak crossover and Move-alpha in Japanese. *Natural Language & Linguistic Theory* 1:245–59.

Salmon, N. (1986). Reflexivity. *Notre Dame Journal of Formal Logic* 27:401–29.

Saxon, L. (1984). Disjoint anaphora and the Binding Theory. In M. Cobler, S. MacKaye, and M. Wescoat, eds., *Proceedings of WCCFL 3.* Stanford Linguistics Association, Stanford University, Stanford, Calif.

Schein, B. (1994). *Plurals and events.* MIT Press, Cambridge, Mass.

Schiebe, T. (1971). Zum Problem der grammatisch relevanten Identität. In F. Kiefer and N. Ruwet, eds., *Generative grammar in Europe.* Reidel, Dordrecht.

Sells, P. (1986). Coreference and bound anaphora: A restatement of the facts. In S. Berman, J.-W. Choe, and J. McDonough, eds., *Proceedings of NELS 16.* GLSA, University of Massachusetts, Amherst.

Sells, P. (1987). Aspects of logophoricity. *Linguistic Inquiry* 18:445–79.

Sells, P., A. Zaenen, and D. Zec (1986). Reflexivization variation: Relations between syntax, semantics, and lexical structure. In M. Iida, S. Wechsler, and D. Zec, eds., *Working papers in grammatical theory and discourse structure: Interactions of morphology, syntax and discourse.* Center for the Study of Language and Information, Stanford, Calif.

Sher, G. (1991). *The bounds of logic*. MIT Press, Cambridge, Mass.

Soames, S. (1987). Direct reference, propositional attitudes, and semantic content. *Philosophical Topics* 15:47–87.

Soames, S. (1990). Pronouns and propositional attitudes. *Proceedings of the Aristotelian Society* 1989/90:191–212.

Szabolcsi, A. (1990). Combinatory grammar and projection from the lexicon. In I. Sag and A. Szabolcsi, eds., *Lexical matters*. Center for the Study of Language and Information, Stanford, Calif.

Webber, B. L. (1978). A formal approach to discourse anaphora. Doctoral dissertation, Harvard University.

Weinstein, S. (1974). Truth and demonstratives. *Noûs* 8:179–84.

Williams, E. (1977). Discourse and Logical Form. *Linguistic Inquiry* 8:101–39.

Williams, E. (1988). Is LF distinct from S-Structure?: A reply to May. *Linguistic Inquiry* 19:135–46.

Wyngaerd, G. V., and J.-W. Zwart (1991). Reconstruction and vehicle change. To appear in F. Drijkoningen and A. van Kemenade, eds., *Linguistics in the Netherlands, 1991*.

Zagona, K. (1988). *Verb phrase syntax: A parametric account of English and Spanish*. Kluwer, Dordrecht.

Index